# The Handbook of HUMAN RIGHTS LAW

An accessible approach to the issues and principles

Michael Arnheim
Of Lincoln's Inn and King's Inns, Dublin
Barrister at Law
Sometime Fellow of St John's College, Cambridge

London and Sterling, VA

**Publisher's note**
Every possible effort has been made to ensure that the information contained in this book is accurate at the time of going to press, and the publishers and authors cannot accept responsibility for any errors or omissions, however caused. No responsibility for loss or damage occasioned to any person acting, or refraining from action, as a result of the material in this publication can be accepted by the editor, the publisher or the author.

First published in Great Britain and the United States in 2004 by Kogan Page Limited
Paperback edition 2005

Apart from any fair dealing for the purposes of research or private study, or criticism or review, as permitted under the Copyright, Designs and Patents Act 1988, this publication may only be reproduced, stored or transmitted, in any form or by any means, with the prior permission in writing of the publishers, or in the case of reprographic reproduction in accordance with the terms and licences issued by the CLA. Enquiries concerning reproduction outside these terms should be sent to the publishers at the undermentioned addresses:

120 Pentonville Road
London N1 9JN
United Kingdom
www.kogan-page.co.uk

22883 Quicksilver Drive
Sterling VA 20166-2012
USA

© Michael Arnheim, 2004

The right of Michael Arnheim to be identified as the author of this work has been asserted by him in accordance with the Copyright, Designs and Patents Act 1988.

ISBN 0 7494 4480 0

---

**British Library Cataloguing-in-Publication Data**

A CIP record for this book is available from the British Library.

---

**Library of Congress Cataloging-in-Publication Data**

Arnheim, M. T. W. (Michael T. W.)
The handbook of human rights law : an accessible approach to the issues and principles / Michael Arnheim.
p. cm.
Includes bibliographical references and index.
ISBN 0–7494–3498–8
1. Great Britain. Human Rights Act 1998. 2. Human rights--Great Britain. 3. Human rights--Europe. I. Title.
KD4080.A975 2004
342.4108′5--dc22

2003024859

---

Typeset by Datamatics Technologies Ltd, Mumbai, India
Printed and bound in Great Britain by Creative Print and Design (Wales), Ebbw Vale

Books are to be returned on or before
the last date below.

7 – DAY
LOAN

LIVERPOOL
JOHN MOORES UNIVERSITY
AVRIL ROBARTS LRC
TEL. 0151 231 4022

LIBREX-

LIVERPOOL
JOHN MOORES UNIVERSITY
AVRIL ROBARTS LRC
TEL. 0151 231 4022

LIVERPOOL JMU LIBRARY
3 1111 01280 3480

*In memory of my beloved parents*

# Contents

# Preface

*Law is reason without passion.*

Aristotle, *Politics*

*'When I use a word,' Humpty Dumpty said, in rather a scornful tone, 'it means just what I choose it to mean – neither more nor less.'*

*'The question is,' said Alice, 'whether you can make words mean so many different things.'*

*'The question is,' said Humpty Dumpty, 'which is to be master, that's all.'*

Lewis Carroll, *Through the Looking-Glass, 1871*

What, not another human rights book? The importance of human rights law is not in doubt. But what does it mean in practice? It is probably the most uncertain and most unpredictable of all the branches of law. This is bad news in some respects. Uncertainty is an enemy of justice, and unpredictability is unlikely to contribute to the rule of law or equality before the law. But it is also good news, because this is a highly flexible area of law where everything is up for grabs. Hard-edged definitions are few and far between, and principles tend to be open to a variety of interpretations – a potential gold mine for the bold, but a minefield to the unwary.

I have tried to write this book in as direct and straightforward a style as possible so that it will be accessible to all, including lawyers, businesspeople, civil servants, private citizens and, last but not least, students.

The first three chapters are essentially about how to use human rights law, with Chapter 3 identifying some practical winning strategies and tactics illustrated by case studies. The remaining chapters deal with the various Convention rights in turn, arranged in a question and answer format.

At the time of writing the European Union was in the throes of finalizing a constitution and a 'Charter of Fundamental Rights', which bears more than a passing resemblance to the European Convention on Human Rights. It remains to be seen what its status will be in the United Kingdom and elsewhere, and also how it will relate to the Convention.

I owe a debt of gratitude to my personal assistant, Toran Shaw, and my research assistant, Jan Dormann, without whose help this book would probably never have seen the light of day. But all errors and omissions are entirely my own responsibility.

In the period since the main text of this book was compiled, two important human rights cases have gone to the House of Lords in which the Court of Appeal was reversed and the first instance decisions effectively reaffirmed. They are therefore what may be called 'yo-yo' cases. In both instances the Court of Appeal decision is severely criticised in this book. One of them is subjected to detailed scrutiny in Chapter 9: *Aston Cantlow Parochial Church Council v Wallbank* [2001] EWCA Civ 713 (Court of Appeal); [2003] UKHL 37, [2003] 3 All ER 1213 (House of Lords); and the other in Chapter 3: *Wilson v First Country Trust (No. 2)* [2001] EWCA Civ 633 (Court of Appeal), [2003] UKHL 40, [2003] 4 All ER 97 (House of Lords).

It gives me very little satisfaction to say 'I told you so'. The fact that these cases needed to go to the House of Lords at all is itself a sad commentary on the lack of certainty in the law. In both cases the whole approach adopted by the Court of Appeal was effectively rejected by the House of Lords. This, unfortunately, will not solve the underlying problem of a lack of clear and properly defined principles in human rights law.

Dr Michael Arnheim
Holborn Chambers
6 Gate Street
Lincoln's Inn Fields
London WC2A 3HP
e-mail: ArnheimCounsel@aol.com

# Table of cases

# Table of statutes*

*For references to the European Convention on Human Rights, see the general index, under 'Human Rights'.

# Abbreviations

| | |
|---|---|
| ECHR | European Convention for the Protection of Human Rights and Fundamental Freedoms commonly known as the European Convention on Human Rights |
| ECtHR | European Court of Human Rights |
| The Strasbourg court | European Court of Human Rights |
| HRA | The Human Rights Act 1998 |

# 1

# The Human Rights Act

## WHAT IS THE HUMAN RIGHTS ACT 1998?

Nothing about the Human Rights Act ('HRA') is simple or straightforward. Passed in 1998, it came into force on 2 October 2000, so there has now been just enough time to test its workings and effect.

It is a cross between two kinds of law. On the one hand it is a piece of parliamentary legislation, but on the other hand it incorporates the European Convention on Human Rights. Even that is not quite true, because it does not actually incorporate the whole Convention, only selected articles. That is why, as the long title of the Act says, it is intended 'to give further effect to rights and freedoms (not '*the* rights and freedoms') guaranteed under the European Convention on Human Rights'. Note also: not 'to give effect' but 'to give further effect'. This is because even before the passing of the HRA the judges had effectively come to take the Convention into account:

> The more substantial the interference with human rights, the more the court will require by way of justification before it is satisfied that the decision is reasonable.[1]

The White Paper issued by the British government to pave the way for the legislation was titled *Bringing Rights Home*. Lord Wilberforce's light-hearted comment was, '"Bringing home the rights" is a lovely phrase. It makes us think of the "Ashes", or perhaps the bacon.'[2] There can be no doubt that for some the rights 'brought home' have indeed proved a boon, but, as will be seen in Chapter 3, they are a small proportion of the population and tend to belong to certain all too easily identifiable special interest groups.

## WHAT IS THE EUROPEAN CONVENTION ON HUMAN RIGHTS?

The full name is the rather cumbersome European Convention for the Protection of Human Rights and Fundamental Freedoms ('ECHR'). It has nothing whatsoever to do with the European Union, or European Communities, but is a product of the quite separate body known as the Council of Europe, established by the Allies shortly after the Second World War 'to reconstruct durable civilization on the mainland of Europe'. It is a very loose association now boasting a membership of over 40 states.

The Council of Europe is based in Strasbourg. This was a deliberate choice, as Strasbourg was a city that epitomized the historic see-saw struggle between France and Germany and had come to symbolize the new harmony between them that emerged after the war. Besides being associated with the Council of Europe, Strasbourg also happens to be the seat of the European Parliament, which of course is an institution of the European Union and totally unconnected with the Council of Europe.

Three institutions were set up by the Council of Europe to operate the Convention. These were the European Commission of Human Rights, the European Court of Human Rights ('ECtHR') and the Committee of Ministers. An individual alleging a violation of any of his or her Convention rights needed to have exhausted all domestic remedies before bringing his or her case to Strasbourg. It was considered by the Commission first and only then by the Court, a process that often took five years or more from the date of the alleged violation. In 1998 the system was slightly slimmed down by abolishing the Commission, which meant that once a case had exhausted all domestic remedies it could go directly to the Court.[3]

## WHERE DO THE RIGHTS COME FROM?

It is important to note that the Convention does not give or confer any rights on anyone. It treats the rights as already existing. That is why the preamble to the HRA refers to them as 'rights and freedoms guaranteed under the European Convention on Human Rights'. The preamble to the Convention itself talks about 'the maintenance and further realization of human rights and fundamental freedoms'. Above all, the Convention is stated to be one of the first steps towards 'the collective enforcement of certain of the rights stated in the Universal Declaration [of Human Rights].' Article 1 of the Universal Declaration, proclaimed by the General Assembly of the United Nations in 1948, reads as follows:

**Article 1**

All human beings are born free and equal in dignity and rights. They are endowed with reason and conscience and should act towards one another in a spirit of brotherhood.

This has a long pedigree going all the way back to the American Declaration of Independence of 1776 and beyond:

We hold these truths to be self-evident, that all men are created equal, that they are endowed by their Creator with certain unalienable Rights, that among these are Life, Liberty and the pursuit of Happiness.

This is all part of the concept of 'natural law' or 'the law of nature' tracing its origins from ancient times. Rights are seen as deriving from God or nature and as being 'inalienable' or 'imprescriptible'. This school of thought was by no means universal, however, and was savagely attacked by, among others, the radical reformer Jeremy Bentham (1748–1832), whose famous comment on the French Declaration of the Rights of Man in 1793 was, '*Natural rights* is simple nonsense: natural and imprescriptible rights, rhetorical nonsense – nonsense upon stilts.'

The main problems with the doctrine of natural rights are: how do you know what these rights are, and even if they can be reduced to writing, how are they to be interpreted and applied? These problems are still very much in evidence today, as we shall see.

## SOME KEY CONCEPTS

Some of the articles of the ECHR that have not been incorporated into the HRA are as important as the ones that have been, if not more so. Articles 1 and 13 are in this category:

**Article 1**

***Obligation to respect human rights***

The High Contracting Parties shall secure to everyone within their jurisdiction the rights and freedoms defined in Section I of this Convention.

**Article 13**

***Right to an effective remedy***

Everyone whose rights and freedoms as set forth in this Convention are violated shall have an effective remedy before a national authority notwithstanding that the violation has been committed by persons acting in an official capacity.

The reason that these articles were omitted from the HRA is not because they are unimportant but because their function is effectively performed in the United Kingdom by the HRA itself. The flowery phrase 'the High Contracting Parties' simply means the states that are signatories to the ECHR. What Article 1 is saying is essentially that each member state, including of course the United Kingdom, is under an obligation to make sure that the rights and freedoms in Section I (that is, the substantive rights) are actually enjoyed by its population. And Article 13 takes this one step further by obliging member states to offer a domestic 'effective remedy'.

Articles 17 and 18 of the Convention, which are incorporated into the HRA, are relevant here:

> **Article 17**
>
> ***Prohibition of abuse of rights***
>
> Nothing in this Convention may be interpreted as implying for any State, group or person any right to engage in any activity or perform any act aimed at the destruction of any of the rights and freedoms set forth herein or at their limitation to a greater extent than is provided for in the Convention.

This article is intended to restrict or even ban political activity designed to curtail the rights or to abolish the whole rights-based culture altogether. It is naive to imagine that words on paper could possibly have any such effect in the face of violent revolution, or possibly even in the face of widespread popular disaffection reflected in a shift in the power structure or in ideological orthodoxies.

> **Article 18**
>
> ***Limitation on use of restrictions on rights***
>
> The restrictions permitted under this Convention to the said rights and freedoms shall not be applied for any purpose other than those for which they have been prescribed.

This restricts the restrictions on the rights to their 'prescribed purpose' – which is usually so vague and uncertain as to lay it open to a variety of interpretations. However, it sends a message to the courts to keep the restrictions within close bounds.

## WHAT STATUS DID THE CONVENTION ENJOY UNDER UK LAW BEFORE THE COMING INTO FORCE OF THE HRA?

By contrast with certain other countries, under United Kingdom law a treaty or a convention to which the United Kingdom is a signatory does not automatically form part of UK law. It is binding on the UK government in terms of international law, but rights under it cannot be claimed in the UK domestic courts until or unless it is incorporated into an Act of Parliament. It is in fact very rare for such international agreements to become part of UK law.

The Convention came into existence in 1950 and the United Kingdom ratified it the following year. British lawyers played a leading role in drafting the

Convention, but as it was felt that the rights it contained were already largely enshrined in UK domestic law, there seemed to be no point in incorporating them into UK law. The Convention came into force in 1953, and in 1966 the United Kingdom allowed the right of 'individual petition' to Strasbourg. But this still did not entitle individuals to claim any of the Convention rights in the UK domestic courts.

## HORIZONTAL EFFECT – STRASBOURG

All Strasbourg applications are complaints against a state, in the form *Hogg v UK* or *Duck v Italy*, even where the alleged violation is not directly the fault of the state or government authorities concerned. *Young, James and Webster v UK* is a case in point.[4]

The three applicants had been sacked from their jobs by British Rail in 1976 because they refused to join a trade union. Under English law in force at the time the 'closed shop' was lawful and their dismissals were therefore deemed not to be unfair. So although their dispute was with British Rail, their application to Strasbourg took the form of a complaint against the United Kingdom for having legislation in place that violated their rights under Article 11 of the Convention to 'freedom of assembly and association'. This case is a prime example of how, though the Convention is ostensibly concerned only to protect private individuals (including corporations) against the state, it could also have indirect 'horizontal effect'. This was put very clearly by the Human Rights Commission in *Young*:

> It is well established by now that apart from protecting the individual against State action, there are articles of the Convention which oblige the State to protect individual rights even against the action of others.

## WHAT IS THE STATUS OF THE CONVENTION UNDER THE HRA?

### *'Public authority'*

Since the implementation of the Human Rights Act in 2000 it has become easier to give the Convention horizontal effect, but with one notable exception: the Act, as well as the Convention itself, is couched in terms of strictly vertical effect. So HRA s 6(1) provides: 'It is unlawful for a public authority to act in a way which is incompatible with a Convention right.'

This means that for a private person to act in a way that is incompatible with a Convention right is not in itself unlawful. But what exactly is a 'public authority'? S 6(3) explains the term in a not particularly helpful way:

In this section 'public authority' includes –

(a) a court or tribunal, and
(b) any person certain of whose functions are functions of a public nature, but does not include either House of Parliament or a person exercising functions in connection with proceedings in Parliament.

But then in s 6(5) comes a further qualification:

In relation to a particular act, a person is not a public authority by virtue only of subsection (3) (b) if the nature of the act is private.

And in s 6(4) the House of Lords sitting as a court is separated out from the concept of 'Parliament' for the purposes of this section:

In subsection (3) 'Parliament' does not include the House of Lords in its judicial capacity.

It is important to note that none of this adds up to a definition of 'public authority', as the word used is 'includes' rather than 'means'. And what is meant by 'certain of whose functions'? This is far too vague to be of any real help. It leaves a void at the heart of the Act, which can only be filled by the judges. And judicial definitions are rarely precise.

In other words, what might have been thought to be an elementary preliminary question turns out to be yet another of the many issues up for grabs in the courts. Is, for example, a statutory sewerage undertaker a 'public authority'? Yes.[5] What about the RSPCA? No.[6]

The Court of Appeal has rather unhelpfully suggested that:

the definition of who is a public authority, and what is a public function, for the purposes of section 6, should be given a generous interpretation . . . As is the position on applications for judicial review, there is no clear demarcation line which can be drawn between public and private bodies and functions. In a borderline case, such as this, the decision is very much one of fact and degree.[7]

This vague non-definition has only fuelled further litigation. In the case in question, a housing association, Poplar Housing and Regeneration Community Association Ltd ('Poplar'), was held by the Court of Appeal to be performing a public function as a 'registered social landlord' providing accommodation in housing stock transferred to it by a local authority. But in a similar case heard only a few months later, another housing association was held not to have been acting as a public authority. The facts of the case were as follows.[8]

Two elderly people were entitled to free accommodation provided by their local authority under the National Assistance Act 1948. The local authority arranged for the accommodation to be provided on its behalf by a charity, the Leonard Cheshire Foundation (LCF). The two elderly people concerned were long-stay patients in a home owned by LCF, which LCF had decided to close in its then form. The two patients applied for judicial review of LCF's decision on the ground that, as LCF was exercising functions of a 'public nature', it was a 'public authority' within HRA s 6. The relevance of this, they contended, was that by closing the home LCF would be acting in a way that was incompatible with their rights under ECHR Article 8 (right to respect for private and family life), which it was unlawful for a public authority to do.

In this case, as in the Poplar case, the issue before the court was whether the housing association in question was a public authority or not. Unlike Poplar, in LCF both the judge and the Court of Appeal held that the housing association was not a public authority.

Needless to say, the test for a 'public authority' under the HRA is not the same as that for a 'public body' exercising 'public decision-making powers' under the general law applicable to judicial review. Here the *Datafin* case involving a challenge to a decision of the Panel on Take-overs and Mergers remains the leading authority. The question before the court was whether the decisions of a quasi-public body such as the Panel could be subjected to judicial review. Lord Donaldson put forward this test:

> Possibly the only essential elements are what can be described as a public element, which can take many different forms, and the exclusion from the jurisdiction of bodies whose sole source of power is a consensual submission to its jurisdiction.[9]

Not all human rights cases will be decided by judicial review, and not all judicial review cases will involve human rights. But, where a case combines both these elements it will presumably have to satisfy both sets of criteria. In other words, only decisions taken by a 'public body' exercising 'public decision-making functions' will be subject to judicial review. But, only 'public authorities' as defined in terms of HRA s 6 are obliged to act in a way that is not incompatible with a Convention right.

Do all these distinctions really make any difference in practice? Unfortunately, yes. One of the most significant questions in this regard is whether the Press Complaints Commission (PCC) is a 'public authority' within HRA s 6. Newspapers of course are not, so if a newspaper violates somebody's Convention rights, it cannot be held liable specifically for that.[10] The victim of the newspaper can, however, lodge a complaint with the PCC, a body made up of newspaper editors, who, not surprisingly perhaps, are not noted for coming down hard on their fellow editors. If the PCC dismisses the complaint, the aggrieved person can take it (that is, the PCC but not the newspaper) to court for violating the person's Convention rights. But this can only be done if the PCC is a 'public authority' within HRA s 6. Well, is the PCC a 'public authority' or not? This has been left undecided by the courts.[11]

So where does that leave you if your Convention rights have been trampled underfoot by the press? Unfortunately, in limbo. You will not even know in advance whether you can get to square one in any human rights case against the PCC.

Perhaps the most important provision of HRA s 6 is the inclusion of the courts as 'public authorities'. This has several significant consequences. First, it means that it is 'unlawful' for a court 'to act in a way which is incompatible with a Convention right'. This means that the loser in a court case can appeal on the ground that the court's decision was itself unlawful.

This provision also gives an extra fillip to the already tremendous power exercised by the judiciary. What it really means is that judges can effectively scupper any law that they consider to be 'incompatible' with the Convention. Judges are not allowed to declare a law void or invalid on the ground that it is incompatible with a Convention right. All they can do is issue a 'declaration of incompatibility' (see below). But in practice such a declaration consigns the legislation in question to outer darkness. So in the recent *Anderson* case, for example, when the House of Lords held that the law giving the Home Secretary the power to set a 'tariff' for murderers was 'incompatible' with Article 6 of the Convention (right to a fair trial), this effectively put paid to that power.[12] In terms of the HRA the offending provision could have remained on the statute book indefinitely if the government had wanted it to, notwithstanding that it was now branded as 'incompatible' with the Convention. But the murderers concerned would simply have taken their case to Strasbourg (at the taxpayer's expense). If they had won there too, which would have been a foregone conclusion, the UK government would then have been placed under irresistible pressure to change the law. As it was, after first proclaiming his intention to brazen it out, the Home Secretary, David Blunkett, backed down but subsequently announced his intention to introduce new legislation that would give the judges sentencing guidelines on murder without falling foul of the Convention. It remains to be seen whether this new legislative initiative fares any better.[13]

## HORIZONTAL EFFECT UNDER THE HRA

If the Press Complaints Commission (PCC) is a public authority, a matter which, as we have seen, is still not finally decided, this will automatically give at least indirect horizontal effect to Article 8 (respect for private and family life) as well as to Article 10 (freedom of expression). If the PCC dismisses a complaint from an alleged victim of press intrusion, a human rights claim can be brought: against the PCC even if it cannot be brought directly against the newspaper, journalist or photographer concerned.

But HRA s 12(4) can be interpreted as giving direct horizontal effect to ECHR Article 10. HRA s 12 applies 'if a court is considering whether to grant any relief which, if granted, might affect the exercise of the Convention right to freedom of expression'. HRA s 12(4) itself says:

> The court must have particular regard to the importance of the Convention right to freedom of expression and, where the proceedings relate to material which the

respondent claims, or which appears to the court, to be journalistic, literary or artistic material (or to conduct connected with such material), to –

(a) the extent to which –

(i) the material has, or is about to, become available to the public; or

(ii) it is, or would be, in the public interest for the material to be published;

(b) any relevant privacy code.

The 'respondent' mentioned here must obviously be a publisher of some kind. What the subsection is referring to, therefore, is an application made, for example, by someone who wishes to stop publication of a newspaper article that allegedly infringes his or her privacy – a horizontal relationship.

In the words of Sedley LJ, this subsection 'puts beyond question the direct applicability of at least one article of the convention as between one private party to litigation and another – in the jargon, its horizontal effect. Whether this is an illustration of the intended mechanism of the entire Act, or whether it is a special case (and if so, why), need not detain us here.'[14]

Sedley LJ here leaves open the possibility that the HRA as a whole may be intended to give the Convention horizontal effect. This has not yet been tested, but it is clear that there is plenty of scope for this.

The inclusion of the courts as 'public authorities' in HRA s 6 has also made it easier for the Convention to be given horizontal effect. An unsettling example of this is to be found in a recent case involving a pawnbroker and a consumer credit agreement. Here, on the basis of a strained literal interpretation of the statutory provisions, the Court of Appeal held the agreement void and of its own motion issued a declaration of incompatibility stigmatizing the relevant legislation as being non-compliant with Article 6 of the Convention. In this way the Convention came to be applied in an action between two private persons, thereby having a form of horizontal effect.[15]

## 'VICTIM'

As we have seen, although it is only 'public authorities' that are meant to be subject to the Convention, horizontality has gone some way towards negating this restriction. What we are talking about here are the parameters determining who can and cannot be a defendant to a human rights claim.

But what about the rules for claimants? The requirement is that you may bring a human rights claim or rely on Convention rights only if you yourself are (or would be) the victim of an act of a public authority that is unlawful by virtue of the fact that it is incompatible with a Convention right: HRA s 7(1). This is what is commonly referred to as the 'victim test'. And, for once, in HRA s 7(7), we are given a definition – of sorts:

> For the purposes of this section, a person is a victim of an unlawful act only if he would be a victim for the purposes of Article 34 of the Convention if proceedings were brought in the European Court of Human Rights in respect of that act.

This simply adopts the Strasbourg understanding of 'victim', which, needless to say, is not actually defined in Article 34 or anywhere else. Do you actually have to have suffered the effects of some 'unlawful' act before you can apply? There are two main exceptions.

First, the damage does not have to have been done by the time you lodge your claim. It is enough if you 'run the risk of being directly affected'. So in *Marckx v Belgium* an unmarried mother and her daughter successfully stigmatized Belgian illegitimacy laws as being in violation of Article 8 ('right to respect for private and family life') and Article 14 ('prohibition of discrimination') – even though there was no specific act or decision that affected the applicants directly. The Strasbourg court rejected the Belgian government's objection that there was no victim here.[16]

Similarly, in *Norris v Ireland* a homosexual complaining about the Irish law criminalizing homosexual relations between consenting adults was held by Strasbourg to be a victim even though he had never been prosecuted and the impugned legislation was not enforced in practice.[17]

In a case brought against the United Kingdom objecting to corporal punishment in Scottish schools as repugnant to Article 3 ('Prohibition of inhuman or degrading punishment') and Article 2, Protocol 1 ('right to education'), neither of the two boys concerned had actually been subjected to a beating (strapping with the tawse), although one had been suspended for refusing to accept such punishment. Yet Strasbourg recognized them – or, to be more precise, their parents – as victims.[18]

The fact that the parents were allowed to bring the case on behalf of their children is the second main exception to the 'victim test', though hardly a surprising one. Similarly, in the 'Death on the Rock' case brought against the United Kingdom, the parents of three IRA members shot dead by the British SAS were held to be victims for the purpose of claiming that this constituted a violation of Article 2 ('right to life'). In the event the United Kingdom lost the case by 10 votes to 9.[19]

## 'VICTIM TEST' IN JUDICIAL REVIEW

How does the 'victim test' operate in judicial review applications, the chief vehicle for human rights claims? HRA s 7(3) spells this out:

> If the proceedings are brought on an application for judicial review, the applicant is to be taken to have a sufficient interest in relation to the unlawful act only if he is, or would be, a victim of that act.

The point is that in order to be permitted to bring an application for judicial review in pre-HRA days it was necessary to have 'standing' (formerly *locus standi*) or 'sufficient interest', which was so broadly interpreted as to leave the court 'an unfettered discretion to decide what in its own judgment it considers to be a "sufficient interest" on the part of an applicant in the particular circumstances in the case before it.'[20]

In this case an association of small businesses sought to challenge the tax amnesty given to Fleet Street casual workers who used to avoid paying income tax by signing in as 'Mickey Mouse', 'Donald Duck' and the like. The court decided that the association did not have a 'sufficient interest' to bring the application, but it actually represents one of the more restrictive interpretations of the doctrine.

The 'sufficient interest' rule (if it can be called that) still applies in non-human rights judicial review, but where human rights are involved the stricter 'victim test' has to be used.

## HOW TO BRING A HUMAN RIGHTS CLAIM

The HRA identifies two routes for bringing a human rights claim against a public authority that has acted (or proposes to act) in a way that is made unlawful by being 'incompatible with a Convention right'. You can either 'bring proceedings against the authority under this Act in the appropriate court or tribunal' or you can 'rely on the Convention right or rights concerned in any legal proceedings'. In other words, you can go to court specifically with a human rights claim or you can raise a human rights issue in any court case regardless of its cause of action. You can also raise human rights issues in an appeal against the decision of a court on the ground that that decision is unlawful by virtue of being incompatible with a Convention right.

## LIMITATION

The two different types of claims have different time limits. If you bring a specifically human rights claim you have to do so within a year of 'the date on which the act complained of took place', or 'such longer period as the court or tribunal considers equitable having regard to all the circumstances': HRA s 7(5). And, to complicate matters still further, the time limit 'is subject to any rule imposing a stricter time limit in relation to the procedure in question'.

What this means is that if your case is a specifically human rights claim you have a year to bring it – unless there is some rule imposing a stricter time limit. The prime example of this is judicial review, where the time limit is three months. But any time limit can be extended by the court on grounds of 'equity': HRA s 7(5)(b). It is not clear how this will play in relation to the general procedural rule that 'Except where these Rules provide otherwise, the court may . . . extend or shorten the time for compliance with any rule.'[21] The exception applies only where the Civil Procedure Rules (CPR) themselves 'provide otherwise'. The time limits laid down by the HRA are not in the CPR. Further room for argument!

However, if you are raising human rights issues as part of some other cause of action, then the normal limitation periods will apply. So, for example, if it is a personal injury case it will be subject to a three-year limitation period, while other torts and contractual claims will enjoy their usual six-year limitation period.

## STATUS OF STRASBOURG DECISIONS

One of the oldest and most important principles of English common law is the doctrine of binding precedent, or *stare decisis*. What this means is that courts are bound by relevant decisions previously taken by a higher court, or even by one on the same level. Even the House of Lords, the highest court in the United Kingdom, was traditionally bound by this doctrine until it unilaterally freed itself from it in 1966.

In the domestic courts of mainland Europe, however, the doctrine of binding precedent is unknown. The same applies to the Strasbourg court. The relevant law before the Strasbourg court is contained in the Convention, and the court is permitted to look at it afresh each time. In practice previous decisions are frequently referred to and often followed, but not necessarily, and there have been some quite clearly discernible shifts in Strasbourg jurisprudence in recent years.

The position was well put by the Strasbourg court in a recent case:

> While the Court is not formally bound to follow its previous judgments, it is in the interests of legal certainty, foreseeability and equality before the law that it should not depart, without good reason, from precedents laid down in previous cases. However, since the Convention is first and foremost a system for the protection of human rights, the Court must have regard to the changing conditions within the respondent State and within Contracting States generally and respond, for example, to any evolving convergence as to the standards to be achieved. It is of crucial importance that the Convention is interpreted and applied in a manner which renders its rights practical and effective, not theoretical and illusory.[22]

This flexibility – and uncertainty – is now also enshrined in the HRA. First, although some articles of the Convention are now incorporated into UK law, that does not apply to Strasbourg case law. HRA s 2 provides only that a UK 'court or tribunal determining a question which has arisen in connection with a Convention right must take into account any' relevant Strasbourg judgments, decisions or other pronouncements. The phrase 'must take into account' sounds peremptory but is in reality pretty vague, as all it means is that the domestic courts must look at the relevant Strasbourg jurisprudence while remaining free to depart from it if they choose.

What about the doctrine of binding precedent within the United Kingdom itself? Are the UK courts bound by UK domestic decisions on the Convention in the same way as in ordinary domestic cases? The answer must be yes, although the whole concept of binding precedent has been considerably watered down of late.

What then about uniformity of interpretation of the Convention? In general, as Lord Browne-Wilkinson explained, 'An international Convention, expressed in different languages and intended to apply to a wide range of differing legal systems, cannot be construed differently in different jurisdictions. The Convention must have the same meaning and effect under the laws of all contracting states.'[23] The Convention referred to here was the Hague Convention on the Civil Aspects of International Child Abduction, and the general doctrine expressed here clearly has no application to the Human Rights Convention. The Strasbourg court itself does not decide cases uniformly for all member states but allows a 'margin of appreciation' (see below), which may differ from one state to another.

## INTERPRETATION

The importance of the HRA can be seen from the provision in s 3(1) that:

> So far as it is possible to do so, primary legislation and subordinate legislation must be read and given effect in a way which is compatible with the Convention rights.

This again looks more peremptory than it really is in practice. The effect of 'must' is greatly weakened by 'possible', which is often a matter of opinion. Lord Steyn remarked, 'Traditionally the search has been for the one true meaning of a statute. Now the search will be for a possible meaning that would prevent the need for a declaration of incompatibility.'[24] Too strained an interpretation will, however, be likely to produce an example of what Lord Bingham in a memorable phrase has termed 'not judicial interpretation but judicial vandalism'.[25]

It is worth noting that the requirement to interpret legislation as far as possible so as to comply with the Convention applies equally to legislation passed before and after the advent of the HRA.[26] Moreover, this provision 'does not affect the validity, continuing operation or enforcement of any incompatible primary legislation'.[27] In the case of subordinate legislation the position is a little more complicated, as the courts do in certain circumstances have the right to set aside offending subordinate legislation.[28]

# REMEDIES

What remedies are available in human rights cases? Once again this is left to the discretion of the court, which 'may grant such relief or remedy, or make such order, within its powers as it considers just and appropriate'.[29]

## *Damages*

There are some restrictions placed on the award of damages. First, damages may be awarded only by a court that has power to award damages or order compensation in civil cases.[30] Even then, an award of damages should be made only if, after taking all circumstances into account, 'the court is satisfied that the award is necessary to afford just satisfaction to the person in whose favour it is made'. In addition, in determining whether to award damages, and if so, how much, the court must take into account what are laughingly referred to as the 'principles' of compensation in Article 41 of the Convention as applied by the Strasbourg court. In fact the closest thing to a principle in Article 41 is the vague concept of 'just satisfaction'. Strasbourg has on occasion awarded compensation for distress, lost opportunities and other heads of damage, but it has quite often also held that the finding of a violation itself constituted sufficient 'just satisfaction'. To its credit the Strasbourg court has sometimes admitted that there was not enough evidence before it to conclude that the Convention breach had indeed been the cause of the alleged loss or damage; or that it did not wish to 'speculate' on whether the alleged adverse consequences of the Convention breach would not have occurred anyway.

To predict the likely quantum of damages to be awarded in human rights cases is therefore, to put it mildly, very difficult. Strasbourg awards, it is worth noting, tend to be modest.

## *Remedies for judicial review*

The traditional remedies for judicial review are available in human rights cases as well. The ancient prerogative writs (or 'prerogative remedies', as they are now called) of certiorari, mandamus and prohibition have now been prosaically renamed 'quashing orders', 'mandatory orders' and 'prohibiting orders' respectively. All remedies in judicial review applications are discretionary, which gives the courts great latitude.

### Quashing orders

Quashing orders, by far the commonest of the three, have the effect of setting aside a judgment, order or other kind of decision. The law provides that:

> If, on an application for judicial review seeking an order of certiorari [ie a quashing order], the High Court quashes the decision to which the application relates, the High Court may remit the matter to the court, tribunal or authority concerned, with a direction to reconsider it and reach a decision in accordance with the findings of the High Court.[31]

The traditional position was that the court had no right to substitute its own decision for that of the original decision maker. Thus Lord Cairns in 1878 described certiorari as 'merely a jurisdiction to leave the order standing or remove it out of the way . . . not a jurisdiction to substitute for it another or a different order'.[32] However, in 2000 a procedural rule was added which greatly increased the court's power:

> (1) This rule applies where the court makes a quashing order in respect of the decision to which the claim relates . . . . (3) Where the court considers that there is no purpose to be served in remitting the matter to the decision-maker it may, subject to any statutory provision, take the decision itself.[33]

Although ostensibly only a rule of procedure, it marks a radical change to the substantive law as well. For if judges are allowed to substitute their own decisions for those of the original decision makers, this changes the whole nature of judicial review, in which that power has always been strictly off-limits to judges. A change of this magnitude should not have been allowed to enter the law by the back door in the shape of an amendment to the Civil Procedure Rules, which are compiled by a committee of judges. As a form of delegated, subordinate or secondary legislation this change has become law without going through Parliament in the form of a bill. It is also contrary to the doctrine of the separation of powers, actually in two respects. First, the actual rule change itself amounts to legislation by the judiciary in its own interest. Even more important, by giving judges the right to substitute their own decisions for those of the original decision makers, the new rule allows the judiciary to usurp the role of the executive or indeed even of Parliament, as the most important quashed decisions were initially taken by government ministers, and in the case of EU law may even include Acts of Parliament.[34]

## Mandatory and prohibiting orders

In Latin *mandamus* means 'we order', and the prerogative writ of that name was so called because this was its opening word. A mandatory order is therefore in a sense the opposite of a quashing order. Whereas a quashing order strikes down a decision, a mandatory order makes a positive order that something should be done that has wrongly been left undone.

A prohibiting order contrasts with a quashing order in a different way. Where a quashing order sets aside a decision that has already been taken, a prohibiting order looks to the future and nips an unlawful action or decision in the bud by prohibiting it from being taken.

In addition to the three ancient prerogative orders, since 1977 it has also been possible in certain circumstances to obtain ordinary remedies such as declarations, injunctions and damages in judicial review applications. Like the traditional remedies, these are also discretionary.

## Judicial review remedies in human rights cases

Judicial review is primarily concerned to determine whether a particular decision is lawful, whereas human rights cases are chiefly concerned to determine compatibility with the Convention. These are distinct but could possibly overlap.

What Anthony Anderson (in the case already mentioned), for example, was asking for was a quashing order against the Home Secretary's decision setting the 'tariff' applicable to himself. In fact, however, the House of Lords did not quash the Home Secretary's decision – because the tariff that he had set was perfectly lawful in terms of the relevant legislation. Instead, the legislation itself (section 29 of the Crime (Sentences) Act 1997) was branded as incompatible with the Convention. Because the court had no power to set the legislation aside, all it could do was to issue a declaration of incompatibility.[35]

This did not really help Anthony Anderson directly, which is why his counsel asked for the relevant legislation to be interpreted so as to exclude the Home Secretary's right to set a tariff for murderers. This would have meant that the legislation was not incompatible with the Convention, but that the Home Secretary's decision on Anderson himself was unlawful. This would then have allowed the court to quash the decision.

The House of Lords rejected the invitation. In Lord Bingham's words:

> To read s 29 [of the Crime (Sentences) Act 1997] as precluding participation by the Home Secretary, if it were possible to do so, would not be judicial interpretation but judicial vandalism: it would give the section an effect quite different from that which Parliament intended and would go well beyond any interpretative process sanction by s 3 of the 1998 [Human Rights] Act.[36]

In certain circumstances, however, it would be possible for a single judicial review application to result in a quashing order plus a declaration of incompatibility. If, for example, the Home Secretary had set a tariff for Anthony Anderson which was held by the court to have been disproportionate, then that decision could have been quashed. That would still have left it open to the court to declare the legislation under which the Home Secretary's decision had been taken to be incompatible with the Convention.

### *Remedies against judicial decisions*

What if the act or decision that a claimant contends is unlawful is a judgment by a court? As we have seen, the courts are themselves 'public authorities' within

HRA s 6(3). But here HRA s 9(1) warns prospective claimants off the turf. The only way a judge's decision can be challenged is 'by exercising a right of appeal', or where that is allowed, by judicial review: HRA s 9(1–2). In fact, it is only magistrates' courts and county courts whose decisions can be subjected to judicial review. In short, there is no way of challenging judges' decisions except by going cap in hand to other judges! This is hardly in keeping with that great judicial favourite, the doctrine of the separation of powers. Whatever happened to impeachment? In the United States, where separation of powers is a reality, impeachment – a procedure borrowed from English law – has been employed successfully against many judges over the years. Here, however, though never formally abolished, it has not been used for over 150 years.

Another provision that flies in the face of the doctrine of the separation of powers is Article 24: 'No judge may be dismissed from his office unless the other judges decide by a majority of two-thirds that he has ceased to fulfil the required conditions.' Only judges have the power to dismiss other judges – and even then only by a two-thirds majority! This is of course applicable only to judges of the Strasbourg court. But in a sense even this is more democratic than the British system, where the position of senior judges is impregnable, requiring an address by both Houses of Parliament to remove them.

## NON-CONVENTION RIGHTS

Perhaps the most important provision in the HRA is section 11, which preserves pre-existing rights:

> A person's reliance on a Convention right does not restrict –
>
> (a) any other right or freedom conferred on him by or under any law having effect in any part of the United Kingdom; or
>
> (b) his right to make any claim or bring any proceedings which he could make or bring apart from sections 7 to 9 [of the HRA].

The rights preserved here include statutory and common law rights alike, and are also clearly not restricted to pre-existing rights. But why is the section worded in such a way as to suggest that these rights are preserved only for litigants relying on a Convention right? In other words, what it seems to be saying is that if a Convention right that you wish to rely on is narrower than a corresponding non-Convention right, you can still rely on the broader right. So, for example, if there was a Convention right to pick your nose in private and a statutory right to pick your nose anywhere, you would still be protected if you chose to pick your nose in Piccadilly Circus.

But what if the Convention right is relied upon by one party and the non-Convention right by the other, and the two rights are in conflict? If the party relying on the non-Convention right is a public authority, then the rule in HRA s 6(1) would presumably apply: 'It is unlawful for a public authority to act in a way which is incompatible with a Convention right.' Even then, however, there is a let-out clause in HRA s 6(2), which makes it lawful for a public authority to act in accordance with an Act of Parliament that was incompatible with the Convention but was still on the statute book.

A further question is, when talking of 'reliance on a Convention right', does HRA s 11 include the exceptions contained within the particular article in question? It is commonly maintained in Strasbourg that these are an integral part of the right.

Let us imagine a hypothetical case of an asylum seeker who on entering the United Kingdom without leave is arrested and placed in detention. Who will prevail? The asylum seeker, relying on the rights established in his or her favour by judicial precedent, or the government relying on Article 5(1)(f) justifying 'the lawful arrest or detention of a person to prevent his effecting an unauthorised entry into the country'? In practice the judges have a wide discretion.

Article 53 of the Convention is both wider (and narrower?) than HRA s 11 but is not incorporated into the HRA. So, in theory at least, it can only be relied upon once the case gets to Strasbourg:

**Article 53**

***Safeguard for existing human rights***

Nothing in this Convention shall be construed as limiting or derogating from any of the human rights and fundamental freedoms which may be ensured under the laws of any High Contracting Party or under any other agreement to which it is a Party.

On the basis of its title Article 53 appears narrower than HRA s 11 in being limited to 'existing human rights'. But what exactly does this mean? Does it mean rights available in the member states prior to their accession to the Convention? If not, 'existing' is misleading. But the word is not repeated in the body of the text of the article. HRA s 11 says nothing about when the non-Convention rights have to have come into force.

Unlike HRA s 11, Article 53 is not restricted to a person relying on a Convention right. It can be used by anyone. In this respect Article 53 is wider.

## Freedom of expression

HRA s 12 singles out a Convention right, freedom of expression, the subject of Article 10, and gives it extra protection.[37] Or does it? Remarks made by the then Home Secretary, Jack Straw, seem to support this view: 'We have taken the opportunity to enhance press freedom in a wider way than would arise simply from the incorporation of the Convention into our domestic law.'[38] And again, 'So far as we are able in a manner consistent with the Convention and its jurisprudence, we are saying to the courts that whenever there is a clash between Article 8 [privacy] rights and Article 10 [freedom of expression] rights, they must pay particular attention to the Article 10 rights.'[39] If this does not mean that press freedom is to be favoured over privacy rights, what does it mean? Moreover, if this is not what HRA s 12 means, then why was the section enacted at all?

It is worth noting that Article 10 makes no specific mention of press freedom at all, but quite rightly guarantees a general right of free expression to all, as is emphasized in its opening sentence: 'Everyone has the right to freedom of expression.' HRA s 12, by contrast, accords special protection to 'journalistic, literary or artistic material', and Jack Straw frankly admitted the government's intention 'to enhance press freedom'. As will be seen in Chapter 6, not only is freedom of the press not the same thing as freedom of expression for all, but the two may even conflict with each other.

Some judges have rejected the interpretation of the section as favouring the press – or even as favouring the right to freedom of expression over other rights – by claiming that the reference to Article 10 must include not only the positive right to freedom of expression contained in Article 10(1) but also the exceptions to that right contained in Article 10(2).[40] But if this view is right, HRA s 12 adds nothing to Article 10 of the Convention, and we can only wonder why it was necessary to enact HRA s 12 at all. In that case it would be hard to disagree with the comment made by Lord Lester and David Pannick QC that HRA s 12 'serves no sensible purpose'.[41]

## *Freedom of thought, conscience and religion*

The next section, HRA s 13, is likewise branded by the same commentators as serving no useful purpose.[42] The wording is modelled on that of HRA s 12 but is much vaguer. All it says is that:

> If a court's determination of any question arising under this Act might affect the exercise by a religious organisation (itself or its members collectively) of the Convention right to freedom of thought, conscience and religion, it must have particular regard to the importance of that right.

Does this add anything to the relevant Convention right as set out in Article 9 (discussed in Chapter 6)? In particular, does it give priority to Article 9 rights over conflicting rights? No, because the court would find it necessary, in the interests of that fashionable but suitably vague concept, proportionality, to strike 'a fair balance' between the rights in question and the public interest. So it would have no hesitation in bringing into play the exceptions listed in Article 9(2).

At the time of writing the possibility had been mooted of the introduction of a statute banning Jewish and Muslim ritual slaughter as inhumane.[43] Could such legislation be certified as compatible with Article 9 of the Convention? Article 9(2) subjects religious freedom 'to such limitations as are prescribed by law and are necessary in a democratic society in the interests of public safety, for the protection of public order, health or morals, or for the protection of the rights and freedoms of others'.

It would be hard to justify such legislation as 'necessary' for any of these ends – unless the word 'morals' were given a very broad interpretation indeed so as to include the treatment of animals, and then only if it could be proved that strict halal slaughter and shechita amounted to cruelty.

But the inclusion of s 13 in the HRA would not do anything to help Muslims and Jews to preserve their ancient rituals. Here the contrast with HRA s 12 is stark, and this is confirmed by parliamentary materials. For unlike s 12, which was sponsored by the government, the idea of including special protection for religious beliefs and practices was opposed by the government. The House of Lords actually adopted an amendment in the teeth of government opposition making it 'a defence for a person to show that he has acted in pursuance of a manifestation of religious belief in accordance with the historic teaching and practices of a Christian or other principal religious tradition represented in Great Britain'.[44] In the House of Commons the government managed to get this and several other similar amendments removed by replacing them with a sop in the shape of HRA s 13.

## DECLARATIONS OF INCOMPATIBILITY

If a higher court is 'satisfied' that a provision of primary legislation (that is, an Act of Parliament) is incompatible with a Convention right, it 'may' make a declaration of incompatibility: HRA s 4. The word 'may' is worth noticing, as it means that there is no obligation on the court to make such a declaration: it is a discretionary matter. This right is restricted to the higher courts: in England and Wales, the High Court, the Court of Appeal and the House of Lords.

It does not apply to criminal trials because, in the words of the Lord Chancellor, Lord Irvine, the government did not believe that criminal trials 'should be upset, or potentially upset, by declarations of incompatibility that may go to the very foundations of the prosecution'.[45] This rather begs the question why it is more 'upsetting' for such a declaration to be made in a criminal trial than in a civil trial in the High Court. It also sidesteps the problem that will arise where a Crown Court judge finds an incompatibility but is not allowed to issue a declaration to that effect.

The rules governing subordinate (or delegated) legislation are slightly different from those applicable to primary legislation. In the case of subordinate legislation, the court must not only be 'satisfied' that the legislative provision in question is incompatible with a Convention right, but must also be satisfied that 'the primary legislation concerned prevents removal of the incompatibility'. Otherwise the court can set aside the offending subordinate legislation.[46]

## *Effect of declaration*

The effect of a declaration is very limited indeed, and intentionally so. The British government was anxious not to give the judges the power to strike down Acts of Parliament on the ground of incompatibility with the Convention, as was explained in the White Paper *Rights Brought Home*, presented to Parliament in October 1997:

> The Government has reached the conclusion that the courts should not have the power to set aside primary legislation past or future, on the ground of incompatibility with the Convention. This conclusion arises from the importance which the Government attaches to parliamentary sovereignty. In this context, parliamentary sovereignty means that Parliament is competent to make any law on any matter of its choosing and no court may question the validity of any Act that it passes. In enacting legislation, Parliament is making decisions about important matters of public policy. The authority to make those decisions derives from a democratic mandate. Members of Parliament in the House of Commons possess such a mandate because they are elected, accountable and representative. To make provision in the Bill for the courts to set aside Acts of Parliament would confer on the judiciary a general power over the decisions of Parliament which under our present constitutional arrangements they do not possess, and would be likely on occasions to draw the judiciary into serious conflict with Parliament.[47]

The White Paper likewise rejected the idea that what was to become the HRA should be 'entrenched' by giving it special protection against subsequent repeal or amendment. The White Paper specifically cited the US Constitution in this connection, which can be amended only by a highly elaborate process involving a two-thirds majority of both houses of Congress and ratification by three-quarters of the state legislatures.

'But', comments the White Paper, 'an arrangement of this kind could not be reconciled with our own constitutional traditions, which allow any Act of Parliament to be amended or repealed by a subsequent Act of Parliament. We do not believe that it is necessary or would be desirable to attempt to devise such a special arrangement for this Bill.'

Indeed, whether any UK statute could ever be 'entrenched' is extremely doubtful. For a necessary concomitant of the principle of parliamentary sovereignty, or, better, the legislative supremacy of Parliament, is the doctrine that no Parliament can bind a future Parliament or be bound by a previous Parliament. So, for example, if today's Parliament were to pass legislation setting the basic rate of income tax at 60 per cent 'forever', and if it was permissible for one Parliament to bind a future Parliament, that would mean that no future Parliament could ever lower (or raise) the tax rate – which would make a nonsense of the whole concept of parliamentary legislative supremacy.[48]

All that a declaration of incompatibility does is to flag up the problem without resolving it. A declaration, we are told in section 4(6), 'does not affect the validity, continuing operation or enforcement of the provision in respect of which it is given'. In addition, it 'is not binding on the parties to the proceedings in which it is made'. As Lord Irvine explained:

> A declaration of incompatibility will not itself change the law. The statute will continue to apply despite its incompatibility. But the declaration is very likely to prompt the Government and Parliament to respond.[49]

For the same reason a declaration is not even 'binding on the parties to the proceedings in which it is made', which can prove frustrating to both.[50]

As we have seen, a court does not have to make a declaration of incompatibility, but if it is so minded, section 5 provides that the court has to notify the responsible government minister, who is entitled either to be joined as a party in person or to nominate someone else to be joined as a party. But the minister will presumably take this offer up only if he or she wishes to oppose the issue of a declaration of incompatibility. What if the minister does not wish to oppose it? The declaration will then be duly issued by the court, but it will still have no effect until or unless the legislation is amended.

As the Crown Court cannot issue declarations of incompatibility, the Court of Appeal (Criminal Division) is the lowest criminal court in England and Wales that can notify the relevant minister under section 5. Where this happens, s 5(4) provides that, in England and Wales and Northern Ireland, any such minister or their nominee joined as a party to criminal proceedings 'may, with leave, appeal to the House of Lords against any declaration of incompatibility made in the proceedings'.[51]

## *Fast-track procedure after declaration of incompatibility*

A declaration of incompatibility does not strike down the offending piece of domestic legislation, but it allows the setting in motion of a special fast-track procedure for amending the provision that has been found to be incompatible with the Convention.[52] The same fast-track amendment process can also be used where there has been an adverse judgment against the United Kingdom by the ECtHR.

The procedure is quick and simple: 'If a Minister of the Crown considers that there are compelling reasons' for doing so, 'he may by order make such amendments to the legislation as he considers necessary to remove the incompatibility.' This gives the Executive the power to amend by means of delegated legislation not only the offending Act of Parliament itself but also other primary legislation.[53]

If the offending provision is a piece of subordinate legislation, then the minister may, if he or she considers it 'necessary', use the fast-track process to amend not only the relevant subordinate legislation but even the primary legislation under which that subordinate legislation was made.[54] The minister's powers in regard to the offending subordinate legislation itself are even wider, as he or she may by remedial order not only amend it but even revoke it altogether.

Although it is left to a minister to initiate the fast-track remedial procedure if he or she finds it 'necessary', the final decision rests with Parliament. Unlike most other items of delegated legislation, which become law automatically if not challenged, except in cases of urgency these orders have to be laid before Parliament for 60 days and be approved by affirmative resolution of both Houses to become law.[55]

Does the fast-track remedial process amend the law retrospectively? The normal effect of a statutory amendment is to change the law only with effect from the time when the amendment is passed, or from some later commencement date. Judge-made law, by contrast, takes effect as if it had always been the law. Ironically, this is because in theory there is no such thing as judge-made law: the judge is supposedly only declaring the law, not changing it. So, what the judge declares to be the law must be taken always to have been the law! However, the HRA specifically allows a remedial order to have retrospective effect – as long as this does not result in anyone being found guilty of an offence that was not a crime at the time it was committed.[56]

## STATEMENTS OF COMPATIBILITY

In order to avoid challenges to the validity of future legislation, s 19 of the HRA provides for a 'statement of compatibility' to be made by the minister steering a bill through either House of Parliament. The statement must be made before second reading of the bill and must be in writing and be published 'in such manner as the Minister making it considers appropriate'. In the statement the minister must say that 'in his view the provisions of the Bill are compatible with the Convention rights'.[57] If the minister cannot make a statement of compatibility, then the minister must issue a published written statement 'to the effect that although he is unable to make a statement of compatibility the government nevertheless wishes the House to proceed with the Bill'.[58]

It is still too early to tell what effect these provisions are likely to have, but it is doubtful that they will altogether prevent challenges to future legislation from being pursued through the courts. The passage through Parliament of the great majority of bills will no doubt be heralded by statements of compatibility. This will at least mean that the responsible minister has taken legal advice and been assured that the bill in question is indeed compatible with the HRA. However, a statement of compatibility only expresses the minister's opinion: it certainly cannot prevent a court from finding that the legislation in question is not actually compatible with the Convention rights. As for the negative type of statement, this is intended to signify that, while the government fully recognizes the incompatibility of the legislation with the Convention, it still wishes it to be enacted and enforced. Such cases will no doubt be rare, but even so the government will have to have good justification for taking such a course, otherwise there will be bound to be pressure for the law to be brought into line with the Convention.

# IMPLIED REPEAL

What effect, if any, does the HRA have on the fundamental old doctrine of implied repeal, under which a statutory provision is held to have been automatically repealed by a later inconsistent Act of Parliament? This doctrine is illustrated by many cases, a simple example being *Smith v Benabo*,[59] in which the Divisional Court of King's Bench held that certain provisions contained in an 1817 Act were impliedly repealed by ss 122 and 123 of the Metropolis Management Act 1855. This case is by no means unique, but it is worth noting that, in finding the earlier provisions impliedly repealed, the court was upholding a decision taken by a magistrate's court. This feature is likewise far from unique. Indeed, any court may declare a statutory provision impliedly repealed by another. Does the HRA abrogate the doctrine of implied repeal in regard to Convention rights?

There appear to be some attempts in the HRA to fetter the discretion of the courts in this regard. There is, for example, the pointed omission of the Crown Court from the courts competent to issue a statement of incompatibility. How then is a defendant in a criminal trial to challenge a statutory provision that he or she claims is inconsistent with a Convention right? Neither the magistrates' courts nor the Crown Court can issue a declaration of incompatibility. Does this mean that these courts cannot even consider the question of incompatibility? Even if they are not competent to do so in regard to legislation passed after the coming into force of the HRA, what about earlier statutes? Can a Crown Court judge not pronounce an earlier statutory provision impliedly repealed by the HRA? On general principles, there would seem to be no reason why not. Otherwise, any criminal case in which such a defence was run would have to go on appeal on that point, hardly a satisfactory solution.

# DEROGATIONS

Article 15(1) of the Convention expressly allows states to 'derogate' from (that is, opt out of) obligations under the Convention 'in time of war or other public emergency threatening the life of the nation'. The United Kingdom has done this in only one instance, namely in regard to the right in Article 5(3) allowing anyone lawfully arrested or detained 'to be brought promptly before a judge' or equivalent.

In *Brogan v UK*[60] the four applicants had been arrested by police under the Prevention of Terrorism (Temporary Provisions) Act 1984 and taken to holding centres, where they were kept for between four and a half and nearly seven days. None of them were brought before a judge while in custody. Interestingly, however, none of them chose to avail himself of the remedy of habeas corpus, an application for release from illegal custody or detention. As there was no bar to their applying for habeas corpus, the Strasbourg court found no violation of ECHR Article 5(4):

> Everyone who is deprived of his liberty by arrest or detention shall be entitled to take proceedings by which the lawfulness of his detention shall be decided speedily by a court and his release ordered if the detention is not lawful.

However, because the authorities did not bring them before a judge 'promptly' enough, the Strasbourg court held there had been a violation of their rights under Article 5(3). On the basis of this somewhat technical judgment, the UK government immediately decided to derogate from Article 5(3). Though subsequently challenged, this derogation is still in force.[61] The challenge failed on the basis of proportionality.[62]

## RESERVATIONS

Where a state is prepared to observe a particular Convention right, but only on certain conditions, this is referred to as a reservation. Here too, as far as the United Kingdom is concerned, only one Convention right is affected. This is the second sentence of Article 2 of the First Protocol:

> **The First Protocol – Article 2**
>
> ***Right to education***
>
> No person shall be denied the right to education. In the exercise of any functions which it assumes in relation to education and to teaching, the State shall respect the right of parents to ensure such education and teaching in conformity with their own religious and philosophical convictions.

The United Kingdom had no quarrel with the general right in the first sentence. But the second sentence is accepted 'only so far as it is compatible with the provision of efficient instruction and training, and the avoidance of unreasonable public expenditure'. The principle behind this reservation (in force since 1952) is now enshrined in s 9 of the Education Act 1996.

## RESTRICTIONS, LIMITATIONS AND EXCEPTIONS

It is important not to confuse these with derogations or reservations. The structure of most articles of the Convention is to have a statement of the relevant right in paragraph 1 and then, in the second and following paragraphs, a list of circumstances justifying a breach of the right. These latter are variously labelled restrictions, limitations or exceptions. And as we are often told by Strasbourg, they form an integral part of the Convention right in question. It is more realistic to regard them instead as belonging to a rival set of values competing with those of the Convention right itself. To be fair, Strasbourg does recognize that sometimes too, though not in those terms. It prefers to talk about striking 'a fair balance' between the rights of the individual applicant and the public interest.

Article 8(1), for example, guarantees everyone's 'right to respect for his private and family life, his home and his correspondence'. This is unspecific enough as it is, but the waters really become muddied by Article 8(2), which subjects these amorphous rights to some supremely vague exceptions. To be justifiable, we read, any interference with the rights in Article 8(1) must be 'in accordance with the law' and 'necessary in a democratic society' in the interests of certain objectives, namely 'national security, public safety or the economic well being of the country' for certain purposes, such as 'for the prevention of disorder or crime, for the protection of health or morals, or for the protection of the rights and freedoms of others'.

Similar restrictions are to be found in Articles 9, 10 and 11. It is worth noting that according to Strasbourg jurisprudence the rights themselves are meant to be interpreted broadly but the exceptions narrowly.[63]

This doctrine can be traced to Articles 17 and 18 of the Convention quoted above.

## *'Prescribed by law'*

'In accordance with the law' in Article 8(2) is generally equated with 'prescribed by law' in Articles 9(2) , 10(2) and 11(2). What this means is that for 'interference' with the Convention right in question to pass muster it must be lawful in terms of the law of the state concerned. That seems pretty obvious and straightforward, but, needless to say, it is only the starting point.

There are supposedly two (sometimes said to be three) 'principles' applicable here. First, the law in question must be 'adequately accessible' and, second, it must be precise enough to have foreseeable consequences.[64]

In *Silver v UK*[65] it was held by Strasbourg that the stopping or delaying of prisoners' letters was 'in accordance with the law' in a few instances but not in accordance with the law and therefore a violation of Article 8 in the case of other letters. This was partly on the ground that the law relied upon by the prison authorities included Standing Orders and Circular Instructions which were not published. The Prison Rules 1964, which were published, gave prison governors a wide discretion to read or examine prisoners' mail and 'to stop any letter or communication on the ground that its contents are objectionable or that it is of inordinate length'. Other basic rules were concerned with the identity of a prisoner's correspondents. Thus, Rule 33(2): 'Except as provided by statute or these Rules, a prisoner shall not be permitted to communicate with any outside person, or that person with him, without the leave of the Secretary of State.'

*Silver* is only one of a long list of human rights cases won by convicted prisoners. The whole debate in *Silver* over the legality of such rules and orders has an air of unreality about it. One point that does not appear anywhere in the Strasbourg judgment in this case is a recognition that there could perhaps be some intrinsic justification for not allowing convicted prisoners the full range of rights available to others; that this less favourable treatment might even be considered as a justifiable part of their punishment; and that the legality of such rules and orders should be viewed in this light.

## *'Legitimate aim'*

The restrictions listed in Articles 8–11 are the only 'legitimate aims' justifying 'interference' by public authorities with those rights. But, unlike UK domestic law (such as proof 'beyond reasonable doubt' in criminal cases or 'on a balance of probabilities' in civil), Strasbourg has no standard of proof beyond vague phrases such as the need for a restriction to be 'convincingly established'. But the restrictions are very loosely worded, so that, in spite of Articles 17 and 18 and occasional interpretation guidelines, the outcome of a case is often unpredictable. In 1979 the Strasbourg court clarified the relationship between Convention rights and restrictions.

> The Court is faced not with a choice between two conflicting principles, but with a principle of freedom of expression that is subject to a number of exceptions which must be narrowly interpreted . . . . It is not sufficient that the interference belongs to that class of the exceptions listed in article 10(2) which has been invoked; neither is it sufficient that the interference was imposed because its subject-matter fell within a particular category or was caught by a legal rule formulated in general or absolute terms: the Court has to be satisfied that the interference was necessary having regard to the facts and circumstances prevailing in the specific case before it.[66]

Probably the most important of all the 'legitimate aims' is 'the protection of the rights and freedoms of others'. This is a restriction found in Articles 8, 9 and 11, and with a slight variation in Article 10 as well. But what if the 'rights of others' engaged in a particular case also happen to be substantive rights under another article of the Convention?

This is what happened in *Otto-Preminger-Institut v Austria*,[67] where a complaint under Article 10 (freedom of expression) was met by a defence of 'rights of others', which, besides being a restriction under Article 10(2), is also a substantive right under Article 9 (freedom of religion). The basis of the complaint to Strasbourg was that the seizure and forfeiture of a film under an Austrian law which criminalized 'disparaging religious doctrine' was a violation of Article 10 (freedom of expression). The Strasbourg Human Rights Commission found that this did indeed constitute a violation, but the Strasbourg court disagreed.

## *'Necessary in a democratic society'*

The key to the list of 'legitimate aims' in Articles 8–11 is the phrase 'necessary in a democratic society'. 'Necessary' is a very strong word, but it has never been properly defined. We do, however, have an unhelpful string of non-definitions:

> 'Necessary' is not synonymous with indispensable', neither has it the flexibility of such expressions as 'admissible', ordinary', 'useful', 'reasonable' or 'desirable', and . . . it implies the existence of a 'pressing social need'.[68]

So is 'necessary in a democratic society', which does at least appear in the Convention (four times over), to be read as meaning 'pressing social need', which is not to be found in the Convention at all? And how is that phrase to be interpreted? No definition of it has been vouchsafed to us.

Some clue to its relationship to 'necessary in a democratic society' may possibly be gleaned from a remark in the *Sunday Times (Thalidomide)* case in 1979, where it was said that, in determining whether a particular restriction on a specific Convention 'right was 'necessary in a democratic society' the court must assess 'whether the interference complained of corresponded to a pressing social need, whether it was proportionate to the legitimate aim pursued, whether the reasons given by the national authorities to justify it are relevant and sufficient . . . '.[69] What an impressive line-up we have here of all the usual suspects: 'pressing social need', 'legitimate aim' and – the most fashionable of them all – 'proportionality'.

## *Proportionality*

Sometimes termed a 'doctrine' and at other times a 'principle' or even a 'general principle of law', proportionality has long been a great favourite in European jurisprudence, both in the EU and in the Human Rights court, and also in mainland European domestic jurisdictions.

In its original sense it is quite a simple concept, encapsulated in the adage that one should not use a sledgehammer to crack a nut. Imposing the death penalty for jay-walking would be a good example of a disproportionate sentence. Proportionality was more formally defined by the Committee of Ministers of the Council of Europe (the umbrella body for the European Human Rights Convention) in 1980 as requiring an administrative body exercising a discretionary power to 'maintain a proper balance between any adverse effects which its decision may have on the rights, liberties or interests of persons and the purpose which it pursues.'[70]

There are said to be two (or sometimes three) relevant tests for proportionality in general: the 'balancing test' and the 'necessity test' (with the possible addition of the so-called 'suitability test'). The balancing test requires a comparison between ends and means, so that the end is not disproportionate to the means used to attain it. Costs of £100,000 in a court case worth only £10,000 would be a good example. The necessity test asks whether the measure in question was the only one that could have been used to achieve the desired objective. An example of this is the charming old German decision that exempted an innkeeper from being fined for excessive noise if the noise level could have been reduced by allowing the inn longer opening hours.[71]

In the specific context of human rights law longer lists of criteria for proportionality have been compiled, including:

(1) whether 'relevant and sufficient' reasons have been advanced in support of it;
(2) whether there was a less restrictive alternative;
(3) whether there has been some measure of procedural fairness in the decision-making process;
(4) whether safeguards against abuse exist; and
(5) whether the restriction in question destroys the 'very essence' of the Convention right in issue.[72]

On the face of it these criteria seem fair enough, but they are also vague enough to be open to a variety of interpretations. So, for example, in *Campbell v UK*[73] a case involving the opening of a convicted murderer's mail (yes, another one of those cases!), the Strasbourg court held that, though some control over a prisoner's correspondence was not in itself incompatible with the Convention,[74] opening all letters was 'disproportionate', as the same objective could have been achieved by opening only those letters where there was 'reasonable cause' to suspect that a particular letter may not have been as innocent as it looked. What exactly would justify opening a letter on the basis of 'reasonable cause'? No guidance was forthcoming.

## CAN YOU STILL TAKE YOUR CASE TO STRASBOURG?

UK cases will still be able to go to Strasbourg provided they have exhausted all domestic remedies, as laid down by ECHR Article 35. This has always been the rule, but, as we have seen, once the HRA came into force many more domestic remedies became available in the United Kingdom.

One difference between Strasbourg's approach and that of the domestic courts is that, strictly speaking, the important doctrine of 'the margin of appreciation' is available only from a Strasbourg vantage point (see below).

## MARGIN OF APPRECIATION

The 'margin of appreciation' is a movable feast – or perhaps a Cheshire cat. 'Margin of appreciation' is a favourite Strasbourg buzz-phrase. To call it a principle is probably going too far, as it fluctuates a great deal from case to case and sometimes vanishes almost completely, like the Cheshire cat in *Alice in Wonderland*. It refers to the discretion allowed by Strasbourg to the national authorities to determine how and to what extent human rights are to be safeguarded and what restrictions are to be imposed upon them. Is it available in domestic courts in the post-HRA era at all or only once a case reaches Strasbourg? (See below.)

The width or scope of the margin is not fixed but varies in accordance with the 'context', or the nature of the right in issue, and also to some extent with fashions in social values. Whatever the scope of the margin allowed in any particular case, it is subject to 'European supervision', that is, review by the Strasbourg court to determine whether the national decisions are compatible with the Convention and proportionate to the legitimate aims pursued. The concept of supervision is the flip-side of the concept of the margin of appreciation itself, and will vary in inverse proportion to the scope of the margin allowed. Or, in the words of Lord Hope, 'The extent of this supervision will vary according to such factors as the nature of the convention right in issue, the importance of that right for the individual and the nature of the activities involved in the case.' And again:

> This doctrine [of the margin of appreciation] is an integral part of the supervisory jurisdiction which is exercised over state conduct by the international court. By conceding a margin of appreciation to each national system, the court has recognised that the convention, as a living system, does not need to be applied uniformly by all states but may vary in its application according to local needs and conditions.[75]

It is worth noting that the margin accorded to one country may be different from that allowed to another – a licence for Strasbourg to discriminate in favour of some states and against others. In terms of 'context', that is, subject matter of the right concerned, moral considerations have tended to enjoy the widest margin, but this is now changing and margins have been contracting generally, with a corresponding increase in Strasbourg assertiveness. In 1976 the Strasbourg court actually went so far as to hold that 'the machinery of protection established by the Convention is subsidiary to the national systems safeguarding human rights'. The position has changed perceptibly since then. The Strasbourg decision that, despite the special measures taken by the UK authorities to allow for their youth, Venables and Thompson, the murderers of little Jamie Bulger, had not had a fair trial, is a case in point. Although it might have been thought to be very much in point, the concept of the margin of appreciation does not even appear to have been referred to in these judgments, in which the whole approach of the UK court was pilloried.[76]

In determining the appropriate margin of appreciation Strasbourg also has regard to the procedural safeguards provided to the applicant by the state in question. Where a national authority claimed the right to 'interfere' with a Convention right, the procedure involved had to be fair.

Strasbourg's 'supervision' to which the margin of appreciation is subject is sometimes described as a 'review' in terms similar to those applicable to judicial review in English law, giving the Strasbourg court the right to determine whether the national authorities have infringed the relevant Convention rights but without giving it the right to substitute its own (Strasbourg's) views for those of the national authorities.

## *Balance*

The purpose underlying the setting of the margin of appreciation is sometimes described in terms of striking a 'fair balance' between public and private interests, that is, the interests of the community at large as against the protection of the fundamental rights of the individual. This position was well put in a case involving town planning:

> In an area as complex and difficult as that of the development of large cities, the Contracting States should enjoy a wide margin of appreciation in order to implement their town-planning policy. Nevertheless, the Court cannot fail to exercise its power of review and must determine whether the requisite balance was maintained in a manner consonant with the applicants' right to the 'peaceful enjoyment of [their] possessions', within the meaning of the first sentence of Article 1.[77]

## *Margin of appreciation in the UK courts?*

The margin of appreciation is a Strasbourg doctrine. But what about domestic cases? This is particularly relevant now that Convention rights are accessible in the UK domestic courts. In October 1999, after the HRA had been passed but before it came into force, Lord Hope expressed the view that the doctrine of the margin of appreciation 'is not available to the national courts when they are considering convention issues arising within their own countries'. He went on to qualify this:

> In some circumstances it will be appropriate for the courts to recognise that there is an area of judgment within which the judiciary will defer, on democratic grounds, to the considered opinion of the elected body or person whose act or decision is said to be incompatible with the convention.[78]

This view was based on an extract from a book written by two senior barristers:

> This doctrine of margin of appreciation does not apply when a national court is considering the Human Rights Act. However, an analogous doctrine should be recognised by national courts. Just as there are circumstances in which an international court will recognise that national institutions are better placed to assess the needs of society, and to make difficult choices between competing considerations, so national courts will accept that there are some circumstances in which the legislature and the executive are better placed to perform those functions.[79]

It seems now to be accepted in the United Kingdom that the doctrine of the margin of appreciation is not applicable in the domestic courts, although 'an analogous doctrine', labelled 'the discretionary area of judgment', is available. Where did this dogma come from? It is the creation of a couple of legal commentators – not a particularly reassuring fact. There is no explanation of why the doctrine is not available to the UK domestic courts, which is all the more baffling as a doctrine that appears indistinguishable from it is supposedly available!

The proper starting point should be the fundamental constitutional principle of parliamentary sovereignty, or more accurately, the legislative supremacy of Parliament:[80]

> The sovereignty of Parliament is (from a legal point of view) the dominant characteristic of our political institutions . . . . Parliament means, in the mouth of a lawyer . . . the Queen, the House of Lords and the House of Commons; these three bodies acting together may be aptly described as the 'Queen in Parliament', and constitute Parliament.
>
> The principle of parliamentary sovereignty means neither more nor less than this, namely that Parliament thus defined has, under the English constitution, the right to make or unmake any law whatsoever; and, further, that no person or body is recognized by the law of England as having a right to override or set aside the legislation of Parliament.

No court can therefore set aside an Act of Parliament, except in the case of a clash with European Union law.[81] But this exception does not apply in the case of human rights law. This has been recognized even by Lord Steyn, who has expressed the view that the Human Rights Act has 'higher order law' status.[82] Yet even Lord Steyn is on record as accepting the principle of parliamentary sovereignty in regard to human rights law:

> It is crystal clear that the carefully and subtly drafted 1998 [Human Rights] Act preserves the principle of parliamentary sovereignty. In a case of incompatibility . . . the courts may not disapply the legislation. The court may merely issue a declaration of incompatibility which then gives rise to a power to take remedial action: see s 10.[83]

What then did Lord Hope mean in the passage quoted above about the judges' discretion to 'defer on democratic grounds' in the event of such incompatibility? Lord Hope is not here talking about setting aside or disapplying an Act of Parliament if it is said to be incompatible with a Convention right. It is fully admitted on all hands that no court has any such power in regard to human rights law. What Lord Hope is referring to is presumably the possibility that, in recognition of the democratic provenance of a particular law or decision, it will be found that it is not incompatible with the Human Rights Convention.

How different is the exercise of this judicial discretion from what the Strasbourg court does under the label of 'margin of appreciation'? Hardly at all. So, to deny that the concept of the margin of appreciation has any applicability to domestic courts is less than helpful.

A case in which anti-terrorist legislation was challenged as being incompatible with the Human Rights Convention is a good example of a UK domestic application of this doctrine (after a false start), although the case in question was actually decided in the period between the passing of the Human Rights Act in 1998 and its coming into force in October 2000.[84]

## Terrorism

How do you prove that someone is a terrorist? If he or she is found, say, with large sums of money, a false passport, a rubber mask and radio equipment, could that possibly be enough to give rise to a 'reasonable suspicion' that he or she is planning an act of terrorism? A 1989 law said that if there was any 'reasonable suspicion' of terrorism arising out of articles or documents in a person's possession, then the person concerned was guilty of an offence carrying a maximum penalty of 10 years' imprisonment.[85] However, the same law provided that it was a defence for the accused to prove that the articles in question were not in his or her possession for the purposes of terrorism, or in the case of documents, that he or she had lawful authority or a reasonable excuse for having them in his/her possession.

In other words, the burden of proof in cases of this kind rested not on the prosecution, which is the usual position in criminal cases, but on the defendant. Did this amount to a violation of the presumption of innocence contained in Article 6(2) of the Human Rights Convention? This was the issue before the English courts in the *Kebeline* case.[86]

In the Divisional Court Lord Bingham CJ held that the sections in question 'undermine, in a blatant and obvious way, the presumption of innocence'.[87] He added that 'Whenever a criminal intention is an essential ingredient of a crime the defendant is better placed to prove his intention than anyone else, but this does not relieve the prosecution of the need to prove a criminal intention against him in the overwhelming majority of cases.'[88]

In the House of Lords, however, Lord Hope made the important point that under the doctrine of parliamentary sovereignty there is nothing to stop Parliament from shifting the burden of proof if it feels like it. So although this principle is commonly referred to as a 'golden thread' running 'throughout the web of the English Criminal Law'[89] Parliament is not bound by it. Lord Hope cited Glanville Williams's observation that 'Parliament regards the principle with indifference',[90] adding however, 'That may be overstating the matter; but it is clear that until now, under the doctrine of sovereignty, the only check on Parliament's freedom to legislate in this area has been political. All that will now change with the coming into force of the Human Rights Act 1998.'[91]

This is slightly puzzling. In what sense has the coming into force of the Human Rights Act affected Parliament's freedom to legislate as it pleases? In terms of law, it has not done so at all. For as the Act itself makes clear, and as even radical judges have admitted, the courts have no power to strike down any parliamentary legislation on the ground of incompatibility with human rights law. All they can do is to flag up this incompatibility by means of a declaration of incompatibility, leaving it up to the government and Parliament to decide whether they wish to amend the offending law or not.

As evidence of Parliament's freedom to legislate on this important matter Lord Hope reeled off no fewer than 11 Acts of Parliament that contain provisions reversing the burden of proof in regard to a variety of serious criminal offences, including riot, drug trafficking and of course terrorism. These provisions all sought to address the legislative problem of 'how to curb a grave evil which postulates a guilty mind or mental element on the part of the offender, when proof of that guilty mind or mental element is likely to be a matter of inherent difficulty'.[92]

This is a practical consideration of some importance, for in Lord Hope's words, 'Society has a strong interest in preventing acts of terrorism before they are perpetrated – to spare the lives of innocent people and to avoid the massive damage and dislocation to ordinary life which may follow from explosions which destroy or damage property.'[93]

Was the shifting of the burden of proof in the 1989 anti-terrorism legislation incompatible with Article 6(2) of the Human Rights Convention, as the Divisional Court had held? Such a finding, said Lord Hope, was not 'inevitable'. As this case was decided before the Human Rights Act had actually come into force, the issue of compatibility with the Convention did not have to be decided. But it is clear that there is more than one possible answer to this question.

It is instructive to compare *Kebeline* with *Salabiaku*, a French case which went to Strasbourg a few years earlier. Here too the issue was the presumption of guilt. Amosi Salabiaku was arrested at a French airport after collecting a trunk containing a large amount of cannabis. Charged with smuggling prohibited goods, he claimed that he had picked up the trunk by mistake. After appealing without success all the way up to the highest French court, the Cour de Cassation, he took his case to Strasbourg claiming that the French Customs Code under which he had been convicted was incompatible with the presumption of innocence guaranteed by Article 6(2). Under the Code, if a person entering France from outside was in possession of prohibited goods he or she was deemed to be guilty of smuggling. This was an irrebuttable presumption and no defence was stipulated in the Code. Nevertheless, allowing a wide margin of appreciation to the French authorities, the Strasbourg court held that there had been no infringement of Article 6(2), on the ground that, despite the peremptory wording of the Customs Code, the French courts in practice did not rely automatically on the presumption of guilt but took all the evidence into account in reaching their verdict.[94]

Citing *Salabiaku*, Lord Hope in *Kebeline* commented, 'The cases show that, although Art 6(2) is in absolute terms, it is not regarded as imposing an absolute prohibition on reverse onus clauses, whether they be evidential (presumptions of fact) or persuasive (presumptions of law). In each case the question will be whether the presumption is within reasonable grounds.'[95]

## Wide margin

How can you tell in advance what margin of appreciation is likely to be applied in your particular case? This is not always easy to predict. At one time moral issues enjoyed the widest margin, but this is likely to vary with the current fashions in social values. The case of the *Little Red Schoolbook* is a good example.

The book, aimed at a teenage market, contained a graphic description of a variety of sexual practices. Richard Handyside, its publisher, fell foul of the British obscenity laws. The book was banned and the print matrix and remaining copies of the book were destroyed by court order. He took his case to Strasbourg claiming that this infringed his right to freedom of expression guaranteed by Article 10(1) of the Convention. Relying on the restrictions on this right contained in Article 10(2), the United Kingdom argued that the legislation complained of was 'necessary in a democratic society' for 'the protection of morals'. Yet the book had been published in Denmark and several other countries without incident – and even in Scotland, where a bookseller was charged under Scots indecency laws, he was acquitted because the court found that the book was not obscene or indecent. By 13 votes to 1 the Strasbourg court nevertheless accepted the United Kingdom's defence and held that there had been no violation of Article 10. Handyside's claim that the confiscation and destruction of the books was a breach of his right to the peaceful enjoyment of his property under Article 1 of Protocol 1 was even more unceremoniously dismissed.[96]

This case represents the high-water mark of the margin of appreciation, with Strasbourg accepting the right of the UK authorities to set the relevant moral standards, even though it was clear that the UK standards were much less tolerant than those of many other countries. Convention protection, it was held, was subsidiary to national systems safeguarding human rights. In the absence of a uniform conception of morals there had to be a considerable domestic margin of appreciation, subject to European supervision. This judgment was given in 1980, but it is by no means certain that *Handyside* would be decided differently today. In general the trend has been for the margin of appreciation to become narrower, not wider.

## Notes

1 *R v Ministry of Defence, ex parte Smith* [1996] QB 517 at 554, per Bingham MR for the Court of Appeal.
2 582 House of Lords Official Report (5th series), col 1279 (3 November 1997).
3 These bodies must be distinguished from the similarly named but totally unconnected institutions of the European Union: the European Commission (based in Brussels) the European Court of Justice (based in Luxembourg) and the European Council (previously known as the Council of Ministers of the European Communities, which usually meets in Brussels).
4 *Young, James and Webster v UK* (1982) 4 EHRR 38, (1983) 5 EHRR 201 81/3.
5 *Marcic v Thames Water Utilities Ltd* [2001] 3 All ER 698.
6 *RSPCA v Attorney General* [2001] UKHRR 90S (§ 37).
7 *Poplar Housing and Regeneration Community Association Ltd v Donoghue* [2001] EWCA Civ 595 [2001], 3 WLR 183 [2001], 4 All ER 604 (§§ 58, 66).
8 *R (on the application of Heather and others) v Leonard Cheshire Foundation* [2002] EWCA Civ 366, [2002] 2 All ER 936.

9 *R v Panel on Take-overs and Mergers, ex parte Datafin plc* [1987] 1 All ER 564 at 577.
10 There may of course be some ordinary common law cause of action that would be applicable, such as trespass or breach of confidence, but that is another matter.
11 *R (on the application of Ford) v Press Complaints Commission* (31 July 2001 – unreported).
12 *R (on the application of Anderson) v Secretary of State for the Home Department* [2002] UKHL 46, [2002] 4 All ER 1089.
13 At the time of writing, the new legislation had not yet been presented to Parliament. In view of a recent decision by the Strasbourg court it is open to doubt whether any such legislation would be likely to succeed: *Egon von Bulow v UK*, ECtHR, 7 October 2003, Application no 00075362/01.
14 *Douglas v Hello!* [2001] 2 All ER 289 at 322 (§133)..
15 *Wilson v First County Trust* [2001] EWCA Civ 633, [2001] 3 All ER 229. See Chapter 3, Case Study A.
16 *Marckx v Belgium* (1979) 2 EHRR 330 at 340 79/2.
17 *Norris v Ireland* (1988) 13 EHRR 186 88/14.
18 *Campbell and Cosans v UK* (1980) 3 EHRR 531, (1982) 4 EHRR 293 82/1.
19 *McCann v UK* (1995) 21 EHRR 97 95/28.
20 *R v Inland Revenue Commissioners, ex parte National Federation of Self-Employed and Small Businesses Ltd* [1982] AC 617 at 642 (Lord Diplock).
21 Civil Procedure Rules 1998 (CPR) 3.1(2)(a).
22 *Christine Goodwin v UK* (2002) 28957/95 (§74).
23 *Re H (Minors) (Abduction: Acquiescence)* [1998] AC 72 at 87.
24 Lord Steyn (1998) Incorporation and devolution: a few reflections on the changing scene, *European Human Rights Law Review* 153 at 155.
25 *R (on the application of Anderson) v Secretary of State for the Home Department* [2002] UKHL 46, [2002] 4 All ER 1089 at 1102 (§30).
26 HRA s 3(2)(a).
27 HRA s 3(2)(b).
28 HRA ss 3(2)(c), 6(1).
29 HRA s 8(1).
30 HRA s 8(3).
31 Supreme Court Act 1981, s 31(5).
32 *Overseers of the Poor of Walsall v London & North Western Railway Co* [1878] 4 AC 30 at 39–40.
33 Civil Procedure Rules 1998 (CPR) 54.19.
34 See Chapter 2.
35 *R (on the application of Anderson) v Secretary of State for the Home Department* [2002] UKHL 46, [2002] 4 All ER 1089.
36 *R (on the application of Anderson) v Secretary of State for the Home Department* [2002] UKHL 46, [2002] 4 All ER 1089 at 1102 (§30).
37 See the discussion in Chapter 6.

38 315 House of Commons Official Report (6th series) col 536 (2 July 1998).
39 315 House of Commons Official Report (6th series) col 543 (2 July 1998).
40 Sedley LJ in *Douglas v Hello!* [2001] 2 All ER 289 at 323 §136.
41 Lord Lester and David Pannick (1999) *Human Rights Law and Practice*, London, p 50.
42 *Ibid.*
43 See *The Times*, 15 May 2003.
44 585 House of Lords Official Report (5th series) cols 747–813 (5 February 1998).
45 583 House of Lords Official Report (5th series) col 551, 18 November 1997.
46 HRA ss 4(4), 6(1).
47 *Rights Brought Home: The Human Rights Bill* (Cm 3782), §2.13.
48 Cf Ian Loveland (2000) *Constitutional Law: A critical introduction*, 2nd edn, p 33.
49 582 House of Lords Official Report (5th series) col 1231 (3 November 1997).
50 See, for example, *Wilson v First County Trust* [2001] EWCA Civ 633, [2001] 3 All ER 229.
51 It has been suggested by a commentator that this provision applies only to private prosecutions or local authority prosecutions and the like, where the Crown is not the prosecutor: Christopher Baker, *Human Rights Act 1998: A practitioner's guide*, p19. The section certainly does not say anything like that, nor is there any reason to interpret it in this narrow fashion.
52 HRA s 10 (1) (a).
53 HRA s 10(2), Sch 2.
54 HRA s 10 (3) (a).
55 HRA Sch 2 SS2–4.
56 Sch 2, S1(1)(b).
57 HRA s 19(l)(a).
58 HRA s 19(l)(b).
59 *Smith v Benabo* [1937] 1 KB 518.
60 *Brogan v UK* (1989) 11 EHRR 117 88/17.
61 HRA, Schedule 3, Part I.
62 *Brannigan v UK* (1994) 17 EHRR 539.
63 *Niemietz v Germany* (1992) 16 EHRR 97 at 112 (§31) 92/76; *Sunday Times v UK* (1979) 2 EHRR 245 at 281 (§65) 79/1.
64 *Sunday Times v UK* (1979) 2 EHRR 245 at 271 (§49) 79/1.
65 *Silver v UK* (1983) 5 EHRR 347 83/2.
66 *Sunday Times v UK* (1979) 2 EHRR 245 at 281 (S65) 79/1.
67 *Otto-Preminger-Institut v Austria* (1995) 19 EHRR 34 94/25.
68 *Sunday Times v UK* (1979) 2 EHRR 245 at 275 (§59) 79/1; *Handyside v UK* (1976) 1 EHRR 737 at 753–754 (§62) 76/5.
69 *Sunday Times v UK* (1979) 2 EHRR 245 at 277–278 (S62) 79/1.
70 Quoted in Stanley de Smith, Lord Woolf and J Jowell (1995) *Judicial Review of Administrative Action*, 5th ed, p 594.
71 Cited in de Smith, Woolf and Jowell, *op cit*, p 596.

72 Keir Starmer (1999) *European Human Rights Law*, p 171.
73 *Campbell v UK* (1993) 15 EHRR 137 92/41.
74 Cf *Silver v UK* (1983) 5 EHRR 347 83/2.
75 *R v DPP, ex parte Kebeline* [1999] 4 All ER 801 at 844.
76 *V v UK* 99/122; *T v UK* 99/121, Application no 24724/94.
77 *Sporrong and Lönnroth v Sweden* (1982) 5 EHRR 35 at 52 §69 82/5.
78 *R v DPP, ex parte Kebeline* [1999] 4 All ER 801 at 844.
79 Lord Lester and David Pannick (1999) *Human Rights Law and Practice*, p74 §3.21.
80 Dicey (1959) *Introduction to the Study of the Law of the Constitution (1885–1914)*, 10th edn, pp 39 ff.
81 EU law is now regarded as 'higher law' in the sense that if there is a clash between UK domestic law and EU law, EU will prevail and the offending domestic law will be set aside. See *Factortame Ltd v Secretary of State for Transport (No. 1)* [1990] 2 AC 85; (1989) 2 All ER 692 (HL); *(No. 2)*, Case C-213/89 [1991] 1 All ER 70 (ECJ & HL); [1991] 1 AC 603. However, it is important to recognize that as far as the United Kingdom is concerned the whole edifice of EU law itself rests on a UK domestic law, namely the European Communities Act 1972. If this Act were to be repealed – which would happen if the United Kingdom ceased to be a member of the EU or if the EU ceased to exist – then the whole huge apparatus of EU law would collapse and no longer have any effect in the United Kingdom.
82 See the discussion in Chapter 3 under 'Fuzzy logic'.
83 *R v DPP, ex parte Kebeline* [1999] 4 All ER 801 at 831.
84 *R v DPP, ex parte Kebeline* [1999] 4 All ER 801.
85 Sections 16A & B of the Prevention of Terrorism (Temporary Provisions) Act 1989.
86 *R v DPP, ex parte Kebeline* [1999] 4 All ER 801.
87 *Ibid* at 815.
88 *Ibid* at 816.
89 *Woolmington v DPP* [1935] AC 442 at 481.
90 *R v DPP ex parte Kebeline* [1999] 4 All ER 801 at 841, citing Glanville Williams (1963) *The Proof of Guilt*, 3rd edn.
91 *R v DPP, ex parte Kebeline* [1999] 4 All ER 801 at 841–842.
92 *Ibid* at 846.
93 *Ibid* at 850.
94 *Salabiaku v France* (1988) 13 EHRR 379 88/12.
95 *R v DPP, ex parte Kebeline* [1999] 4 All ER 801 at 847.
96 *Handyside v United Kingdom* (1979–80) 1 EHRR 737 76/5.
97 Some UK judges have gone well beyond any interpretation ever proposed by Strasbourg. In *London Borough of Harrow v Qazi* [2003] UKHL 43, the House of Lords split 3:2, with the minority going so far as to interpret Art 8(1) as conferring a right to a home. Lord Steyn characterized the approach of the majority as suffering from a 'basic fallacy'.

# 2

# Judicial review

## HOW TO USE JUDICIAL REVIEW TO BRING A HUMAN RIGHTS CLAIM

Judicial review is the most important and commonest way of bringing a human rights claim. It is available only from the High Court, or to be more precise, from what is now known as the Administrative Court. Judicial review can be used to challenge the legality of a decision taken by a public authority such as a government minister or department, a local authority, a lower court or a statutory body such as the Monopolies and Mergers Commission or the Human Fertilisation and Embryology Authority. If your claim is specifically based on an alleged violation of a Convention right, then you can bring it only if you are a victim of the decision.

Judicial review is different from an appeal. In order to have the right to appeal against a decision there has to be a statute, an Act of Parliament, specifically providing for it. Appeals are mostly made against court judgments, although there also are certain administrative bodies from whose decisions it is possible to appeal. There is a hierarchy of courts, with the possibility of appeal lying from one level to the next and culminating in the House of Lords. You will generally need permission to lodge your appeal. The court hearing the appeal will normally have the right to decide the whole case again, and if it wishes, to substitute its own decision for that of the court below.[1]

This is precisely where a judicial review differs from an appeal. The court conducting a review is concerned to determine the lawfulness, but not the merits, of the decision under review. The natural corollary to this is that though the court could quash the impugned decision, that is, set it aside, it could not substitute its own decision for that of the original decision maker. However, a recent procedural change now allows the court to do just that, with the result that the substantive law has been changed by the back door.[2]

Does the distinction between a review and an appeal have any practical meaning any more, or is it merely a distinction without a difference? If properly respected, the distinction is an important one with very real practical effects. But the recent 'procedural' change is only the latest of a series of nails which have been driven into the coffin of judicial self-restraint.

Nevertheless, the very clear way that Lord Brightman put the position in 1982 is still supposedly the law today:

> Judicial review is concerned, not with the decision, but with the decision-making process. Unless that restriction on the power of the court is observed, the court will in my view, under the guise of preventing the abuse of power, be itself guilty of usurping power.[3]

## WEDNESBURY

In the most famous judicial review case of all, commonly known as *Wednesbury*, decided in 1947, the issue was the lawfulness of a decision taken by a local authority. The Sunday Entertainments Act 1932 gave local authorities the power to grant a licence to cinemas to show films on Sundays 'subject to such conditions as the authority think fit to impose'. A cinema in the Wednesbury area applied to the local council for such a licence. The council agreed to grant them a licence but attached to it the condition that no children under 15 were to be admitted to the Sunday shows even if accompanied by an adult. This condition made the licence practically useless to the cinema. What was the point of Sunday cinema if children could not attend? It has to be remembered that this all happened in the days when English family life still existed.

The cinema proprietors challenged the lawfulness of this restrictive condition. In his judgment Lord Greene was at pains to stress that the question was not whether he or his fellow judges would have allowed children in, but the very different and much narrower question of whether the local authority had been acting lawfully in taking the decision that they took. In short, the court engaged in a judicial review is not allowed to 'second guess' the original decision. In a review the power of the court is much less than in an appeal.

In the words of Lord Greene MR:

> The power of the court to interfere in each case is not as an appellate authority to override a decision of the local authority, but as a judicial authority which is concerned, and concerned only, to see whether the local authority have contravened the law by acting in excess of the powers which Parliament has confided in them.[4]

This last phrase is fundamental: the right to make the decision under review was given by Act of Parliament not to the courts but to the local authority. For a court to substitute its own decision for that of the local authority would amount to a usurpation of the right of the local authority, and could even be seen as an attempt to subvert the intention of Parliament.

*Wednesbury* is now over half a century old and has been subjected to a tremendous onslaught from judicial activists or judicial supremacists who want to expand the power of the judiciary. One senior judge has gone so far as to predict that 'the day will come when it will be more widely recognised that the *Wednesbury* case was an unfortunately retrogressive decision in English administrative law, in so far as it suggested that there are degrees of unreasonableness and that only a very extreme degree can bring an administrative decision within the legitimate scope of judicial invalidation.'[5]

This remark appears to miss the point that Lord Greene was at such pains to make. In cases of this kind, said Lord Greene, '[t]he law recognises certain principles. . . . What, then, are those principles? They are perfectly well understood.' Lord Greene then goes on to set out these principles. They are really quite simple.

- **Illegality.** Is the decision under review lawful? In *Wednesbury* itself, as we have seen, Parliament had allowed the local authority to grant Sunday licences 'subject to such conditions as the authority think fit to impose'. This is a very wide discretion indeed. Was the local authority acting within what Lord Greene called 'the four corners' of this discretion? If it had stepped outside these four corners, it would have been acting *ultra vires,* or beyond its powers, and its decision could have been quashed by the court. But so wide was the discretion granted to it by Parliament that this was not the case here at all. Its decision to include the restriction against children under 15 was therefore lawful and could not be set aside by the court even if the judges had disagreed with it.
- **Unreasonableness.** Once it is found that the decision under review is not unlawful, that would normally be the end of the matter – unless the decision was perverse or unreasonable in the extreme. Lord Greene's formulation of what is still termed 'Wednesbury unreasonableness' echoes down the years. For a decision to be set aside as 'unreasonable', said Lord Greene, it has to be 'so unreasonable that no reasonable authority could ever have come to it'. The word 'ever' emphasizes just how extreme the degree of unreasonableness has to be before the court can act. This is deliberate. If the threshold of unreasonableness were lowered, judges would be allowed to set aside administrative decisions simply because they did not happen to agree with them. This would amount to a usurpation of the power of the original decision maker by the judge concerned. Lord Greene explained this important point as carefully as he could:

> Some courts might think that no children ought to be admitted on Sundays at all, some courts might think the reverse. All over the country, I have no doubt, on a thing of that sort honest and sincere people hold different views. The effect of the

legislation is not to set up the court as an arbiter of the correctness of one view over another. It is the local authority who are put in that position and, provided they act, as they have acted here, within the four corners of their jurisdiction, the court, in my opinion, cannot interfere.

- **Procedural impropriety.** This third ground of judicial review is concerned not with the actual decision itself but with the way the decision was taken. In short, it is about natural justice. As this was not in issue in Wednesbury it is not mentioned there, but it is a very ancient and important ground.

**Q. Is *Wednesbury* still good law? And does it really make any difference whether it is or not?**

**A. *Wednesbury* is still supposedly good law, though now under frontal attack from activist judges. And yes, it makes a great deal of difference whether it is in force or not.**

In a lecture given in 1995 Lord Irvine of Lairg, the future Lord Chancellor, delivered a powerful blast against 'judicial supremacism' and in favour of the traditional *Wednesbury* approach, advocating 'judicial self-restraint in public law matters . . . which the vast majority of lawyers would still acknowledge to be the guiding principle of our system of judicial review'.[6]

Lord Irvine took issue with the idea expressed by a High Court judge that 'the greater the intrusion proposed by a body possessing public powers over the citizen into an area where his fundamental rights are at stake, the greater must be the justification which the public authority must demonstrate.'[7]

The main target of attack of those opposed to *Wednesbury* is the high threshold of '*Wednesbury* unreasonableness'. Such critics favour what Lord Irvine described as 'a lower standard of *Wednesbury* unreasonableness in fundamental rights cases' and a more 'interventionist role' for the courts. 'On this approach, the court would be invited to exercise a much tighter control over the merits of a decision where it perceives a threat to fundamental rights.' Lord Irvine warned that this approach led the judges 'into dangerous territory':

> The political and legal choices which import consideration of fundamental rights protection are among the most difficult and the most subjective, and offer immense scope for political and philosophical disagreement. It cannot be right that such questions should be regarded as more rather than less suitable to judicial determination. The approach adopted in *Brind*,[8] which states conclusively that the Wednesbury threshold of unreasonableness is not lowered in fundamental rights cases, must prevail.[9]

Those words were written before the passing of the Human Rights Act. With the Act in place the anti-*Wednesbury* forces have been able to draw sustenance from the European Convention on Human Rights insofar as it is incorporated into English law by the Act.

**Q. Do the courts now have greater powers in judicial review cases involving human rights? If so, what practical effect does this have?**

**A. *The courts have tended to arrogate greater powers to themselves where 'fundamental rights' are concerned. But the law on judicial review is in disarray, with several approaches competing with one another.***

In a leading case four homosexual members of the armed forces challenged their discharge from the service as irrational. At first instance the approach adopted was described as follows:

> I approach the case . . . on the conventional *Wednesbury* basis adapted to a human rights context and ask: can the minister show an important competing public interest which he could reasonably judge sufficient to justify the restriction? The primary judgment is for him. Only if his purported justification outrageously defies logic or accepted moral standards can the court, exercising its secondary judgment, properly strike it down.[10]

Except for the requirement that 'the most anxious scrutiny is accorded when fundamental rights are in issue' the standard of irrationality applied here is, if anything, stricter than the well-known definition of *Wednesbury* unreasonableness.

The Court of Appeal adopted the position that where fundamental human rights were involved a 'heightened scrutiny' test was applicable: 'The more substantial the interference with human rights, the more the court will require by way of justification before it is satisfied that the decision is reasonable' in the sense that it is within 'the range of responses open to a reasonable decision-maker.'[11]

Nevertheless the Court of Appeal upheld the first instance decision against the four service personnel, who then took their case to Strasbourg, where a unanimous court found a 'grave violation' of their rights under Article 8.[12]

Subject to the doctrine of the margin of appreciation the Strasbourg court had no hesitation in judging the merits of the ministry's decision:

> The court recognises that it is for the national authorities to make the initial assessment of necessity, though the final evaluation as to whether the reasons cited for the interference [with the applicants' private lives] are relevant and sufficient is one for this court. A margin of appreciation is left open to contracting states in the context of this assessment, which varies according to the nature of the activities restricted and of the aims pursued by the restrictions.[13]

The Strasbourg court took the opportunity of aiming a broadside at what they saw as the undue restrictions placed on the domestic courts by the conventional approach to judicial review:

> The threshold at which the High Court and the Court of Appeal could find the Ministry of Defence policy irrational was placed so high that it effectively excluded any consideration by the domestic courts of the question of whether the interference with the applicants' rights answered a pressing social need or was proportionate to the national security and public order aims pursued, principles which lie at the heart of the Court's analysis of complaints under Article 8 of the Convention.[14]

Now that the HRA and the Convention can be applied directly by the domestic courts, can they too go for the jugular as the Strasbourg court did here?

## 'PROPORTIONALITY APPROACH'

The last-quoted passage was cited with approval in *Daly,* a case involving the rights of convicted prisoners. Lord Steyn there identified two alternative approaches to judicial review: the traditional *Wednesbury* approach and the 'proportionality approach', which he admitted may 'sometimes yield different results'. What exactly is the difference? 'The intensity of review,' according to Lord Steyn, 'is somewhat greater under the proportionality approach'. And: 'Even the heightened scrutiny test developed [by the Court of Appeal in the case on homosexual service personnel] is not necessarily appropriate to the protection of human rights.' Does this mean that in human rights cases the courts should exercise even greater powers than envisaged there to set aside administrative decisions?

Apparently recognizing that this 'proportionality approach' looked very much like an attempt on the part of the court to judge the merits of the decision under review – which was totally forbidden under the traditional approach as a usurpation of the position of the original decision maker – Lord Steyn found it necessary to state quite starkly, 'This does not mean that there has been a shift to merits review.'[15]

## 'MERITS REVIEW'?

Yet is that not exactly what *Daly* was: a 'merits review'? George Daly, a long-term prisoner, objected to the new policy requiring a prisoner's privileged legal correspondence to be searched in the prisoner's absence. Daly lost in the Court of Appeal, which held 'that the policy represented the minimum intrusion into the rights of prisoners consistent with the need to maintain security, order and discipline in prisons.'[16]

But this decision was reversed by a unanimous House of Lords. The relevant legislation, section 47(1) of the Prisons Act 1952, provides that: 'The Secretary of State shall make rules for the regulation and management of prisons . . . and for the classification, treatment, discipline and control of persons required to be detained therein.' This is a very widely drawn power indeed. Moreover, there was no challenge to the right of prison officers to search a prisoner's cell, including his privileged documents. In other words, there was a tacit recognition by the applicants themselves that convicted prisoners were not entitled to the same rights of 'respect for their private and family life' as everybody else. The only objection was to the requirement that the prisoner step outside his cell while the search was being conducted. In these circumstances it is hard to see the House of Lords judgments in *Daly* as anything other than an attempt to substitute their own decision for that of the Home Secretary.

## 'CONTEXT IS EVERYTHING'

Lord Steyn adopted the view that 'the intensity of review in a public law case will depend on the subject matter in hand', adding, 'That is so even in cases involving Convention rights. In law context is everything.'[17]

Context is everything? What does this mean? If this means that principles are subordinate to facts and that the courts should decide matters 'on a case by case basis' (to use a phrase much beloved of some members of today's judiciary), then it is less than reassuring, as it threatens to increase subjectivity and uncertainty at the expense of objectivity, certainty, predictability and therefore of justice.

Context is everything? If this means that the subject matter of the case is all-important, then it becomes even more disquieting. For what this implies is that a case will be treated differently according to the identity of the applicant. And this is arguably borne out by an examination of court decisions. Is it entirely fanciful to suggest that the courts appear unduly concerned to protect the rights of convicted killers and other criminals, prisoners in general and asylum seekers? The recent cases of Venables and Thompson (the murderers of little Jamie Bulger), the child-killer Mary Bell, the murderer Anthony Anderson and the Afghan hijackers differ in many respects but all have one thing in common: victory for convicted criminals.[18]

## 'POLICY DECISIONS' v 'DETERMINATION OF RIGHTS'

Yet another fashionable approach to judicial review was suggested by Lord Hoffmann, who drew a distinction between 'policy decisions' and 'a determination of rights'. In the interests of democracy, policy decisions, or decisions as to what the public interest (or general interest) requires, should be made 'by democratically elected bodies or persons accountable to them'. Examples of such decisions are questions of taxation, town and country planning, and road construction. 'In that way,' said Lord Hoffmann, 'democratic principle is preserved.'[19]

When it comes to individual rights, however, Lord Hoffmann recommends a different approach:

> There is no conflict between human rights and the democratic principle. Respect for human rights requires that certain basic rights of individuals should not be capable in any circumstances of being overridden by the majority, even if they think that the public interest so requires. Other rights should be overridden only in very restricted

> circumstances. These are rights which belong to individuals simply by virtue of their humanity, independently of any utilitarian calculation. The protection of these basic rights from majority decision requires that independent and impartial tribunals should have the power to decide whether legislation infringes them and either (as in the United States) to declare such legislation invalid or (as in the United Kingdom) to declare that it is incompatible with the governing human rights instrument. But outside these basic rights, there are many decisions which have to be made every day (for example, about the allocation of resources) in which the only fair method of decision is by some person or body accountable to the electorate.[20]

Unfortunately, however, the distinction between 'policy decisions' and 'determinations of rights' is not as clear-cut as Lord Hoffmann's classification might lead us to believe. Immigration policy is a good example. Is it a matter of public interest or of individual rights? If it is treated as a matter of public policy, the appropriate approach by the courts should be judicial self-restraint, with a reluctance on the part of the judges to interfere with decisions taken by the elected legislature and democratically accountable executive. In fact, however, this is one of the prime areas of particularly marked judicial activism or even judicial supremacism, presumably on the assumption that it concerns fundamental individual rights.

Lord Hoffmann's assertion that 'there is no conflict between human rights and the democratic principle' is really an expression of an elitist theory of democracy, which is at loggerheads with the normal 'electoral' theory of democracy. The electoral view sees democracy as a system of government designed to give voice to the wishes of the majority. By contrast, the elitist view sees democracy as a system of government embodying certain 'liberal' or even 'politically correct' social and political values, whether they are held by the majority or not. The problem with the elitist theory of democracy is that it is an attempt to impose certain values on society regardless of the views of the majority. In the normal sense, therefore, this elitist approach can be seen as fundamentally undemocratic or even anti-democratic.

To return to our example, is it wrong for Parliament and the government to seek to control the influx of asylum seekers? Seen as a policy decision with wide popular support, such measures should surely be subject to minimal interference from the courts. Instead we find that it is an area where the courts are more inclined than in almost any other to strike down government policy. The justification for this is that, when looked at from the point of view of individual asylum seekers, which is how the courts tend to view it, it is an area of fundamental human rights entitling the courts to maximum interference.

Which view is correct? It cannot be stressed enough that a right enjoyed by one person necessarily entails a reciprocal obligation owed to him or her by another. So, if asylum seekers are accorded the right to be supported at public expense, this right imposes an obligation on taxpayers to support them. Likewise, one person's rights will be likely to compete with those of others. So, for example, if asylum seekers are given the right to free housing, this cannot but detract from others' rights to free housing.

Upon examination, therefore, the assertion that there are some human rights that are so fundamental that they have to be upheld by the courts in the face of opposition by the majority turns out in reality to be a doctrine giving judges the power to impose their own social and political values on society.[21]

## Notes

1 See the discussion of the meaning of these terms in Chapter 1.
2 See Chapter 1.
3 *Chief Constable of North Wales v Evans* [1982] 3 All ER 141 at 154 (HL).
4 *Associated Provincial Picture Houses v Wednesbury Corp* [1948] 1 KB 223, per Lord Greene MR.
5 *R v Secretary of State for the Home Department, ex parte Daly* [2001] UKHL 26, [2001] 3 All ER 433 at 447, para 32, per Lord Cooke of Thorndon.
6 Lord Irvine of Lairg [1996] Judges and decision-makers: the theory and practice of Wednesbury review, *Public Law* 59 at 63.
7 Sir John Laws (1993) Is the High Court the guardian of fundamental constitutional rights?, *Public Law* 59 at 69.
8 *R v Secretary of State for the Home Department, ex parte Brind* [1991] 1 AC 697.
9 Lord Irvine of Lairg (1996) Judges and decision-makers: the theory and practice of Wednesbury review, *Public Law* 59 at 65.
10 *R v Ministry of Defence, ex parte Smith* [1995] 4 All ER 427 at 447.
11 *R v Ministry of Defence, ex parte Smith* [1996] 1 All ER 257 (CA), per Bingham MR.
12 *Lustig-Prean and Beckett v UK* (1999) 29 EHRR 548 99/53.
13 *Ibid*, at §81.
14 *Smith and Grady v UK* (1999) 29 EHRR 493 at 543, para 138.
15 *R v Secretary of State for the Home Department, ex parte Daly* [2001] UKHL 26, [2001] 3 All ER 433 at 446, para 28, per Lord Steyn.
16 Quoted by Lord Bingham, *ibid*, p 444 para 21.
17 *R v Secretary of State for the Home Department, ex parte Daly* [2001] UKHL 26, [2001] 3 All ER 433 at 446, para 28, per Lord Steyn citing *R (Mahmood) v Secretary of State for the Home Department* [2001] 1 WLR 840.
18 See the discussion in Chapter 3.
19 *R (Alconbury) v Secretary of State for the Environment* [2001] UKHL 23, [2001] 2 All ER 929 at 980, para 69.
20 *Ibid*, para 70.
21 Lord Hoffmann at least recognizes that, by contrast with both the legislature and the executive, judges are not democratically accountable. Cf the views of Sedley LJ, discussed in Arnheim, *Principles of the Common Law*, Duckworth, London (forthcoming).

# 3

# Winning strategies and tactics

## PLAYING TO WIN

At no time has English law been in a greater state of disarray than it is today. There is less certainty and therefore less predictability or foreseeability of the outcome of cases than ever before, which inevitably affects the quality of justice. For if cases that ought to be treated in the same way have different outcomes, how can that be squared with the fundamental principles of equality before the law and the rule of law?

This uncertainty has given rise to a number of what might be called yo-yo cases: cases decided one way at first instance, reversed on appeal and then with a reaffirmation of the original decision on further appeal. Even when all the judges sitting on a particular case agree on the result, their reasons for reaching that result may differ.

The judges' function was traditionally supposed to be to declare and interpret the law but not to make law, as that would amount to a usurpation of the role of Parliament. The fine line separating interpretation from legislation has always been hard to detect, and it has never been possible to avoid the creation of judge-made law altogether. But this fine line has lately become much more blurred. Judicial activism or even judicial supremacism has been on the rise, with the result that judge-made law is now rampant. At no time has there been as much judge-made law as in recent years; at no time have more changes to the law been made in this way; and at no time have such changes been more radical.

These developments have been accompanied by an eclipse of many of the fundamental principles of law which, together with the doctrine of binding precedent, are what gave the common law of England the stability, certainty and justice that it used to manifest and which invested it with an aura of majesty. But binding precedent has likewise suffered at the hands of judicial activism. With a welter of cases from several different jurisdictions to choose from, it has become easier than ever to depart from earlier decisions. Previous domestic judgments can often be distinguished on the ground that they are not in keeping with EU or human rights law, and it has become increasingly fashionable to cite decisions from a variety of foreign jurisdictions to back up the line that the court wishes to take.

However, when they do not suit the prevailing mood of the court foreign judgments can just as easily be ignored. This is particularly noticeable in regard to the law on judicial bias, where even after a serious lapse, English law still lags behind other common law jurisdictions.[1]

Continuity always used to be one of the greatest strengths of English law. But the break with the past in substantive law is matched by recent changes in civil procedure which mean that decisions made under the old rules are largely irrelevant.

Changes in terminology are only the tip of the iceberg. 'Certiorari' is admittedly a bit of a tongue-twister, but the changes are likely to cut present-day English law off from its long and glorious past and also from other common law jurisdictions around the world. Even the time-honoured, simple and easily pronounceable 'plaintiff' has been abandoned in favour of the dull 'claimant'.

But behind these ostensibly purely procedural innovations lurk some really far-reaching changes, which add up to a yet further boost to the already highly inflated power of the judges. One of the most significant of these changes is the new right of the court in a judicial review application to substitute its own decision for that of the original decision maker. So, for example, if – as happens all the time – a court finds a decision by the Home Secretary to be unlawful, not only can it quash that decision as it could in the past, but it can now also step into the shoes of the minister and decide the matter afresh itself. This always used to be totally prohibited. Indeed, it was what differentiated a review from an appeal. This prohibition supposedly still stands, as the change allowing substitution as well as quashing is meant to be purely procedural. In practice, however, it marks a major change in the substantive law introduced by the back door in the shape of secondary legislation compiled by a committee of unelected judges.

Disquieting as these changes are from the point of view of democracy and justice alike, the resulting increase in the uncertainty of the law provides new opportunities for litigants and their lawyers. Of no area of the law is this more true than human rights law. The vague wording of the Convention is an open invitation to interpretative gymnastics, not to mention the added ambiguity created by the restrictions contained within several of the articles. As we have already seen, even the definitions of the basic terms are up for grabs. What, for example, is a 'public authority'? Plus that, there is the wonderfully subjective judge-made doctrine that 'in law context is everything', which appears to mean (for this phrase too is nowhere properly defined) that similar cases can be treated differently.

If this is the basis for treating convicted killers and other criminals with special favour, it is hard to justify. But it also serves as a warning, for although the vagueness and uncertainty of human rights law can easily lend itself to a variety of interpretations, only an interpretation that chimes in with the mood of the court will be likely to succeed.

The descent of the law, and especially human rights law, into a morass of vagueness, uncertainty, subjectivity and conflicting concepts is not all bad news, however. It presents lawyers and their clients with opportunities for using the law for their own benefit. The rest of this chapter shows how they can take advantage of the situation. The best strategy may well be to combine several of the tactics discussed here.

## SOME WINNING TACTICS

### *1. Scope*

The very boundaries of human rights law are so flexible as to allow plenty of room for manoeuvre. How this can be used as a practical tactic in a lawsuit is more fully explained in Case Study A.

### *2. Rights versus rights*

Assert your rights against the conflicting rights of others. This proactive approach may be seen as a whole strategy in itself. See Case Study B.

### *3. Fuzzy logic*

In human rights law it is possible for less than strictly logical arguments to pass muster. Some examples of this tactic are given in the discussion in Case Study C.

### *4. Special interest groups*

Is it unduly cynical to see human rights law as going out of its way to favour certain identifiable special interest groups, such as convicted murderers, some other criminals and, to a lesser extent, asylum seekers? The practical problem here is that if it is true that certain types of claimants are favoured, and if you do not yourself belong to one of these groups, your chances of success may be reduced – especially if you are up against someone from one of these special groups.

There has certainly been no shortage of cases involving these groups, including some UK domestic decisions dating from a time well before the HRA. See the discussion in Case Study D.

## *5. 'The commuter on the London Underground'*

A law lord, Lord Steyn, has suggested a new test for justice: distributive justice and moral acceptability as measured by public opinion.

A man had a vasectomy. Six months later his sperm count was found to be negative and he was advised by his surgeon that he and his wife did not need to use contraception any more. They acted on this advice, but the wife subsequently fell pregnant and gave birth to a healthy daughter. The couple sued the health board, seeking damages for the pain and distress involved in the pregnancy, and also for the cost of bringing up the child to the age of 18. This latter claim was rejected by the House of Lords. Lord Steyn's reasoning was as follows:

> It is possible to view the case simply from the perspective of corrective justice. It requires somebody who has harmed another without justification to indemnify the other. On this approach the parents' claim for the cost of bringing up Catherine must succeed. But one may also approach the case from the vantage point of distributive justice. It requires a focus on the just distribution of burdens and losses among members of a society. If the matter is approached in this way, it may become relevant to ask of the commuters on the Underground the following question: Should the parents of an unwanted but healthy child be able to sue the doctor or hospital for compensation equivalent to the cost of bringing up the child for the years of his or her minority, i.e. until about 18 years? My Lords, I have not consulted my fellow travellers on the London Underground but I am firmly of the view that an overwhelming number of ordinary men and women would answer the question with an emphatic No. And the reason for such a response would be an inarticulate premise as to what is morally acceptable and what is not.[2]

Lord Steyn's commuter is obviously inspired by the 19th century 'man on the Clapham omnibus' created by Lord Bowen as an example of 'the reasonable man'. In the circumstances of the case in question, Lord Steyn was probably right in thinking that public opinion would have been unlikely to support the award of compensation to cover the upbringing of a child for the whole of her first 18 years.

Lord Steyn's identification of moral acceptability with public opinion is as surprising as it is salutary. This 'principle' has been notable by its absence in human rights cases, where it is arguably even more relevant but cuts right across the belief that 'context is everything', another of Lord Steyn's doctrines.[3] Yet now that the commuter 'principle' has been propounded and indeed applied in at least one case, it must surely be open to litigants to contend for its use in other cases as well.

LIVERPOOL JOHN MOORES UNIVERSITY
LEARNING SERVICES

Would public opinion have agreed that the child-murderers Venables and Thompson had an unfair trial? Or that they should be let free after seven-and-a-half years in a juvenile home before serving a single day in a real prison? Or that they or the child-killer Mary Bell should be given new identities and guaranteed anonymity and lifelong protection at the taxpayers' expense? Or, for that matter, that an intruder shot by a householder while attempting to burgle his home should have the right to sue the householder for damages? Public opinion would probably have had little sympathy with any of these propositions.

## 6. *Principles*

It always helps if you can pray in aid (that is, invoke) a principle of law. But the term 'principle' is now used so loosely as to drain it of most of its meaning.[4]

In what has long been taken as an authoritative statement of the law, Lord Diplock in 1984 identified the grounds of judicial review as 'illegality', 'irrationality' and 'procedural impropriety'. These were all well-established principles which had formed the basis of judicial review for centuries. But Lord Diplock then added:

> That is not to say that further development on a case by case basis may not in course of time add further grounds. I have in mind particularly the possible adoption in the future of the principle of 'proportionality', which is recognised in the administrative law of several of our fellow members of the European Community.[5]

Two points are worth noting here. First, Lord Diplock was not immediately seeking to add proportionality as a ground of judicial review. Secondly, however, he airily assumed that the principles governing judicial review could be amended 'on a case by case basis'. This reminds one of the old adage 'Those are my principles, but if you don't like them I have others.' Or here perhaps: 'Those are my principles, but if they don't suit the circumstances of a particular case I have others.'

The common law of England developed for hundreds of years on the basis that the task of the courts was to apply principles to facts. No two cases are the same. However similar, their facts will always differ in some way. It is for the court to decide what the material facts are in any particular case, to identify the appropriate principles and rules that are applicable to it, and then to apply them. This is no easy task. But it is no part of the judges' task to invent or create new principles. Facts vary from case to case; principles remain fixed in the firmament, although they must obviously be adaptable to changing circumstances. They are the standards of justice. If principles keep changing there can be no certainty in the law, and without certainty there can be no predictability and no justice.[6]

If principles are to change, on whose authority is this to be done? In referring to the future possible addition of the principle of proportionality Lord Diplock appears to have assumed that this could simply be done by the judges 'on a case by case basis'. Yet for judges to create new principles would amount to legislation, something that is reserved to Parliament. Judicial legislation flies in the face of the most fundamental of all principles of the British constitution, namely the sovereignty (or better, the legislative supremacy) of Parliament, a doctrine that has been specifically safeguarded in the Human Rights Act.

Judicial legislation would also be contrary to the doctrine of the 'separation of powers', much beloved of the Strasbourg court and of certain UK judges – including Lord Diplock, who once even went so far as to identify this doctrine as the bedrock of the British constitution:

> [I]t cannot be too strongly emphasised that the British Constitution, though largely unwritten, is firmly based on the separation of powers: Parliament makes the laws, the judiciary interpret them.'[7]

This dictum is interesting from at least three points of view. First, it gives only a partial view of the doctrine, namely the aspect of it that deals with the relationship between the judiciary and the legislature. There is no mention of the other equally important aspects: the relationship between the executive and the judiciary and that between the executive and the legislature. Upon a full examination especially of this last aspect it is clear that the British constitution is very far from being 'firmly based on the separation of powers'.

Secondly, Lord Diplock's extremely strongly worded dictum on the status of the separation of powers is unfortunately only too typical of judicial attempts at legislating. Legislation needs to be carefully worded and must try to cover as many angles as possible. His lopsided analysis of the separation of powers inevitably led Lord Diplock to make a sweeping and insupportable assertion on a fundamental but elementary legal question.

Thirdly, however, Lord Diplock did at least recognize that it was not for the judges to make the law, only to interpret it. In practice the line separating interpretation and legislation is a fine line indeed, and it is very difficult if not impossible to prevent judicial decisions from crossing this line. Nevertheless, there is a big difference between a situation where a judge inadvertently strays over this dividing line and a situation where he or she deliberately sets about making up new legal principles.[8] It is hardly surprising that judge-made law has now simply added proportionality to the list of grounds for judicial review.[9]

A related more recent judicial *obiter dictum* on the separation of powers is even more disquieting than Lord Diplock's:

> The proper constitutional relationship of the executive with the courts is that the courts will respect all acts of the executive within its lawful province, and that the executive will respect all decisions of the courts as to what its lawful province is.[10]

On the face of it, this statement appears to be depicting an even-handed reciprocal 'checks and balances' relationship between the executive and the judiciary. But that impression is quickly dispelled upon closer examination. According to this formulation, all that the courts (that is, the judges) have to do is 'respect all acts of the executive within its lawful province', but the corresponding obligation on the executive – to 'respect all decisions of the courts as to what its lawful province is' – is far more onerous, and indeed different in kind. For what this does is to give power to the courts to determine the scope of executive authority. This amounts to a usurpation by the judiciary of the position of both the legislature and the executive. Determining what the executive may and may not do is legislation, which is the province of Parliament. And by reducing the power of the executive the courts would be usurping that power too.

Where did this statement come from? It was a formulation 'adopted' in the highly controversial case of *M v Home Office* by Nolan LJ (as he then was), 'tentatively advanced' by Stephen Sedley QC (as he then was) as counsel in that case.[11] On what authority? None is cited, for the very simple reason that there is none. Not only does this formulation attribute to the judiciary powers that it has never possessed, but the formulation is itself an example of constitutional law-making, something which is the strict prerogative of Parliament. Most disquietingly of all, this formulation has been quoted uncritically in legal texts as an authoritative statement of a constitutional principle.

### 7. *Scattergun*

It can never do any harm to frame your claim under as many different Convention rights as possible. This has long been standard practice in Strasbourg. There are some constraints militating against doing the same before the domestic courts. So, for example, if you come to court complaining of the violation of your rights under, say, ECHR Articles 3, 6 and 8, and you succeed only under Article 3, the fact that you failed under the other two articles may have serious negative costs implications for you. Nevertheless, the scattergun approach will still be worth considering, depending on your chances of success under each head. And this is a game that can be played by both sides. If you are a defendant or respondent, you can rely on as many of the available restrictions on the Convention rights as you like.

## CASE STUDY A: THE SCOPE OF HUMAN RIGHTS LAW

### *The unlucky pawnbroker*

A recent Court of Appeal decision[12] provides useful pointers to some unlikely applications of human rights law:

## 1. Try to extend or narrow the scope of the Convention to protect yourself. The scope of the Convention and of each individual right within it is a movable feast

This is a good example of a case which on the face of it appears light years away from anything to do with human rights. But the whole case took on a whole new complexion when the Court of Appeal decided it on human rights grounds – which neither party had requested!

## 2. Beware of the possibility of the introduction of a human rights dimension into your case if you do not think it is relevant

The Court of Appeal here turned an ordinary little commercial case into a major human rights production. This was done by the court 'of its own motion'. Is that allowed? It is certainly not possible in Strasbourg, because no case can find its way there without an application claiming a violation of a Convention right. It is also practically unheard of in UK domestic law. It is true that the Civil Procedure Rules 1998 give judges the duty of furthering the objectives of justice by 'actively managing cases', but to let judges decide the subject matter of the case appears to go well beyond this.

## 3. This case shows that legislation is always at risk in any court case, no matter how unlikely that may seem at the outset

The courts do not have the power to set aside any primary legislation (an Act of Parliament) on the ground that it does not agree with the Human Rights Convention. All that a court can do is to issue a 'declaration of incompatibility', but this is likely in practice to have a pretty devastating effect on the particular law in question. This danger is all the greater if, as in this case, a court can decide to challenge the validity of legislation not at the behest of either of the parties but entirely 'of its own motion'.

## 4. Is it not true that legislation is now routinely interpreted 'purposively', and all the more so now in order to avoid the need for a 'declaration of incompatibility'?

Because HRA s 3 expressly requires that 'so far as it is possible to do so', legislation 'must' be interpreted 'in a way which is compatible with the Convention rights', it was predicted by at least one senior member of the judiciary that the courts would go out of their way to interpret legislation so as to avoid the need for a declaration of incompatibility. But what we find in this case is that, after the county court judge had found no incompatibility with the Convention, the Court of Appeal disagreed, and as a result prevented the actual issues in the case from being resolved.

## 5. Do not lose sight of pre-existing fundamental common law rights

As discussed in Chapter 1, HRA s 11 together with Article 53 of the Convention preserves pre-existing common law (and other) rights. One such fundamental principle which was relevant here is the presumption of regularity, meaning in this instance that where the sense of an agreement is clear, the law should give effect to it. (See below.) This principle was not referred to by the Court of Appeal.

## 6. It is increasingly possible to argue successfully in favour of giving Convention rights horizontal effect

This case is a good example of the development of human rights law in a horizontal direction. It was a dispute between pawnbrokers and their customers, neither of whom could remotely be thought of as a public authority. Yet it became a human rights case simply because of the inclusion of the courts as public authorities in HRA s 6(3). As it is unlawful for a public authority 'to act in a way which is incompatible with a Convention right', it can be argued that if a court wrongly held legislation to be in keeping with the Convention, the court itself would be acting unlawfully. The fact that neither of the parties in the particular case before the court was making a human rights claim would not make any difference.

## 7. Above all, do not expect the introduction of a human rights dimension into a case to favour the interests of justice

In this case the pawnbroker ought to have been allowed to claim his money under the contract, as was decided at first instance. But the injection of a massive dose of human rights into the case meant that this question – which was the issue before the court – was put to one side and that the pawnbroker therefore effectively lost. And all on the basis of a minor clerical omission in the contract. This result was reached, in the words of the Court of Appeal, 'notwithstanding that no prejudice has been caused to anyone by that omission' – quite an admission!

## 8. Even 'proportionality', that favourite human rights doctrine, which should in this case have come to the aid of the pawnbroker, can be interpreted in unexpected ways

See below for a discussion of this.

## *The facts and judgments in the case*

Penelope Wilson pledged her car to pawnbrokers. She signed a loan agreement with them which stated the loan amount to be £5,250. In fact, however, £250 of this amount was a 'document fee', so the loan amount was really only £5,000.

Did this misstatement of the amount invalidate the agreement under the Consumer Credit Act 1974, which requires the agreement to include 'a term stating the amount of the credit'? Mrs Wilson applied to the county court for a declaration that the agreement was void and unenforceable.[13]

Despite the mistake it was clear to all concerned exactly how much was owed. The judge held that the agreement was in conformity with the legislation, which meant that Mrs Wilson had to pay what was due. There was a time when this case would have been resolved quickly on the basis of the old principle that 'Everything is presumed to have been done rightly and properly', or, in its original Latin, *omnia praesumuntur rite et sollemniter acta esse*. What this means is that technical errors are to be ignored in the interests of justice. It is not known whether the judge cited this maxim in his judgment, but it would have corroborated his eminently sensible decision.

That should have been the end of the matter. But, to coin a phrase, not only was it not the beginning of the end, it turned out to be only the end of the beginning. It went to the Court of Appeal, where Mrs Wilson again contended for a literal interpretation of the 1974 law, while the pawnbrokers naturally favoured the common-sense approach which had given them victory at first instance.

What did the Human Rights Act have to do with this really trivial case? Apparently, nothing at all – and neither party raised it. But the Court of Appeal decided to bring it up anyway. The court decided that the 1974 legislation not only invalidated the loan agreement but also gave no power to the court to enforce a defective loan agreement – which is contrary to the right to a fair trial under Article 6(1) of the Human Rights Convention and also to Article 1 Protocol 1 ('Protection of Property') . So, after handing down interim judgments indicating that they were considering making a declaration of incompatibility, they delivered a final judgment in which they did indeed make such a declaration, to the effect that section 127(3) of the Consumer Credit Act 1974 was incompatible with the Convention rights guaranteed under Art 6(1) of the Convention and Article 1 of the First Protocol.

What about the money? Although it was clearly owed, by reversing the judge's decision the Court of Appeal deprived the pawnbrokers of their claim. Sympathy for pawnbrokers is not a common emotion, but it is hard not to sympathize with them in this case, even though they were presumably responsible for the innocent clerical error which lies at the heart of this case.

The decision raises more questions than it answers:

**Q. What effect did the declaration of incompatibility have on the issues in the case itself?**

***A. None, except that it lost the pawnbrokers their claim by default.***

The only effect that such a declaration has is to flag up a problem regarding the impugned legislation. Once such a declaration is made, it is left to the UK government to decide whether it wishes to change the law so as to bring it into line with the Convention right with which it is supposedly incompatible. If it does decide to change the law in this way, there is a special fast-track procedure available to it under section 10 of the Human Rights Act. But any change, however quickly it is implemented, can only have prospective, that is future, effect. As it does not have retrospective effect it cannot affect the actual issue in this case, namely whether the pawnbrokers can get their money. And if the government chooses not to change the law, then the position remains as it is – with a supposedly invalid loan agreement.

**Q. Why was it necessary to make a declaration of incompatibility at all? Could the Court of Appeal not have interpreted the legislation concerned so as to comply with the Convention?**

**A. *The Court of Appeal held that it was not possible to interpret the legislation in a way which was compatible with the Convention.***

Section 3(1) of the Human Rights Act actually says that 'so far as it is possible to do so', legislation 'must be read and given effect in a way which is compatible with the Convention rights'. Only if this cannot be done does a declaration of incompatibility come into play: section 4. In fact, both parties agreed with the County Court judge that the relevant legislation could indeed be interpreted to comply with the Convention, and it is really only because the Court of Appeal adopted a narrowly literalistic interpretation that it found this impossible to do.

**Q. On what basis did the Court of Appeal decide that the legislation was incompatible with the Convention?**

**A. *On the basis of a narrowly literalistic interpretation.***

The Court of Appeal's tortuous logic appears to run along the following lines:

1. The loan agreement signed by Penelope Wilson and the pawnbrokers was regulated by the Consumer Credit Act 1974. Section 61(1)(b) of that Act says that for such an agreement to be 'treated as properly executed' it must include 'a term stating the amount of the credit'.
2. The figure given as 'the amount of the credit', £5,250, was incorrect, as it included a £250 'document fee'. The figure that should have been entered as the 'amount of the credit' was £5,000.
3. As the agreement therefore did not include 'a term stating the amount of the credit', the agreement was not properly executed.
4. However, section 65 (1) of the 1974 Act 'provides that an improperly executed regulated agreement is enforceable against the debtor on an order of the court only'.
5. But unfortunately section 127(3) prevented a court from making an enforcement order:

> The court shall not make an enforcement order under section 65(1) if section 61(1)(a) (signing of agreements) was not complied with unless a document (whether or not in the

prescribed form and complying with regulations under section 60(1)) itself containing all the prescribed terms of the agreement was signed by the debtor or hirer (whether or not in the prescribed manner).

The Court of Appeal concluded from this that it could not make an enforcement order.

6. But by stopping courts from enforcing improperly executed agreements s 127(3) is itself in conflict with Article 6(1) of the Convention, which guarantees a fair trial.
7. So, by applying s 127(3) the court would itself be acting contrary to a Convention right. As a court is a 'public authority' within HRA s 6(3)(a), it would therefore be acting unlawfully: 'It is unlawful for a public authority to act in a way which is incompatible with a Convention right': HRA s 6.

**Q. Does the Court of Appeal's interpretation of the relevant sections of the 1974 Act not make a nonsense of them?**

***A. Yes, arguably so.***

The Act was trying to make it possible to enforce 'improperly executed' agreements, but the literal way it was read by the Court of Appeal nullified this attempt. The bracketed phrases in the quoted extract are clearly intended to give latitude to the court in the interests of enforcement. But the sticking point for the Court of Appeal was the phrase 'containing all the prescribed terms of the agreement'. Where was the £250 'document fee' mentioned? It is not clear from the judgment. But if this figure appeared anywhere – it would not matter where – in the agreement, it would be obvious that it had to be deducted from the £5,250 shown as 'the amount of the credit'. The point is that the document was clear enough for there to be no disagreement between the parties on the amount of the loan.

**Q. Then could the agreement not have been saved by the rule of interpretation in *Pepper v Hart*?**

***A. Quite possibly, but this rule was not even mentioned in the Court of Appeal's final judgment.***

When interpreting legislation which is 'ambiguous or obscure, or leads to an absurdity' this rule now allows a court to refer to 'statements by a Minister or other promoter of the Bill' and other 'parliamentary materials'. In other words, it is now possible for a court to refer to the debates as reported in Hansard in order to find out what the legislators' intention was in passing the legislation in question.[14] This approach might have helped to make sense of the relevant provisions of the 1974 Act, which were self-defeating as interpreted by the Court of Appeal.

**Q. Do courts have the right to make a declaration of incompatibility when neither party has asked for one and when human rights law has not even been mooted by either side?**

***A. This case represents a disquieting precedent to this effect.***

A court is meant to address the particular issue in the case before it, and judges are not even expected to go in search of authorities that have not been cited to them by either party. Yet here we find the Court of Appeal going off at a tangent from the issue before them. Their justification for this, as we have seen, was the unimpressive argument that unless the appeal judges issued a declaration of incompatibility they would be acting unlawfully themselves. In reality, the only reason that the Court of Appeal was in danger of acting unlawfully was self-induced paralysis resulting from its own unduly literalistic interpretation of the legislation. If it had interpreted it – with the help of *Pepper v Hart* – in a way that made sense and was also compatible with the Convention – in accordance with HRA s 3 – then there could have been nothing unlawful about making an enforcement order to give effect to an agreement whose terms were well understood by all concerned. Even the Court of Appeal, referring to the trivial omission from the agreement which was the basis of the whole case, admitted that 'no prejudice has been caused to anyone by that omission'.[15]

**Q. How could the Human Rights Convention be applicable to a case like this where both parties are private persons?**

***A. This case is an example of the growing number of cases where human rights law has 'horizontal effect'.***

The Convention was intended to protect private persons against 'public authorities', such as departments of state, local authorities, the police, the courts and other bodies performing a public role.[16] This is termed 'vertical effect', as against 'horizontal effect', which refers to conflicts between two private persons (including corporations). As we have seen, this case was not brought as a human rights case at all. It got its human rights dimension from the fact that courts are classified as public authorities. This could easily result in many more essentially non-Convention horizontal cases being sucked into the human rights orbit.

**Q. Could the fuss made over this case by the Court of Appeal possibly be justified in terms of proportionality?**

***A. It is hard to see how.***

'Proportionality' is a European buzz-word. Using a sledge-hammer to crack a nut is the classic definition of a disproportionate response. A favourite Strasbourg way of putting it is in terms of striking 'a fair balance between the demands of the general community and the fundamental right of the individual'.[17] In this case the Court of Appeal actually did consider the question of proportionality, but it applied it rather strangely. What it should have asked was whether turning a little case over a small sum of money and with clear-cut rights into a major human rights production could possibly be proportionate to the objective. After a County court hearing the case went to two hearings before the Court of Appeal involving no fewer than six barristers, including three QCs, a representative of the government and an amicus curiae! The costs must have amounted to many times the paltry £5,000 that it was supposedly all about, contrary to 'the overriding objective' set out in the Civil Procedure Rules 1998, which says that the courts must deal with cases 'justly', meaning, among other things, 'dealing with the case in ways which are proportionate to the amount of money involved'.[18]

**Q. So who won in the end?**

**A. *The debtor won by default, as the loan agreement was invalidated by the court of Appeal. But the real winners were the judges.***

The pawnbrokers lost out badly, though they were clearly in the right as the County court judge had held. The real loser therefore was justice.

By making a declaration of incompatibility, albeit in regard to an insignificant and unknown little sub-section, the Court of Appeal scored a signal success over the government and Parliament alike. Although the HRA was carefully drafted so as to prevent the courts from striking down primary legislation, this case shows that the practical effect of a declaration of incompatibility, which was intended to be a lame signal only, is effectively to nullify the legal provisions that are made subject to it.[19]

## CASE STUDY B: RIGHTS VERSUS RIGHTS

### *Assert your rights against the conflicting rights of others*

The rights of one person often conflict with those of another. The conflicting rights may be either of the same type or different. So one person's right to freedom of expression may clash with another person's right to freedom of expression, as for example where a heckler armed with a bullhorn drowns out a politician's speech. But it is equally possible that one person's right to X may conflict with another's right to Y. A journalist's right to freedom of expression, for instance, can easily come into conflict with someone else's 'right to respect for his private and family life' within Article 8.

Do you have the right to shout 'Fire!' in a crowded theatre when there is no fire? Seen as part of your right to freedom of speech, whether under the common law or under Article 10 of the Convention, the answer may appear to be 'Yes'. But when it is realized that your irresponsible act may well result in a stampede and cause injury or even death, then the position becomes less clear-cut. Your right to shout 'Fire!' may then be seen to conflict with the right to life of the rest of the audience. This case is hypothetical. But if it were to become the subject of a real lawsuit, the court would, as judges like to say, have to conduct a 'balancing exercise'.

Where there is a clash of rights it is not always easy to predict the outcome. But there is no better way of countering a rights claim than by asserting one of your own.

## *Freedom of expression versus freedom of the media*

The ProLife Alliance, an anti-abortion British political party entitled under the relevant election laws to a party election broadcast in Wales, was refused transmission of its video by the BBC on its own behalf and on behalf of the independent television companies as well. The reason given for the refusal was that the images of aborted foetuses contained in the video were too 'offensive' to be broadcast.

The ProLife Alliance went to the High Court to challenge the television companies' decision by means of judicial review, but their application fell at the preliminary hurdle. They were refused permission to apply for judicial review, on the ground that the broadcasters' decision was not even close to being irrational. Their appeal against this refusal was, however, allowed, but by a four to one majority the House of Lords restored the first instance decision.

This case is interesting for several reasons. First, it exemplifies two different approaches to judicial review. The judge who refused ProLife's leave application was thinking in terms of the traditional grounds for judicial review. Whether one agreed with the broadcasters' objections to the video images or not, could the decision not to broadcast be labelled as irrational? Probably not. But the Court of Appeal applied a different set of criteria, based on human rights law. Branding the television companies' refusal to transmit the video as 'censorship', Laws LJ concluded that the broadcasters had 'failed altogether to give sufficient weight to the pressing imperative of free political expression. . . . There is no recognition of the critical truth, the legal principle, that considerations of taste and decency cannot prevail over free speech by a political party at election time save wholly exceptionally'.[20]

Secondly, the television companies were effectively using their own right to freedom of expression to deny the same right to others. This underlines the crucial distinction between media freedom and freedom of expression generally. The media like to equate the two, which enables them to portray any attack on themselves as an attack on everyone's right to freedom of expression. This case, however, shows not only that media freedom is not equivalent to freedom of speech or expression for everyone, but more than that, that in certain circumstances media freedom can actually be inimical to freedom of speech for all.

In this connection it is worth quoting an extract from the judgment of Simon Brown LJ:

> It is an irony of these proceedings that the respondent broadcasters, natural campaigners for media freedom and ordinarily concerned to resist complaints about programmes

which they themselves have thought suitable for transmission, are here in the very different position of defending a decision not to broadcast.[21]

Simon Brown LJ then went on to cite three television programmes put out by the television companies themselves. All these programmes contained shocking and offensive images, the same criticism as was now being levelled by the broadcasters themselves against ProLife. All three programmes cited by the judge were the subject of complaints to the Broadcasting Standards Commission (BSC), which, however, rejected all the complaints. One of these programmes showed footage 'of animals being killed for their fur', which the BBC successfully defended on the basis of 'a strong public interest in making viewers aware of the full horror of the situation'. The second one showed the killing of badgers, which was successfully justified by Channel 5 on the ground that it 'secured the conviction of those involved and brought about a change in the law'. The third programme cited by the judge showed harrowing scenes of the victims of a Nairobi bomb blast, which was justified by the BSC as 'representing the true horror of terrorism'.

What is interesting is that all three of these programmes were politically motivated. The two about animals were seeking a change in the law, but the third one is perhaps the most interesting of all – not because of what it showed, but because of the contrast that it presented with what is usually shown on television. In its adjudication the BSC commented that '[The] images shown were, indeed, shocking, with a level of explicitness not usually depicted by broadcasters when acts of terrorism have occurred in the United Kingdom'.[22] Why was UK terrorism played down in this way? And could this not possibly have helped to soften up the British public for the amnesty to terrorist murderers in Northern Ireland?

In reversing the Court of Appeal's unanimous decision, the House of Lords made no reference to these three trenchant examples. If the party seeking to make a party election broadcast had been pro-choice instead of pro-life, would it have been subjected to censorship by the television companies? One can only wonder.

## *Effective rights against the press*

English law still lacks any comprehensive law of privacy, although there is patchy protection under the law of trespass, confidentiality and ECHR Article 8, which, however, is concerned not with privacy as such but rather with 'respect for private and family life', which is not the same thing at all.[23]

There are a couple of examples of more far-reaching privacy protection against the press and 'the whole world', but this has unfortunately so far been used to benefit only the convicted murderers Venables and Thompson and the child-killer formerly known as Mary Bell.[24] It will probably be a very long time before the advantages now restricted to child-killers are more widely available.

# CASE STUDY C: FUZZY LOGIC

## *In human rights law it is possible for less than strictly logical arguments to pass muster*

A good example of this sort of argument concerns the status of the Human Rights Act itself and the Convention rights that it incorporates. In a lecture delivered in October 2000, just after the Human Rights Act 1998 had come into force, Lord Steyn, a law lord, had this to say:

> Now we have a true Bill of Rights, in the shape of the European Convention on Human Rights, incorporated into our law by the carefully and subtly crafted Human Rights Act 1998. It is a Bill of Rights akin to similar measures in many constitutions. In *Reynolds* I said that the Human Rights Act has a *constitutional or higher order legal order foundation*. The Human Rights Act 1998 is now part of what is otherwise an unwritten constitution.
>
> One may then legitimately ask why does it matter whether the Human Rights Act has a constitutional or higher legal order status. It matters greatly. The fact that a right is *entrenched* in a Bill of Rights is compelling testimony that it is to be accorded *a higher normative status than other rights*. This will be particularly important in regard to the interpretation and application of the Convention and the Act. Constitutional adjudication needs to be approached generously in order to afford citizens the full measure of the protections of a Bill of Rights. By contrast, decisions taken day by day by commercial judges in respect of the meaning of, say, standard forms of letters of credit may sometimes employ relatively strict methods of construction. The Human Rights Act as a constitutional measure will influence not only the interpretation of statute law but also the development of common law. Decisions under it are not to be regarded as a separate stream of jurisprudence. The common law, statute law and the Human Rights Act coalesce in one unified legal system. [Emphasis added.][25]

Lord Steyn's argument appears to run as follows:

1. The fact that the European Human Rights Convention is now incorporated into English law automatically makes the Convention part of the British constitution.
2. The fact that the Convention is part of the constitution automatically gives the Convention higher law status.
3. The Convention rights are therefore 'entrenched in a Bill of Rights'.
4. Which means that the Convention rights are 'to be accorded a higher normative status than other rights'.
5. The judicial approach to these rights must be less strict than in ordinary commercial matters.

Upon examination, as we shall see, although the first of these statements is unassailable, assertions 2, 3 and 4 do not follow from it and fly in the face of centuries of UK law and also of evidence drawn from other countries; and if statement 5 is an exhortation for judges to favour those claiming rights against those resisting such claims, this would be unjust.

## *Does the European Human Rights Convention now form part of the British constitution?*

Yes, undoubtedly. But this does not mean much. Any law that has some bearing on constitutional matters may be considered to be part of the constitution. But, the fact that a particular statute forms part of the British constitution does not 'entrench' it or set it above any other statute or give it any special 'higher law' status. Such concepts are totally alien to the British constitution and to English law as a whole.

The British constitution is commonly said to be 'unwritten'. This is somewhat misleading, as large parts of the constitution are in fact written down, whether in the form of statutes, case law or other rules and regulations. There are really two respects – one superficial and the other of crucial importance – in which Britain's 'unwritten' constitution differs from the 'written' constitutions now found in most other countries around the world.

The superficial point is that, unlike a written constitution, which is normally codified (that is, contained in a single document), Britain's unwritten constitution is made up of a whole host of disparate sources scattered in a variety of documents, practices and customs. There is no single identifiable document or book or series of books to which one can point and say 'This is the British constitution.' That is the superficial difference between a written and an unwritten constitution.

There is also a much more important and deep-seated difference, and that is in the status enjoyed by a written constitution by contrast with Britain's unwritten one. For a written constitution is almost invariably invested with the status of a higher form of law than ordinary laws. Such constitutions are commonly referred to as containing the 'fundamental law' or 'basic law' of the state concerned. Another way of putting it is that a written constitution is often accorded the status of a 'higher law' or 'higher form of law'. In order to protect this higher status enjoyed by the constitution, two further features are generally found.

The key feature of written constitutions is that if any 'ordinary' law conflicts with the constitution, the constitution prevails. Or, to put it simply, where there is a clash the constitution will 'trump' ordinary law every time. It is this that has given the courts such great power in states with written constitutions, because it falls to them to strike down laws which are 'unconstitutional'.

In addition, written constitutions are generally deliberately made difficult to amend or repeal. The degree of protection with which a constitution is hedged about can be expressed in terms of 'flexibility' or 'rigidity': the more 'rigid' a constitution is the more difficult it is to change. One can also say that a particular constitution, or a particular article or provision of a constitution, is 'entrenched', by which is meant that it is specially protected against alteration. This may mean that it needs, say, a two-thirds majority in the legislature to amend it, or possibly even a popular referendum.

There is no parallel in the British constitution to the entrenchment or the higher law status enjoyed by written constitutions. Many constitutional changes have been made over the years, all by means of ordinary statutes. Every Act of Parliament can be amended or repealed at any time by the same ordinary procedure as was used to pass it: a simple majority in the House of Commons, a simple majority in the House of Lords, and the Queen's assent.

Even so ancient and sacrosanct a part of the British constitution as Magna Carta, dating back to 1215, could be repealed at any time by exactly the same procedure as is needed to pass, amend or repeal any statute. Indeed, this is true not only in theory but also in practice. The Bill of Rights 1688, for example, one of the most important constitutional enactments, was amended by a perfectly ordinary statute called the Defamation Act 1996. And the right to jury trial in Magna Carta itself has been greatly eroded in recent decades, and at the time of writing is under threat of being restricted yet further. What procedure has been used to make these constitutional changes? As always, just a simple majority in the House of Commons, a simple majority in the House of Lords and the Queen's assent.

Because of the non-entrenchment and non-higher status of the British constitution it really makes no difference whether a particular statute is part of the constitution or not, or whether part of it is concerned with constitutional issues and the rest is not. Are the laws governing divorce part of the British constitution or not? Under the constitution of the Republic of Ireland divorce was strictly forbidden until the constitution was amended to allow it. As the Irish constitution is an entrenched written instrument, this change required a popular referendum. In the United Kingdom, by contrast, the statutes relating to divorce can be changed with the same ease as any other Acts of Parliament – and have been on several occasions. So are the UK laws of divorce part of the British constitution or not? This is not a question that need exercise anyone, because it makes absolutely no difference whether they are so considered or not.

What then about the Human Rights Act? Because of its subject matter it must obviously now be regarded as part of the British constitution. But that does not give it a status any different from that of any other statute that forms part of the constitution – which is exactly the same as the status enjoyed by all other statutes, whether they are concerned with constitutional matters or not.

## *Does the fact that the European Human Rights Convention is now part of the British constitution automatically give the Convention higher law status?*

The answer, as we have already seen, is a resounding 'No'. The doctrine of a constitutional law 'trumping' any other inconsistent law has no application in the United Kingdom. There is no hierarchy of 'higher' and 'lower' laws. All laws are equal. If there is a conflict between two statutes, the applicable rule is that of implied repeal: the later one will be preferred to the earlier one. This has nothing to do with the 'status' of the two laws but is concerned only with the dates when they were passed.

In the lecture quoted above, Lord Steyn cited a letter to *The Times* by a senior barrister claiming that the Human Rights Act enjoyed no higher a status than the Dangerous Dogs Act 1991. Lord Steyn rejected this out of hand, adding that the 1991 Act 'has been widely condemned as an appallingly drafted piece of legislation'. This is irrelevant. Indeed, the unnamed barrister no doubt chose an apparently trivial and much-criticized statute deliberately to make the point that under English law all statutes have equal status. Lord Steyn does go on to concede that 'other commentators have also expressed the view that the Human Rights Act is no more than an ordinary statute', but he simply dismisses this view as 'wholly misconceived'. Yet he gives no reason for his assertion other than that 'the European Convention on Human Rights, incorporated into our law by the carefully and subtly crafted Human Rights Act 1998 . . . is a Bill of Rights akin to similar measures in many constitutions.' This is true enough of the *contents* of the Convention but it says nothing about its *status*.

It is also a non sequitur to say, as Lord Steyn does elsewhere in the same lecture, that: 'The fact that a right is entrenched in a Bill of Rights is compelling testimony that it is to be accorded a higher normative status than other rights.' If a right were entrenched it would indeed have 'higher normative status' or 'higher legal order status', but, as shown above, the whole point about the British constitution is that nothing in it is entrenched: the whole concept of entrenchment is alien to the British constitution.

## *Europe*

The fact that a country has a Bill of Rights does not automatically invest it with higher law status. In Germany, for example, the European Convention on Human Rights does form part of German domestic law, but it only enjoys the status of an ordinary statute. It specifically does not have any kind of higher law status. In addition, the decisions of the Strasbourg Court and the Committee of Ministers are merely persuasive, not binding. Germany does of course also have its own set of 'Basic Rights' (*Grundrechte*), which are part of the constitution or 'Basic Law' (*Grundgesetz*), and which therefore do enjoy higher law status. But the European Convention certainly does not do so. The position of the Convention is similar in Italy and Turkey.[26]

## *New Zealand*

New Zealand likewise has a Bill of Rights which specifically does not have higher law status. This is laid down in the Bill of Rights Act 1990, section 4 of which provides as follows:

> No court shall, in relation to any enactment (whether passed or made before or after the commencement of this Bill of Rights), (a) Hold any provision of the enactment to be impliedly repealed or revoked, or to be in any way invalid or ineffective; or (b) Decline to apply any provision of this enactment by reason only that the provision is inconsistent with any provision of this Bill of Rights.

## *Human Rights Act 1998*

The UK Human Rights Act was also carefully drafted so as to prevent it from being accorded higher law status. The British government was anxious not to give the courts the power to set aside Acts of Parliament on the ground of incompatibility with the European Convention, as was frankly explained in the White Paper *Rights Brought Home: The Human Rights Bill*[27] presented to Parliament in October 1997.[28] The White Paper likewise rejected the idea that what was to become the HRA should be 'entrenched' by giving it special protection against subsequent repeal or amendment.[29]

Section 3 of the Human Rights Act provides that the courts must try as far as possible to interpret any legislation, primary and subordinate alike, in a way that is compatible with the Convention rights. But if a court is 'satisfied' that a statutory provision is incompatible with a Convention right, it may issue a 'declaration of incompatibility' under section 4(2). What this means is that, far from being able to set aside legislation inconsistent with the Human Rights Convention, all that the courts can do is flag up the inconsistency – and it is then up to the government to decide whether to remedy the incompatibility or not.

In order to avoid challenges to the validity of future legislation, s 19 of the HRA provides for a 'statement of compatibility' to be made by the minister steering a bill through either House of Parliament. In the statement the minister must say that 'in his view the provisions of the Bill are compatible with the Convention rights'.[30] If he or she cannot make a statement of compatibility, then the minister must issue a published written statement 'to the effect that although he is unable to make a statement of compatibility the government nevertheless wishes the House to proceed with the Bill'.[31] The Act here goes out of its way specifically to allow legislation incompatible with the Convention to be enacted if the government so wishes – which could hardly be the case if the Convention enjoyed higher law status!

What then about section 6(1), which states categorically that 'It is unlawful for a public authority to act in any way which is incompatible with a Convention right'? The term 'public authority' is defined in section 6(3) as including courts and tribunals. So if an Act of Parliament incompatible with the Convention is allowed to remain on the statute book, will it not be 'unlawful' under section 6(1) for the court to continue to recognize and enforce it? No, because there is also section 6(2)(a), which says that section 6(1) does not apply where the court in question has no choice in the matter 'as the result of one or more provisions of primary legislation'. The purpose of this less than pellucid subsection is obviously to preserve the right of Parliament (that is, in practice of the government) to allow legislation incompatible with Convention rights to remain valid. It covers new incompatible legislation introduced by the government after the coming into force of the Human Rights Act as well as pre-existing incompatible legislation.

## *'Parliamentar.sovereignty'*

The passage quoted above from the 1997 White Paper, *Rights Brought Home*, will repay close examination. The points made there are essentially as follows:

1. The Human Rights Act does not allow the courts to set aside Acts of Parliament on the ground of incompatibility with the Human Rights Convention.
2. The Human Rights Act was deliberately drafted in this way.
3. If it were not so drafted it would conflict with the important principle of Parliamentary sovereignty.
4. 'In this context, Parliamentary sovereignty means that Parliament is competent to make any law on any matter of its choosing and no court may question the validity of any Act that it passes.'
5. Parliament's power 'derives from a democratic mandate'.
6. Members of Parliament in the House of Commons possess such a mandate because they are elected, accountable and representative.
7. If the Human Rights Act were to give the courts the right to set aside Acts of Parliament, this 'would confer on the judiciary a general power over the decisions of Parliament which under our present constitutional arrangements they do not possess, and would be likely on occasions to draw the judiciary into serious conflict with Parliament'.
8. In addition, as mentioned above, the government also set its face against 'entrenching' the Human Rights Convention.

If the Human Rights Convention had the higher law status that Lord Steyn claims it has, then that would automatically give the courts the right to set aside statutes incompatible with it. Yet it is clear that the Convention does not have higher law status and is not entrenched. This is clear not only from government statements but also from a reading of the Human Rights Act itself (see above). Any suggestion that the Human Rights Act can be interpreted to mean that the courts have the power to set aside other statutes on the ground that they conflict with the Human Rights Act or the Convention could only be based on a wholesale scrapping and rewriting of the Human Rights Act as it appears on the statute book.

The doctrine of the sovereignty of Parliament, or better, the legislative supremacy of Parliament, has been a fundamental principle of the British constitution for over 300 years. It has to some extent become a legal fiction, as legislation is in practice under the control not of Parliament, however defined, but of the executive government, namely the Prime Minister and Cabinet. The government can normally ensure that any law that it wishes Parliament to pass will be passed, and any bill that lacks government backing is practically doomed to failure. This is because the British constitution has been hammered out over the years on the anvil of practical politics. The executive is the executive because it commands a majority in the House of Commons.

The fact that the driving force behind legislation is the executive rather than the legislature does not make any difference to the issue we are considering here. The executive is made up of Members of Parliament (who have been elected to the House of Commons) together with some members of the House of Lords.

This is what the White Paper meant by 'democratic mandate'. But, it may be objected, ministers are not elected as ministers, and some of them are not elected at all. Because of the close interlocking relationship between executive and legislature, this is a pedantic point. The electorate has the power to turn out an unpopular government at a general election – and it has exercised this power on numerous occasions. Although voters are ostensibly voting only for a Member of Parliament, in reality they are voting for a party and for a government, which is why small parties which are not perceived by the electorate as having a genuine chance of forming a government do poorly in elections. What about ministers who are not in the Commons but in the Lords? Because the outcome of at general election is in reality the people's verdict on the government, these ministers are effectively accountable to the electorate as well, and if the government is turned out of office these ministers will be out of a job.[32]

## *Are the Convention rights 'to be accorded a higher normative status than other rights', as Lord Steyn claims?*

As the Convention rights clearly do not have higher law status and are not entrenched (see above), with one possible exception there is no basis for giving them 'higher normative status' than other rights. The one exception is freedom of expression, and more particularly freedom of the press, which, however, owes its special status – if any – not to the Convention but to section 12 of the Human Rights Act itself.[33]

## *Should the interpretation of the Convention rights be less strict than that applicable to documents in ordinary commercial matters, as Lord Steyn suggests?*

The interpretation of a document as vaguely worded as the European Convention on Human Rights inevitably gives more latitude to the judiciary. There is plenty of room for divergent interpretations. Not surprisingly, the Strasbourg court is rarely unanimous when deciding whether a particular set of circumstances amounts to a breach of a Convention right or not. But Lord Steyn appears to be going further when he adds: 'Constitutional adjudication needs to be approached generously in order to afford citizens the full measure of the protections of a Bill of Rights.'[34] If this means that judges should interpret Convention rights in a way that favours those claiming such rights, then it is a less than reassuring example of judicial activism. Every right has a reciprocal duty – something which rights-based lawyers sometimes appear to lose sight of. Moreover, several of the Convention rights contain restrictions, limitations or exceptions. Even the right to life (Article 2), for example, is subject to the qualification that 'deprivation of life' is permissible 'when it results from the use of force which is no more than absolutely necessary'. Should judges automatically favour those claiming rights against those resisting their claim? This would be unjust in the extreme.[35]

## SUMMARY OF ARGUMENTS

The following is a summary of the arguments contained in this part:

1. The European Human Rights Convention is now part of the British constitution.
2. But this most certainly does not invest the Convention with higher law status.
3. The Convention rights are not entrenched.
4. There is therefore no basis for the Convention rights (except freedom of expression) 'to be accorded a higher normative status than other rights'.
5. It would be unjust for the judiciary to favour litigants claiming rights against those opposing such a claim.

Practical realities, however, may have an impact on these legal points.

### *Practical effect*

No government would like to appear to be flying in the face of human rights, so even if the courts interpret such rights in ways that are hard to justify in terms of either logic or fairness, it is highly unlikely that either the government or Parliament would be emboldened to challenge them. As a result human rights law – as interpreted by the judges – may well in practice come to be treated as enjoying higher law status, which is unlikely to serve the interests of ordinary law-abiding citizens as much as it will contribute to the victory of the judiciary in its long-running battle against the executive. The ultimate casualties will be democracy and the rule of law.

#### **Tariff for mandatory lifers**

A recent example is the case of Anthony Anderson, a convicted murderer, in which it was held by a unanimous seven-judge panel of the House of Lords that it was incompatible with Article 6 of the European Convention on Human Rights for the Home Secretary to have the right to determine how long a convicted murderer serving a mandatory 'life' sentence should spend in prison for purposes of punishment.[36] This was widely reported in the press as meaning that the Home Secretary had 'lost' this right or been 'stripped' of it by the court. In fact, however, all that the House of Lords had done was to issue a 'declaration of incompatibility' under HRA s 4, which, as we have seen, is all that they could do.

The Home Secretary's sentencing power was granted to him by Act of Parliament, namely section 29 of the Crime (Sentences) Act 1997. The significance of this case is therefore that convicted murderers were mounting a challenge to an Act of Parliament. But not even Lord Steyn suggested that the legislation in question could be set aside on the grounds of incompatibility with human rights.

So could the Home Secretary not simply ignore the declaration of incompatibility and carry on as before? In theory, yes. But, if he did so Anderson would take his case to Strasbourg, where he would be bound to score a victory against the United Kingdom. Under Article 46 of the Convention the United Kingdom is bound 'to abide by the final judgment of the [Strasbourg] Court in any case to which it is a party'. Ignoring a Strasbourg judgment would earn the government the opprobrium of flying in the face of human rights law, and in fact no UK government has ignored a Strasbourg ruling before.

In practice, therefore, all the government's carefully contrived wording of the Human Rights Act designed to prevent the Convention from becoming a higher form of law is likely to be thwarted. A victory for fuzzy logic? Perhaps.

## CASE STUDY D: SPECIAL INTEREST GROUPS?

Are there any special groups that enjoy special favour in human rights law? Let us conduct a brief survey of some landmark cases involving convicted criminals.

Prisoners retain all their civil rights that are not taken away expressly or by necessary implication. So held the House of Lords as long ago as 1983.[37] In 1993 the Court of Appeal struck down as unlawful the provision in the Prison Rules 1964 allowing a prison governor to read every letter to or from a prisoner and to stop any letter whose contents in his opinion were 'objectionable or of inordinate length'.[38] This latter decision went well beyond the Strasbourg judgment in *Golder v UK*,[39] though Strasbourg became more favourably disposed towards the correspondence rights of convicted criminals in *Silver v UK*[40] and *Campbell v UK*.[41]

As far as sentencing is concerned, there has been a long line of decisions favouring convicted criminals, again going back to domestic cases predating the HRA. One issue that has exercised the courts over a long period is the setting of a 'tariff' for convicted murderers, for whom there is a mandatory sentence of life imprisonment, where, however, 'life' does not mean life. The power to set the tariff in each such case belonged by statute to the Home Secretary, who 'fixes the period which, in his view, is appropriate by way of punishment (i.e. retribution and deterrence) and says that he will not refer the matter to the Parole Board until just before that period has elapsed': *Pierson v Secretary of State for the Home Department*.[42] In *Doody*, involving four convicted murderers, the Court of Appeal decided in 1993 that though the setting of the tariff and the procedure adopted for doing so were within the Home Secretary's discretion, he was expected to consult the judiciary and had to give reasons for departing from their recommendations. In addition, he had to inform the murderers of the judges' recommendations and had to give the murderers the opportunity of making representations on how long they should serve! In *Doody* itself the Home Secretary's decisions were held to be unlawful and quashed.[43] In the case of *Pierson*, who had murdered both his parents, the Home Secretary's 20-year tariff was struck down as 'unlawful' by a 3:2 majority in the House of Lords.[44]

However, in *Stafford*[45] a murderer lost his appeal to the House of Lords on the question of whether it was lawful for the Home Secretary to refuse to release him after he had served the tariff part of his sentence, on the ground that there was a risk that he might after release commit serious (but non-violent) crimes. But Stafford then took his case to Strasbourg, where he won a great victory. A new principle was now applied, namely that the Home Secretary's role in fixing the tariff was a sentencing exercise and not a purely administrative function, which was therefore contrary to ECHR Article 5(4) guaranteeing the right of anyone in detention to 'take proceedings by which the lawfulness of his detention shall be decided speedily by a court'.[46]

The stage was now set for the final onslaught on the Home Secretary's role in sentencing convicted murderers. This came in the House of Lords decision in *Anderson*[47] discussed above. By setting the tariff for the punitive element of a convicted murderer's sentence, it was held, the Home Secretary was actually involving himself in the trial process. And as he was not a judge but a member of the executive, this was a violation of the right to a fair trial under ECHR Article 6!

The Home Secretary's power in regard to juvenile murderers suffered a similar fate at the hands of Venables and Thompson, the young killers of little Jamie Bulger, who were released after less than eight years and before they had spent a single day in an adult prison or even in a young offenders' institution.[48] This revised tariff was based on the Practice Note issued by Lord Woolf following the decision by the Strasbourg court in the cases of Venables and Thompson that government ministers should not set tariffs for juvenile murderers.[49]

One of the mitigating circumstances listed in the Practice Note is 'age', which is obviously relevant to Venables and Thompson. Another is 'hard evidence of remorse or contrition', which Lord Woolf held was present in their cases. But among the aggravating factors, besides 'the killing of a child', is 'evidence of sadism, gratuitous violence, or sexual maltreatment, humiliation or degradation before the killing' – which fits the Bulger murder precisely. Why then were Venables and Thompson released so early?

It was undoubtedly in no small measure the public outrage at the lenient treatment of the perpetrators of what even Lord Woolf described as an 'exceptionally horrific' murder that prompted another act of benevolence by the judiciary towards the two murderers, namely the grant of an injunction intended to guarantee their anonymity against the whole world for ever.[50] The two young murderers themselves received death threats, and it was in the interests of their safety that they received special protection. However, there would probably not have been the same degree of public outrage had they served, say, 15 years' imprisonment before being released. The judge made the point that 'until now the courts have not granted injunctions in the circumstances which arise in this case', adding, 'It is equally true that the claimants are uniquely notorious'. On this basis one might have thought it unlikely that any further such injunctions would be issued.[51]

## *'Mary Bell'*

However, two years later similar protection was accorded the child-killer originally known as Mary Bell. The injunction opens with a warning (printed in bold capitals) as stern as the curse on any Egyptian pharaoh's tomb:

> IF YOU THE RECIPIENT OF THIS ORDER AND ANY OTHER PERSON WITH NOTICE OF THIS ORDER DISOBEY THIS ORDER YOU MAY BE HELD TO BE IN CONTEMPT OF COURT AND LIABLE TO IMPRISONMENT OR TO BE FINED OR TO HAVE YOUR ASSETS SEIZED.[52]

This order is 'contra mundum', that is, against the whole world, and 'until further order', that is, of indefinite duration. The injunction then spells out in some detail what it is that is prohibited on pain of imprisonment. Among other things, there is a prohibition on 'publishing or causing to be published . . . any information likely to lead to the identification' of the woman formerly known as Mary Bell or her daughter. '[A]ny depiction, image in any form, photograph, film or voice recording . . . which is likely to lead to the identification' of either mother or daughter.

Why? Why did the court find it necessary to afford this kind of protection to a child-killer? Amazingly, neither the newspapers, who were the chief defendants in the case, nor the Attorney General nor even the Home Secretary opposed this order.

In 1968 Mary Bell, then aged 11, strangled two small boys aged three and four. Her conviction was not for murder but for the lesser crime of manslaughter on the ground of diminished responsibility. She was sentenced to 'detention for life' and actually served 12 years, first in young offender institutions and later in prison. On her release in 1980 she was granted a new identity. In 1984 she had a daughter, who was made a ward of court. A court order granted both mother and daughter anonymity until the daughter turned 18.

The question then was whether to continue this protection, and if so on what terms and for how long. Or, as it was put by the judge, Dame Elizabeth Butler-Sloss, President of the Family Division: 'The question which I have to answer is whether X and Y's cases are so exceptional that they should be granted lifetime protection contra mundum.'[53] It was in response to this question that the injunction outlined above was granted on 21 May 2003.

But why? The reasons were considered under the following headings.

## 1. Confidentiality

The court cited a passage from the Court of Appeal's judgment in the *Naomi Campbell* case, involving press intrusion into the private life of a leading model who, having won at first instance, lost in the Court of Appeal on the ground that publication of her story was in 'the public interest'. The passage quoted was as follows:

> The development of the law of confidentiality since the Human Rights Act 1998 came into force has seen information described as 'confidential', not where it has been confided by one person to another, but where it relates to an aspect of an individual's private life which he does not choose to make public. We consider that the unjustifiable publication of such information would better be described as breach of privacy rather than as breach of confidence.[54]

Whether labelled 'confidentiality' (as in Mary Bell's case) or, more daringly, 'privacy' (as suggested by the Court of Appeal in *Campbell*), why was Mary Bell allowed to rely on this doctrine while Naomi Campbell's claim was rejected? Yet Naomi Campbell was concerned to keep private only one aspect of her life, while Mary Bell was seeking lifelong anonymity. And of course, above all, while Naomi Campbell was a highly admired model, Mary Bell was a child-killer. Moreover, why is it in 'the public interest' to know about Naomi Campbell's private life but not about Mary Bell's? The court offered no explanation.

## 2. ECHR Article 2

A possible answer to this question might have been in terms of risk. If Mary Bell had been subjected to death threats, her Article 2 right to life could have been engaged. Then, as the court is a 'public authority', if it made a decision that placed her life in danger, that decision could be held to have been 'unlawful' under HRA s 6. Yet it was admitted by the judge that there was 'no cogent evidence of a threat to her life and, in my judgment, this is not a case in which there is a real risk of a breach of Article 2 if the public were to become aware of the identity or whereabouts of X.'[55]

## 3. ECHR Articles 8 and 10

It was primarily under ECHR Article 8 ('right to respect for private and family life') that Mary Bell's claim succeeded, a rare instance where this right trumped the press's right to freedom of expression under Article 10. Why? No fewer than eight 'exceptional circumstances' were put forward in support of her claim for lifetime anonymity, most of which appear to have been accepted by the court. These include all the obvious factors such as 'the young age at which she committed the offences', her 'abusive childhood', the length of time that had elapsed since the offences were committed, 'her present mental state', and the need for her to be rehabilitated.[56]

Can it seriously be suggested that any of these factors, or indeed all of them together, warrant lifelong anonymity at the taxpayer's expense? If so, probably half the population, comprising people with personal problems but who have not killed anyone and have not been convicted of any criminal offence, would qualify even more.

Two of these 'exceptional circumstances' call for comment. One is 'Her concerns for the welfare of her daughter', which is linked to the daughter's own need of protection. The daughter's situation, we read, 'is so inextricably linked with that of her mother that it is not . . . possible to treat them separately. The identification of one will lead for certain to the identification of the other. The Attorney General supports the granting of an injunction to protect Y [ie the daughter]. I am satisfied that if I grant anonymity to X, I must also grant anonymity to Y.'[57]

Is this not putting the cart before the horse? Is it the mother's 'concerns' about the daughter that are paramount, or is it the daughter's own need of protection? If the former, as the judgment appears to suggest, it is hard to see how this could possibly justify anonymity for both of them. 'No suggestion has been made', we read, that the daughter's rights under Article 2 (right to life) or Article 3 (inhuman or degrading treatment) 'are at risk through disclosure of her identity or whereabouts'.[58]

If, on the other hand, it was the daughter's need that was uppermost, then why not give anonymity to her alone? After all, there is no suggestion of any protection for the daughter's stepfather, who apparently formed part of the same household. If he does not need anonymity, why the daughter? And above all, why the child-killer herself?

So far we have not identified a single good reason for the lifelong protection accorded the killer. But we now come to a most remarkable 'exceptional circumstance': 'She has . . . a semi-iconic status, a special degree of notoriety, and I have no doubt from the evidence that, if she is not protected from publicity, she is at serious risk of identification and publicity.'[59] If not protected from publicity, what 'serious risk' does she run? Answer: the 'serious risk of identification and publicity'. But is that really enough to justify lifelong protection?

If protection against publicity is given to a 'semi-iconic' killer, why not to some more positive full icons? Many famous sportspeople, film stars and other entertainers serve as positive role models to their fans. But such 'icons' are also often targeted by killers, kidnappers and other criminals. Do they not deserve protection against unwanted intrusion into their private lives much more than a child-killer?

The stock answer to this is of course, 'But these celebrities have placed themselves in the public eye and often go out of their way to court publicity.' However, why should that entitle the media and the public at large to know exactly where they live or to intrude on their private lives?

This example is all the more apt in view of the publication (in 1998) of a book on the life story of Mary Bell – written with the killer's collaboration, 'for which she was paid a substantial sum'.[60] This is the sole reference to the matter in the recent judgment, where the point made is not that this was wrong but that the appearance of the book resulted in the killer's address being discovered. And so even her (indirect) self-publicization and her profiting from her crimes (reputedly to the tune of £50,000)[61] becomes a reason for protecting her from publicity![62]

There is a genuine principle of law here, which, however, was totally ignored: 'Nobody should profit from his own wrongdoing.'[63] Not only was this ignored at the time the book appeared,[64] but it has also been totally ignored now.

Why could the sweeping injunction in favour of Mary Bell not have made her protection conditional upon her not making any more money out of her killings? This was something that the families of Mary Bell's victims suggested, and it would have been the least that the court could have done to show that it too understood who the real victims in this story were.

## Victims

For human rights law is supposed to protect and compensate *victims*. In what sense can murderers and other killers be seen as victims? If the court had refused to offer protection to Venables and Thompson, and these two murderers had then themselves been murdered, this could conceivably have resulted in the court itself being held to have acted 'unlawfully' as a 'public authority' under HRA s 6, because its inaction could have been construed as being incompatible with the two murderers' right to life under ECHR Article 2. This is a pretty far-fetched argument, and raises the fundamental question of whether public authorities owe any duty positively to protect the lives of convicted murderers. But not even this unconvincing argument could possibly avail Mary Bell or her daughter, neither of whom, it was admitted by the court, was in danger of losing her life (Article 2) or even of suffering 'inhuman treatment' (Article 3).[65]

What about the real victims, the killers' innocent victims and their families? Ralph Bulger, Jamie's father, did actually try to challenge Lord Woolf's decision on the early release of Venables and Thompson – but to no avail. The attempt was made by way of judicial review, but it did not even succeed in clearing the preliminary hurdle of 'permission' to apply for judicial review! It was held that Ralph Bulger did not have 'a sufficient interest' or 'standing' to challenge the new tariff – even though he had been invited by Lord Woolf to make representations. 'The invitation extended to him to make representations as to the impact of the offence on him was not an invitation to indicate views at to the appropriate tariff.'[66]

Ralph Bulger would not qualify as a 'victim' within HRA s 7(1)(b), because the decision that he sought to challenge was not directly about himself, nor indeed even about his murdered little boy. However, it is important to note that he was not bringing his challenge under human rights law at all but under the ordinary rules of judicial review, for which the hurdle of 'sufficient interest' or 'standing' is generally set very low – but not in his case.

In the United States it is not unknown for a murder victim's family even to appear in court and be heard on the appropriate sentence to be meted out to the murderer. And the decision in such cases, especially where the death penalty is available, is generally made not by a judge but by a jury – precisely because it is a reflection of public opinion, the very reason that is so excoriated in Europe as being political and 'populist'.

## *'Bloody Sunday'*

It is instructive to compare the treatment of Mary Bell and the Bulger killers with that of the British soldiers called to give evidence before the so-called 'Bloody Sunday Inquiry', a judicial tribunal set up to re-investigate the events of 'Bloody Sunday', in which 13 civilians were killed and an equal number injured by British paratroopers during an illegal march in Londonderry, Northern Ireland, on 30 January 1972.

In April 1972 Lord Chief Justice Widgery, who had headed a tribunal that looked into these events, reported that the soldiers had not initiated the firing, although their return fire on occasion 'bordered on the reckless' and was 'sometimes excessive'. But Lord Widgery's conclusion was that 'There would have been no deaths . . . if those who organised the illegal march had not thereby created a highly dangerous situation in which a clash between demonstrators and the security forces was almost inevitable.'[67]

From the outset the Widgery Report had been dismissed by Irish nationalists as a 'whitewash'. After the initiation of the Northern Ireland 'peace process', the British government bowed to pressure for a fresh investigation of the events of 30 January 1972. In 1998 Prime Minister Tony Blair announced the setting up of a new tribunal – under the ominous official title of 'the Bloody Sunday Inquiry' – made up of a British law lord and two Commonwealth judges, one from Canada and the other from New Zealand.

With the exception of senior officers, the soldiers who testified before the Widgery Tribunal in 1972 had done so anonymously. The Ministry of Defence asked for the same arrangement before the new tribunal on the ground that otherwise these soldiers' lives would be in danger. The tribunal accepted that the soldiers' fears were reasonable. It also admitted that 'the proper fulfilment' of its task of 'ascertaining, through an inquisitorial process, the truth about what happened on Bloody Sunday . . . does not necessarily require that the identity of everyone who gives evidence to the Inquiry should be disclosed in public. . . . Indeed we think that there are likely to be circumstances in which granting anonymity will positively help us in our search for the truth.' However, after a flurry of toings and froings the tribunal ultimately refused the soldiers' request for anonymity on the ground that it 'would represent a material derogation from the Tribunal's public investigative function.'[68]

The soldiers applied for judicial review of the tribunal's decision refusing them anonymity and were successful both in the Divisional Court and then in the Court of Appeal, whose judgment, delivered by Lord Woolf MR, amounted to a scathing rejection of the tribunal's position:

> When what is at stake is the safety of the former soldiers and their families . . . the risk is extremely significant. After all, the individual's right to life is . . . the most fundamental of all human rights. It does appear that the tribunal may well have failed to attach sufficient significance to this.[69]

And in conclusion:

> Examining the facts as a whole, therefore, we do not consider that any decision was possible other than to grant the anonymity to the soldiers.[70]

After the mauling it received from the Court of Appeal in this judgment, the 'Bloody Sunday Inquiry' might have been expected to be a little more sensitive to the very real risks confronting these soldiers. But this was not the end of the story. The next dispute between the soldier witnesses and the tribunal was over the place where they were to give their evidence. The tribunal insisted on Londonderry, but the Ministry of Defence and the soldiers, none of whom lived in Northern Ireland, once again pointed to the 'lethal danger' involved and offered to testify in London or anywhere else in Great Britain.

The Administrative Court quashed the tribunal's insistence on Londonderry, holding that the tribunal had 'misdirected itself in law, with the result that their decision was fundamentally flawed'.[71] Nothing daunted, the tribunal appealed against this, supported by the families of those killed or wounded on 'Bloody Sunday', who were 'desperately concerned that the soldier witnesses should give evidence in the city where the tragedy occurred and where the families will be able to listen to their evidence.'[72] The Court of Appeal once again came to the rescue of the soldier witnesses by dismissing the tribunal's appeal:

> No-one has suggested that changing the venue of the soldier witnesses' evidence would reduce the likelihood of the tribunal getting at the truth of what happened on Bloody Sunday, and that must be the primary object of the Inquiry. Nor would a

> change of venue prevent the families and others in Londonderry from seeing what transpires when the soldier witnesses give their evidence.[73]

The court then explained the by now all-too-familiar possibilities of video links and the like and concluded:

> The Administrative Court was correct to conclude that the Tribunal's ruling on venue did not comply with the requirements of Article 2 and of fair procedure and that it should accordingly be quashed.[74]

It is instructive to compare the 'Bloody Sunday' soldiers' saga with the privacy cases concerning Venables and Thompson and Mary Bell.

1. It is important to remember that, like the child-killers, the soldier witnesses did in the end get the protection that they were seeking.
2. But why did it take two judicial review applications and two trips to the Court of Appeal for the soldiers to get this protection?
3. Venables and Thompson had been convicted of murder and Mary Bell of manslaughter; the 'Bloody Sunday' soldiers have never been convicted of anything.
4. Venables and Thompson and Mary Bell were granted lifelong anonymity; all that the soldier witnesses were asking for was anonymity while testifying before the 'Bloody Sunday' tribunal.
5. Above all, the danger that the killers needed protection against (and in the case of Mary Bell it was admitted that her life was not likely to be in danger) was the product of their own crimes; the very real mortal danger confronting the soldier witnesses arose purely from the decisions of the tribunal, first, obliging them to reveal their names when testifying and then to come to Londonderry to give their evidence.
6. These decisions by the tribunal which placed the soldier witnesses' lives at risk were quite unnecessary.

## Notes

1 See *R v Bow Street Metropolitan Stipendiary Magistrate, ex parte Pinochet Ugarte* [1998] 4 All ER 897 and [1999] 1 All ER 577, discussed in Chapter 11.

2 *McFarlane v Tayside Health Board* [1999] 4 All ER 961 at 977.

3 See the discussion above.

4 See Michael Arnheim, *Principles of the Common Law*, Duckworth, London (forthcoming).

5 *Council of Civil Service Unions v Minister for the Civil Service* [1984] 3 All ER 935 at 949 ff.

6 See Michael Arnheim, *Principles of the Common Law*, Duckworth, London (forthcoming). Some of these have lately been ignored or lost sight of and some have been replaced by 'principles' which are not principles at all.

7 *Duport Steels v Sirs* [1980] 1 All ER 529 at 541. The relationship in the British constitution between the executive and the legislature, to cite but one example, is incompatible with any true separation of powers system. Cf the US Constitution. Montesquieu in his *Esprit des Lois* (1748) held up the British constitution as an exemplar of the separation of powers and used it as a stick with which to beat the French monarchy. But Montesquieu's knowledge of the British constitution left much to be desired.

8 See Lord Reid (1972) 'The judge as lawmaker', 12 *Journal of the Society of Public Teachers of Law* 22 at 27.

9 See *R v Secretary of State for the Home Department, ex parte Daly* [2001] UKHL 26, [2001] 3 All ER 433 at 445 (§27).

10 *M v Home Office* [1992] QB 270 at 314; (1992) 4 All ER 97 at 146, per Nolan LJ.

11 Sir Stephen Sedley (1997) The common law and the constitution, in Lord Nolan and Sir Stephen Sedley, *The Making and Remaking of the British Constitution*, p 27. On the possible origin of this doctrine see Arnheim, *Principles of the Common Law.*

12 *Wilson v First County Trust Ltd* [2001] EWCA Civ 633, [2001] 3 All ER 229. This case has since been to the House of Lords, which revised the Court of Appeal holding that no declaration of incompatibility was called for: [2003] UKHL 40, [2003] 4 All ER 97. See comment in the Preface, page xii, above.

13 *Wilson v First County Trust Ltd* [2001] EWCA Civ 633, [2001] 3 All ER 229.

14 *Pepper v Hart* [1993] 1 All ER 42 at 69.

15 *Wilson* at 235 §9.

16 See above.

17 *Stran Greek Refineries and Stratis Andreadis v Greece* (1994) 19 EHRR 293 at 328 (S69).

18 Had they considered this at all (it is not mentioned), the Court of Appeal might have fastened on to another aspect of proportionality in the same rule, namely 'proportionate to the importance of the case' or 'proportionate to the complexity of the issues'. Yet in fact the case was really pretty insignificant in itself and the impugned sections of the 1974 Act have very rarely been used in practice. As for complexity, as we have seen the real issue in the case was very simple indeed.

19 *Wilson v First County Trust Ltd* [2001] EWCA Civ 633, [2001] 3 All ER 229.

20 *ProLife Alliance v BBC* [2002] EWCA Civ 297, [2002] 2 All ER 756 at 775 §44.

21 *Ibid*, at 778/9 §61.

22 *Ibid*. The House of Lords judgment reversing the Court of Appeal is reported at [2003] UKHL 23, [2003] 2 All ER 977.

23 See Chapter 8.

24 See Case Study D.

25 Paper kindly sent to the author by Lord Steyn, based on a lecture given by Lord Steyn at a conference organized and held by Justice and Sweet & Maxwell on 19 October 2000. In fact, as is pointed out in Chapter 1, the HRA

does not incorporate the whole Convention but omits certain rights, although this does not affect Lord Steyn's argument.

26 Andrew Z. Drzemczewski (1983) *European Human Rights Convention in Domestic Law: A comparative study*, Oxford University Press, Oxford, p 281 (Germany), p 286 (Italy), p 302 (Turkey).

27 *Rights Brought Home: The Human Rights Bill* (Cm 3782), para 2.13.

28 See Michael Arnheim, *Principles of the Common Law*, Duckworth, London (forthcoming), Chapter 4–2.

29 By contrast with Human Rights law, EU law does enjoy higher law status, subject to the European Communities Act 1972. It was clearly in order to prevent the ECHR from gaining the same status as EU law that the HRA was drafted the way it is. See discussion in Michael Arnheim, *Principles of the Common Law*, Duckworth, London (forthcoming).

30 HRA s 19 (1) (a).

31 HRA s 19 (1) (b).

32 Cf Sedley LJ, discussed in Michael Arnheim, *Principles of the Common Law*, Duckworth, London (forthcoming).

33 See discussion in Chapter 6.

34 See note 25.

35 See discussion on interpretation in Chapter 1.

36 *R v Secretary of State for the Home Department, ex parte Anthony Anderson* [2002] UKHL 46.

37 *Raymond v Honey* [1983] AC 1.

38 *R v Secretary of State for the Home Department ex parte Leech* [1993] 4 All ER 539.

39 *Golder v UK* (1979–80) 1 EHRR 524 75/1.

40 *Silver v UK* (1983) 5 EHRR 347 83/2.

41 *Campbell v UK* (1993) 15 EHRR 137 92/41.

42 *Pierson v Secretary of State for the Home Department* [1997] 3 All ER 577 at 588.

43 *R v Home Secretary, ex parte Doody* [1993] 1 All ER 151.

44 *Pierson v Secretary of State for the Home Department* [1997] 3 All ER 577.

45 *R v Secretary of State for the Home Department, ex parte Dennis Stafford* [1998] 4 All ER 7.

46 *Stafford v UK* [2002] 35 EHRR 32.

47 *R (on the application of Anderson) v Secretary of State for the Home Department* [2002] UKHL 46, [2002] 4 All ER 1089 (HL).

48 *R v Secretary of State for the Home Department, ex parte Venables & Thompson* [1997] 3 All ER 97 (HL) *T v UK; V v UK* [2000] 2 All ER 1024; *Re Thompson and another (tariff recommendations)* [2001] 1 All ER 737.

49 Practice Note [2000] 4 All ER 831.

50 *Venables and another v News Group Newspapers* [2001] 1 All ER 908.

51 *Ibid* at 931 (§76).

52 *X, A Woman Formerly Known as Mary Bell and Y v O'Brien, News Group Newspapers and MGN Ltd* [2003] EWHC QB 1101.

53 *Ibid*, at §10.
54 *Campbell v MGN Ltd* [2002] EWCA Civ 1373, [2003] WLR 80 (§70).
55 [2003] EWHC QB 1101, at §16.
56 *Ibid*, at §36.
57 *Ibid*, at §50.
58 *Ibid*, at §18.
59 *Ibid*, at §40.
60 *Ibid*, at §6.
61 BBC News – http://news.bbc.co.uk – 26 April 1998.
62 [2003] EWHC QB 1101 at §6.
63 See Michael Arnheim, *Principles of the Common Law*, Duckworth, London (forthcoming).
64 On the ground that it was superseded by a statute that could only be used to stop a criminal from profiting from his crime within a period of six years from the time when the crime was committed: Criminal Justice Act 1988 s 74A(10) as amended by the Proceeds of Crime Act 1995, s 5.
65 *X, A Woman Formerly Known as Mary Bell and Y v O'Brien, News Group Newspapers and MGN Ltd* [2003] EWHC QB 1101 at §§16–18.
66 *R (on the application of Bulger) v Secretary of State for the Home Department* ([2001] EWHC Admin 119, [2001] 3 All ER 449 at 455 (§23).
67 Lord Widgery, *Report of the tribunal appointed to inquire into the events of Sunday 30 January 1972*, HL 101, HC 220, HMSO 1972.
68 *R v Lord Saville of Newdigate and others, ex parte A and others* [1999] 4 All ER 860 at 865 f.
69 *Ibid* at 882.
70 *Ibid*. Even this ruling, however, applied only 'to those soldiers who are most at risk, namely the soldiers who either admitted firing rounds or are alleged to have fired rounds'.
71 *Lord Saville of Newdigate and Others v Widgery Soldiers and others* [2001] EWCA Civ 2048 (19 December 2001), §3.
72 *Ibid*.
73 *Ibid* §55.
74 *Ibid* §57.

# 4

# Right to life

**Article 2**
***Right to life***

1. Everyone's right to life shall be protected by law. No one shall be deprived of his life intentionally save in the execution of a sentence of a court following his conviction of a crime for which this penalty is provided by law.
2. Deprivation of life shall not be regarded as inflicted in contravention of this article when it results from the use of force which is no more than absolutely necessary:
   a in defence of any person from unlawful violence;
   b in order to effect a lawful arrest or to prevent the escape of a person lawfully detained;
   c in action lawfully taken for the purpose of quelling a riot or insurrection.

**Article 3**
***Prohibition of torture***

No one shall be subjected to torture or to inhuman or degrading treatment or punishment.

## THE SIXTH PROTOCOL

**Article 1**
***Abolition of the death penalty***

The death penalty shall be abolished. No one shall be condemned to such penalty or executed.

**Article 2**

***Death penalty in time of war***

A State may make provision in its law for the death penalty in respect of acts committed in time of war or of imminent threat of war; such penalty shall be applied only in the instances laid down in the law and in accordance with its provisions. The State shall communicate to the Secretary General of the Council of Europe the relevant provisions of that law.

## PRINCIPLES IN PRACTICE

1. Article 2(1) is twofold:
   - It makes it obligatory for each state to pass laws to protect human life; and
   - It protects individuals against intentional killing by public authorities.

2. Article 2 is concerned not only with intentional killing but also with death resulting from the lawful use of force in certain circumstances.
3. Article 2(2) excludes from the general prohibition in Article 2(1) death resulting 'from the use of force which is no more than absolutely necessary':
   - 'in defence of any person from unlawful violence;
   - in order to effect a lawful arrest or to prevent the escape of a person lawfully detained;
   - in action lawfully taken for the purpose of quelling a riot or insurrection.'

4. The phrase 'no more than *absolutely* necessary' (emphasis added) in Article 2(2) indicates a stricter test than the test of necessity in Articles 8, 9, 10 and 11.
5. In its original form Article 2(1) allowed the death penalty, but this is no longer the case. Article 1 of the Sixth Protocol not only obliges each state to abolish the death penalty but also categorically forbids anyone from being condemned to death or from being executed.
6. The only exception to this prohibition of capital punishment is contained in Article 2 of the Sixth Protocol, which allows states to pass laws imposing the death penalty 'in respect of acts committed in time of war or of imminent threat of war'.
7. Article 3 prohibits torture or 'inhuman or degrading treatment or punishment'.
8. Article 3 allows of no exceptions.
9. Less extreme cases of ill-treatment have been held to fall under the protection of private life in Article 8, which is a qualified right. (Article 8 is considered later in this chapter).

# Q&A: SUMMARY

**Q. Is it permissible for the police or army to kill suspected terrorists who have not yet committed a violent offence?**

A. *The applicable principle is that of proportionality. Lethal force is justified only when it is proportionate to the objective in view, provided that objective is legitimate. But the actual decisions in this highly sensitive area reveal just how difficult this principle is to interpret and how subjective it is.*

**Q. In what circumstances is it permissible for the police to kill someone unintentionally in the course of their ordinary duties?**

A. *Here too the appropriate test is that of proportionality, with the same problem of subjectivity.*

**Q. In what circumstances is it permissible for someone to kill another in self-defence?**

A. *Under English law this would be permissible only if the person defending him- or herself used no more than 'reasonable force', which has recently been interpreted to the detriment of the person so defending him- or herself. The Convention test allowing no more force than is 'absolutely necessary' appears even stricter.*

**Q. Is capital punishment now banned forever in the United Kingdom?**

A. *The death penalty was abolished in the United Kingdom for murder in 1965 and for treason in 1998. It is open to the United Kingdom to pass legislation reintroducing it 'in respect of acts committed in time of war or of imminent threat of war', but even this is highly unlikely.*

**Q. Do states have a positive duty to protect or preserve life?**

A. *The wording of Article 2(1) appears to point in this direction, but where state agents have failed to prevent a murder or suicide no violation of Article 2 has been found, although claims under other Convention rights have sometimes been upheld.*

**Q. Is it permissible to have as many children as you like?**

A. *Yes, provided they are born 'naturally' and not by means of artificial insemination or in vitro fertilization.*

**Q. How does the law view in vitro fertilization?**

A. *With a pretty jaundiced eye.*

**Q. Is there a right of abortion?**

A. *There is a limited right of abortion for the mother, but the father and the unborn child itself have no rights.*

# PRACTICAL PROBLEMS

**Q. Is it permissible for the police or army to kill suspected terrorists who have not yet committed a violent offence?**

*A. The applicable principle is that of proportionality. Lethal force is justified only when it is proportionate to the objective in view, provided that objective is legitimate. But the actual decisions in this highly sensitive area reveal just how difficult this principle is to interpret and how subjective it is.*

The leading case involving the United Kingdom is the so-called 'Death on the Rock', involving the killing of three members of an 'active service unit' of the Provisional IRA by the crack British anti-terrorism unit known as Special Air Service, or SAS, which had been tipped off about an impending terrorist attack in Gibraltar.[1] Two of the three IRA members had convictions for offences involving explosives and the third was regarded by the SAS as an expert bomb-maker. In the words of the majority opinion of the Strasbourg court, the SAS considered 'that it was likely that the suspects would detonate the bomb if challenged; that they would be armed and would be likely to use their arms if confronted. In the event, all of these crucial assumptions, apart from the terrorists' intention to carry out an attack, turned out to be erroneous.'[2] The suspects all turned out to be unarmed and there were no explosives in their car in Gibraltar, but one of the suspects had in her handbag keys to another car parked just across the Spanish border in which 64 kg of Semtex was found. The issue before the Court was whether the killing of the three IRA members violated their right to life or whether it was sanctioned under Article 2(2). In short, was the force involved 'no more than absolutely necessary in defence of any person from unlawful violence'? Unlike Articles 8–11, where the test is whether the infringement of the rights concerned was 'necessary in a democratic society', in Article 2(2) the test is the much stricter one of showing that the infringement was 'absolutely necessary'.

By 11 votes to 6, rejecting the claim that the killing of the three suspects was premeditated, the Commission held that there had been no violation of Article 2, but in the court there was a photo-finish, with 10 judges finding against the United Kingdom and 9 dissenting, the minority including the president and the four most senior members of the court.

The practical question is whether security services are to be permitted to pre-empt violence or terrorism or whether they have to wait for a terrorist to kill them before retaliating, something normally only possible in the Hollywood version of the Wild West! The outcome of the Death on the Rock case has severely hampered security operations and has also opened the way for individual serving soldiers and police to be charged with murder.

Yet an earlier case involving suspected Irish terrorism had a different outcome.[3] British soldiers shot at a car breaking through a roadblock, killing the driver. In a civil action brought against the Ministry of Defence it was held that, as the soldiers had reasonably believed that the car contained terrorists who had to be stopped to prevent them from committing a crime, the Ministry of Defence was not liable for the death.

The Strasbourg Commission rejected the complaint brought by the dead man's father, finding the soldiers' use of force 'strictly proportionate, having regard to the situation confronting the soldiers, the degree of force employed in response and the risk that the use of force could result in the deprivation of life', and therefore 'absolutely necessary' for effecting a lawful arrest within ECHR Article 2(2)(b). The case never went to the Strasbourg court.

**Q. In what circumstances is it permissible for the police to kill someone unintentionally in the course of their ordinary duties?**

***A. Here too the appropriate test is that of proportionality, with the same problem of subjectivity.***

In a Cyprus case a failed police rescue mission was at issue.[4] This was something of a Romeo and Juliet tragedy. Lefteris and Elsie were an engaged couple who had a quarrel, resulting in Lefteris's taking Elsie hostage. In an attempt by the police to rescue her, both lovers were killed. Was the use of force by the police 'no more than absolutely necessary' as required by Article 2(2)? By a majority of 15 to 3 the Human Rights Commission found a violation of Article 2, but this was reversed by a narrow majority of 5 to 4 in the Strasbourg court itself. The court contrasted the phrase 'absolutely necessary' with the more usual get-out wording 'necessary in a democratic society' found in Articles 8–11. It was held by the majority that the police had been entitled to use lethal force in the circumstances, so there was no violation of Article 2.

**Q. In what circumstances is it permissible for someone to kill another in self-defence?**

***A. Under English law this would be permissible only if the person defending him- or herself used no more than 'reasonable force', which has recently been interpreted to the detriment of the person so defending him- or herself. The Convention test allowing no more force than is 'absolutely necessary' appears even stricter.***

Unlike most of the other Convention rights, Article 2 is not only concerned to protect the individual against the state but also seeks to protect individuals against one another. 'Everyone's right to life shall be protected by law.' Every country has laws against homicide, but what are of particular interest are the circumstances in which killing is lawful. The law must protect people against murder, but it must also protect those who kill in those very limited circumstances when killing is justified. This is reflected in Article 2(2)(a), which provides that killing 'in defence of any person from unlawful violence' is justifiable provided 'it results from the use of force which is no more than absolutely necessary'.

Does this include self-defence? This has never been tested in Strasbourg, though it has been the subject of some high-profile English domestic cases, notably one in which a householder, Tony Martin, shot at two intruders to his remote home, aptly named Bleak House, killing one and wounding the other. Martin based his case on self-defence but was convicted of murder and wounding with intent, and was sentenced to life imprisonment. On appeal his conviction was downgraded from murder to manslaughter and his sentence reduced from life to five years' imprisonment.[5] The judgment of the Court of Appeal was delivered by Lord Woolf CJ, who remarked that:

> At the time the offences were committed, Mr Martin was being burgled by the two people whom he shot. Because he was being burgled at the time there was considerable public sympathy for Mr Martin and media interest in his case. There were also suggestions that the law was in need of change.

To say that Tony Martin had attracted 'considerable public sympathy' was an understatement. The reaction to his conviction for murder was little short of a public outcry. As for the state of the law, the main authority cited by the Court of Appeal was *Beckford v R*[6], a Privy Council advice on an appeal from Jamaica. Solomon Beckford was a police officer who had shot and killed a suspect in the belief that the man was armed and posed a threat to the police officer's life. Like Tony Martin, therefore, Solomon Beckford pleaded self-defence but was found guilty of murder. However, his conviction was quashed by the Privy Council on the ground that the trial judge had misdirected the jury on the test for self-defence.

Solomon Beckford's case was the only authority on self-defence cited by the Court of Appeal in Tony Martin's case. Yet the circumstances of that case were very different from those of Martin. In particular, Solomon Beckford was not in his own home at the time of the shooting. Yet even in that case it was specifically stated by the Privy Council that '[A] man about to be attacked does not have to wait for his assailant to strike the first blow or fire the first shot: circumstances may justify a pre-emptive strike.'[7]

Was it not relevant that the man shot dead by Tony Martin was an intruder in the process of burgling his home? Traditional English common law certainly took this into account, giving rise to the adage 'An Englishman's home is his castle.' In *Semayne's* case, heard in 1605, Sir Edward Coke CJ explained that although killing in self-defence or even accidentally is normally a felony, this is not the case when a householder or his servants kill 'in defence of himself and his house' a thief who has come to rob or murder him. Backing this up with authority, he then goes on to cite a statute dating from the reign of Henry VII (1485–1509), a century earlier, which specifically allows a householder to assemble his friends and neighbours 'to defend his house against violence'. The statute draws a sharp distinction between gathering supporters together at the house – which is allowed – and taking them on a vigilante expedition around the streets.[8]

Judging by the fate of Tony Martin, we would have to conclude that this kind of thinking no longer represents the law of England. But a comparison with the situation in the United States is instructive, where the law still recognizes that:

> The right of a person to defend his home from attack is a substantive right governed by rules analogous to those applicable to defense of the person, with the major exception that a person faced with danger of attack in his own home is under no duty to retreat. The modern rule as to homicide in defense of the habitation is that if an assault on a dwelling and an attempted forcible entry are made under such circumstances as to create a reasonable apprehension that it is the design of the assailant to commit a felony or to inflict on the inmates a personal injury which may result in the loss of life or great bodily harm, and the danger that the design will be carried into execution is imminent and present, the lawful occupant of the dwelling may lawfully prevent the entry, even by the taking of the life of the intruder. In such case, the occupant may meet the assailant at the threshold and prevent him from breaking in by any means rendered necessary by exigency, and upon the same ground and reason that one may defend himself from peril of life or great bodily harm by means fatal to the assailant, if rendered necessary by the exigency of the assault. This permits the taking of life in case the assailant purposes the commission of any felony, or other crime of violence to the person. In some jurisdictions statutes have been enacted expressly justifying homicides committed in defense of the habitation. Generally, however, a householder is deemed to have no right to take life to prevent a mere unlawful entry into his house, if the entry is not under such circumstances as to afford reasonable grounds for apprehension that the intruder's purpose is to take life, or to inflict serious bodily harm on the inmates, or to commit a felony.[9]

Under US common law, therefore, Tony Martin would probably have been entitled to kill the intruder as he did.

**Q. Is capital punishment now banned forever in the United Kingdom?**

***A. The death penalty was abolished in the United Kingdom for murder in 1965 and for treason in 1998. It is open to the United Kingdom to pass legislation reintroducing it 'in respect of acts committed in time of war or of imminent threat of war', but even this is highly unlikely.***

Article 2 recognizes capital punishment as long as it is 'provided by law'. However the Sixth Protocol, which has been ratified by the United Kingdom, declares that 'The death penalty shall be abolished. No one shall be condemned to such penalty or executed.' A state may, however, pass a law providing for the death penalty 'in respect of acts committed in time of war or of imminent threat of war'.

Does this mean that, with this narrow exception, the death penalty can never be reintroduced in the United Kingdom? It has certainly been interpreted in that way by commentators. However, as was discussed in Chapter 1, the Human Rights Act goes out of its way to stress that the UK Parliament is entitled, if it so wishes, to pass legislation that is incompatible with the Convention, although this represents a theoretical principle rather than a practical reality.

It is also perhaps worth mentioning that the Sixth Protocol itself contains four articles, only two of which are incorporated into the Human Rights Act. The two that are omitted are the ones that do not permit any reservation or derogation from the Protocol. Does this omission give the United Kingdom more leeway in case it decides to reintroduce capital punishment? Possibly, though the question is probably academic, as it seems unlikely that the UK Parliament will vote for a return of the death penalty in the foreseeable future.

Capital punishment for murder was abolished in 1965, and periodic votes in Parliament – where MPs have always been allowed a free vote – confirmed this decision. However, treason and setting fire to the royal dockyards continued in theory to carry the death penalty until the law was changed in 1998 in the wake of the Human Rights Act.

If capital punishment ever came back in the United Kingdom it would probably be within the terms allowed by the Sixth Protocol 'in respect of acts committed in time of war or of imminent threat of war'. In the light of the 'war on terror' or 'war on terrorism' declared by United States President Bush in the immediate aftermath of the cataclysm of '9/11', in 2001, the phrase 'imminent threat of war' may become more relevant. But it is probably unlikely that the death penalty will be reintroduced even for such cases. The main problem with capital punishment is that it is irreversible: it is difficult to unhang someone whose conviction turns out later to have been unsafe or unsatisfactory. There is also the political problem that executing a terrorist or revolutionary, however bloody his or her misdeeds, is a sure-fire way of turning him or her into a martyr.

**Q. Do states have a positive duty to protect or preserve life?**

**A.** ***The wording of Article 2(1) appears to point in this direction, but where state agents have failed to prevent a murder or suicide no violation of Article 2 has been found, though claims under other Convention rights have sometimes been upheld.***

Does the state have a positive duty to protect the life of a convicted killer who may be at risk from angry vigilantes? Amazingly, the English courts have granted lifelong anonymity to the child-killers Venables and Thompson and also to Mary Bell, a child-killer whose life was not considered to be in danger. This is not just a question of a name change but the equivalent of a witness protection programme applied to people who are at risk only because of their own criminal acts. The court orders concerned bristle with threats of condign punishment for anyone who invades the privacy of these specially protected personages. Why? Is it because the court is afraid that as a 'public authority' within HRA s 6(1) it would be acting incompatibly with these killers' right to life under ECHR Article 2 if it did not extend this kind of hospitality to them at public expense?

Why, then, did the judicial tribunal known as the 'Bloody Sunday Inquiry' not take the same view of the right to life of the soldier witnesses – never convicted of any offence – who were called to testify before it? Quite the reverse, in fact, as in this case the risk arose specifically from the fact that the tribunal actually refused the soldiers anonymity and then insisted that they testify in Londonderry – both of which would have placed the soldiers in mortal danger, and quite needlessly so, as the Court of Appeal subsequently held. As the

LIVERPOOL JOHN MOORES UNIVERSITY
LEARNING SERVICES

'Bloody Sunday' tribunal is of course a 'public authority' within HRA s 6(1), it would have been unlawful for it to place the life of these soldier witnesses in peril in this way, as this would clearly have been incompatible with their right to life under ECHR Article 2. (See Chapter 6 for a fuller discussion of Venables and Thompson and Chapter 3 for Mary Bell and 'Bloody Sunday'.)

## Strasbourg

How do these UK decisions relate to previous cases brought under the Convention? Besides the negative obligation on states not to take lives except where 'absolutely necessary', is there in Strasbourg jurisprudence a positive obligation on them to protect or preserve life? In a recent case brought against Italy,[10] 40 inhabitants of a town situated close to a chemical plant claimed that the Italian government had infringed their right to freedom of information under Article 10 by failing to inform them of the hazards and how to handle them. By the same token there was a claim under Article 8 (right to respect for private and family life) and also under Article 2. These overlapped. The Strasbourg court found that there had been a violation of Article 8 and found it unnecessary to consider Article 2 separately. However, two of the judges specifically addressed the Article 2 claim.

This may be a sign of things to come. So, for example, in the admissibility decision in another case involving Italy,[11] one of the issues raised was the State's liability for murder at the hands of a dangerous prisoner on parole.

A similar issue arose in the extremely unusual case of *Osman v United Kingdom*.[12] After a long series of bizarre incidents to which the police were called, a schoolteacher shot and killed Ali Osman and seriously wounded his son Ahmet Osman. 'Why didn't you stop me before I did it?' pleaded the distraught schoolteacher on his arrest. 'I gave you all the warning signs.' Were the police liable for the shootings? The English courts held that in cases alleging negligence for failure to investigate or suppress crime the police enjoyed immunity from suit. The Strasbourg court, however, found unanimously that this purported immunity amounted to a violation of the right to access to justice contained in Article 6(1), but the claim under Article 2 failed.

This ruling will nevertheless be likely to expand the scope of state liability for deaths caused by the actions of one private person against another, which at the time of writing has still not been recognized by the domestic courts.

## Clunis

This was demonstrated in another sad and bizarre case: *Clunis v Camden & Islington Health Authority*.[13] Jonathan Zito was innocently standing on the platform in a London Underground station when he was fatally stabbed in the eye by Christopher Clunis, a mental patient who had recently been discharged from Guy's Hospital, where he had been briefly detained under s 3 of the Mental Health Act 1983. To a charge of murder Clunis pleaded guilty to manslaughter on grounds of diminished responsibility. Clunis then sued the health authority for professional negligence in allowing him to be at large at the time of the attack. His argument in simple terms was that had he been confined to a psychiatric hospital he would not have killed Mr Zito.

This argument was rejected by the Court of Appeal on three grounds. First, there was the public policy ground that nobody should be allowed to benefit from his own wrong – based on an ancient maxim enshrining a fundamental principle of law. Secondly, there was the rather technical point that as s 117 of the 1983 Act provided a route of complaint via the Secretary of State, the wording of the section was not 'apposite' to create a private law claim as well. Thirdly, in view of this it would not be 'fair, just and reasonable' to impose a common law duty of care on the health authority.

Will this reasoning survive the Strasbourg decision in *Osman*? Only time will tell. *Should* it survive? A claim on all fours with *Clunis* is unlikely to be decided differently in the future, because the claimant would clearly be trying to benefit from his own criminal act. But what if the claim against the health authority were to be brought instead by the victim's family? Here it could be argued that the damage was too remote. Yet there are precedents in English law for liability to be found in similar cases, most notably *Home office v Dorset Yacht Co Ltd*,[14] where a duty of care was found to exist on the part of the Home Office towards the owners of a yacht damaged by borstal trainees who had escaped as a result of the negligence of the three borstal officers in whose custody they were. Though *Dorset Yacht* has never been overruled, the tide of tort liability has receded drastically since it was decided, and the new lamentably vague 'fair, just and reasonable' test may well be used to defeat a claim by victims or their families, just as it was in *Clunis* itself.

## Suicide

Until 1961 suicide was a criminal offence under English law. This aroused a certain amount of amusement, for what sentence can be passed on a successful suicide? The Suicide Act 1961, however, left 'complicity in another's suicide' as a crime: 'A person who aids, abets, counsels or procures the suicide of another, or an attempt by another to commit suicide' is guilty of an offence carrying a maximum sentence of 14 years' imprisonment. As a safeguard there is a provision that a prosecution for this offence requires the consent of the Director of Public Prosecutions – so as to introduce an element of discretion.

In *Dunbar v Plant*[15] an engaged couple made a suicide pact to kill themselves by jumping simultaneously from a ladder. In the event, the male partner died but his fiancée survived. In keeping with the spirit of the 1961 Act she was not prosecuted for any criminal offence. But her late fiancé's father, as administrator of his son's estate, took her to court to stop her from becoming sole owner of the house that she had shared with the dead man and from claiming on his life insurance policy, of which she was the named beneficiary. By a majority the Court of Appeal decided that, though never prosecuted, she was guilty of aiding and abetting her fiancé's suicide but that in the interests of 'trying to do justice between the parties' she should be allowed to have the whole of the house and the insurance moneys.

## *Euthanasia*

The law making complicity in suicide an offence clearly covers euthanasia of any kind, regardless of whether the person assisting the would-be suicide is medically qualified or not. The most high-profile case of its kind to date was that of Diane Pretty, a sufferer from motor neurone disease, an inexorable and invariably fatal wasting condition: *R (on the application of Pretty) v DPP*.[16] She wished to die with dignity, and although her mental faculties were unimpaired, she was physically incapable of committing suicide, so she asked her husband to assist her to end her life. As this would have constituted a criminal offence under the Suicide Act 1961, Mrs Pretty asked the Director of Public Prosecutions (DPP) to give an undertaking not to prosecute her husband if he assisted her to commit suicide. This request was refused. Mrs Pretty then took the unprecedented step of applying for judicial review of the DPP's decision.

Mrs Pretty sought two remedies in the alternative:

- A declaration that the DPP's decision was unlawful under the Human Rights Act 1998 because it infringed Articles 2, 3, 8, 9 and 14 of the Human Rights Convention.
- Alternatively, a declaration that by making assisted suicide a criminal offence s 2(1) of the Suicide Act 1961 was incompatible with her rights.

Mrs Pretty was given permission to apply for judicial review – in itself a radical departure from precedent – but her substantive application was rejected by a unanimous House of Lords. A right to life, it was held, did not imply a right to die, or a right to die at the time and in the manner of one's own choosing. Quite the reverse. The contentions put forward on Mrs Pretty's behalf under Articles 3, 8, 9 and 14 were also rejected.

Although the Suicide Act gave the DPP a discretion whether or not to prosecute in a particular case, it was held that there was nothing in the Act that gave him or her the right to exercise discretion before any relevant death had even occurred. However, it was added, the DPP was entitled if he or she so wished to issue policy statements indicating how he or she would exercise discretion in specific circumstances. This left the door open for undertakings not to prosecute to be given in advance in suitable cases in the future.

The *Pretty* case was the first to reach Strasbourg after going through the UK domestic courts. Here once again the claim was framed in terms not only of Article 2 but also of Articles 3, 8, 9 and 14. The argument was again advanced on Mrs Pretty's behalf that the right to life under Article 2 must be understood as including a corresponding right to die. A comparison was drawn with the right of freedom of association and assembly in Article 11, where it had been successfully pleaded that the right to join a trade union must include the right to refuse to join one: *Young, James and Webster v. United Kingdom*.[17] The court did not accept this parallel and held that there had been no violation of Article 2. The claims under other Articles of the Convention were likewise rejected – including that under Article 8, which probably had the best chance of success of all.

Less than two weeks after her case had been rejected by the Strasbourg court Diane Pretty died. Her husband Brian's poignant words encapsulated the futility of her legal struggle: 'Diane had to go through the one thing she had foreseen and was afraid of going through and there was nothing I could do to help.'[18]

In sharp contrast with Diane Pretty's case was that of a tetraplegic who successfully sought to have her life-support system switched off: *Ms B v An NHS Hospital Trust*.[19] The contrast was all the sharper because the two cases were heard within a very short time of each other. On behalf of Ms B it was stressed that the court was not being asked directly to decide whether she should live or die, but only whether she could herself refuse medical treatment which was keeping her alive against her will.

Two equal and potentially conflicting principles were identified by the court: that of the sanctity of life on the one hand, and, on the other, the principle of autonomy, which includes the right to refuse medical treatment.

## Autonomy

The 'principle of autonomy' is traced back to *S v S; W v Official Solicitor*,[20] two paternity suits heard together by the House of Lords. In both cases the putative father was asking for a blood test of the child to be ordered so as to show that he was not in fact the father. In both cases the House of Lords made the order. Lord Reid made the point that, by contrast with the United States, under English law an adult could not be ordered to submit to a blood test:

> The real reason is that English law goes to great lengths to protect a person of full age and capacity from interference with his personal liberty. We have too often seen freedom disappear in other countries not only by coups d'état but by gradual erosion; and often it is the first step that counts. So it would be unwise to make even minor concessions.
>
> . . . But the position is very different with regard to young children. It is a legal wrong to use constraint on an adult beyond what is authorised by statute or ancient

> common law powers connected with crime and the like. But it is not and could not be a legal wrong for a parent or person authorised by him to use constraint to his young child provided it is not cruel or excessive. . . . So it seems to me to be impossible to deny that a parent can lawfully require that his young child should submit to a blood test. And if the parent can require that, why not the court? There is here no overriding requirement of public policy as there is with an adult.[21]

The distinction drawn here between adults and children may now raise a few eyebrows in the wake of the Human Rights Act, and in particular of Article 3 of the Human Rights Convention incorporated into the Act, but that could, if anything, only have broadened the scope of the principle of 'autonomy'. Lord Reid did not cite any sources for this principle or trace its origin. Where then does it come from?

This 'right of autonomy', as it has lately been dubbed, is really the basic right that everyone has to integrity of his person and property. If, as Coke put it, 'every man's house is his castle', giving people the right to defend themselves against burglars even to the extent of killing them,[22] then there must a fortiori be a right to integrity of life and limb. That there is such a right can be seen from the law of trespass – which is precisely a violation of a person or property and therefore akin to the modern concept of *privacy*. Indeed, although the word 'autonomy' does not appear in the Convention, the House of Lords in *Pretty* specifically characterized Article 8 as being 'expressed in terms directed to protection of personal autonomy while individuals are living their lives', but they went on to add that 'there is nothing to suggest that the Article has reference to the choice to live no longer'.

## Sanctity of life

The other 'equally fundamental principle', as it was described by Dame Elizabeth Butler-Sloss P in Ms B's case, was 'the sanctity of life', which she traced back to *Airedale NHS Trust v Bland*,[23] concerning a young man who was in a persistent vegetative state after being severely brain damaged in the Hillsborough disaster three years before. It was an application brought by the hospital, supported by Anthony Bland's parents, to turn off his life-support system and thereby inevitably cause his death.

In *Bland* Lord Goff identified the 'sanctity of life' with the right to life in Article 2 of the European Human Rights Convention, adding that 'this principle, fundamental though it is, is not absolute'. From there it was but a short step to allowing Anthony Bland's life-support system to be turned off, with the caveat that euthanasia in the sense of taking some positive step to end a patient's life remained unlawful.

There are at least two problems with the identification of the 'sanctity of life' with the right to life in Article 2 of the Convention:

- 'Sanctity of life' is plainly not the same thing as 'right to life'.
- Although the right to life under Article 2 is not absolute, ending someone's life without his or her consent in a situation like that in *Bland* is not covered by any of the three exceptions enumerated in Article 2(2) (see above).

## *Right to decide to refuse treatment*

To return to Ms B's case, although it was held that the principle of the sanctity of life and that of autonomy were 'equally fundamental', it was decided that 'the right of the competent patient to request cessation of treatment must prevail over the natural desire of the medical and nursing profession to try to keep her alive'. Having held that Ms B was indeed perfectly competent, the conclusion naturally followed that she should be allowed to refuse treatment even if, as in her case, such refusal would almost inevitably result in her death.

But if the two principles were indeed 'equally fundamental', why should the right of autonomy prevail over that of sanctity of life? No explanation is given.

## *State of the law*

Diane Pretty's case can be distinguished from those of Anthony Bland and Ms B, because she was asking for something positive to be done by her husband to end her life whereas in the other two cases what was sought was something negative, the cessation of medical treatment, albeit 'treatment' that was keeping the patient alive. Once *Bland* was decided the way it was, it was probably inevitable that Ms B's application should have been successful, as Anthony Bland's life was terminated without his consent in a situation where he was mentally incompetent, while Ms B, as was stressed throughout, had the mental capacity to decide her own fate.

It is perhaps worth noting that certain versions of the Hippocratic Oath still taken by medical graduates at some universities, in addition to an undertaking not to administer any 'deadly drug to any, though it be asked of me', continue: 'Nor shall I strive officiously to keep alive.'

Nevertheless, it is a very narrow line that separates 'positive' acts causing inevitable death from 'negative' ones. Smothering the patient in question with a pillow would clearly fall into the category of positive acts and so would giving them a fatal overdose of sleeping tablets.

**Q. Is it permissible to have as many children as you like?**

***A. Yes, provided they are born 'naturally' and not by means of artificial insemination or in vitro fertilization.***

Unlike China, where there are powerful legal constraints against having more than one child, in the United Kingdom it is permissible to have as many children as you like provided they are born 'naturally' and not by means of artificial insemination or in vitro fertilization. There is no restriction on natural-born children no matter how many of them there are, whether their parent(s) are able to support them or are dependent on state benefits – and even if they have been brought into the world specifically for the purpose of generating welfare payments.

By contrast, the courts have tended to look with a jaundiced eye on artificial insemination of all kinds, even though the parents involved are generally highly responsible couples who not only pay for the fertility treatments themselves but are also only too willing to support their children to the best of their ability. A cynic might suggest that this is precisely the reason why left-leaning judges do not like such parents, for fertility treatments are expensive and may possibly be seen as a 'perk' of the rich.

**Q. How does the law view in vitro fertilization?**
***A. With a pretty jaundiced eye.***

The Code of Practice of the Human Fertilisation and Embryology Authority ('HFEA') did not allow more than three eggs or embryos to be placed in a woman in any one cycle. A particular clinic wished to use more than three embryos in the case of a 46-year-old woman who had had numerous unsuccessful treatments. The woman and the clinic applied for judicial review of the inflexible insistence by the HFEA on the three-embryo rule.

The Court of Appeal, upholding the judge, adopted a position of classic self-restraint: Parliament had entrusted the HFEA, not the courts, with the power to regulate in vitro fertilization treatments.

> Like any public authority [the HFEA] is open to challenge by way of judicial review if it exceeds or abuses the powers and responsibilities given to it by Parliament; but where, as is manifest here from an examination of the facts, it considers requests for advice carefully and thoroughly, and produces opinions which are plainly rational, the court, in our judgment, has no part to play in the debate and certainly no power to intervene to strike down any such decision.[24]

Rosalind English, a barrister, aptly comments:

> This case simply furnishes more evidence of the attitude of the courts towards reproductive medical technology; that it is in general the slippery start to a very precipitous slope that leads to a Brave New World of clones and designer babies. Whether this attitude is scientifically justified (and the author tentatively ventures the view that it is not), it is still clearly a waste of time and energy for claimants to enlist the help of Art 12 European Convention on Human Rights. Remember: in the Humpty Dumpty world of human rights these provisions will only ever mean what the current custodians of our morals and values want them to mean.[25]

The same commentator remarks more generally and equally pointedly:

As the court observed, it is not the role of applicants seeking judicial review to canvass the merits of the decision before the court. However, this is a rule more often evident in the breach than in the observance. A cursory survey of many leading Judicial Review decisions reveals an overwhelming judicial tendency to re-run the merits of an administrative decision, particularly where that decision relates to immigration or asylum (for example the case law on safe third country challenges by asylum seekers).[26]

**Q. Is there a right of abortion?**

***A. There is a limited right of abortion for the mother, but the father and the unborn child itself have no rights.***

Probably the best known case on abortion is the American case of *Roe v Wade*[27] 410 US 113 (1973), decided by the US Supreme Court by a 7:2 majority. It is primarily concerned not with the right to life but with privacy – the mother's right to choose whether to have the baby or not. 'Jane Roe' brought the case to challenge two anti-abortion statutes, one from Texas and another rather more liberal one from Georgia. The leading opinion for the majority was delivered by Justice Harry Blackmun, whose position was briefly encapsulated in one sentence: 'The right of privacy . . . is broad enough to encompass a woman's decision whether or not to terminate her pregnancy.' Interestingly, perhaps, this was Justice Blackmun's second stab at the case. His original opinion sought to strike down both statutes on the rather weak ground that they were 'unconstitutionally vague'. After reargument he enunciated his now famous doctrine invoking the right of privacy which he found lurking in the 'due process' clause of the Fourteenth Amendment. Even Justice Potter Stewart in his concurring opinion made the point that this approach enforced a right that was not specifically mentioned in the Constitution. Opponents of the decision have been considerably less kind. Judge Robert Bork commented: 'Whatever one's feelings about abortion, the decision has no constitutional foundation, and the court offered no constitutional reasoning.'[28]

Although *Roe v Wade* allowed only a restricted right of abortion after the first trimester, it unleashed a massive 'right to life' lobby championing the cause of the unborn child. The legal foundation of this challenge was also based on the Fourteenth Amendment, in which the key word was seen to be 'person': 'No state shall . . . deprive any person of life, liberty, or property without due process of law.' When does a foetus become a person? Opinions range over the whole period from the moment of conception (the Roman Catholic Church's position) to birth (the traditional common law view).

If a foetus becomes a person at any stage before birth, then it must have its own right to life, and abortion at that stage must amount to murder, or at the very least to manslaughter. It is here that the issue has been joined, with 'pro-choice' campaigners focusing their attention on privacy rights, and 'pro-life' supporters on the right to life. It has not only become one of the most hotly contested areas in contemporary western politics and law, but also provides one of the best examples of how two rights can conflict – or be deemed to conflict – with each other.

## *Abortion Act 1967*

The UK Abortion Act 1967 allows a pregnancy to be terminated only if, in the opinion of two doctors, it has not gone beyond its 24th week and carrying the baby to term 'would involve risk, greater than if the pregnancy were terminated, of injury to the physical or mental health of the pregnant woman or any existing children of her family'. For a pregnancy to be terminated any later than this is subject to the more stringent test, again in the opinion of two registered medical practitioners, 'that the termination is necessary to prevent grave permanent injury to the physical or mental health of the pregnant woman', or else that the pregnant woman's life is in danger if the pregnancy is continued, or finally 'that there is a substantial risk that if the child were born it would suffer from such physical or mental abnormalities as to be seriously handicapped'.

The emphasis on the health of the mother is understandable enough. The one slightly unexpected feature of this legislation is the possibility of terminating a pregnancy on the grounds of a risk to the health of 'existing children'. Children are often afraid that a new baby may rob them of their parents' affection, and it is conceivable that this may affect the children's health in some way. The test, though, is that this risk must be 'greater than if the pregnancy were terminated' – quite a formidable hurdle to clear.

## *Fathers' rights?*

The one person who does not figure in the legislation at all is the father. In US law, where abortion is classified as an aspect of the law of privacy – 'the woman's right to choose' – there is clearly no room for any input by the prospective father. And he is equally shut out from the 'right to life' viewpoint, according to which once conception has taken place neither parent has any right to choose.

The fact that the British law of abortion is statute based means that it can adopt a value-neutral position. However, in the absence of any statutory rights for the father, the courts have also refused to accord him any recognition in the abortion process.[29]

In *C v S*[30] a father applied unsuccessfully for an injunction to prevent the unmarried mother, who was under 24 weeks pregnant at the time, from having an abortion. As required by the Abortion Act 1967, two doctors had certified that continuing the pregnancy would involve a greater risk to her health than if the pregnancy were terminated. The father, who applied both on his own behalf and as next friend of the unborn child, contended that an abortion would amount to the offence of child destruction, carrying a maximum sentence of life imprisonment, under section 1(1) of the Infant Life (Preservation) Act 1929. The offence occurs where 'any person who, with intent to destroy the life of a child capable of being born alive, by any wilful act causes a child to die before it has an existence independent of its mother'.

In *Kelly v Kelly*[31] a father failed to obtain an interim interdict (the Scots equivalent of an interlocutory injunction) restraining his wife from having an abortion. The question before the Court of Session was whether an abortion could amount to an actionable wrong against the father. If so, the father would be entitled to take legal proceedings on behalf of the foetus. It was held, however, that it was not an actionable wrong. Treating the foetus as a person with actionable rights was the 'fatal flaw' in the father's argument. For under Scots law the foetus was part of the mother's body and had no independent right to remain in the womb. The pursuer's case was therefore without foundation and his application was dismissed.

There seems to be a conflation here of two quite separate issues: the rights of the foetus and the rights of the father. The fact that the foetus has no rights does not need to mean that the father has none either. The application in Kelly appears to have been based on the concept of the father as bringing the action on behalf of his unborn child. This was automatically doomed to failure as the unborn child had no rights. But why could the father not have rights of his own, simply in his capacity as a father, similar to those that a father has over minor children after birth and corresponding to a father's onerous legal obligations towards his children? In the absence of any statutory provision to this effect or any common law precedent, fathers' rights are doomed to lag well behind their obligations.

## Rights of the unborn child

Both English and US law have set their face firmly against recognizing that a foetus has any legal rights at any stage prior to birth. So, in *R v Tait*[32] it was held that it was not a criminal offence under section 16 of the Offences Against the Person Act 1861 to threaten a pregnant woman with the words 'I am going to kill your baby'. The section makes it an offence to threaten another person 'to kill that other or a third person'. It was held, however, that an unborn child was not 'a third person'. This seems a rather narrow view. It was assumed by the Court of Appeal that 'the threat would, if spelt out in full, have been on the following lines "I will inflict such injuries on you as will cause the foetus which you are carrying to miscarry."' However, the threat could also have meant: 'I will wait until you are delivered of the baby which you are now carrying, and if it is born alive I will kill it.' Yet, even on this interpretation of the threat it was held that no offence under the section was made out.

In *McKay v Essex Area Health Authority*[33] a woman contracted rubella (German measles) in the early stages of her pregnancy and as a result gave birth to a severely disabled child, who then sued the doctor and health authority concerned for failing to advise her mother to have an abortion – what has been termed a 'wrongful life' suit. It was held that although the doctor owed the mother a duty to advise her to have an abortion in these circumstances, it did not follow that he owed the unborn child a duty to terminate its life, which would have given the foetus a right to die.

At first glance *Burton v Islington Health Authority*[34] may appear to be at variance with this decision, but this is not in fact the case. Here a child who was born with disabilities sued the health authority for causing her abnormalities by carrying out a gynaecological operation on her mother while pregnant and thereby injuring the daughter while still a foetus. The crucial difference between this case and *McKay* is that in *McKay* the disabilities were caused by the mother's rubella, whereas in *Burton* they were the result of surgery performed on the mother.

As the injuries in *Burton* were suffered at a time when the claimant was as yet unborn, the question before the court was, does an unborn child have any rights under the law? The matter was decided by applying an ancient maxim of Roman Law from Justinian's *Digest*: 'Qui in utero est, perinde ac si in rebus humanis esset, custoditur, quotiens de commodis ipsius partus quaeritur.'[35] 'The unborn child is treated just as if he were a fully fledged human being whenever benefits accruing to him at birth are in issue.' This somewhat obscure maxim, attributed to the illustrious jurist Paulus, who lived during the Severan age (c. AD 200), was cited by Lord Westbury LC in *Blasson v Blasson*[36], by Lord Atkinson in *Villar v Gilbey*[37] and by the Supreme Court of Canada in *Montreal Tramways Leveille*.[38]

This last case provides a good example of the application of the maxim. A pregnant woman thrown from a tram as a result of the negligence of the tramway company's motor man gave birth to a baby girl who was born with club feet. The operative principle was succinctly expressed by Cannon J in French: 'On peut dire que son droit est né en même temps qu'elle' ('One may say that her right was born at the same time as she was') . In other words, although the unborn child has no rights, its rights crystallize at birth, allowing it to bring claims relating even to the time when it was still in the womb. The justification for this was put in an eloquent and emotive passage by Lamont J in the same case:

> If a child after birth has no right of action for prenatal injuries, we have a wrong inflicted for which there is no remedy, for, although the father may be entitled to compensation for the loss he has incurred and the mother for what she has suffered, yet there is a residuum of injury for which compensation cannot be had save at the suit of the child. If a right of action be denied to the child it will be compelled, without any fault on its part, to go through life carrying the seal of another's fault and bearing a very heavy burden of infirmity and inconvenience without any compensation therefor. To my mind it is but natural justice that a child if born alive and viable, should be allowed to maintain an action in the Courts for injuries wrongfully committed upon its person while in the womb of its mother.[39]

It is worth mentioning that, as the unborn child's rights are on ice, as it were, until birth, so for limitation purposes time begins to run only once the child in question has reached the age of majority. That is why in *Burton* the claim was still in time although brought when the claimant was nearly 21 years old.

It should now be clear that the doctrine derived from Paulus's ancient maxim is not actually an exception to the principle that the unborn child has no rights, but adds a rider to it. The principle as a whole can therefore be restated as follows: the unborn child has no rights until birth, when its rights crystallize even in regard to events occurring while it was as yet unborn.

No discussion of the rights of the unborn child can be considered complete without consideration of wills and inheritance. *Villar v Gilbey*[40] went all the way to the House of Lords on the meaning of the simple phrase 'born in my lifetime'. The will in question left property to the testator's brother's two sons, followed by: 'But I declare my intention to be that any third or other son or sons of my said brother born in my lifetime shall not take a larger interest in my said estates than for life only with remainder to his issue in tail male and then in tail female . . . '

The testator's two eldest nephews died without issue, so the property devolved upon the third nephew, who was born just three weeks after the testator's death. The question before the court was a practical one: was this third son entitled to an estate tail (that is, one that would pass to his own children) or merely to a life interest? Although clearly born only after the testator's death he was equally clearly en ventre sa mère (that is, in his mother's womb) at that time. Unborn children in this special category are indeed protected by the law, but did that give a whole new meaning to the phrase 'born in my lifetime' as the Court of Appeal had ruled? The House of Lords said no. In the words of Lord Loreburn LC:

> It is certain that a child en ventre sa mère is protected by the law, and may even be party to an action . . . but I do not think that it helps to establish a rule that the words born in my lifetime, include persons born some weeks or months later.

## Notes

1 *McCann v UK* (1996) 21 EHRR 97.
2 *Ibid*, paras 206–207.
3 *Kelly v UK* (1993) 16 EHRR CD 20.
4 *Lefteris Andronicou and Elsie Constantinou v Cyprus*, Case no 97/76 (1998) EHRR 491.
5 *R v Anthony Edward Martin* [2001] EWCA Crim 2245, [2002] 2 WLR 1.
6 *Beckford v R* [1987] 3 All ER 425.
7 *Ibid*, at 431.
8 5 Coke Reports 92
9 *American Jurisprudence 2d* (40 AmJur 2d §174, 1968 as updated to 2000).
10 *Anna Maria Guerra v Italy*, Case 98/8 (1998) 26 EHRR 357.

11 *Mastromatteo v Italy* (2000).
12 *Mulkiye Osman v United Kingdom* (2000) 29 EHRR 245 98/91.
13 *Clunis v Camden & Islington Health Authority* [1998] 3 All ER 180 (CA).
14 *Home Office v Dorset Yacht Co Ltd* [1970] 2 All ER 294.
15 *Dunbar v Plant* [1997] 4 All ER 289.
16 *R (on the application of Pretty) v DPP* [2001] UKHL 61, [2002] 1 All ER 1.
17 *Young, James and Webster v UK* [1981] 4 EHRR 38.
18 Justis database – Context Ltd – from Voluntary Euthanasia Society web site.
19 *Ms B v An NHS Hospital Trust* [2002] EWHC 429 (Fam), [2002] 2 All ER 449.
20 *S v S; W v Official Solicitor* [1970] 3 All ER 107.
21 *Ibid*, at 111.
22 5 Coke Reports 92.
23 *Airedale NHS Trust v Bland* [1993] 1 All ER 821.
24 *R v Human Fertilisation & Embryology Authority, ex parte Assisted Reproduction & Gynaecology Centre* [2002] EWCA Civ 20.
25 Lawtel doc CC0101361. This extract is reproduced with kind permission of the author, Rosalind English, 1 Crown Office Row.
26 *Ibid*. However, in *R v Human Fertilisation & Embryology Authority, ex parte Quintavalle* [2002] EWCA Civ 667, the Court of Appeal, reversing the Administrative Court judge, allowed the *in vitro* fertililization of a 'designer baby', which in this instance was approved by the HFEA.
27 *Roe v Wade* 410 US 113 (1973).
28 Robert Bork (1996) *Slouching Towards Gomorrah*, p 103.
29 *Paton v Trustees of BPAS* [1978] 2 All ER 987.
30 *C v S* [1987] 1 All ER 1230.
31 *Kelly v Kelly* [1997] 2 FLR 828.
32 *R v Tait* [1989] 3 All ER 682.
33 *McKay v Essex Area Health Authority* [1982] 2 All ER 771.
34 *Burton v Islington Health Authority* [1992] 3 All ER 833.
35 Digest 1, 5, 7.
36 *Blasson v Blasson* (1864) 46 ER 534 at 536.
37 *Villar v Gilbey* [1907] AC 139, [1904–7] All ER Rep 779 at 783–84.
38 *Montreal Tramways Leveille* [1933] 4 DLR 337.
39 *Ibid*, at 345.
40 *Villar v Gilbey* [1904–7] All ER Rep 779.

# 5

# Prohibition of torture

Article 3 is the shortest of all the articles in the Convention. It is also one of the few expressed in absolute terms without any restrictions or get-out clauses: 'No one shall be subjected to torture or to inhuman or degrading treatment or punishment.'

There are three degrees of forbidden treatment here, in descending order: (i) torture; (ii) inhuman treatment or punishment; (iii) degrading treatment or punishment. The fact that 'punishment' is specifically mentioned means that even judicial sentences are covered if deemed to be 'inhuman' or 'degrading'. The article therefore covers quite a wide range of activities, the test laid down by Strasbourg for the Article as a whole being that for any conduct to fall foul of the Article it must exceed 'a certain roughness of treatment' – a lamentably vague phrase: the *Greek Case*.[1]

## TORTURE

The only state found guilty of 'torture' by the Strasbourg court is Turkey. A prime example is *Aydin v Turkey*.[2] A 17-year-old Kurdish girl claimed to have been stripped, spun round in a car tyre, beaten, blindfolded and raped by village guards and police. Although these allegations were denied by Turkey, they were accepted as true by the Commission. By a majority of 14 to 7 the Strasbourg court found a violation of Article 3. Because of the cruel suffering caused by the rape this was classified as torture rather than as merely inhuman or degrading treatment.

## INHUMAN TREATMENT AND PUNISHMENT

In *Tomasi v France*[3] (1993) a Corsican political activist was arrested by police, and while held in custody on charges of murder and other offences was subjected to inhuman and degrading treatment. What is surprising about this case is that by the time it came to Strasbourg the applicant had been awarded compensation by the Compensation Board of the French Cour de Cassation. Nevertheless, the Strasbourg court unanimously upheld the claim in regard to Article 3 and also in regard to Articles 5(3) and 6(1).

*Heczegfalvy v Austria*[4] (1993) explored the fine line between deliberate humiliation and bona fide medical treatment. Here a patient detained in a psychiatric institution claimed a violation of his rights under Articles 3, 5, 8, 10 and 13. He succeeded under Articles 5(4) and 10, but failed under the rest, including Article 3. In general, it was held, genuinely essential medical treatment could not be deemed inhuman or degrading, even if apparently cruel. The applicant had been force-fed and handcuffed to his bed for long periods. In the circumstances, however, it was held that this was justified for medical reasons, and no violation of Article 3 was found.

## DEGRADING TREATMENT OR PUNISHMENT

*Hurtado v Switzerland*[5] (1994) was a case where a Colombia national was allegedly beaten up by Vaud cantonal police after a pretty violent arrest struggle. He was convicted on drugs charges and prohibited from re-entering Switzerland for 15 years. His complaints of ill-treatment at the hands of the police were rejected by the Swiss courts and also by the Strasbourg court. The only aspect of his claim that succeeded was in relation to his being refused immediate medical attention and having to continue to wear his soiled clothing after the arrest battle. The matter was amicably settled by payment to the applicant of 14,000 Swiss francs.

## CORPORAL PUNISHMENT

No fewer than three cases have been brought against the United Kingdom in connection with corporal punishment.

*Tyrer v United Kingdom*[6] was a complaint by a 15-year-old boy who had been sentenced to three strokes of the birch by an Isle of Man court. The applicant had to take down his trousers and underpants and bend over a table. The birching raised weals without actually breaking the skin and the boy was sore for about 10 days. Having lodged an application with the Strasbourg Commission, the applicant subsequently changed his mind and sought to withdraw it. Interestingly, although Anthony Tyrer took no further part in the case, the

Commission decided to go ahead with it anyway on the basis that it raised important questions relating to the observance of the Convention! By 14 to 1 the Commission found a violation of Article 3, and this was confirmed by the Court by 6 votes to 1. The fact that the caning was done on the boy's bare buttocks was seen as a factor contributing to the 'degrading' nature of the punishment.

It is worth pointing out that although *Tyrer* was brought against the United Kingdom it was actually defended by the Manx authorities, the Isle of Man being in fact a Crown possession with its own parliament (the ancient House of Keys) and courts (notably the Tynwald). It has its own laws and is not subject to Westminster statutes unless specifically mentioned in them. By the time this case was heard corporal punishment had long been abandoned as a judicial sentence in the United Kingdom proper.

*Tyrer* was concerned with punishment meted out in pursuance of a court sentence. The other two complaints about corporal punishment brought against the United Kingdom were *horizontal* cases, in the sense that the alleged perpetrators of the conduct complained of were not agents of the state. *In Costello-Roberts v United Kingdom*[7] a seven-year-old schoolboy at an independent preparatory school was beaten by the headmaster with a rubber-soled gym shoe. As in *Tyrer* the 'cuts' were administered to the boy's bottom, but unlike *Tyrer*, he was allowed to keep his shorts and underpants on. The case was decided in the Strasbourg court by a majority of 5 to 4. The degree of severity, the majority felt, was not sufficient to warrant its being considered a violation of Article 3. This is perhaps surprising, as the boy in this case was only seven years old, by contrast with Anthony Tyrer, who was 15 at the time of his ordeal.

The most recent of these cases was *A v UK* (1999).[8] Here the applicant was a boy who at the age of nine had been beaten by his stepfather with a garden cane. Charged with assault occasioning actual bodily harm, the stepfather was acquitted by an English jury (by a majority). However, a unanimous Strasbourg court found a violation of Article 3 here.

Like so many Strasbourg decisions, these cases are troubling. For one thing, it is hard to extract any clear-cut principle from them. The case involving the youngest boy (*Costello-Roberts*) was dismissed, while that concerning the oldest (*Tyrer*) was upheld even though that was a case of judicial punishment. Moreover, the acquittal of the perpetrator in *A*'s case had no effect on the Strasbourg decision. So much for the principle of the margin of appreciation!

## THIRD-PARTY CASES

Besides vertical and horizontal human rights cases there are what may be termed third-party cases. In a vertical case the conduct complained of is that of the state against which the application is being brought. For example, in *Tomasi* what was at issue was the conduct of the French police. On the face of it the Convention's applicability is restricted to vertical cases. However, as we have seen, the

Strasbourg court has expanded its scope to embrace horizontal cases as well: that is, cases where the alleged perpetrator is a private person, supposedly on the same level as the applicant – hence the label 'horizontal'. But there has been a yet further extension to cases where it is really a third party that is at fault. One of the best examples of this type of case is *Soering*.

## *Death row*

*Soering v UK*[9] was brought by a German national who was detained in prison in the United Kingdom pending extradition to the United States where he was wanted for capital murder by the state of Virginia. The British government sought an assurance from the US government that he would not be executed even if sentenced to death! No such assurance was forthcoming. The applicant's case in Strasbourg was that the 'death row phenomenon' meant that he would probably have to spend between six and eight years in prison awaiting execution, and it was this that constituted 'inhuman and degrading treatment' under Article 3. Amazingly, a unanimous court found in his favour!

This decision raises some serious issues.

### 1. The possibility of the applicant's having to suffer the 'death row phenomenon' was dependent upon a threefold contingency

The presumptions were:

- that he would be convicted of murder;
- if so, that he would be sentenced to death; and
- that he would spend a long period in prison awaiting execution.

None of the states of the United States that have capital punishment for murder impose it automatically. This applies as much to Virginia as to any other state.[10]

As for the 'death row phenomenon', that is by no means inevitable but is the result of the lodging of repeated appeals. As the death penalty is controversial and has been the subject of a number of challenges in the Supreme Court, which at one time held it to constitute 'cruel and unusual punishment' contrary to the Eight Amendment of the US Constitution, most condemned murderers embark on a protracted process of appeals, judicial review and requests for clemency, which only prolongs their stay on death row.

### 2. Did imprisonment pending execution automatically amount to 'inhuman' or 'degrading' treatment under Article 3?

The Strasbourg court seems to have taken this for granted. Yet it is hard to see why it inevitably qualifies under Strasbourg's own test mentioned above for violations of Article 3: conduct exceeding 'a certain roughness of treatment'.

Imprisonment is never intended to be a rest-cure, and the condemned prisoner's awareness of his impending fate is unlikely to lift his spirits. Yet, so far as one knows, the sort of violence that is endemic in ordinary US prisons appears to be absent from death row, where their common plight tends to create a certain camaraderie amongst the inmates.

## 3. How does this decision affect extradition and the comity of nations?

The decision of the Strasbourg court pre-empted the English court's decision under the extradition treaty between Britain and the United States. It effectively prevented the United Kingdom from honouring its obligations under this treaty, which is contrary to the whole international law concept of the comity of nations. This may have been understandable if Jens Soering was facing trial by a kangaroo court followed by torture on the rack and public execution by being hanged, drawn and quartered!

The Federal Republic of Germany was also seeking his extradition for the same murders. As Germany did not have the death penalty, there could be no objection to this request. But what if he was being sought only by the United States? Would this have meant that he would have been allowed to escape justice altogether? For as none of the alleged offences were committed in the United Kingdom, no British court would have been competent to try him.

## 4. Is there not a conflict of rights here?

The tenor of recent decisions is such as to lead a cynic to suggest that convicted murderers are now the darlings of the judicial system. Jens Soering had not been convicted of murder or anything else, yet his application was predicated on a conviction for murder. If he was not extradited to stand trial in Virginia, would this not have been a slap in the face to his alleged victims and their families? Did they not have any rights in this matter? There is certainly no mention of this aspect of the case in the Strasbourg record.

## 5. Does this decision mean that Contracting States are responsible under the Convention for contingencies that might arise in other countries?

Besides the fact that the 'inhuman' or 'degrading' treatment upon which Jens Soering based his claim was not only in the future but also hypothetical, it was also treatment at the hands of a third party. Does it really make any sense to hold a state responsible for the activities of some other state, as here the United Kingdom was for the (hypothetical) conduct of Virginia?

This approach not only places a huge burden on Contracting States but may also result in an interpretation of the law that hampers or even nullifies government policy as enacted by statute or delegated legislation. *Soering* was an extradition case involving a German national, so no immigration issues arose. But it is in immigration law, and especially that part of it concerned with asylum, that this problem is most frequently encountered.

# IMMIGRATION

**Q. Is it a violation of asylum seekers' rights under Article 3 for the United Kingdom to send them back to their country of origin?**

The case of *Chahal* (discussed below) represents something of an exception in Strasbourg jurisprudence. In general the Strasbourg court has been reluctant to allow applications by asylum seekers under Article 3. Such applications seek to blame the United Kingdom (or another European country) for the possibility that the asylum seekers might be 'subjected to torture or to inhuman or degrading treatment for punishment' if they are returned to their country of origin. Is it fair to blame one country for what might happen in another? And why did the asylum seeker choose the United Kingdom (or another European country) for asylum in any event, often after passing through several others? Moreover, such claims are both indirect and difficult to prove.

A fairly typical case of this sort involved five young male Sri Lankan Tamils who sought asylum in the United Kingdom alleging ill-treatment by Sri Lankan government forces. Their applications for asylum were rejected by the UK authorities and they were returned to Sri Lanka. After further allegations of ill-treatment they were granted exceptional leave to enter the United Kingdom, but by this time their application had already been lodged with Strasbourg. The ECtHR accepted that states have the right to control the entry, residence and expulsion of aliens. It also stressed that there was no right to political asylum in the European Human Rights Convention. For the expulsion of an alien to engage his or her rights under Article 3 there would have to be evidence of substantial grounds for believing that the applicant in question faced a real risk of being 'subjected to torture or to inhuman or degrading treatment or punishment'. In order to qualify under Article 3 the ill-treatment would have to reach a certain minimum level of severity, and the evidence of such alleged ill-treatment would have to be subjected to rigorous scrutiny. A mere possibility of ill-treatment was not enough. In this case the Strasbourg court found that there was insufficient evidence to show that the applicants' position was any worse than that of the Tamil community as a whole.[11]

Despite these strict guidelines the UK domestic courts have adopted a much laxer approach.[12] The UK courts had already adopted a similar position well before the coming into effect of the HRA. A good example of this is *Bugdaycay v*

*Secretary of State for the Home Department* [13] involving a Ugandan asylum seeker who had entered the United Kingdom via Kenya. The Home Office decided that he should be returned to Kenya, a signatory to the Geneva Convention on Refugees 1951 and therefore a 'safe' third country. However, the House of Lords granted the applicant certiorari of the Home Secretary's decision on the ground that there was a real danger that if deported to Kenya he might be returned by the Kenyan authorities to Uganda. In the words of Lord Templeman:

> In my opinion where the result of a flawed decision may imperil life or liberty a special responsibility lies on the court in the examination of the decision-making process.

This decision predates the incorporation of the Human Rights Convention into English law. It is based therefore not on Article 3 of the Human Rights Convention but purportedly on the Geneva Convention on Refugees. Article 33 of this Convention provides that: 'No Contracting State shall expel or return a refugee in any manner whatsoever to the frontiers of territories where his life or freedom would be threatened on account of his race, religion, nationality, membership of a particular social group or political opinion.' The word 'frontiers' has simply been taken over from the French and is probably better rendered 'boundaries'. What this article is saying, therefore, is that Contracting States of the Geneva Convention must not deport people to a country where their life or liberty is likely to be at risk. It says nothing about the more indirect risk that if deported to country X, a 'safe' country, they may be returned by that country's authorities to country Y, where their life or liberty may be under threat. To construe the Geneva Convention so as to broaden the scope of the duty owed by the United Kingdom was the work of the English courts.

## *Chahal*

By contrast with this, in *Chahal* the UK courts took a firm line, but it was Strasbourg that came to the applicant's rescue. Chahal was a Sikh activist who entered the United Kingdom illegally from India in 1971. On a visit to India in 1984 he claimed to have been arrested, detained and tortured by the Indian police. On his return to Britain he was briefly detained under the Prevention of Terrorism (Temporary Provisions) Act 1984 on suspicion of being involved in a conspiracy to assassinate Mr Rajiv Gandhi, the Indian Prime Minister, but was never charged. In 1990 he was notified that the Home Secretary had decided to deport him. His claim for political asylum was refused both by the Home Secretary and by the English High Court. However, a unanimous Strasbourg court found that his rights under Article 3 would be violated if he was deported back to India. As there were 'substantial grounds' for believing that there was a 'real risk' that he would be subjected to treatment contrary to Article 3 on his return there, his deportation was prohibited under Article 3. This prohibition was held to be 'absolute', regardless of the applicant's conduct.[14]

## TERRORISM

Does the characterization of Article 3 protection as 'absolute' mean that a Contracting State would be prohibited from deporting even a known terrorist? The horrendous and brutal murder of thousands of innocent people in the attacks on the World Trade Center in New York and the Pentagon in Washington, DC on 11 September 2001 had a huge impact on public consciousness not only in the United States but also in Britain, though probably considerably less so elsewhere in Western Europe.

The Anti-Terrorism, Crime and Security Act 2001 was passed in the immediate aftermath of the atrocities. It gives the authorities extended powers. If the Home Secretary 'reasonably suspects' that a person is a terrorist and 'reasonably believes that the person's presence in the United Kingdom is a risk to national security', then the person concerned can be deported or at least be denied leave to enter the country, and can also be detained for examination or pending deportation. There is an attempt to get around the restrictions placed on government action by international agreements and by 'practical considerations'. But this is in itself an admission that the government's hands are tied to some extent. And at the time of writing, the courts have not yet been let loose on this new legislation. If previous examples are anything to go by, there is a good chance that the purpose of the Act – to prevent, or at least reduce the possibility of, terrorist activities in the United Kingdom – will be frustrated. For, if Article 3 is 'absolute', as the Strasbourg court has held, then the fact that someone served with a deportation order is a terrorist – however defined – will make no difference. It will still be prohibited under Article 3 to deport him or her. The question will then be: which takes precedence, Article 3 or the Anti-Terrorism Act? The doctrine propagated by certain judges that the Human Rights Convention as incorporated in the Human Rights Act is now 'entrenched' and has 'higher order law' status is plainly wrong, but if this view is enforced by the courts, then no legislation will ever be able to trump Convention rights as interpreted by the courts.

## POLITICAL DECISIONS

**Q. Are the courts allowed to make political decisions?**

***A. They are not supposed to, but some of their decisions undoubtedly stray into the area of politics.***

In *R v Secretary of State for the Home Department, ex parte Asif Javed, Zuifiqar Ali & Abid Ali,*[15] the inclusion of Pakistan in the 'White List' of 'safe countries' for asylum seekers was declared illegal by the Court of Appeal. This characterization of Pakistan (together with Bulgaria, Cyprus, Ghana, India, Poland and Romania) as a country 'in which it appears to the Secretary of State that there is in general no serious risk of persecution' appeared in the Asylum (Designated Countries of Destination and Designated Safe Third Countries) Order 1996 SI 1996/2671, made by the Secretary of State pursuant to para 5(8) of Schedule 2 to the Asylum and Immigration Appeals Act 1993.

We are here dealing with a statutory instrument, a form of delegated legislation. It is legislation made by the executive as authorized by an Act of Parliament, in this case the 1993 Act. Schedule 2 to the Act provides that a special fast-track appeals procedure is to apply in the case of an asylum seeker 'if the Secretary of State has certified that, in his opinion, the person's claim on the ground that it would be contrary to the United Kingdom's obligations under the Convention for him to be removed from, or be required to leave, the United Kingdom is one to which' the Order designates this asylum seeker's country of origin as one 'in which it appears to him [the Secretary of State] that there is in general no serious risk of persecution.' And the Schedule specifically authorizes the Secretary of State to make such an Order. But the Schedule stipulates that the Order will not be valid 'unless a draft of the Order has been laid before and approved by a resolution of each House of Parliament' – a requirement which is by no means usual for delegated legislation.

The Order in question was duly approved by an affirmative resolution of the House of Commons and by a separate affirmative resolution of the House of Lords, in each case after considerable debate. However, in *Javed* the validity of the Order was successfully challenged in court.

The basis of the challenge was that the Home Secretary had been 'unreasonable' in identifying Pakistan as a safe country. In the words of Lord Phillips MR, delivering the judgment of the Court of Appeal in May 2001:

> The argument of the applicants . . . was that no reasonable Secretary of State, directing himself properly to the issues, could have come to the conclusion that there was in general no serious risk of persecution bearing in mind in particular (i) what was known about the position of women in Pakistan and (ii) what was known about the attitude of the Pakistan authorities towards Ahmadis.

Lord Phillips conceded: 'We should record that because of the political situation in Pakistan, the Secretary of State did not in fact certify any cases under the Order after October 1999, and that as a result of the Immigration and Asylum Act 1999, the power to designate countries on the ground here in question was repealed with effect from 2 October 2000.' He nevertheless went on to strike down the Order. Why? Was this not an academic exercise at best, as the Order had already been repealed?

Nigel Pleming QC for the Home Secretary contended that there were limits to the court's power to review an Order approved by both Houses of Parliament under the affirmative resolution procedure. The argument put forward for the Home Secretary was summarized by Lord Phillips as follows:

> [Mr Pleming QC] has submitted that binding authority establishes that the Court can only review such an Order if it can be shown that the Secretary of State did not act in good faith or 'had taken leave of his senses' in putting it before Parliament. He has further submitted that, whatever the test that falls to be applied when reviewing the making of the Order, the Secretary of State was entitled to come to the conclusion that there was in general no serious risk of persecution in Pakistan on the material that was available to him. Finally, he has submitted that nothing has occurred subsequent to the making of the Order during the period relevant to these applications which has required the Secretary of State to remove Pakistan from the Order.

On the basis of several cited cases the Court of Appeal concluded: 'For these reasons we reject Mr Pleming's submission that there is a principle of law which circumscribes the extent to which the Court can review an Order that has been approved by both Houses of Parliament under the affirmative resolution procedure.'

This case therefore turned on a disagreement on the governing principle of law relating to the restrictions, if any, on the court's powers to review delegated legislation. Is the law in this area so unclear, then, as to beg this fundamental question?

There is an even more fundamental principle of judicial review, which is not mentioned in the Court of Appeal judgment in *Javed*. This principle is that there is an important difference between a review and an appeal, which prohibits the court from substituting its own decision for that of the legally designated decision maker (in this case the Home Secretary). For a court to ignore this fundamental principle amounts to a usurpation of the role of the decision maker.

Much of the judgment in *Javed is* taken up with the court's own assessment of the human rights status of Pakistan – a highly political question. It is on the basis of this assessment that the conclusion is reached that the Home Secretary's inclusion of Pakistan in his order was 'unlawful'. Whether the court's assessment of Pakistan's human rights status is or is not to be preferred to that of the Home Office is really irrelevant. The question is whether the court was entitled to substitute its own assessment for that of the Home Secretary, which is what it did. In so doing, was it not descending into the political arena? Or, to put it in its legal context, had it not crossed that all-important dividing line between review and appeal and usurped the power entrusted by Parliament to the Home Secretary?[16]

**Q. Is there such a thing as a 'law of humanity'? If so, what does it say and what is its status?**

A. ***The 'law of humanity' is not a statute, nor indeed a law in any real sense at all. It was mentioned in an obiter dictum (a passing remark) in a single case dating from 1803. It did not form the basis of the decision in that case or any other. After being totally submerged for nearly 200 years it has recently been rediscovered and used to block legislation designed to reduce the influx of asylum seekers. But it has no more legal status now than it had in 1803. It supposedly gave any destitute foreigner the right to claim maintenance in the United Kingdom. This has never been the law.***

A 200-year-old 'law of humanity' has recently been rediscovered by the courts and applied to scupper legislation intended to control the influx of asylum seekers. The first modern appearance of this supposed old law was in 1996, when by a two to one majority the Court of Appeal used it to strike down regulations disqualifying asylum seekers from entitlement to benefit payments unless they claimed asylum immediately on arrival in the United Kingdom.[17]

An impassioned plea was made here for the rights of all asylum seekers to claim benefits based on 'the law of humanity' as adumbrated by Lord Ellenborough CJ in *R v Inhabitants of Eastbourne*[18] (1803). Interestingly enough, the dissenting voice was that of Neill LJ, the most senior judge present, who did not even find it necessary to mention the 'law of humanity'.

The regulations struck down were a form of delegated, subordinate or secondary legislation. But it was admitted that if the same provision were enacted by primary legislation, that is, by Act of Parliament, the court could not touch it.[19]

In order to make this provision judge-proof Parliament did indeed subsequently incorporate it into primary legislation, namely the Asylum and Immigration Act 1996. But a High Court judge, Collins J, tried to block this too by means of the 'law of humanity' (as well as by invoking another more recent but equally disused law, the National Assistance Act 1948). While admitting that the 'law of humanity' could not possibly withstand the clear words of a statute, Collins J argued that it was to be presumed that in passing the 1996 Act Parliament had legislated in accordance with it.[20]

The case was brought by four asylum seekers who had been refused welfare by four different London councils. Collins J found in favour of the applicants, and this was upheld by the Court of Appeal, which however based its decision solely on the National Assistance Act 1948 (discussed below). The 1803 'law of humanity' was not even mentioned.[21]

In response to this onslaught from the courts the government passed through Parliament the Nationality, Immigration and Asylum Act 2002, section 55 of which tried to stop asylum seekers from drawing social security benefits unless they had claimed asylum 'as soon as reasonably practicable' after their arrival in the United Kingdom. But it took hardly any time at all before this new government initiative likewise fell prey to the courts.

Six claimants challenged Home Office decisions taken under section 55. The case came once again before Collins J, who, however, after laying great stress on the 'law of humanity'[22], made a surprise admission that 'Parliament has now in terms removed the law of humanity in s 55(1)'[23]. A further concession followed: 'It is clear that there is no duty on a state to provide a home. It may even be that there is no duty to provide any form of social security.'[24] Collins J nevertheless found in favour of the applicant asylum seekers on the basis of ECHR Articles 3, 8 and 6, stiffened with a final passing reference to the 'law of humanity':

> It would be surprising if the standards of the ECHR were below those believed 200 years ago to be applicable to the law of humanity, although I recognise that in those days the possibility of any charitable assistance would have been extremely remote.[25]

But what exactly is the 'law of humanity' and what does it say? Despite the grandiose title, the 'law of humanity' is not statutory but owes its existence to the judgment in a single case decided in 1803, *R v Inhabitants of Eastbourne*.

A German baker lived with his English wife of seven years and their four young children in Seaford, Sussex. For two years the family had occupied a house at a rent of more than £10 a year. The baker's trade declined and he decided to move to the nearby town of Eastbourne, his wife's birthplace. Because of his poverty his wife and children became 'chargeable' (that is, entitled to public support), and they were removed from Seaford to Eastbourne by order of two justices of the peace.

The question before the 1803 court was 'whether a foreigner can gain a settlement in this country'. This was crucial, because only those paupers who had a 'settlement' had a claim to become a charge on the rates of a parish. Under the 'Old Poor Law' dating back to 1601 the burden of maintaining the poor fell on individual parishes. If you were not 'settled' in a particular parish you could not become a charge on the rates there and might have to move back to a parish where you had previously been settled. The rules governing settlement were restrictive, but it was held that two years' residence, carrying on a trade and occupation of a tenement of £10 a year were enough to qualify the German baker as being 'settled' in Seaford.

That decided the case, but Lord Chief Justice Ellenborough added a flourish at the end of his judgment, which is the only time he mentioned the 'law of humanity':

> As to there being no obligation for maintaining poor foreigners before the statutes ascertaining the different methods of acquiring settlements, the law of humanity, which is anterior to all positive laws, obliges us to afford them relief, to save them from starving; and those laws were only passed to fix the obligation more certainly and point out distinctly in what manner it should be borne.

This remark, it has to be stressed, is purely *obiter*. In other words, it does not form part of the *ratio decidendi* of the case. But what exactly does it mean? Lord Ellenborough appears to be suggesting that a foreign pauper could claim maintenance at public expense even if he or she was not 'settled' in this country. But that would have created a serious practical problem, namely: which parish was to pay for the maintenance of such a foreigner? Or could foreigners choose to become a charge on the rates of any parish they liked? There is no suggestion that that idea was entertained in any quarter in 1803. And Lord Ellenborough's concluding words indicate that, far from overriding the statutes laying down the rules for establishing a settlement, the 'law of humanity' was qualified by these statutes, which determined 'in what manner' the obligation to maintain the poor should be carried out.

Why then was it necessary for Lord Ellenborough, a diehard conservative, to mention the 'law of humanity' at all? He was really using it to bolster his interpretation of the statute law that actually governed the case. The key point about the 'law of humanity' is that it was, as Lord Ellenborough put it, 'anterior to all positive laws'. In other words, it formed part of 'natural law' or 'the law of nature', a fashionable concept to which to pay lip-service in 1803.

The problem was that Lord Ellenborough's interpretation of the relevant statute law did not follow the precedent of a very similar case, *St Giles v St Margaret*,[26] decided nearly a century earlier, in 1715. In this earlier case Lord Holt had supposedly held that 'an Englishwoman, the wife of a foreigner, continuing unremovable in a parish for forty days' had not 'gained a settlement', adding 'that he did not know that a foreigner had a right to be maintained in any place to which he came; but that they might let him starve'. As the 1803 case raised the same issue, Lord Ellenborough ought really to have found against the applicants. Instead, he impugned the authenticity of the 1715 law report by appealing to Lord Holt's better nature: 'We owe it to the memory of Lord Chief Justice Holt to believe that he never uttered such a sentiment.'

The only snag here was that Lord Chief Justice Holt died in 1710, fully five years before the *St Giles* case was heard! In any event, rejecting a precedent on the basis that the report was wrong is hardly a persuasive argument. That is no doubt why Lord Ellenborough decided to throw the 'law of humanity' in for good measure.

Several points need to be emphasized:

- Neither the 1803 case itself nor any other case was ever decided on the basis of the 'law of humanity'. The 1803 case was decided on the basis that the German baker and his family had acquired a 'settlement' in England.
- In 1803 there were no passports and no immigration control.
- By the time of the case the German baker had been living perfectly lawfully in England for at least seven years.
- Could a foreigner acquire a settlement in England and thereby become entitled to maintenance at public expense? There was some doubt about it at the time, especially in view of the 1715 decision in *St Giles v St Margaret*, but this question was answered by the 1803 court in the affirmative.
- It is hard to see the relevance of this case to a present-day asylum-seeker who is expressly prohibited by statute from claiming maintenance at public expense.
- As for the 'law of humanity', if it is interpreted in the way that it appears to be understood by Collins J, does it mean that any destitute foreigner who is able to find his or her way on to British soil can claim to be maintained at public expense? This would be a very novel concept indeed, and one that has never been the law and still is not.

- Is it unduly cynical to attribute (at least to some extent) the exceptional attractiveness of the United Kingdom among asylum seekers to the ready availability of social security benefits?
- It cannot be emphasized enough that every right has a reciprocal obligation. If someone has a right to a handout, then somebody else must have an obligation to pay for it. In the case of social security benefits paid to asylum seekers, this obligation rests on the shoulders of local authorities – which of course means their taxpayers. Is this an obligation that these councils or their taxpayers have voluntarily undertaken? Far from it.
- It is one of the most fundamental principles of English law that an Act of Parliament takes precedence over common law (that is, decisions of the courts). Another equally sacred principle is that a later law takes precedence over an earlier one. These two reasons mean that the 'law of humanity' cannot possibly have any effect today (if it ever did).
- Counsel for the local authorities in the Hammersmith and Westminster cases decided in 1996 made the point that 'to allow these applications would be to frustrate the will of Parliament which has been so clearly and unequivocally set out in the 1996 Act'.[27] The 2002 Act is, if anything, even clearer and more unequivocal.
- Moreover, by blocking parliamentary legislation intended to reduce the influx of asylum seekers, is a court not itself usurping the role of Parliament? And, if so, is this in keeping with democracy?

The cases considered so far all concerned applicants whose right to asylum in the United Kingdom had yet to be determined. But the 'law of humanity' has even been applied by the courts to assist those unlawfully present in the United Kingdom – expressly overriding the fundamental principle that a person may not take advantage of his or her own wrongdoing.[28]

**Q. Are asylum seekers entitled as of right to financial support?**

***A. No, but the statutory system intended to deny support to those who have not claimed asylum 'as soon as reasonably practicable' has been held to have been 'vitiated by deficiencies in the procedure'.***

The Prime Minister is the only person who can claim defeat in the Court of Appeal as a triumph.[29]

Thus Iain Duncan Smith, the then Leader of the Opposition, referring to a Court of Appeal decision in an important recent asylum case. Who was right? Was the decision a victory for the government or a defeat?

The real question is: how could there be such doubt about the meaning of a judgment? The whole case turned on the interpretation of a single subsection of the Nationality, Immigration and Asylum Act 2002 intended to control the influx of asylum seekers. The relevant words, in section 55(1), state that the Home Secretary 'may not provide or arrange for the provision of support' to anyone claiming asylum where he/she 'is not satisfied that the claim was made as soon as reasonably practicable after the person's arrival in the United Kingdom'.[30]

The Court of Appeal admitted that when interpreting a statute:

> The judge has no discretion of his own. Rules of law prescribe what can and what cannot be considered when seeking to interpret a statute. The starting point must always be the words of the statute itself, but where there is any uncertainty there is other material to which it is legitimate to have regard and principles of construction which fall to be applied.[31]

The mention of 'other material' is presumably a reference to the use of 'parliamentary materials' permitted under *Pepper v Hart*,[32] to which only a passing reference was made by the Court of Appeal.[33] Yet the argument in the case, centring on the meaning of this one subsection, lasted three-and-a-half days.

The main bone of contention was the meaning of the phrase 'as soon as reasonably practicable'. For the government the Attorney-General argued that 'practicable' meant 'possible', and that for the vast majority of those arriving by air it would be 'reasonably practicable' to claim asylum at the airport. This was not accepted by the Court of Appeal, which held that 'the state of mind of the person concerned can have relevance'.[34] But it is hard to understand what 'state of mind' would make a genuine asylum seeker fail to mention asylum at the port of entry. 'Oh, I was in such a state that it slipped my mind that I was looking for asylum'? Much is said in the judgment about the control that agents or 'facilitators' exert over asylum seekers, but why would such agents be unwilling to allow their charges to claim asylum at passport control? What about the possibility that those entering the United Kingdom on false EU passports – a common way of getting in – are initially intending to live in the United Kingdom with the full benefits of EU citizenship? This possibility is not even alluded to in the judgment.

The Court of Appeal's own test of whether an asylum seeker has claimed asylum 'as soon as reasonably practicable' is as follows:

> On the premise that the purpose of coming to this country was to claim asylum and having regard to both the practical opportunity for claiming asylum and to the asylum seeker's personal circumstances, could the asylum seeker reasonably have been expected to claim asylum earlier than he or she did?[35]

The Court of Appeal then identified two issues: '(1) Can failure to provide support ever constitute *subjecting* an asylum seeker to inhuman or degrading *treatment*? If yes, (2) in what circumstances will the failure constitute such treatment?'[36]

The first instance judge, Collins J, answered the first question in the affirmative, the Court of Appeal went on to say 'although the basis upon which he did so is a little opaque'.[37] The judge had also found a 'tension' between Article 8 and the refusal of support to destitute asylum seekers.[38] The Court of Appeal did not uphold his view on this either, citing *Marzari v Italy*[39] for the proposition that: 'Certainly, Article 8 without more does not entitle the applicant to a roof over his head.'

> Unlike Collins J we do not consider that the fact that there is a real risk that an individual asylum seeker will be reduced to this state of degradation of itself engages Article 3. It is not unlawful for the Secretary of State to decline to provide support unless and until it is clear that charitable support has not been provided and the individual is incapable of fending for himself.[40]

However, the Court of Appeal held that the judge 'was correct to conclude that each of the six decisions under consideration was vitiated as a result of deficiencies in the procedure'. It added: 'We were told by the Attorney-General that these procedures are being radically overhauled. When they have been put in order we can see no reason why section 55 should not operate effectively.'

So who won in the end? Was it a defeat for the government, as Iain Duncan Smith maintained, or a victory, as Tony Blair claimed? Or was it a bit of each, as the judgment of the Court of Appeal suggests? It remains to be seen whether any changes to the system that the government introduces will ever succeed in satisfying the judges.

**Q. Do foreigners who are unlawfully present in the United Kingdom have a right to be housed at public expense?**

***A. No, although the courts have lately reinterpreted the legislation in favour of such applicants.***

Lord Denning posed the question in characteristically forthright terms:

> When a man or woman with children come from a foreign country and are homeless here, and are also homeless in their own country, are the local authority here bound under our statute to secure accommodation for them here, and their children?[41]

His answer was no less robust:

> Of course if he is an illegal entrant, if he enters unlawfully without leave, or if he overstays his leave and remains here unlawfully, the housing authority are under no duty whatever to him. Even though he is homeless here, even though he has no home elsewhere, nevertheless he cannot take advantage of the 1977 [Housing (Homeless Persons)] Act. As soon as any such illegality appears, the housing authority can turn him down and report his case to the immigration authorities. This will exclude many foreigners.[42]

This was further explained by the Court of Appeal in 1996:

> Those who enter the country without leave or in breach of a deportation order, or who overstay after a limited leave was given, and who do so knowingly, commit a criminal offence under section 24 of the Immigration Act. It is not suggested by [counsel] for the present appellants that persons who have committed any such offence are owed any duty by the housing authority under the Act.[43]

The legal position was most clearly put by Bingham MR in 1993:

> It is common ground that housing authorities owe no duty to house those, homeless or not, priority need or not, who require leave to enter and illegally enter without any leave. I agree with this view. It would be an affront to common sense if those who steal into the country by unlawful subterfuge were then to be housed at public expense.[44]

However, the judges then suddenly rediscovered the National Assistance Act 1948, s 21(1) of which provided that 'a local authority . . . to such extent as [the Secretary of State] may direct shall make arrangements for providing – (a) residential accommodation for persons aged eighteen or over who by reason of age, illness, disability or any other circumstances are in need of care and attention which is not otherwise available to them . . . ' So, for example, the Court of Appeal held that, although section 21(1) of the National Assistance Act was not a 'safety net' on which anyone who was short of money or accommodation could rely, asylum seekers had a special claim on the section:

> Asylum seekers are not entitled merely because they lack money and accommodation to claim that they automatically qualify under section 21(l)(a). What they are entitled to claim . . . is that they can as a result of their predicament after they arrive in this country reach a state where they qualify under the subsection because of the effect upon them of the problems under which they are labouring. In addition to the lack of food and accommodation is to be added their inability to speak the language, their ignorance of the country and the fact that they have been subject to the stress of coming to this country in circumstances which at least involve their contending to be refugees. Inevitably the combined effect of these factors with the passage of time will produce one or more of the conditions specifically referred to in section 21(1)(a).[45]

In other words, anyone claiming asylum will inevitably qualify for benefit. This marks a sharp contrast with Lord Bingham's pointed remark quoted above: 'It would be an affront to common sense if those who steal into the country by unlawful subterfuge were then to be housed at public expense.'

In order to stop the courts from thwarting the laws aimed at stemming the influx of asylum seekers, the section was amended by s 116 of the Immigration and Asylum Act 1999, which removed the right to residential accommodation from anyone whose 'need for care and attention has arisen solely – (a) because he is destitute; or (b) because of the physical effects, or anticipated effects, of his being destitute'.

Despite this clear wording the Court of Appeal nevertheless found in favour of two overstayers, one of whom was suffering from 'severe depression with psychotic features' and the other of whom had had an operation for cancer of the stomach. This decision was taken partly on the basis of the 'law of humanity',[46] but chiefly on the ground that section 21(1) of the National Assistance Act 1948 'affords the very last possibility of relief, the final hope of keeping the needy off the streets. Not even illegality should to my mind bar an applicant who otherwise qualifies for support. . . . [T]he applicants' needs should have been assessed without regard to their immigration status.'[47]

Overstaying one's leave to remain in the country is a criminal offence (see above). So besides the strained interpretation of the relevant legislation, this decision also rejects the fundamental principle of the common law that nobody may benefit from his own wrongdoing.[48]

**Q. Could refusing someone free accommodation amount to 'inhuman or degrading treatment' within Article 3 of the Human Rights Convention?**

***A. In general, Strasbourg case law does not support this view.***

After his release from a two-year prison sentence for rape and indecent assault, Peter O'Rourke applied to Camden Council for accommodation. Temporary hotel accommodation was provided, and because of his health problems the council gave him priority status. But there were complaints about his behaviour towards female residents and he was evicted. Camden's offers of alternative temporary accommodation and of permanent accommodation were turned down, and he slept on the street for some months, to the detriment of his already bad health, before eventually accepting temporary and then later permanent accommodation.

O'Rourke sued Camden Council for breach of statutory duty. Amazingly, this was a yo-yo case, with the action first being struck out by the county court judge, then reinstated by the Court of Appeal and finally struck out again by a unanimous House of Lords.[49] But that was not the end of the story. Peter O'Rourke took his case to Strasbourg, where he claimed violations of his rights under ECHR Article 3 (inhuman or degrading treatment), Article 8 (respect for private and family life) and Article 13 (right to an effective remedy).

The Human Rights Court gave him short shrift. It refused even to entertain his application, finding it 'manifestly unfounded' and therefore inadmissible. As far as the Article 3 claim was concerned the finding was as follows:

> The Court recalls that, in order to fall within the scope of Article 3, mistreatment must attain a minimum level of severity (see *Ireland v UK*).[50] The Court does not consider that the applicant's suffering following his eviction attained the requisite level of severity to engage Article 3. Even if it had done, the Court notes that the applicant failed to attend a night shelter pending a decision on permanent housing, contrary to the advice he was given by [Camden] following his eviction. He also indicated an unwillingness to accept temporary accommodation and refused two specific offers of accommodation prior to his acceptance of temporary accommodation in June 1992. The applicant was therefore largely responsible for his own deterioration following his eviction.[51]

What was this 'minimum level of severity' that was needed to engage Article 3? In *Ireland v UK* it was described as follows:

> Ill-treatment must attain [a] minimum level of severity if it is to fall within the scope of Article 3. The assessment of this minimum is, in the nature of things, relative; it depends on all the circumstances of the case such as the duration of the treatment, its physical or mental effect and, in some cases, the sex, age and state of health of the victim, etc.[52]

This typically vague and subjective non-definition is none too helpful. Nevertheless, the general impression created by Strasbourg is that Article 3 is not easily engaged and it is not to be regarded as merely a social or economic right.

As for Article 8, it was long ago established by the Strasbourg court that while 'respect for private and family life' might be translated as 'respect for the home', it did not give anyone a right to be provided with a home.[53] This position has been reiterated on a number of occasions, most recently in *Chapman v UK*:[54]

> It is important to recall that Article 8 does not in terms recognise a right to be provided with a home. Nor does any of the jurisprudence of the Court acknowledge such a right. While it is clearly desirable that every human being have a place where he or she can live in dignity and which he or she can call home, there are unfortunately in the Contracting States many persons who have no home. Whether the State provides funds to enable everyone to have a home is a matter for political not judicial decision.[55]

All in all, it is clear that in this area of law Strasbourg remains much less radical than some of the more activist members of the British judiciary.

## MEDICAL TREATMENT

**Q. Are Article 3 rights engaged where the 'inhuman treatment' complained of is the expected future result of poor medical service in a foreign country?**
***A. Amazingly, yes.***

In *D v United Kingdom* [56] the applicant had been sentenced to six years' imprisonment for possession of cocaine with a street value of about £120,000 and after his release on licence was ordered to be deported back to his home country of St Kitts. Diagnosed as HIV positive and as suffering from AIDS, for which the treatment that he was on was not available in St Kitts, he claimed that his removal to St Kitts would shorten his life and therefore amounted to a violation of Article 3. The English Court of Appeal refused him leave to apply for judicial review, but in Strasbourg a unanimous court citing 'very exceptional circumstances' found in his favour.

The court made it clear that D's case turned on its own facts. The trouble with that approach is that it makes it difficult, if not impossible, to predict the outcome of other cases and leaves the law in an uncertain state. In a similar case, *X v Secretary of State for the Home Department*,[57] decided shortly after the Human Rights Act had come into force, the English Court of Appeal rejected an application in a similar case. Here a paranoid schizophrenic from Malta entered the United Kingdom without permission. He was detained in hospital under the Mental Health Act 1983 but was then refused exceptional leave to remain in the United Kingdom. He applied for judicial review against an order for his deportation, adducing evidence that he would harm himself or even commit suicide if he was returned to Malta. Despite this, the Court of Appeal refused the application.

The Court of Appeal distinguished *D*, but it is by no means certain that the Strasbourg court would do the same were X's case to reach there. In some respects, indeed, X's case was stronger than D's. X was an illegal immigrant, but D arrived in the United Kingdom with cocaine worth £120,000, for which he was tried, convicted and imprisoned. Also, although D had AIDS, X was supposedly in danger of committing suicide if he was returned to his home country. The one factor that makes D's case stronger than X's is the fact that D appears to have got AIDS in prison. If so, there may well be an element of blame attaching to the British authorities for not screening prisoners in such a way as to avoid this kind of thing from happening. However, this does not appear to have been argued on D's behalf in Strasbourg.

Cases like this are a far cry from what must surely have been the intention behind Article 3, namely to give the victims of deliberate acts of cruelty a remedy against the perpetrators of those acts. By entertaining such applications the Strasbourg court is actually flying in the face of democracy, as it is clear that Western European governments are under pressure from their electorates to control immigration. In other words, we are, as so often, in the realm of conflicting rights: the rights of the applicant against the rights of others. There was no acknowledgment of this problem in *D*.

## Notes

1 *The Greek Case* (1969) Application nos 00003321–3/67, 11 Yearbook of the ECHR 501.
2 *Aydin v Turkey* (1998) 25 EHRR 251 97/71.
3 *Tomasi v France* (1993) 15 EHRR 1 92/53.
4 *Heczegfalvy v Austria* (1993) 15 EHRR 437 92/58.
5 *Hurtado v Switzerland* (1994) 94/1.
6 *Tyrer v UK* (1979–80) 2 EHRR 1 78/2.
7 *Costello-Roberts v UK* (1995) 19 EHRR 112 93/14.
8 *A v UK* (1999) 27 EHRR 611 98/80.
9 *Soering v UK* (1989) 11 EHRR 439 89/15.
10 In a recent case the US Supreme Court has ruled that the decision to sentence anyone to death has to be made by a jury, not a judge. But in any event, it is an issue which is always determined quite separately from the guilty verdict: see *Ring v Arizona* Case no 010–488, 24 June 2002. <http://laws.findlaw.com/us/000/01-488.html>
11 *Vilvarajah v UK* (1991) 14 EHRR 248 91/46.
12 Returning the appellant to Iran would constitute a violation of Articles 2, 3 and 6 of the ECHR: *Hari Dhima v Immigration Appeal Tribunal* [2002] EWHC 80

(QBD Administrative Court); *Ijaz Russell v Secretary of State* (Uxbridge County Court) 30/1/2002.

13 *Bugdaycay v Secretary of State for the Home Department* [1987] 1 All ER 940.
14 *Chahal v United Kingdom* (1996) 23 EHRR 413 96/54.
15 *R v Secretary of State for the Home Department, ex parte Asif Javed, Zuifiqar Ali and Abid Ali* [2001] EWCA Civ 789, [2001] 3 WLR 323.
16 See Chapter 2.
17 *R v Secretary of State for Social Security, ex parte Joint Council for the Welfare of Immigrants* [1996] 4 All ER 385.
18 *R v Inhabitants of Eastbourne* (1803) 4 East 103 at 107, 102 ER 769 at 770.
19 *R v Secretary of State for Social Security, ex parte Joint Council for the Welfare of Immigrants* [1996] 4 All ER 385, at 402c.
20 *R v Hammersmith & Fulham LBC, ex parte M, et al* LTL 10/10/96.
21 *R v Westminster City Council, ex parte A, et al* [1997] EWCA Civ 1032.
22 *R (on the application of Q and others) v Secretary of State for the Home Department* [2003] EWHC at §§ 59–61.
23 *Ibid*, at §§62.
24 *Ibid*, at §v67.
25 *Ibid*, at §§72.
26 *St Giles v St Margaret* 93 ER 31.
27 *R (on the application of Q and others) v Secretary of State for the Home Department* [2003] EWHC 195, at para 61.
28 *R v Brent London Borough Council, ex parte D* (1997) 31 HLR 10 as cited in *R v Wandsworth London Borough Council, ex parte 0; R v Leicester City Council, ex parte Dhikha* [2000] 4 All ER 590 (CA) at 601.
29 HC Hansard 19 March 2003: Column 935–Q 4 (103490).
30 *R (on the application of Q and others) v Secretary of State for the Home Department* [2003] EWCA Civ 364.
31 *Ibid*, §4.
32 *Pepper v Hart* [1993] AC 539 at 593.
33 *R (on the application of Q and Others) v Secretary of State for the Home Department* [2003] EWCA Civ 364, at §24.
34 *Ibid*, at § 36.
35 *Ibid*, at §§37 & 119(i).
36 *Ibid*, at §46.
37 *Ibid*, at §47.
38 *Ibid*, at §14.
39 *Marzari v Italy* (1999) 28 EHRR CD 175.
40 *R (on the application of Q and others) v Secretary of State for the Home Department* [2003] EWCA Civ 364, at S63.
41 *R v Hillingdon LBC ex parte Streeting* [1980] 3 All ER 413 at 418, per Lord Denning MR.
42 *Ibid*, at 420.

43 *R v City of Westminster ex parte Castelli* [1996] 3 FCR 383.
44 *R v Environment Secretary ex parte Tower Hamlets* [1993] 3 All ER 439 at 447 (CA).
45 *R v Hammersmith & Fulham LBC ex parte M; R v Westminster City Council ex parte A* [1997] EWCA Civ 1032.
46 See above.
47 *R v Leicester City Council, ex parte Bhikha* [2000] 4 All ER 590 at 603.
48 See *R v Chief National Commissioner ex parte Connor* [1981] QB 758 – where, in the words of Staughton LJ in *Castelli*, 'a widow was held not to be entitled to social security benefits brought about by the death of the husband whom she had unlawfully killed'.
See also *R v Brent London BC ex p D* (1997) 31 HLR 10 at 20, where Moses J held that 'In my judgment the applicant's right to life, and at least a minimum standard of health overrides the principle that a man may not take advantage of his own wrongdoing. (Note: this is the case where *Castelli* is cited.)
49 *O'Rourke v Camden London Borough Council* [1997] 3 All ER 23 (HL).
50 *Ireland v UK* (1979–80) 2 EHRR 25 78/1 §162.
51 *O'Rourke v UK* 39022/97–26/6/2001 §2.
52 *Ireland v UK* (1979–80) 2 EHRR 25 78/1 §162.
53 *X v Germany* (1956) 1 YB 202. See also *Burton v UK* (1996) 22 EHRR CD 135 (Commission decision).
54 *Chapman v UK* (No. 27238/95–18/01/2001).
55 *Ibid*, at §99.
56 *D v United Kingdom* (1997) 97/24.
57 *X v Secretary of State for the Home Department* [2001] 1 WLR 740.

# 6

# Freedom of expression

**Article 10**
***Freedom of Expression***

1. Everyone has the right to freedom of expression. This right shall include freedom to hold opinions and to receive and impart information and ideas without interference by public authority and regardless of frontiers. This Article shall not prevent States from requiring the licensing of broadcasting, television or cinema enterprises.
2. The exercise of these freedoms, since it carries with it duties and responsibilities, may be subject to such formalities, conditions, restrictions or penalties as are prescribed by law and are necessary in a democratic society, in the interests of national security, territorial integrity or public safety, for the prevention of disorder or crime, for the protection of health or morals, for the protection of the reputation or rights of others, for preventing the disclosure of information received in confidence, or for maintaining the authority and impartiality of the judiciary.

## PRINCIPLES IN PRACTICE

- Article 10 protects the right to freedom of expression in the very broadest sense.
- Protection is accorded to individuals as well as to the press, but in practice the press and other media tend to enjoy special treatment.
- Where a particular publication is illegal in its own country, this fact may be respected by the European Court of Human Rights. The degree of respect known as the 'margin of appreciation' varies, with the widest margin until recently applying to moral issues.
- Where freedom of expression conflicts with other rights, freedom of expression generally prevails.

# Q&A: SUMMARY

**Q. What is the scope of expression protected by ECHR Article 10?**

A. *Extremely wide protection is provided but, in theory at least, only against 'public authorities'.*

**Q. What is the relationship between freedom of expression and freedom of the press?**

A. *It is a serious mistake to equate these two concepts. In practice the rights of the press are favoured under Article 10 and even more so in the United Kingdom by HRA s 12.*

**Q. What if the publication in question is illegal in the country concerned?**

A. *This is governed by the so-called margin of appreciation, which varies but is widest where issues of morality are involved.*

**Q. What if there is a conflict between one person's freedom of expression and other rights enjoyed by another?**

A. *Taken together with HRA, 12, Article 10 gives freedom of expression precedence over all other rights. However, there are a few notable exceptions, but they are not always easy to predict or justify.*

**Q. Is it possible to obtain a court order prohibiting publication in advance (that is, prior restraint)?**

A. *With some surprising exceptions, HRA s 12 makes prior restraint very difficult to obtain.*

**Q. Is there a right to shout 'Fire' in a crowded theatre when there is no fire?**

A. *No, because this would allow anyone to subvert the rights of others in the name of his or her own right to freedom of expression.*

**Q. Is there legal protection for the expression of revolutionary or anti-social views?**

A. *Yes, unless they are seen to pose a threat to national security.*

**Q. What is the relationship between freedom of expression and equality?**

A. *The right to freedom of expression is eroded in practice by the very disparate means available to the different players. A private citizen on a soap-box is no match for a press baron.*

**Q. Is there a right to freedom of expression on the Internet?**

A. *The Internet has done something to reduce the disparity between all those wishing to makes their voices heard, but the trend is against the rights of the small voices.*

**Q. Do licensing laws conflict with freedom of expression?**

A. *Not unless they help to create or maintain a monopoly system.*

**Q. Can press freedom ever be subordinated to a harassment claim?**

A. *Yes, this has happened in an English case involving allegations of racism, though there are no comparable decisions from Strasbourg.*

**Q. How does the law of defamation impinge on freedom of expression?**

**A. *Although the English law of defamation has been attacked for having a 'chilling effect' on press freedom, this is less so in practice than in theory, and press freedom tends to be protected in Strasbourg.***

# PRACTICAL PROBLEMS

***The Strasbourg approaches to these problems are given together with those adopted by the UK courts.***

**Q. What is the scope of expression protected by ECHR Article 10?**

**A. *Extremely wide protection is provided but, in theory at least, only against 'public authorities'.***

The ambit of Article 10 is very wide indeed, covering not only political views but the expression of information and ideas on any subject and in any medium, including not only words but also pictures, whether still or moving, and even physical activities. See for example *Müller v Switzerland* (1991) 13 EHRR 212 88/5 [1] (paintings); *Otto-Preminger-Institut v Austria* (1995) 19 EHRR 34 94/25[2] (film); and *Hashman and Harrup v UK* 99/90[3] (demonstration).

This article covers the rights not only to hold opinions and to impart information and ideas, but also to receive information and ideas from others. Both activities, disseminating and receiving information and ideas, are protected regardless of international frontiers.

However, as is the case with all Convention rights, this protection is given only against 'interference by public authority'. In broad terms what this means is that protection is granted only against state and government organs and agencies and the like. The term 'public authority' has never been properly defined. In practice, however, there is a growing tendency for the Convention to be accorded horizontal effect, which was clearly not the original intention.

See also the discussion on *Douglas v Hello!* below.

**Q. What is the relationship between freedom of expression and freedom of the press?**

**A. *It is a serious mistake to equate these two concepts. In practice the rights of the press are favoured under Article 10 and even more so in the United Kingdom by HRA s 12.***

There is no specific protection for freedom of the press, which indeed is not even mentioned in the Convention. On the face of it, therefore, the Convention treats individuals with the same respect as the press barons and media moguls. In practice this is not actually the case. This comes through occasionally in Strasbourg pronouncements. For example:

> The nature of the speech that we have been called upon to protect in this case does not necessarily belong to the highest echelon, of the speech that, according to Strasbourg case-law, merits protection under Article 10 of the Convention. Indeed, it does not enter within the sphere of the freedom of the press; it is not even, properly speaking, political speech.[4]

Although this was a dissenting opinion, there is no disagreement with the majority in the cited extract. See also the unanimous judgment in *Informationsverein Lentia v Austria*:[5]

> The Court has frequently stressed the fundamental role of freedom of expression in a democratic society, in particular where, through the press, it serves to impart information and ideas of general interest, which the public is moreover entitled to receive.

The idea that there are different 'echelons' or levels of speech which are entitled to differing degrees of protection is the product of Strasbourg jurisprudence rather than anything in the Convention itself. According to this doctrine the press is entitled to enjoy the highest degree of protection, which must mean that where there are competing interests those of the press will be favoured – a thought that is likely to be as unsettling to some as it is reassuring to others.

## HUMAN RIGHTS ACT s 12

As far as UK law is concerned, the rights of the press in Article 10 of the Convention are supplemented by section 12 of the Human Rights Act itself, which 'applies if a court is considering whether to grant any relief which, if granted, might affect the exercise of the Convention right to freedom of expression'.

Section 12(2) makes it very difficult to obtain an ex parte injunction against the press without notice. It provides that:

> If the person against whom the application for relief is made ('the respondent') is neither present nor represented, no such relief is to be granted unless the court is satisfied –
>
> (a) that the applicant has taken all practicable steps to notify the respondent; or
> (b) that there are compelling reasons why the respondent should not be notified.

This goes well beyond the ordinary rule generally applicable in these circumstances, as contained in Civil Procedure Rules 25.3:

> (1) The court may grant an interim remedy in an application made without notice if it appears to the court that there are good reasons for not giving notice.

In general, therefore, it is possible to obtain an injunction without alerting the other side to what you are doing as long as there are 'good reasons' for not letting them know. But when freedom of expression is involved there have to be 'compelling reasons' for not notifying the other side in advance, which makes it much more difficult for the applicant. What would such 'compelling reasons' be? During the committee stage of the Human Rights Bill through the House of Commons the then Home Secretary, Jack Straw, helpfully suggested that there might be 'compelling reasons' 'in a case raising issues of national security where the mere knowledge that an injunction was being sought might cause the respondent to publish the material immediately. We do not anticipate that that limb would be used often.'[6] This last throw-away sentence is the key to the purpose behind the phrase 'compelling reasons'. It is clearly intended to make it so difficult for applicants to go ex parte as to be virtually impossible.

What about the hybrid type of application traditionally known as 'ex parte on notice'? This means that only the applicant is officially represented but the other side can come along and raise points of law, though it is not an 'inter partes' hearing properly so called. This has the advantage from the respondents' point of view that they are not kept in the dark, but it is frustrating for them as well as they are not permitted to make proper submissions. Would this hybrid solution pass muster under s 12 of the HRA? Probably not.

Even if the applicant were able to persuade the court that there were compelling reasons why the respondent should not be notified, that would be unlikely to help the applicant very much, as subsection 12(3) provides:

> No such relief is to be granted as to restrain publication before trial unless the court is satisfied that the application is *likely* to establish that publication should not be allowed. (Emphasis added)

This restriction on what is termed 'prior restraint' is clearly intended to assist the press. The scenario it is concerned with is where a person gets wind of the fact that a newspaper is about to publish a damaging article about him or her, and he or she then applies to the court for an injunction to stop publication. This subsection makes it very difficult to obtain such an injunction.

Why is the word 'likely' used here instead of 'probable', which is the normal *American Cyanamid* test for interlocutory injunctions? In *Imutran Ltd v Uncaged Campaigns Ltd*[7] the defendants argued that 'likely' represented a higher standard of probability than 'probable', and this was not disputed by the applicants, though the judge felt that 'the difference between the two is so small that I cannot believe that there will be many (if any) cases which would have succeeded under the *American Cyanamid* test but will now fail because of the terms of s 12(3)'.

Subsection 12(4) goes much further in favour of the press:

> The court must have particular regard to the importance of the Convention right to freedom of expression and, where the proceedings relate to material which the respondent claims, or which appears to the court, to be journalistic, literary or artistic material (or to conduct connected with such material), to –

(a) the extent to which –

(i) the material has, or is about to, become available to the public; or

(ii) it is, or would be, in the public interest for the material to be published;

(b) any privacy code.

This effectively elevates the right to freedom of expression above all other Convention rights (except for freedom of thought, conscience and religion, which is given similar but much vaguer protection by HRA s 13). In reality it is not freedom of expression that is protected here but freedom of the press. This is clear from the phrase 'journalistic, literary or artistic material' as well as from the practical application of the section to litigation.

It has to be remembered, though, that section 12 comes into operation only 'if a court is considering whether to grant any relief which, if granted, might affect the exercise of the Convention right to freedom of expression'. Does this refer only to prior restraint? Obviously not, because that is the subject of a separate subsection, s 12(3) 'No such relief is to be granted so as to restrain publication before trial unless the court is satisfied that the applicant is likely to establish that publication should not be allowed.' To what, then, does the rest of section 12 apply? Could it apply even where publication has already taken place? It is by no means clear. But s 12(5) does specify that '"relief" includes any remedy or order (other than in criminal proceedings)'. So this would presumably include an award of damages, which of course could only be obtained after trial and therefore inevitably after publication has already occurred.

During the passage of the legislation through the House of Commons the then Home Secretary, Jack Straw, explained that s 12 'applies to the press, broadcasters or anyone whose right to freedom of expression might be affected. It is not limited to cases to which a public authority is a party. We have taken the opportunity to enhance press freedom in a wider way than would arise simply from the incorporation of the Convention into our domestic law.'[8] In other words, section 12 was intended to give Article 10 horizontal as well as vertical effect. The admission in the last sentence of the government's intention 'to enhance press freedom' – not, it should be observed, freedom of expression generally – is particularly remarkable (see below).

What is the relevance of the question whether the 'journalistic, literary or artistic material' in question 'has, or is about to, become available to the public'? This is a reference to the 'public domain' defence. If the newspaper or publisher concerned can say that the material complained of is already in the public domain, there would clearly be little point in suppressing its publication. This was a problem encountered in the *Spycatcher* saga (see below). Amazingly, however, section 12 extends the same protection even to material that is 'about to become available to the public', presumably from another source, though that is by no means clear from the wording.

Then comes the 'public interest' defence. If the publisher can show that it is or would be in the public interest for the material to be published, it must not be suppressed. Unfortunately, the press – and particularly those parts of the press least entitled to adopt such a stance – frequently don the mask of the guardians of morality when their true motive is probably profit derived from public prurience. There is no satisfactory definition of 'public interest', which plays into the hands of an already over-mighty press. The *Naomi Campbell* case is but one recent example of this, where at first instance it was accepted that there was no overriding public interest in finding out about the private life of a leading model, but on appeal it was decided that there was such a public interest, with the resulting tail-wags-dog situation where costs greatly outweigh the value of the claim.

The only apparent concession that the section makes to the rights of applicants is the reference in section 12(4)(b) to 'any relevant privacy code'. But this too is designed to protect the press, not their victims. It is noteworthy that the reference is not to 'the right to respect for private and family life' contained in Article 8 of the Convention but only to 'privacy codes'. These are the codes applicable to the press and broadcasting media, compiled by their own self-regulating complaints commissions. During the passage of the Human Rights Bill through Parliament Jack Straw revealed that the government's intention in inserting this provision was to bolster press and broadcasting self-regulation. 'The fact that a newspaper has complied with the terms of the code operated by the Press Complaints Commission – or conversely, that it has breached the code – is one of the factors that we believe the courts should take into account in considering whether to grant relief.'[9] The Press Complaints Commission has been notoriously slow to find a newspaper in breach of the privacy code, so if the courts act in accordance with the government's intention and treat these codes with the same scant respect that is evinced in decisions of the Press Complaints Commission, this provision will prove cold comfort to applicants.

It is clear therefore that HRA section 12 offers the press additional protection over and above that already provided by the Convention. As remarked above, the British government has freely admitted that that was their purpose in adding section 12: 'We have taken the opportunity to enhance press freedom in a wider way than would arise simply from the incorporation of the Convention into our domestic law.' Why was it felt necessary to take this 'opportunity'? And what about the rights of others, which would inevitably suffer as a result of this enhancement of press freedom? There is no mention of this.

**Q. What if the publication in question is illegal in the country concerned?**

***A. This is governed by the so-called margin of appreciation, which varies but is widest where issues of morality are involved.***

How much respect should be shown to decisions taken by the authorities of the country concerned? The greater the deference shown, the greater the *margin of appreciation*. This doctrine is of particular relevance here, but the degree of deference shown to domestic authorities varies. Where moral values are concerned the margin of appreciation is likely to be greater.

## OBSCENITY: *THE LITTLE RED SCHOOLBOOK*

Richard Handyside was convicted in an English court under the Obscene Publications Acts 1959 and 1964 for publishing *The Little Red Schoolbook,* aimed at teenagers and containing information on a variety of sexual practices. The print matrix and the remaining copies of the book were also ordered to be confiscated and destroyed. The aim of the British legislation was 'the protection of morals' within Article 10(2). But was this 'necessary in a democratic society'? By a majority of 8 to 5 the Human Rights Commission found that there was no violation of Article 10, and the Human Rights Court agreed with this result by 13 votes to 1: *Handyside v United Kingdom.*[10]

This case represents the high-water mark of the margin of appreciation. Convention protection, it was held, was subsidiary to national systems safeguarding human rights. In the absence of a uniform conception of morals there had to be a considerable domestic margin of appreciation, subject to European supervision.

In addition, the fact that *The Little Red Schoolbook* was intended for a teenage market no doubt told against it. But it is worth noting that the book had been published in Denmark and several other countries without incident – and that even in Scotland, where a bookseller was charged under Scots indecency laws, he was acquitted because the court found that the book was not obscene or indecent.

## OBSCENITY: SWISS ARTIST

There was a similar outcome, albeit by a narrower margin, in a more recent case involving a Swiss artist convicted of obscenity for exhibiting paintings depicting sodomy, fellatio and bestiality, and whose paintings had been confiscated by law. Both the Human Rights Commission and the Court agreed that the conviction did not constitute a violation of Article 10. By a majority of 5 to 2 the Court also held that the confiscation of the paintings did not infringe Article 10, though the Commission, by 11 votes to 3, had found that it did. The chief issue was whether the convictions were 'necessary in a democratic society' within Article 10(2) . The artist also argued that confiscation of the pictures (which had been returned only after seven years) was disproportionate to the legitimate aim of protecting public morals: *Müller v Switzerland.*[11]

This case illustrates just how unpredictable the outcome is likely to be where something as subjective as morality is left in the hands of a court.

## BAN ON ADVERTISING

An example where a limited margin of appreciation was allowed concerned a German veterinary surgeon who had given an interview in which his photograph appeared, together with details of the emergency service he provided. He was accused by his professional body of advertising, which was contrary to that body's code of conduct. The veterinary surgeon was subjected to court orders to prohibit him from repeating his alleged offence. In Strasbourg the Commission found unanimously in his favour, and the court did so by five votes to two. Would there have been the same outcome if the veterinary surgeon had been guilty of blatant advertising, that is, if he had deliberately flouted the prohibition on advertising? Probably not. It was accepted that there was a legitimate purpose behind the professional body's ban on advertising, but that the injunctions imposed on the applicant were disproportionate to this aim and were not therefore 'necessary in a democratic society': *Barthold v Germany*.[12]

**Q. What if there is a conflict between one person's freedom of expression and other rights enjoyed by another?**

***A. Taken together with HRA s 12, Article 10 gives freedom of expression precedence over all other rights. However there are a few notable exceptions, but they are not always easy to predict or justify.***

> It cannot be too strongly emphasised that outside the established exceptions (or any new ones which Parliament may enact in accordance with its obligations under the Convention) there is no question of balancing freedom of speech against other interests. It is a trump card which always wins.[13]

The last sentence is often quoted out of context. Nevertheless, the dismissive tone in which the exceptions are referred to is significant. And in practice they are not accorded as much respect as might have been expected even from the wording of Article 10 itself.

A case where confidentiality prevailed over press freedom was *X Ltd v Morgan-Grampian Ltd*.[14] A draft business plan stolen from a company (Tetra Ltd, whose identity was protected in the English proceedings, where it was referred to as X Ltd) was communicated to a journalist on a magazine published by Morgan-Grampian. The journalist telephoned the company to check certain facts. The company sought an injunction to stop publication, and an injunction under s 10 Contempt of Court Act 1981 for an order disclosing the identity of the journalist's source. It was held that the damage to the company's business outweighed the public interest in publication, so not only was publication prohibited but it was also held that the disclosure of the journalist's source was in the interests of justice, especially as the information had been imparted in breach of confidence. Disclosure was accordingly ordered, as it 'overrode the policy underlying the statutory protection of sources'. In fact the journalist never disclosed his source and was fined £5,000 for contempt of court.

This victory of confidentiality over freedom of expression was short-lived. The journalist in *Morgan-Grampian* took the case to Strasbourg on the ground that the order to disclose his source infringed Article 10. By 11 votes to 6 the Human Rights Commission upheld his complaint, and this was confirmed by the ECtHR by a majority of 11 to 7. The Court accepted that the aim of the disclosure order was 'legitimate', but held that the company's interests in knowing the identity of the source were outweighed by the journalist's right to protect his source:

> In sum, there was not, in the Court's view, a reasonable relationship of proportionality between the legitimate aim pursued by the disclosure order and the means deployed to achieve that aim. The restriction which the disclosure order entailed on the journalist's exercise of his freedom of expression cannot therefore be regarded as having been necessary in a democratic society, within the meaning of Article 10(2), for the protection of Tetra's rights under English law, notwithstanding the margin of appreciation available to the national authorities.

However, 7 of the 18 judges dissented on the ground that the domestic court was in a better position to evaluate the strength of the conflicting interests, and that the House of Lords decision was within the margin of appreciation allowed to national authorities: *Goodwin v UK*.[15]

This decision plainly subordinated any conflicting rights to freedom of expression, and in particular freedom of the press, which was bolstered still further by HRA s 12 (see below).

## *INTERBREW v FINANCIAL TIMES AND OTHERS*

However, in a more recent case involving the leaking to the press of sensitive confidential (and in this case allegedly partially forged) company documents, the Court of Appeal followed the House of Lords in *X Ltd v Morgan-Grampian Ltd* rather than the Strasbourg court in *Goodwin v UK*. The newspapers concerned were ordered to reveal the source of the leak: *Interbrew v Financial Times and others*.[16]

Does this mean that the UK courts are free to ignore a Strasbourg judgment in favour of a House of Lords decision? Supposedly not, as section 2 of the HRA requires that 'A court or tribunal determining a question which has arisen in connection with a Convention right' to 'take into account' any judgments, decisions, declarations and advisory opinions made by the European Court of Human Rights, the Human Rights Commission and even the Committee of Ministers of the Council of Europe. The operative phrase here is 'take into account', which is so vague as to beg the whole question of the status that Strasbourg jurisprudence should enjoy in the UK courts. This is discussed in Chapter 1.

The key issue in these cases was whether the curbs placed on freedom of expression were 'necessary in a democratic society' within Article 10(2). There has been some unintentionally amusing judicial discussion of the relationship between *X Ltd* and *Goodwin* in this regard. There are essentially two questions here:

- Are the principles applied by the Strasbourg court in *Goodwin* and by the House of Lords in *X Ltd* the same or different?
- If different, which set of principles should the English courts follow?

Some have maintained that the Strasbourg court in *Goodwin* established 'a stricter standard of necessity' than the House of Lords in *X Ltd*, while others insisted that the principles in both cases were the same. But, if so, why did the two courts reach diametrically opposed conclusions? Schiemann LJ explained this difference quite simply in yet another case involving the leaking to the press of confidential company information: *Camelot Group v Centaur Ltd*:[17]

> In my judgment the tests which the Court of Human Rights and the House of Lords applied were substantially the same. I am conscious that they reached different conclusions on the same facts but this is a no more surprising legal phenomenon than this court concluding that a particular course of conduct amounted to negligence when the court of first instance concluded that the very same course of conduct did not amount to negligence. This phenomenon of judges coming to different conclusions although applying the same principles to the same facts is illustrated in Goodwin's case.

Not only, therefore, was there a difference of opinion about whether the principles informing *Goodwin* were the same as those set out in *X Ltd*. In addition, if there was a difference there was the question of which set of principles should be followed. It is less than reassuring that there should be such uncertainty on such important questions.

Even more remarkable is the view expressed in the passage from *Camelot* quoted above that appears to see nothing untoward in different courts reaching different conclusions on the same principles even when applied to the same facts. What is the value of principles if this sort of thing is regarded as normal, or at least as not abnormal? And what does it do to the certainty of the law? Or to the whole concept of justice? For the more uncertain the law is, the more unpredictable it inevitably becomes; and the more unpredictable the law is, the less justice there is. If equality before the law means anything at all, it must include the principle that the law is the same for all; and this must surely mean that the appropriate principles must be readily identifiable, and must be applied in the same way to all relevant cases. What hope is there for this if different results are reached even when the same principles are applied to the same facts? But if principles count for little and the outcome of litigation is unpredictable, what determines the outcome of a case? By a process of elimination what we are left with is the power of the judiciary to make law. But is the rule of lawyers – or, more particularly, the rule of judges – the same thing as the rule of law? And for that matter, what does this say about the level or indeed the existence of democracy?

Even if these really big issues can be addressed satisfactorily, this still leaves unanswered the question, how did it happen that two courts reached opposite conclusions on the basis of the same principles applied to the same facts? And more important, what can be done about it? The inescapable answer to the first question is that the principles of human rights law (to mention but one affected area of the law) are not sufficiently clear. This points to an equally obvious solution, namely to clarify those principles. That is something to which this book is attempting at least to make a modest contribution. However, as long as the courts, both domestic and European, continue to take the law into their own hands by making it up as they go along, and as long as there is either no power or not enough determination on the part of any other institution or group in society to challenge the judiciary, the situation is inevitably going to go from bad to worse, at the expense of the rule of law and democracy alike.

## *NAOMI CAMPBELL v MIRROR GROUP NEWSPAPERS*

Even where there is a claim for damages without any attempt to stop publication in advance, the rights of the press are still likely to prevail over confidentiality. Naomi Campbell, a well-known fashion model, launched an action against Mirror Group Newspapers, which had published articles indicating that the model was a drug addict, including photographs showing her attending meetings of Narcotics Anonymous. Naomi Campbell argued that her connection with this organization and her attendance at their meetings was confidential, and that there was 'no overriding public interest justifying publication'. She won at first instance but was awarded only £2,500 in compensatory damages plus a further £1,000 in aggravated damages: *Naomi Campbell v Mirror Group Newspapers Ltd.*[18]

This was overturned on appeal on the basis of 'public interest': *Naomi Campbell v Mirror Group Newspapers Ltd,*[19] following the guidelines laid down by the Court of Appeal in *A v B & Another, sub nomine Garry Flitcroft v Mirror Group Newspapers Ltd.*[20] A newspaper had been approached by two women who claimed to have had sexual affairs with a married professional footballer. The footballer sought injunctions to restrain publication of these accounts on the ground that this was a breach of confidentiality and would infringe the footballer's privacy. The court's ruling on this was:

> Where an individual is a public figure he is entitled to have his privacy respected in the appropriate circumstances. A public figure is entitled to a private life. The individual, however, should recognise that because of his public position he must expect and accept that his actions will be more closely scrutinised by the media. Even trivial facts relating to a public figure can be of great interest to readers and other observers of the media. Conduct which in the case of a private individual would not be the appropriate

> subject of comment can be the proper subject of comment in the case of a public figure. The public figure may hold a position where higher standards of conduct can be rightly expected by the public. The public figure may be a role model whose conduct could well be emulated by others. He may set the fashion. The higher the profile of the individual concerned the more likely that this will be the position. Whether you have courted publicity or not you may be a legitimate subject of public attention. . . . The courts must not ignore the fact that if newspapers do not publish information which the public are interested in, there will be fewer newspapers published, which will not be in the public interest. (Emphasis added)

There appears to be a blurring here of two meanings of the word 'interest'. They both have the same Latin etymological origin but they have come to be quite distinct. The difference is best illustrated by an example: 'There can be little doubt that the public – or a large part of it at any rate – have an interest in pornography, but does it follow that publication of pornography is in the public interest?' Few would maintain that it does. Yet that appears to be the argument in the *Flitcroft* case: namely, that as the public is interested in the peccadilloes of so-called celebrities there is a public interest in not suppressing publication of such material. This is a non-sequitur. As for the point about public figures as role models, that too seems somewhat strained. Does the fact that someone is a well-known football player turn him into a role model of morality? That footballers are role models to the young is undoubted, in areas such as fashion, hairstyles and drinking habits, but morality? Hardly. Does anybody really expect a footballer to lead an exemplary home life just because he is a 'celebrity'? And the point about the number of newspapers is equally strange. It is doubtless true that if a newspaper does not pander to the tastes of the public it may have to fold. But, first of all, would this be such a bad thing? And moreover, is this an argument for a court? Why should the courts be concerned to protect the proliferation of newspapers on the basis of cheap intrusive sensationalist reporting?

Yet the approach to the 'public interest' set out in *Flitcroft* was applied to Naomi Campbell's case, with the result that the first instance judgment in her favour was reversed. The fact that the model had initially denied involvement with drugs before it emerged that she was attending meetings of Narcotics Anonymous certainly did not do her any good. Against the background of Article 10 of the Convention coupled with HRA s 12 the decision of the Court of Appeal ought not to have come as a great surprise. But why then was the first instance decision different? This only underlines the alarming uncertainty pervading the whole of human rights law.

## BANNED RALLY

A rare example where 'protection of the rights and freedoms of others' succeeded in trumping the rights of free speech and assembly occurred in 1995 in a case involving a group calling itself 'Negotiate Now', which promoted the view that there should be immediate peace talks in Northern Ireland even without a cease-fire. Their application to hold a rally in Trafalgar Square had been refused by the British government on the recommendation of the Metropolitan Police. Although the rights of freedom of thought, freedom of expression and freedom of peaceful assembly are fundamental rights in any democratic society and specifically protected under Articles 9, 10 and 11 of the Convention, the European Commission of Human Rights were not even prepared to entertain the application brought by 'Negotiate Now' but found it 'inadmissible', which is Strasbourg jargon for saying that it had no merit whatsoever.

The ban, it was found, fell within the British government's margin of appreciation, and moreover, was proportionate to its legitimate aim, namely the prevention of disorder and the protection of the rights and freedoms of others – both of these restrictions being specifically mentioned in Articles 10(2) and 11(2). The conclusion was therefore that the ban was 'necessary in a democratic society'[21].

**Q. Is it possible to obtain a court order prohibiting publication in advance (that is, prior restraint)?**

***A. With some surprising exceptions, HRA s 12 makes prior restraint very difficult to obtain.***

As we have seen, one case where an order for prior restraint succeeded was *X Ltd v Morgan Grampian*, but this decision by a unanimous House of Lords was later disapproved by a majority of the ECtHR in *Goodwin v UK*.[22] As mentioned above, section 12 of the HRA now makes it far more difficult than ever before to obtain prior restraint:

> (1) This section applies if a court is considering whether to grant any relief which, if granted, might affect the exercise of the Convention right to freedom of expression.
>
> . . .
>
> (3) No such relief is to be granted so as to restrain publication before trial unless the court is satisfied that the applicant is likely to establish that publication should not be allowed.

If section 12(3) provides tacit protection of the press, section 12(4) is quite open about it:

> The court must have particular regard to the importance of the Convention right to freedom of expression and, where the proceedings relate to material which the respondent claims, or which appears to the court to be journalistic, literary or artistic material (or to conduct connected with such material) to –
>
> (a) the extent to which –
>
> (i) the material has, or is about to, become available to the public; or
> (ii) it is, or would be, in the public interest for the material to be published;
>
> (b) any relevant privacy code.

In other words, books and newspaper or magazine articles should not be prevented from appearing not only where their subject matter is already in the public domain but also where it is 'about to' become public, and, in addition, there is that favourite journalistic argument that publication is 'in the public interest' – a notoriously difficult and inevitably subjective test. As mentioned above, the reference to privacy codes may appear to work against the press, but in fact the opposite is true. The privacy codes in question are those incorporated into the Code of Conduct of the Press Complaints Commission and other similar bodies, which, with some notable exceptions, have provided little succour to individuals whose privacy has been invaded by the media.

The wording of this legislation clearly owes a good deal to the long and inglorious *Spycatcher* saga. In *Attorney-General v Guardian Newspapers*[23] the House of Lords by three votes to two decided to keep in place interlocutory injunctions restraining newspapers from serializing extracts from *Spycatcher*, a book written by Peter Wright, a former British Secret Service agent. The two dissentients, Lords Bridge and Oliver, were not noted as radicals, yet they were, in Lord Bridge's words, 'in profound disagreement' with the majority. Lord Bridge adopted a characteristically commonsense approach. He fully accepted that *Spycatcher* contained material, publication of which amounted to a breach of confidence on the part of its author. But as the book had already been published in the United States, Lord Bridge rejected the remedy of what he called 'a futile injunction' and instead suggested an action for an account of profits. Moreover:

> The maintenance of the ban, as more and more copies of the book *Spycatcher* enter this country and circulate here, will seem more and more ridiculous. If the government are determined to fight to maintain the ban to the end, they will face inevitable condemnation and humiliation by the European Court of Human Rights in Strasbourg. Long before that they will have been condemned at the bar of public opinion in the free world.

Lord Bridge's comment on the likely outcome at Strasbourg was prophetic. In *The Observer and The Guardian v UK*[24] the ECtHR held that the injunctions were initially justifiable but that their continuation by the House of Lords after *Spycatcher*'s publication in America amounted to a violation of Article 10 of the ECHR.

## *DOUGLAS v HELLO!*

When film stars Michael Douglas and Catherine Zeta-Jones got wind of the fact that *Hello!* magazine was about to publish unauthorized photographs of their wedding they immediately that very evening obtained an injunction from an English High Court judge over the telephone prohibiting publication of the offending pictures. On the following day there was a hearing before another High Court judge, who continued the injunction. *Hello!* immediately appealed against this decision. The case then went to a two-judge Divisional Court, who were unable to agree. So it was then heard by a three-judge Court of Appeal, which unanimously discharged the injunction. Of the seven judges who had considered the matter, therefore, three were in favour of granting the injunction and four were against. In view of the *Goodwin* decision in Strasbourg and, even more so, s 12 HRA, it is surprising that any judge would have entertained the idea of an injunction in these circumstances, especially as the order would have killed the relevant issue of *Hello!* completely, which the Court of Appeal was not prepared to do. Yet the judges indicated that in their opinion the Douglases had 'a powerfully arguable case to advance at trial' – and so indeed it turned out: *Douglas v Hello!*[25]

## *VENABLES AND THOMPSON V NEWS GROUP NEWSPAPERS*

A case with a very different outcome was *Venables and Thompson v News Group Newspapers*.[26] The application was made by Robert Thompson and Jon Venables, the two Bulger murderers, by then aged 18, shortly before the two were released on licence with new identities and possibly even some plastic surgery to disguise their appearance. The killers were successful in obtaining perpetual injunctions *contra mundum* (that is, against the world at large) protecting: (a) their physical appearance; (b) their new identities; (c) their whereabouts; and (d) information about the seven-and-a-half years that they had spent in detention.

So ironclad is the protection afforded Venables and Thompson that when the *Manchester Evening News* published an artist's impression of what they might look like at the age of 18 it was found guilty of contempt of court and fined £30,000 plus costs of £120,000.[27] The scope of these orders is so wide that it is hard to think of any new information about the two murderers that could lawfully be published, and it must also be remembered that these restrictions are enforceable not only against the defendants in the case itself but against anyone at all who dares to contravene them. What if the two murderers were to kill again or commit some other crime? Could that be reported? If at all, presumably only under their new assumed names and without any indication of their true identities. This would mean that the success or failure of treating them in this privileged fashion could never be tested!

On the face of it this seems an astounding result. Why should the perpetrators of the brutal and horrific murder of a two-year-old infant be accorded such exceptional protection – and at public expense to boot? It was admitted by the court that 'until now the courts have not granted injunctions in the circumstances which arise in this case' (§76). So what made this case different? Simply the likelihood that, if their identities and whereabouts were known, the two murderers would be pursued. 'Among the pursuers may well be those intent on revenge' (§82).

But the real question is why these particular murderers should be at such great risk. The gruesome nature of their crime and the youthful innocence of their victim is not enough to explain it. The problem is the widespread public perception that they have not been adequately punished for what they did. Had they emerged from a proper adult prison after 15 years behind bars – the tariff proposed by the Home Secretary – the chances of a revenge attack on them would have been minimal, and there would have been no need for any special measures to protect them. What message does the special treatment that these murderers have enjoyed send to other violent youngsters? Or to the parents of vulnerable young children? Or for that matter, to the public at large? Taken together with some other recent cases it is not difficult to see how this decision may strengthen the cynical observation that convicted murderers belong to a specially favoured class of litigants.

Public perceptions aside, what is the legal basis for this remarkable decision? 'In my judgment,' concluded Dame Elizabeth Butler-Sloss P, 'the case stands or falls on the application to it of the law of confidence' (§111). The law of confidence or confidentiality has come to be used to fill the gap in English law occupied in other systems by a law of privacy. But why should information about convicted murderers be confidential?

The court freely admitted that s 12 HRA and ECHR Article 10 'together give an enhanced importance to freedom of expression and consequently the right to publish' (§33). However, the judgment goes on to attempt to justify the remarkable restrictions on freedom of expression contained in the injunctions granted to the two Bulger killers. Turning first to Article 10 itself, Dame Elizabeth Butler-Sloss P remarked: 'The right to confidence is, however, a recognised exception within Article 10(2) . . . '. In fact, however, the scope of this exception is far narrower than that of the law of confidence as developed by the English courts. '[I]n the vast majority of cases,' said Lord Goff in a leading case on confidentiality, 'the duty of confidence will arise from a transaction or relationship between the parties . . . but it is well settled that a duty of confidence may arise in equity independently of such cases': *Attorney General v Guardian Newspapers (No 2)*.[28] In what circumstances could a duty of confidence arise in the absence of any transaction or relationship between the parties? It is in this area that the law of confidence has expanded to fill the void in English law as a result of the absence of a law of privacy. See the discussion on privacy in Chapter 8.

But Article 10 does not appear to include this extension. Article 10(2) refers specifically to 'preventing the disclosure of information received in confidence'. It is hard to see how this could possibly apply to information obtained by a newspaper about convicted murderers. In normal circumstances, anyone offering such information to the press would be most unlikely to ask for it to be treated as confidential. On the contrary, provided the financial reward was adequate an informant would probably be only too happy to see it in print. But what if this information had originally been imparted to this informant in confidence?

Would the informant's broken duty of confidence automatically pass to the newspaper, so that it could be said that the information was 'received in confidence' by the paper? It is hard to see how it could.

The court even prayed in aid of the protective injunctions ECHR Articles 2, 3 and 8. These articles oblige contracting states to uphold everyone's right to life (Article 2), to prevent anyone from being 'subjected to torture or to inhuman or degrading treatment or punishment' (Article 3), and to maintain everyone's 'right to respect for his private and family life, his home and correspondence' (Article 8). Butler-Sloss P's argument appears to run along the following lines: as the courts are 'public authorities', it is their duty to see to it that the rights of the vulnerable young murderers are not interfered with by vigilantes out for revenge. 'There is a positive duty on the court as a public authority to take steps to protect individuals from the criminal acts of others'(§99).

There is only one thing wrong with this argument and that is: why should the courts be more concerned with the rights of two brutal killers than with those of anyone else? In particular, what about the rights of Jamie Bulger? It is ironic indeed that these three rights should have been singled out, for these are the very rights of which that innocent little child was deprived. He was tortured, killed and torn from the bosom of his family. Admittedly, it is now far too late to protect the little toddler's rights. But what about his family? His father was given short shrift when he tried to have a say on the appropriate sentence for his son's killers.

In a radio interview Lord Woolf CJ specifically expressed his support for the anonymity granted to the young killers: 'It would not bring baby Bulger back to life if one or other of those young men had in turn been killed.'[29] As a statement of biological fact this is incontrovertible, but it is hard to see how it justifies the special protection afforded to the murderers.

If the courts have a 'positive duty' to protect people 'from the criminal acts of others' – a salutary concept indeed – then would it not help if murderers were given really long sentences? This might or might not act as a deterrent to others, but a murderer sitting in prison is not going to be committing any more murders while he or she is there. And it would also reduce the likelihood that those perceived as having 'got away with murder' would themselves be murdered.

**Q. Is there a right to shout 'Fire' in a crowded theatre when there is no fire?**

***A. No, because this would allow anyone to subvert the rights of others in the name of his own right to freedom of expression.***

Do you have the right to shout 'Fire!' in a crowded theatre? This has never actually been tested in a court of law, but it is generally assumed that such a right would not exist, because your cry might cause a stampede, resulting in injury or even death. But are we asking the right question? The proper question to ask should surely be not whether you have the right to shout 'Fire!', but rather whether you could be held legally responsible for any damage resulting from your cry. To establish legal liability it would have to be shown that it was 'reasonably foreseeable' that your cry would result in a dangerous stampede, and that your cry actually caused the stampede and the ensuing injuries. Though ignorant of the legal niceties required for legal liability, most people would nevertheless recognize the danger of shouting 'Fire!' in a crowded theatre.

In *Wilkinson v Downton*[30] a practical joker went round to his friend's house and announced to his wife, 'Your husband has been smashed up in an accident and is lying at the Elms pub with both legs broken.' In fact the whole story was a fabrication, but the wife went into shock. The practical joker was found liable in tort and had to pay the wife £100 in general damages.

Does this mean that there is no right to make remarks to people to which they may react badly? Of course not, but it is as well to consider their likely reaction before embarking on a career as a practical joker. This is common sense, which cannot, however, curtail the legal right of freedom of speech.

Similarly, although there is no doubt a right to shout 'Fire!' in a crowded theatre, reflection upon the likely consequences may well inhibit prospective shouters from actually doing so. In this way, they will be limiting their own rights by reference to the rights of their fellow theatregoers – notably the right to live their lives without interference by others.

ECHR Article 10(2) specifically allows freedom of expression to be 'subjected to such formalities, conditions, restrictions, or penalties as are prescribed by law and are necessary in a democratic society, in the interests of national security, territorial integrity or public safety . . . '. The practical approach to this important question is discussed below under 'National security', but here we consider the theoretical justification of curbing freedom of speech.

So is there a right falsely to shout 'Fire!' in a crowded theatre?[31] The panic and stampede that this is likely to cause might easily result in injury or even death. One person's right to shout 'Fire!' for his or her own personal amusement must be balanced against the right of the theatregoers in general not to have their lives placed in danger. This problem has often been discussed by, among others, the US Supreme Court Justice Oliver Wendell Holmes Jr (1841–1935). Two socialists were convicted in 1917 of attempting to cause insubordination amongst soldiers drafted to fight in the First World War. Although the pamphlet published for this purpose did not call upon the draftees to use unlawful or violent means to oppose the draft, in the circumstances, held Holmes, it created 'a clear and present danger', so their conviction was justified: *Schenk v United States*.[32]

> The most stringent protection of 'free speech would not protect a man in falsely shouting fire in a theater, and causing a panic. It does not even protect a man from an injunction against uttering words that may have all the effect of force.

This is particularly noteworthy in view of Holmes's reputation as a champion of human rights. Alan Dershowitz, a modern American liberal jurist, has gone so far as to suggest that falsely shouting 'Fire!' in at crowded theatre is not speech at all. Characterizing Holmes's view as a 'flawed analogy' and a 'silly argument', he urges:

> So let us hear no more nonsensical analogies to shouting fire in a crowded theater. Those who seek to censor speech will just have to come up with a somewhat more cogent illustration – one that bears at least some relationship to real speech.[33]

But if shouting 'Fire!' is not speech, what is it? Dershowitz recognizes that falsely shouting 'Fire!' in a crowded theatre does not deserve legal protection, but he does not want it to be used as the basis for what he calls 'censorship'. With the shouting of 'Fire' out of the way as irrelevant to the question of freedom of speech, any form of 'real speech' will qualify for legal protection.

This is all the more surprising in view of the wide definition of 'speech' that the US Supreme Court is prepared to accept. Even flag-burning is now classified as speech, and speech which does qualify for First Amendment protection! See for example two cases both decided by a five to four majority: *Texas v Johnson*;[34] *Eichman v United States*.[35]

Falsely shouting 'Fire!' in a crowded theatre clearly is speech, but speech that does not enjoy legal protection. Other examples of speech – including what the US Supreme Court calls 'symbolic speech' or 'nonverbal expression' – will qualify for protection according to their nature and the circumstances in which they are used.

Shouting 'Fire!' is not just a theoretical conundrum but an important practical problem for any democracy: in what circumstances can the right of free expression be curbed, or, to put it another way, to what other right or rights could freedom of expression yield precedence? Perhaps the most important practical manifestation of this problem is in regard to revolutionary or anti-social views. (See below)

**Q. Is there legal protection for the expression of revolutionary or anti-social views?**
***A. Yes, unless they are seen to pose a threat to national security.***

Can a democracy curb the expression of anti-democratic opinions? If it does so, is that not in itself a denial of democracy? But if it takes no action against anti-democratic forces, is there not a real danger that it may be overthrown by them?

The ECtHR has been caught on the horns of this age-old dilemma on more than one occasion. The clearest case was *X v Federal Republic of Germany*,[36] where the banning of neo-Nazi pamphlets was upheld by the Commission as not infringing Article 10. However, in *Jersild v Denmark*[37] the conviction of a Danish journalist for 'aiding and abetting the dissemination of racially prejudicial material' was held to be a violation of Article 10. Mr Jersild had made a film for a television news programme about the so-called 'Greenjackets', an extreme right-wing group, which included a good deal of footage of racist remarks by members of the group. However, the Strasbourg Court drew a distinction between propaganda and information:

> 31. A significant feature of the present case is that the applicant did not make the objectionable statements himself but assisted in their dissemination in his capacity of television journalist responsible for a news programme of Danmarks Radio. (§31)

And:

> 36. It is moreover undisputed that the purpose of the applicant in compiling the broadcast was not racist. Although he relied on this in the domestic proceedings, it does not appear from the reasoning in the relevant judgments that they took such a factor into account.

Another case involving the media and right-wing extremists, this time in Austria, was *News Verlags GmbH v Austria*.[38] Here a magazine called *News* published a picture of 'B', describing him as a brutal neo-Nazi and as the 'perpetrator' of a serious letter-bomb campaign which had severely injured some politicians and other public figures. 'B' successfully applied for an injunction prohibiting *News* from publishing any more pictures of himself. At his trial on the bomb charges 'B' was subsequently acquitted, but he was convicted of certain offences under the National Socialism Prohibition Act. 'B' then took further action against *News* for violating his presumption of innocence. 'B' succeeded in the Vienna Court of Appeal, which ordered the magazine to pay him compensation of 50,000 Schillings.

On the face of it this would not appear to be a very promising basis for the magazine to apply to the ECtHR. Yet, amazingly, it won, on the ground that the Austrian court's interference with its right to freedom of expression had been 'disproportionate' and had not been 'necessary in a democratic society'. There had therefore been a violation of Article 10 by Austria!

This goes much further than *Jersild* in protecting the press. The journalist in *Jersild* was merely acting as a reporter, whereas in the Austrian case the magazine took it upon itself to pronounce someone guilty of a serious crime – of which he was later acquitted – before he had been tried. This would appear to be an obvious violation of that person's right to a fair trial under Article 6 and also to his right of privacy under Article 8, not to mention the possibility that it might have been held to be defamatory. Yet the Strasbourg court was prepared not only to ignore this but indeed to find that the magazine proprietors' rights had been violated by the Austrian court!

## *LEHIDEUX AND ISORNI v FRANCE*

In 1984 the French newspaper *Le Monde* carried a full-page advertisement placed by two associations dedicated to rehabilitating the memory of the Second World War French collaborator, Marshal Petain.[39] The two individuals responsible for the advertisement were subsequently convicted on a charge of 'public defence of war crimes or the crimes of collaboration'. By large majorities both the Human Rights Commission and the Court found that this conviction was a violation of Article 10. As the applicants had not sought to deny or justify Nazi atrocities and persecutions, their convictions were held to be disproportionate and, accordingly, unnecessary in a democratic society.

## NATIONAL SECURITY

Can a government invoke national security to starve certain groups or organizations of what Mrs Margaret Thatcher (as she then was) called 'the oxygen of publicity'? An attempt by her government to do so backfired because of inept wording. In 1988 the government issued notices to the BBC and the Independent Broadcasting Authority requiring them 'to refrain at all times from sending any broadcast matter . . . where the person speaking the words represents or purports to represent' one of the named organizations. The broadcasting media easily got round this over-precise wording by having the offending words dubbed by a 'voice over'. This resulted in the comical spectacle of spokespeople for the named organizations being seen on television but appearing to speak in a beautifully clear actor's voice instead of in their own sometimes less than perfectly modulated tones. As a result, far from starving them of the oxygen of publicity, this exercise gave them greater publicity than ever, plus entertaining novelty value.

One may wonder, then, why a legal challenge was launched against the government's directives. In fact the case, brought by a number of broadcast journalists, went all the way up to the House of Lords: *Brind v Secretary of State for the Home Department*.[40] The government sought to justify its directives on the ground that they were necessary in the public interest to combat terrorism. In the judicial review hearings in the English domestic courts it was held that this reasoning could hardly be regarded as '*Wednesbury* unreasonable'. As the ECHR had not yet been incorporated into English law, an application was then lodged with the European Commission of Human Rights under Article 10 of the Convention: *Brind v UK*.[41] But the applicants were rebuffed again. The Commission recognized 'the need to protect the State and the public against armed conspiracies seeking to overthrow the democratic order which guarantees this freedom and other human rights.' As the UK government's measures were not 'disproportionate to the aim sought to be pursued' and 'bearing in mind the margin of appreciation permitted to States', the Commission found the application inadmissible.

Would these decisions have been any different if the words of the spokespeople of the named organizations had been suppressed altogether, instead of the ludicrous situation that actually obtained where their words were only too clearly heard, as they were spoken by actors? It is hard to say, though the Commission certainly was aware of the true situation.

## *SPYCATCHER*

The *Spycatcher* saga is also in point here. When the interlocutory injunctions mentioned above were put in place against the *Guardian* and the *Observer* three other newspapers began publishing extracts from the disputed book. Did this amount to a contempt of court? On the one hand, it seems strange that someone who is not a party to the original action can be held in contempt for doing something that on the face of things he or she is perfectly entitled to do. On the other hand, however, for one newspaper to contravene a publishing ban placed by a court on another newspaper makes a nonsense of the court ban. In *Attorney-General v Times Newspapers*[42] it was held by the House of Lords that where C knowingly impedes or interferes with the administration of justice in an action between A and B, C is in contempt of court. By publishing extracts of the book, it was held, the three other newspapers had put into the public domain material that the government sought to keep confidential, and for this reason were guilty of a contempt of court.

Though never challenged in the ECtHR, this facet of *Spycatcher* seems also to be under threat, as appears from *Attorney-General v Punch*.[43] In 1997 the Attorney-General had obtained an injunction restraining David Shayler, a former member of the Security Service, from disclosing information obtained by him relating to security or intelligence matters. Some three years later, however, an article by David Shayler on the Bishopsgate bombing appeared in *Punch* magazine. A majority of the Court of Appeal, reversing the judge at first instance, held that this did not amount to a contempt of court as the Attorney-General 'had not established that [Mr Shayler] knew that the publication [of the *Punch* article] would interfere with the course of justice by defeating the purpose underlying the injunctions and had therefore failed to prove the necessary element of mens rea.'

It was also held that an attempt to extend the injunction to cover the *Punch* article was contrary to section 12(3) of the HRA (see above) and, moreover, was 'disproportionate to any public interest' and therefore a violation of Article 10 of the ECHR.

This decision shows how difficult it is likely to be for the UK government to bring proceedings for contempt against anyone who is not directly bound by an injunction. This may seem strange in view of the fact that the derogations from freedom of expression contained in Article 10(2) expressly include 'preventing the disclosure of information received in confidence'.

It should be mentioned on the other side, however, that the government was successful in prosecuting David Shayler for disclosing information and documents contrary to the Official Secrets Act 1989: *R v Shayler*.[44] In a robust judgment Moses J rejected the defence that disclosure had been 'necessary in the public interest'. That defence, it was held, was not available under the relevant sections of the Official Secrets Act, which, however, did not mean that those sections were not compatible with Article 10 of the ECHR, because the Official Secrets Act provided a built-in machinery for security agents to obtain authorization for disclosure; and a refusal of such authorization could always be challenged by way of judicial review.

**Q. What is the relationship between freedom of expression and equality?**

***A. The right to freedom of expression is eroded in practice by the very disparate means available to the different players. A private citizen on a soap-box is no match for a press baron.***

How much freedom of speech is there in reality? As mentioned elsewhere (see the section on Liberty, equality, fraternity), for true freedom to exist there must be equality. Everybody has the right to mount a soap-box at Hyde Park Corner and sound off on whatever subject they fancy, but their voice will soon be drowned out by the person armed with a bullhorn or megaphone, whose freedom of speech will in turn be eclipsed by someone who can reach millions through the printed word or who can command the airwaves of radio or television.

The effect of this disparity is particularly noticeable where people who have been unjustifiably maligned by the media want to set the record straight. They can sue the publishers and journalists concerned for defamation, but, as we shall see below, unless these victims of media attacks are multi-millionaires, this is not usually very practical. There have been several private members' bills introduced into Parliament in recent years to give individuals in this situation a 'right of reply' in the newspaper or publication that wrongly attacked them in the first place. Not one of these bills has ever reached the statute book – further evidence of the power of the media.

The power of the media coupled with the rise of 'political correctness' has drastically reduced the average citizen's freedom of expression. Starting as a jocular, mocking label for expressions such as 'vertically challenged' or 'gender reassignment', political correctness has become a powerful force in itself. One may laugh at the banning of the word 'niggardly', which actually has no etymological or semantic connection whatsoever with the Latin word *niger* ('black'); but political correctness is no joke. It plainly restricts freedom of speech. What is worse, it assumes that the values that it enshrines are indeed correct. It is therefore intolerant of dissent

**Q. Is there a right to freedom of expression on the Internet?**

***A. The Internet has done something to reduce the disparity between all those wishing to makes their voices heard, but the trend is against the rights of the small voices.***

The Internet allows anyone to communicate with potentially vast audiences at little or no expense. For once, as a result of a fluke of technology, the playing field appears just a little more level than before. But inevitably this was perceived as a threat by certain vested interests, who have used the genuine concerns of the public about pornography, paedophilia and violence to campaign for government and legal controls to curb the burgeoning of free expression on the Internet while leaving themselves as free as ever from any external regulation.

The English High Court has also weighed in against Internet freedom. For example, in *Totalise v The Motley Fool Ltd*[45] two Web site operators, The Motley Fool Ltd and Interactive Investor Ltd, were ordered by the court to disclose the true identity of the anonymous author (known only as 'Z Dust') of postings to discussion boards on their Web sites. The judge commented:

> It is clear from the evidence that Z Dust is waging an intensive campaign of vilification against the claimant. Much of the posted material is plainly defamatory. It calls into question both the competence and integrity of the claimant's management and the company's solvency, suggesting that it is on the point of collapse.

The claimant company, Totalise plc, was an Internet service provider. It complained to The Motley Fool about 'Z Dust's' scurrilous postings. The Motley Fool responded by removing the offending postings from its site and by subsequently barring 'Z Dust' permanently from the site. But Totalise was not satisfied with this. It asked The Motley Fool for the identity of the anonymous author, but relying on the Data Protection Act 1998, The Motley Fool refused to disclose it.

Totalise then took the matter to court, asking for disclosure of the full name and address of 'Z Dust' together with all documents relating to his or her identity. In ordering disclosure as requested, the judge remarked:

> I turn then to the exercise of my discretion to grant the relief sought. I am satisfied, first, that much of the content of the Z Dust postings on both defendants' discussion boards is plainly defamatory. Defamation is a tort of strict liability. The claimant has demonstrated a strong prima facie case against Z Dust. Secondly, the defamatory material is of a very serious nature, calling into question the claimant's solvency and the competence and integrity of its management and directors. Third, the concerted campaign waged by Z Dust presents a very considerable threat to the claimant. The potential audience is vast. It has no geographical limit. The claimant, in my judgment, is at serious risk of serious damage. Fourth, Z Dust is hiding behind the anonymity afforded by the defendants' discussion boards. Fifth, the claimant has no other practical means of identifying Z Dust.

The judge here says: 'Defamation is a tort of strict liability.' This used to be correct in the sense that the law of defamation did not concern itself with motive. An unintentionally defamatory statement was as much a defamation as a deliberately defamatory statement. So where a newspaper article imputed immoral activities to a certain 'Artemus Jones', intended as a made-up name, a real person called Artemus Jones sued successfully: *Hulton v Jones*.[46] However, even then the coincidence of using the same name was not enough for liability to be found. See the case of *Blennerhasset v Novelty Sales*,[47] in which it was held that there was no case to go to the jury where a stockbroker claimed to have been defamed by a jocular newspaper advertisement.

Even this kind of strict liability ceased to be automatically defamatory as long ago as 1952, provided the defendant has taken reasonable care to avoid the defamation. If so, it is a complete defence under section 4 of the Defamation Act 1952 to publish a statement that is either not intended to refer to the claimant at all, or that, though intended to refer to the claimant, is on the face of it an innocuous statement and is not intended to defame the claimant. See *Cassidy v Daily Mirror*.[48]

Is there any other respect in which defamation can be described as 'a tort of strict liability'? The only relevant point is that it is a prerequisite to a finding of liability for defamation that the words complained of are 'capable of bearing a defamatory meaning'. This is a question of law for the judge to decide. (See *Tolley v Fry*.[49]) It appears from the judgment in the *Totalise* case that 'Z Dust's' postings were easily capable of bearing such a meaning. But that of course cannot possibly decide liability: it is only the first of several hurdles that have to be cleared on the way to such a finding.

In *Totalise* the most that could be said was that there was, as the judge put it, 'a strong prima facie case against Z Dust'. But was this all that the judge was saying? For he also remarked that Z Dust's postings were 'plainly defamatory' and that 'The claimants are not seeking to discover whether a tort has been committed; that is plain from the evidence of Mr Cross.' And again: 'I have come to the conclusion that it was perfectly plain from the outset that the postings on both websites were highly defamatory and that, accordingly, the claimants were the victims of a sustained campaign amounting to an actionable tort.'

For 'Z Dust' to be found liable for defamation it would not have been enough to examine his or her postings; it would also have been necessary to give him or her the opportunity of putting forward a defence. If he or she pleaded justification, or in other words, that what he or she had said in his or her postings was true, he or she would have had to prove this on a balance of probabilities, and in the meantime there would have been a presumption that what he or she had said was untrue. In short, it might not have been particularly easy for 'Z Dust' to fend off a defamation action. Nevertheless, the information before the court in *Totalise* was certainly not enough to determine the question of his or her liability in a hypothetical future defamation action.

Yet the application by Totalise plc depended on labelling 'Z Dust' as a tortfeasor. The application for disclosure of 'Z Dust's' identity was based largely on *Norwich Pharmacal v Commissioners of Customs & Excise*,[50] which allows a special action to obtain information in certain circumstances: where a defendant 'has got mixed up in the tortious acts of others so as to facilitate their wrongdoing he may incur no personal liability but he comes under a duty to assist the person who has been wronged by giving him full information and disclosing the identity of the wrongdoers'.

In *Norwich Pharmacal* itself a pharmaceutical company's patents were being infringed by overseas manufacturers. The pharmaceutical company sought discovery of documents identifying the importers. This information was in the possession of HM Customs & Excise, and the question before the House of Lords was whether the government agency could or should be ordered to disclose the information requested. In the result, discovery was ordered.

In *Norwich Pharmacal* there was no doubt that a tort had been committed. It was in fact a continuing tort. The only question was who had committed it; and it was only by obtaining this information that Norwich Pharmacal could take action to stop the infringement of its patents and seek damages to compensate it for previous infringements.

On this basis, it is clear, *Totalise* could rely on *Norwich Pharmacal* only if 'Z Dust' was a tortfeasor – not just a potential tortfeasor. Yet as we have seen, despite the language of the judge, it was not: possible to say that 'Z Dust' had actually defamed Totalise.

However, the judge did make a *Norwich Pharmacal* order, and, remarkably, by contrast with previous orders of this kind, ordered the defendants to pay the claimant's costs, on the basis that 'those who operate web sites containing discussion boards do so at their own risk'. In other *Norwich Pharmacal* cases the costs order has been exactly the opposite: the party seeking the order has had to pay the defendants' costs, because the defendants in question – like HM Customs and Excise in *Norwich Pharmacal* itself – have not themselves committed any tort or done anything wrong.

The second defendant, Interactive Investor Ltd, successfully appealed against the costs decision: *Totalise v Motley Fool*.[51] But there was no appeal against the *Norwich Pharmacal* order. The judge in *Totalise* clearly did not regard the defendant Web site operators as blameless. Yet, as 'Z Dust' was not a proven tortfeasor him- or herself, this was hardly an appropriate case for a *Norwich Pharmacal* order in the first place!

A more promising approach for the claimant in *Totalise* to have taken might have appeared to be section 10 of the Contempt of Court Act 1981:

> No court may require a person to disclose nor is any person guilty of contempt of court for refusing to disclose the source of information contained in a publication for which he is responsible, unless it be established to the satisfaction of the court that disclosure is necessary in the interests of justice or national security or for the prevention of disorder or crime.

Surprisingly enough, it was The Motley Fool that invoked this section, claiming to be 'responsible' for the postings on its web site. The problem with this is that it could easily work against it, as it lays it open to an order for disclosure 'in the interests of justice'.

The judge rejected The Motley Fool's contention and concluded that the section had 'no application to the instant facts' as it was 'concerned with the protection of a journalist's sources'. 'The journalist is responsible at law for the material which he publishes. The defendants take no such responsibility. They exercise no editorial control. They take no responsibility for what is posted on their discussion board' and in fact expressly distance themselves from the statements posted on their web site and in one case even warn their readers that such statements may be 'misleading, deceptive or wrong'.

However, the judge added that if the defendants were indeed 'responsible' for the postings, then he was satisfied that disclosure was necessary 'in the interests of justice'.

The judgment in *Totalise v The Motley Fool* is only a first instance decision, but until or unless it is overruled by a higher court, it must presumably be taken to be the law of England. It is unsettling for several reasons:

1. Although it was heard after the coming into force of the Human Rights Act 1998 (on 2 October 2000) there is not a single reference to the right of freedom of expression enshrined in Article 10 of the European Convention on Human Rights. Probably the most relevant decision in this connection is *Goodwin v UK*, discussed above, in which a majority of the European Court of Human Rights agreed with the journalist in *X Ltd v Morgan-Grampian* that the House of Lords had infringed the journalist's right to freedom of expression.
2. In *Goodwin* it was held that the order for disclosure of the identity of the 'mole' was unnecessary as it only duplicated the injunction restraining publication. As 'the disclosure order merely served to reinforce the injunction, the additional restriction on freedom of expression which it entailed was not supported by sufficient reasons for the purposes of Art 10(2) of the Convention'.
3. Why was a similar approach not adopted by the English court in the *Totalise* case? 'Z Dust' was silenced. What more did Totalise want?
4. Why were the defendants not protected by section 1 of the Defamation Act 1996, under which it is a defence for a defendant to show that 'he was not the author editor or publisher of the statement complained of', that 'he took reasonable care in relation to its publication', and that 'he did not know, and had no reason to believe, that what he did caused or contributed to the publication of a defamatory statement'? Section 1(3) goes on to provide that:

> A person shall not be considered the author, editor or publisher of a statement if he is only involved –
>
> (a) in printing, producing, distributing or selling printed material containing the statement;
>
> (b) in processing, making copies of, distributing, exhibiting or selling a film or sound recording . . . containing the statement;
>
> (c) in processing, making copies of, distributing or selling any electronic medium in or on which the statement is recorded, or in operating or providing any equipment, system or service by means of which the statement is retrieved, copied, distributed or made available in electronic form;
>
> (d) as the broadcaster of a live programme containing the statement in circumstances in which he has no effective control over the maker of the statement;
>
> (e) as the operator of or provider of access to a communications system by means of which the statement is transmitted, or made available, by a person over whom he has no effective control.

In a case not within paragraphs (a) to (e) the court may have regard to those provisions by way of analogy in deciding whether a person is to be considered the author, editor or publisher of a statement.

- The purpose of this section appears absolutely tailor-made to the sort of situation commonly found on the Internet, where anyone can post messages to a bulletin or message board without the knowledge of the Web site provider. The section protects Web site providers and the like in such circumstances. The substantive decision in *Totalise,* which still stands, may easily have the effect of forcing Web site operators, Internet service providers and others in a similar position to censor the contents of messages and e-mails sent using their service. This would effectively end the genuine freedom of expression that currently exists on the Internet.

**Q. Do licensing laws conflict with freedom of expression?**
***A. Not unless they help to create or maintain a monopoly system.***

As we have seen, one restriction on media freedom that is specifically sanctioned by Article 10 is the right of the state to license radio, television and cinema enterprises. This power has been used in the past as a form of censorship. Indeed, the famous old *Wednesbury* case itself was an example of this: *Associated Provincial Picture Houses v Wednesbury Corp*.[52] A local authority with the power to license cinemas for Sunday performances granted a licence subject to the condition that no children under 15 were to be admitted even if accompanied by an adult. This was unsuccessfully challenged in court as amounting to an 'unreasonable' restriction.

The approach to licensing adopted in Strasbourg is primarily concerned with the availability of competition. So Austria was held to have violated Article 10 rights by allowing a broadcasting monopoly to the Austrian Broadcasting Corporation and refusing a licence to a private television station: *Tele 1 Privatfernsehgesellschaft mbH v Austria*.[53] This was not the first time that Austria had fallen foul of Strasbourg over broadcasting licensing. In *Informationsverein Lentia v Austria*[54] several applicants, including the right-wing politician Jorg Haider, were held by a unanimous Strasbourg court to have had their rights under Article 10 violated by a refusal of a broadcasting operating licence. The court was prepared to accept that '[T]he monopoly system operated in Austria is capable of contributing to the quality and balance of programmes' and therefore had a legitimate aim. It also accepted that the interference complained of was 'prescribed by law'. The Court likewise recognised that '[T]he Contracting States enjoy a margin of appreciation in assessing the need for interference', but added that 'this margin goes hand in hand with European supervision, whose extent will vary according to the circumstances'. In view of the importance of the Article 10 rights at stake in this case, supervision had to be strict. The court accordingly rejected the Austrian government's contention that the interference was 'necessary in a democratic society'. Having found that there was a violation of Article 10, the court found it unnecessary to consider the application alleging discrimination under Article 14.

Another interesting aspect of this case is the fact that Mr Jorg Haider, the right-wing politician, had never in fact applied for a broadcasting licence. Despite this, the Austrian government had accepted in the proceedings before the Commission that he could be regarded as a 'victim', and this was not disputed before the Court.

As mentioned above, the 'victim test' is an important one in human rights law, as it is only alleged 'victims' who can bring proceedings alleging a violation of their rights under the Convention. And such proceedings can be brought only against 'public authorities'.

These concepts are not entirely clear in regard to UK broadcasting. So, for example, is the BBC a public authority? And if so, does that mean it could never claim to be a victim?

As far as the general law of judicial review is concerned, the BBC can bring proceedings; but at the same time it is a 'public body' against which others can bring proceedings. This is likely to be relevant in two different circumstances: first where there is a complaint that the BBC has infringed someone's privacy, and secondly where the BBC itself wishes to complain that its freedom of expression has been violated.

**Q. Can press freedom ever be subordinated to a harassment claim?**

***A. Yes, this has happened in an English case involving allegations of racism, although there are no comparable decisions from Strasbourg.***

Under English common law anything is legal unless specifically prohibited. Obscenity, blasphemy and defamation were the only curbs on freedom of expression under the common law, supplemented by a few statutory bans on 'malicious communications' and the like.

A new potential curb on freedom of speech has reared its head in the form of the Protection from Harassment Act 1997, which both makes 'harassment' a criminal offence (section 2) and also allows it to form the basis of a civil claim for damages (section 3):

> 1. – (1) A person must not pursue a course of conduct –
>
> (a) which amounts to harassment of another, and
>
> (b) which he knows or ought to know amounts to harassment of the other.

There are a number of exceptions to this rule, notably where the defendant can show 'that in the particular circumstances the pursuit of the course of conduct was reasonable'. 'Harassment' is defined as including 'alarming the person or causing the person distress'.

Though not primarily aimed to curb free speech, the Act expressly states that '"Conduct" includes speech', and this statute has in fact been used in cases involving freedom of expression. So, for example, in *Esther Thomas v News Group*

*Newspapers*[55] involving a newspaper report about three police officers who were disciplined and demoted for remarks made about an asylum seeker after a complaint had been lodged by 'a black clerk', whose name and the police station concerned was also published in the article. This was followed by publication of a number of letters to the newspaper in support of the three police officers and hostile to the clerk, who was blamed in some of the letters for the fact that the police officers had been disciplined. The clerk sued the newspaper under section 3 of the Protection from Harassment Act, claiming damages for distress and anxiety resulting from the publication of the articles and from the hate mail to which she had subsequently been subjected. The articles, she alleged, were 'conduct amounting to racism and harassment'. The newspaper's application to have the claim struck out and, in the alternative, for summary judgment, was based on a plea of freedom of speech and freedom of the press under Article 10 of the ECHR.

While accepting the importance attached in the jurisprudence of the European Court of Human Rights to freedom of expression and freedom of the press, the Court of Appeal rejected the newspaper's appeal on the basis that reference in the initial article to the claimant's colour 'was not reasonable' and the claimant 'had accordingly made out an arguable case of racism'. The Court of Appeal also held that it was 'arguably foreseeable that the readers of *The Sun* would send hate mail after the article and *The Sun* made no attempt to dissociate itself from the contents of those letters'.

What is remarkable about this decision is not just that the Court of Appeal found in favour of an individual and against a major newspaper group, but also that in doing so it effectively ignored the newspaper's rights under Article 10 and also under s 12 of the HRA itself.

This case brings home just how fine a dividing line there is between news and comment, or indeed between information and propaganda. Remarkably few newspaper articles or television news reports are totally neutral. The very act of selection, that is, choosing to run certain stories in preference to others, is itself a preliminary exercise in 'spin'. Then comes the 'angle' that a particular paper or journalist adopts. So dominant is the 'slant' of the reporting that it is not always easy to tell that two articles ostensibly covering the same news event in two different papers are actually on the same subject.

A newspaper that is adjudged not only to be reporting but also to be propagating extreme right-wing views will be unlikely to be able to rely on its rights under Article 10 either in a UK court or in Strasbourg. Could the *Sun*'s treatment of the story in the *Esther Thomas* case conceivably fall into this category? Hardly. Yet the Court of Appeal obviously thought that the *Sun* was not just reporting but was engaged in some sort of campaign. What is wrong with that? If the offending articles had a message, it must surely have been a warning of the potential dangers of 'political correctness'. Is this really enough to justify suppressing freedom of expression? And whose decision should this be in any

LIVERPOOL JOHN MOORES UNIVERSITY
LEARNING SERVICES

event? As it is essentially a political matter, is it really appropriate for unelected judges to determine it? The counter-argument, of course, is that it is a matter of law governed by an Act of Parliament. The Protection from Harassment Act 1997 was actually passed in order to tackle the problem of stalking, but, as 'harassment' is not defined, it is open to any interpretation placed upon it by a court.

It is interesting to speculate whether the *Sun*'s right of freedom of expression would have been quite so airily dismissed if, instead of criticizing 'political correctness', the articles in question had supported it.

This question is not entirely hypothetical, for while curtailing press freedom in the *Esther Thomas* case, the English courts were going out of their way to extend it in *R v Secretary of State for the Home Department, ex parte Simms*.[56] The issue in this latter case was whether convicted prisoners could receive visits in prison from journalists specifically invited by the prisoners concerned to investigate their cases 'as a way of gaining access to justice by way of the reference of their cases to the Court of Appeal, Criminal Division'.[57] The two applicants, Ian Simms and Michael O'Brien, were both convicted murderers serving life imprisonment. In Simms's case, after being refused leave to appeal he wrote to 'a journalist who specialises in the investigation of possible miscarriages of justice',[58] after which the journalist started visiting Simms in prison. The journalist wrote an article suggesting that as no dead body had been found the alleged victim might not have been murdered at all but 'may simply have disappeared'.[59] The Home Secretary then refused the journalist permission to make any further visits unless he signed an undertaking in accordance with prison rules not to publish anything said to him by Simms. The journalist refused to sign the undertaking and Simms sought judicial review of the Home Secretary's decision.

It resulted in the familiar yo-yo pattern of an initial victory for the applicants followed by defeat in the Court of Appeal and ultimate success in the House of Lords. The quality of the arguments used in the House of Lords will be examined in connection with prisoners' rights. For the present it is enough to cite the 'fundamental or basic right' relied upon by Lord Steyn, 'namely the right of a prisoner to seek through oral interviews to persuade a journalist to investigate the safety of the prisoner's conviction and to publicise his findings in an effort to gain access to justice for the prisoner'.[60] Precisely where this 'fundamental or basic right' comes from is hard to tell. However, although couched in terms of prisoners' rights, it also extends the rights of journalists. But these are no ordinary journalists – they are specifically identified as journalists with an interest in overturning what they regard as unjust convictions, or in short, journalists who are fighting a campaign. The freedom of expression of this type of journalist is specifically protected by this strained judgment; and in Lord Steyn's words, 'In a democracy [freedom of expression] is the primary right: without it an effective rule of law is not possible.'[61]

Like the journalist in the *Esther Thomas* case, those in *Simms* were fighting a campaign (as they saw it) for justice. The difference was that the journalist in the *Esther Thomas* case was critical of 'political correctness', whereas those involved in *Simms* were advocates of that most 'politically correct' of all politically correct causes, namely the rights of convicted murderers. See further discussion in the section on special interests in Chapter 3.

**Q. How does the law of defamation impinge on freedom of expression?**

***A. Although the English law of defamation has been attacked for having a 'chilling effect' on press freedom, this is less so in practice than in theory, and press freedom tends to be protected in Strasbourg as well.***

On the face of it the English law of defamation looks as though it favours claimants. This is well illustrated by the tongue-in-cheek summary provided by Tony Weir in his *Casebook on Tort*.[62] Describing defamation as 'the oddest' of torts, he goes on to explain that the claimant 'can get damages (swingeing damages!) for a statement made to others without showing that the statement was untrue, without showing that the statement did him the slightest harm, and without showing that the defendant was in any way wrong to make it (much less that the defendant owed him any duty of any kind).'

This is all perfectly true. What it does not mention, however, is that there is no legal aid for defamation and that bringing a claim can be ruinously expensive. As a result, it is generally only 'celebrities' and the super-rich who can contemplate using this blunt legal instrument. The outcome is frequently unpredictable, making it even less appealing to the ordinary person who has been mauled by the press. And perhaps most important of all, being a claimant in a defamation case is not dissimilar to being a defendant in a criminal prosecution. By bringing such a claim you are effectively putting yourself in the dock. As in a criminal prosecution, the burden of proof is on the other side; but as a defamation claimant, you are practically inviting them to repeat the bad things they said about you – and any report of the court proceedings is privileged!

Yet the press are convinced that they are disadvantaged by the law of libel. A recent academic book on *Libel and the Media*[63] is subtitled *The chilling effect* to reflect the supposedly negative effect that the law of libel has on the media. One recommendation for reform is that the burden of proof should be on the claimant and not the defendants, as it has always been up to now. Under the present law, there is a presumption that the offending statement is false. If the defendants can prove that it is true, they will succeed on the defence of what is termed justification. One can just imagine what would happen if the burden were to shift to the claimant. This would mean that the victim of a scurrilous press campaign alleging, for example, unspeakable sexual excesses, would have to prove a negative, which is difficult enough at the best of times. But in this case the person's whole life would come under scrutiny, putting him or her on the defensive even more than a defendant in a criminal prosecution. This would be quite intolerable. But the arguments for such a reform are first, that the presumption of falsity is incompatible with freedom of speech, and secondly, that 'After all, the plaintiff will always know the truth about his or her conduct.'[64]

This may appear plausible, but it represents a serious threat to the rights of the individual. The following points are worth bearing in mind:

- For the media to equate freedom of the press with freedom of expression generally is seriously misleading. In theory individuals have the same rights as the press barons, but their rights are meaningless unless backed by financial muscle and political clout. If what an individual – or even a group of people – wishes to say does not have the right backing, it will never be heard and may effectively be suppressed. In such circumstances press freedom and individual freedom of speech may actually be opposed to each other. The press is highly protective of its own rights but much less so of the rights of others, especially those who disagree with it.
- If the victims of press attacks had a genuine right of reply, then perhaps the presumption of falsity of any statement which formed the subject of a libel action might be less excusable.
- In addition, there are other rights, such as the right not to have one's name and reputation ruined by inaccurate or misleading reporting – and of course the right of privacy.
- Why is there not some other remedy available to curb press excesses? The self-regulation that is meant to be provided by the Press Complaints Commission simply does not work, which is hardly surprising when it is realized that this body is made up largely of editors of newspapers. A light slap on the wrist is occasionally administered to a newspaper that has overstepped the mark, but it is difficult for a complainant to achieve even this degree of success. The press is one of the last bastions of self-regulation. The situation cries out for a proper independent regulatory regime which strikes a genuine balance between press freedom and the rights of individuals, but the power of the press moguls is far too great to allow any such system ever to be established.
- To oblige a claimant to prove his or her own innocence would be the ultimate indignity and would place individuals at the mercy of the press even more than is already the case.
- Even the authors of *Libel and the Media* recognize that 'some tabloids will carry stories with known libel risks owing to the fear that otherwise their rivals will have exclusive coverage or because the stories are just too good to ignore; it is a nice question whether this on occasion amounts to reckless behaviour'.[65]

If English libel law does indeed have a 'chilling effect' on freedom of expression, it inhibits those parts of the media that least deserve to be affected, and in particular the serious broadsheets and publishers of books. One particularly irksome aspect of the law is the need to check for accidental defamation. In an amusing leading case a Sunday newspaper ran a light-hearted article in which a certain Artemus Jones, described as a churchwarden at Peckham, was said to have been seen at the Dieppe motor races 'with a woman who is not his wife, who must be you know – the other thing!' The author of the piece had assumed that the name Artemus Jones was fictitious, but there was a real Artemus Jones, a barrister, who sued the paper for defamation on the basis that anyone who knew him would have thought it was about him, even though he was not a churchwarden, did not come from Peckham and had not been to Dieppe. He was awarded damages of £1,750 – a lot of money in 1910 – a jury award which was upheld by both the Court of Appeal and the House of Lords: *Hulton & Co Ltd v Jones*.[66] It may seem unfair to penalize the press for an innocent mistake like this – and to force every author and publisher to check every intended fictitious name against records. Yet this is the least that the victim of such a libel would expect. This aspect of libel law is rare and has no effect whatsoever on the most irresponsible branch of the press, namely the tabloids.

## DAMAGES

What the public associates most with libel are the astronomical awards of damages made in some high-profile cases – sometimes for apparently trivial insults. Until recently you were likely to be awarded more for injured pride than for broken bones or paralysis. This was commonly blamed on the libel juries, but it was not really their fault. Ironically, it was at least partly the fault of the very tabloid press against which such awards were most likely to be made. Their sensational style of reporting gave the public the impression that six-figure awards were the norm for libel. As a result, when members of the public found themselves on a libel jury these awards became their model. This was because, unlike judges, juries were not allowed to be given any figures during the trial by either judge or counsel.

This curious rule was established (or, to be more precise, re-established) by the Court of Appeal in *Ward v James*,[67] where it was enunciated with enthusiasm by none other than Lord Denning MR himself. Why is it, he asked, that when a case is heard by a judge sitting alone he may be referred by counsel to conventional awards of damages but that no figures could ever be mentioned to a jury: 'Why should the jury not receive the same guidance as a judge? This sounds well in theory, but in practice it is open to strong objection.' As counsel on both sides would mention different figures, the poor jury would become confused. Yet is this not what happened anyway? For though not permitted to cite specific figures to a jury, counsel could and did attempt to guide them by making cryptic remarks such as, 'If you do find for the plaintiff, think of fridges rather than of Rolls Royces.' Such coded messages were doubly confusing, because not only was the jury caught in a welter of conflicting values but they also had to place a monetary figure on them.

In *John v MGN Ltd*[68] a jury award of £350,000 (£75,000 compensatory damages plus £275,000 exemplary damages) to the musician Elton John for a false allegation that he was on a 'diet of death', was reduced by the Court of Appeal to a total of £75,000 (£25,000 compensatory damages plus £50,000 exemplary damages). The power of the Court of Appeal to intervene in this way dates back only to the Courts and Legal Services Act 1990. In addition, the Court of Appeal held, there was no reason why in future the judge or counsel could not give the jury an indication of what they considered an appropriate level of damages. The resulting reduction in the level of libel damages must be welcomed in terms of proportionality, though it does also of course favour the press at the expense of libel claimants.

## LOCAL AUTHORITIES

Other recent developments have tended in the same direction. So, in *Derbyshire County Council v Times Newspapers Ltd* [1993] 1 All ER 1011 the House of Lords decided that a local authority – or indeed any other organ of government – did not have the right to bring a defamation action, as this would be contrary to public policy:

> It is of the highest importance that a democratically elected governmental body, or indeed any governmental body, should be open to uninhibited public criticism. The threat of civil action for defamation must inevitably have an inhibiting effect on freedom of speech.

This was based on *City of Chicago v Tribune Co*,[69] decided by the Illinois Supreme Court and approved by the US Supreme Court in *New York Times Co v Sullivan*.[70] The Chicago decision rested on a broad principle:

> The fundamental right of freedom of speech is involved in this litigation and not merely the right of liberty of the press. If this action can be maintained against a newspaper it can be maintained against every private citizen who ventures to criticise the ministers who are temporarily conducting the affairs of his government.

While recognizing the important distinction discussed above between freedom of the press and freedom of speech generally, this passage neatly asserts the convergence of interests of the press and the general public in criticizing government institutions. This identity is perhaps more apparent than real. For how would a private citizen set about criticizing public institutions without a media platform? Also, if a government body is unable to sue for libel, this gives carte blanche to the press, which can be as irresponsible as it likes, knowing that it is immune from suit. If individual councillors or government officials were attacked as well, they would of course be entitled to bring a libel claim in their own names. But unless they were extremely rich, they would be unlikely to do so.

## THE HUMAN RIGHTS ACT 1998

The most important recent development in English defamation law is the passing of the Human Rights Act 1998, which besides incorporating the European Human Rights Convention, including of course the right to freedom of expression, into English law, affords special protection to freedom of expression (in section 12), and especially to 'journalistic, artistic or literary material'. This has a broad relevance going well beyond defamation. (See above.)

### *'Political information'*

As far as defamation itself is concerned, the effect of the Human Rights Act was felt even before it came into force, notably in *Reynolds v Times Newspapers Ltd.*[71] The former Irish Taoiseach (prime minister) Albert Reynolds sued the *Sunday Times* newspaper for publishing an article accusing him of making certain dishonest statements. At first instance the jury found in favour of Mr Reynolds but awarded him no damages. The judge substituted an award of one penny, the smallest coin of the realm. The matter went on appeal chiefly on the question of whether 'political information' was protected by what is called qualified privilege. Qualified privilege is an important defence in the law of defamation. What it means is that where, for example, a statement is made in the performance of a legal, moral or social duty, the occasion on which it is made is deemed to be privileged in the sense that even if the statement is untrue it is not an actionable defamation unless the claimant can show that it was made 'maliciously', that is, deliberately. So, where an invigilator at an examination announced to the assembled candidates that 'This fellow Bridgman has cribbed and will get no marks in consequence', it was held that the occasion was privileged, as the invigilator was acting out of a sense of duty. Although the accusation was false, there was no evidence of malice on the invigilator's part, so the action must fail.

But to return to Reynolds, should 'political information' be accepted as a new category of qualified privilege similar to that of the 'public figure' defence enunciated by the United States Supreme Court in *New York Times Co v Sullivan*? By three votes to two the House of Lords said no. In his speech Lord Hobhouse identified the power that such an extension of the qualified privilege defence would put in the hands of the media: 'Such an approach would of course be attractive to the media but it would be handing to what are essentially commercial entities a power which would deprive the subjects of such publications of the protection against damaging misinformation.'

The two dissenters wanted the question of qualified privilege to be remitted to the judge at the retrial of the issue, which had been ordered, which would have thrown the whole law in this area into confusion. One of them, Lord Steyn, went so far as to suggest that with the coming into force of the Human Rights

Act 1998, freedom of expression was now 'a right based on a constitutional or higher legal order foundation':

> Exceptions to freedom of expression must be justified as being necessary in a democracy. In other words, freedom of expression is the rule and regulation of speech is the exception requiring justification. The existence and width of any exception can only be justified if it is underpinned by a pressing social need. These are fundamental principles governing the balance to be struck between freedom of expression and defamation.[72]

The problem, as Lord Hobhouse clearly recognized, is that, far from striking a balance, this approach favours the rights of the press barons over ordinary people. As we have seen, freedom of the press is not the same thing as freedom of expression generally. Those attacked by the press cannot retaliate unless they too have access to the mass media. Their only legal recourse is to the extremely costly blunt instrument of the law of defamation, which is not an option for any other than the super-rich.

## TOLSTOY

Another English defamation case that has had a human rights dimension is one in which Count Nikolai Tolstoy Miloslavsky, a historian, wrote a pamphlet alleging the commission of war crimes at the end of the Second World War on the part of Lord Aldington, Warden of Winchester College. Aldington sued Tolstoy for defamation and won, being awarded damages of £1.5 million plus costs together with an injunction against further publication of the defamatory statements. Tolstoy took the matter to Strasbourg, claiming that the judgment constituted a violation of his right to freedom of expression. The Commission unanimously upheld this allegation. But the Human Rights Court equally unanimously held that the judgment against Tolstoy was 'prescribed by law' and as such did not violate Article 10, but that the level of damages was disproportionate: *Tolstoy Miloslavsky v UK*.[73]

This was an unusual case, not least because the pamphlet in question was privately printed and circulated. This may explain why Tolstoy did not receive the same degree of protection that the corporate press normally enjoys. In that respect the case resembles *Janowski v Poland*.[74] A journalist had insulted municipal guards for ordering street vendors to leave a public square, and was given a suspended sentence of eight months' imprisonment for his pains. Here again the journalist was acting in a private capacity. Once again, too, the Strasbourg Commission took a more sympathetic view than the court, the Commission finding by 8 votes to 7 that the journalist's rights under Article 10 had been infringed, while the court held by 12 to 5 that there had been no violation of his right of freedom of expression.

By contrast, journalists writing in their professional capacity can normally count on support in Strasbourg, though when it comes to a battle between journalists and the judiciary this is rather less likely. Three cases involving the same Austrian journalist but with different results are a good illustration of this: *Oberschlick v Austria; Oberschlick (No 2) v Austria;* and *Prager and Oberschlick v Austria.*[75]

However, in *De Haes and Gijsels v Belgium,*[76] a magazine launched a virulent attack on Belgian Court of Appeal judges for awarding custody of children to their father, who had been accused of incest and child abuse but who had been acquitted. The judges sued the magazine for defamation and won. But in Strasbourg both the Commission (by six votes to three) and the Court (by seven to two) found that this constituted a violation of the magazine's freedom of expression.

## Notes

1 *Müller v Switzerland* (1991) 13 EHRR 212 88/5 (paintings).
2 *Otto-Preminger-Institut v Austria* (1995) 19 EHRR 34 94/25 (film).
3 *Hashman and Harrup v United Kingdom* (1999) 99/90 (demonstration).
4 *Nilsen and Johnsen v Norway* 30 EHRR 878 99/91.
5 *Informationsverein Lentia v Austria* ECtHR 24/11/93, para 5.
6 315 HC Official Report (6th series) col 536 (2 July 1998).
7 *Imutran Ltd v Uncaged Campaigns Ltd* [2002] FSR 20.
8 315 HC Official Report (6th series) col 536, (2 July 1998).
9 315 HC Official Report (6th series) cols 538–9, (2 July 1998).
10 *Handyside v United Kingdom* (1976) 1 EHRR 737 76/5.
11 *Müller v Switzerland* (1991) 13 EHRR 212 88/5.
12 *Barthold v Germany* (1985) 7 EHRR 383, (1991) 13 EHRR 431 85/3.
13 *R v Central Independent Television plc* [1994] 3 All ER 641 at 652, per Hoffmann LJ.
14 *X Ltd v Morgan-Grampian Ltd* [1990] 2 All ER 1 (HL).
15 *Goodwin v UK* (1996) 22 EHRR 123 96/15.
16 *Interbrew v Financial Times and others* [2002] EWCA Civ 274.
17 *Camelot Group v Centaur Ltd* [1998] 1 All ER 251 at 259.
18 *Naomi Campbell v Mirror Group Newspapers Ltd* [2002] EWHC 499 (QB).
19 *Naomi Campbell v Mirror Group Newspapers Ltd* [2002] EWCA Civ 1373.
20 *A v B & Another, sub nomine Garry Flitcroft v Mirror Group Newspapers Ltd* [2002] EWCA Civ 337.
21 *Rai, Allmond and 'Negotiate Now' v UK* (1995) 19 EHRR CD 93.
22 *X Ltd v Morgan Grampian* [1990] 2 All ER 1; *Goodwin v UK* (1996) EHRR 1.
23 *Attorney-General v Guardian Newspapers* [1990] 1 AC 109, [1987] 3 All ER 316.
24 *The Observer and The Guardian v UK* (1991) 14 EHRR 153.
25 *Douglas v Hello!* (2000) 9 BHRC 543; 12. *Michael Douglas & Catherine Zeta-Jones v Hello!* [2003] EWHC 786 (Ch), §229 per Lindsay J. See Chapter 8.

26 *Venables and Thompson v News Group Newspapers* (2001) 9 BHRC.
27 *Daily Telegraph*, 4 December 2001.
28 *Attorney-General v Guardian Newspapers (No 2)* [1990] 1 AC 109 at 281.
29 BBC radio interview as reported in the *Daily Telegraph*, 29 July 2002.
30 *Wilkinson v Downton* [1897] 2 QB 57.
31 See Alan Dershowitz (2002) *Shouting Fire*, Little, Brown, Boston, p 147.
32 *Schenk v United States* 249 US 47 (1919).
33 Alan Dershowitz, *Shouting Fire*, Little, Brown, Boston, 2002, p 147.
34 *Texas v Johnson* 491 US 397 (1989).
35 *Eichman v United States* 496 US 310 (1990).
36 *X v Federal Republic of Germany* 29 DR 194.
37 *Jersild v Denmark* (1995) 19 EHRR 1 94/31.
38 *News Verlags GmbH v Austria* (Application No. 00031457/96 ECtHR 11 January 2000).
39 *Lehideux and Isoori v France* ECHR 98/84.
40 *Brind v Secretary of State for the Home Department* [1991] 1 All ER 720.
41 *Brind v UK Admissibility* Application no 18714/91 <http://hudoc.echr.coe.int>
42 *Attorney-General v Times Newspapers* [1991] 2 All ER 398.
43 *Attorney-General v Punch* [2001] EWCA Civ 403 (Lawtel – 23 March 2001).
44 *R v Shayler* (Lawtel – QBD, 16 May 2001).
45 *Totalise v The Motley Fool Ltd* (Lawtel, Owen J, 19 February 2001).
46 *Hulton v Jones* [1910] AC 20.
47 *Blennerhasset v Novelty Sales* (1933) 175 LTJ 393
48 *Cassidy v Daily Mirror* [1929] 2 KB 331.
49 *Tolley v Fry* [1931] AC 333
50 *Norwich Pharmacal v Commissioners of Customs & Excise* [1974] AC 133
51 *Totalise v The Motley Fool Ltd* [2001] EWCA Civ 1897.
52 *Associated Provincial Picture Houses v Wednesbury Corp* [1947] 2 All ER 680 (CA).
53 *Tele 1 Privatfernsehgesellschaft mbH v Austria* (Lawtel doc no G2000284 – ECTHR 21/9/2000).
54 *Informationsverein Lentia v Austria* (Lawtel doc no G1000418 – ECTHR 24/11/93).
55 *Esther Thomas v News Group Newspapers* (Lawtel, 18 July 2001 CA).
56 *R v Secretary of State for the Home Department, ex parte Simms* [1999] 3 All ER 400.
57 *Ibid*, per Lord Steyn, 403.
58 *Ibid*, per Lord Steyn, 404.
59 *Ibid*, per Lord Steyn, 404.
60 *Ibid*, per Lord Steyn, 411.
61 *Ibid*, per Lord Steyn, 407.
62 Tony Weir (1996) *A Casebook on Tort*, 8th edn, p 525.
63 Eric Barendt, Laurence Lustgarten, Kenneth Norrie and Hugh Stephenson (1997) *Libel and the Media: The chilling effect*, Oxford University Press, Oxford.
64 *Ibid*, p 196.

65 *Ibid*, p 183.
66 *Hulton & Co Ltd v Jones* [1910] AC 20.
67 *Ward v James* [1965] 1 All ER 563 at 575.
68 *John v MGN Ltd* [1996] 2 All ER 35.
69 *City of Chicago v Tribune Co* (1923) 307 Ill 595.
70 *New York Times Co v Sullivan* (1964) 376 US 254 at 277.
71 *Reynolds v Times Newspapers Ltd* [1999] 4 All ER 609.
72 *Ibid* at 629.
73 *Tolstoy Miloslavsky v United Kingdom* (1995) 20 EHRR 442 95/20.
74 *Janowski v Poland* (2000) 29 EHRR 705 99/3.
75 *Oberschlick v Austria* (1995) 19 EHRR 389 91/29; *Oberschlick (No 2) v Austria* (1998) 25 EHRR 357 97/41; *Prager and Oberschlick v Austria* (1996) 21 EHRR 1 95/11.
76 *De Haes and Gijsels v Belgium* (1998) 25 EHRR 1 97/7.

# 7

# Freedom of thought, conscience and religion

## PRINCIPLES

1. There is a long-standing tradition of protection of freedom of thought, conscience and religion under English law.
2. ECHR Article 9(1) protects 'the right to freedom of thought, conscience and religion.' As far as beliefs are concerned, including the right to change one's beliefs, the protection is absolute.
3. ECHR Article 9(1) also protects everyone's right 'to manifest his religion or belief, in worship, teaching, practice and observance'. This right is not absolute, but is subject 'to such limitations as are prescribed by law and are necessary in a democratic society in the interests of public safety, for the protection of public order, health or morals, or for the protection of the rights and freedoms of others': Article 9(2).
4. Besides Article 9 there is now also HRA s 13, though this does not really add anything. See the discussion on it in Chapter 1.

## PROBLEMS

### *What is the scope of Article 9 protection?*

Article 9 protection is extremely wide, including not only religious beliefs in the broadest sense but also political and social views. In a case involving

Jehovah's Witnesses the Strasbourg court specifically described Article 9 as 'a precious asset' not only for believers of all varieties, but also 'for atheists, agnostics, sceptics and the unconcerned. The pluralism indissociable from a democratic society, which has been dearly won over the centuries, depends on it': *Kokkinakis v Greece*.[1]

In a case involving a pacifist campaigner in Northern Ireland the Human Rights Commission accepted that pacifist views were protected under Article 9 but that no infringement had taken place in this case: *Arrowsmith v United Kingdom*.[2]

## *Is the maintenance of an established church or religion automatically a violation of Article 9?*

No. In *Darby v Sweden*[3] it was held that the existence of an established religion or church does not in itself amount to an infringement of Article 9. However, where the position of an established religion is bolstered by means of 'rigid or indeed prohibitive conditions on practice of religious beliefs' by competing faiths, this may amount to a breach of Article 9: *Manoussakis v Greece*.[4]

## *Is there any potential conflict between Article 9 and the traditional protection of the same rights under English law?*

This is the same problem as arises in regard to other rights as well. If the ECHR as incorporated into the HRA enjoys a special 'higher order law' status, as has been suggested by some commentators, including at least one senior judge, then Article 9 will trump any pre-existing common law or statutory rights. This is discussed in Chapter 3, where it is shown that neither the ECHR nor the HRA enjoys any such status in English law. However, if the judiciary were to act on this mistaken assumption, then that could have some far-reaching practical implications. It would mean, in particular, that where there is a conflict between the rights of two persons, one being a Convention right and the other a common law right, the person relying on the Convention right would be bound to win, which might in the circumstances be unfair.

Does this mean that Louise Stedman would have succeeded in her claim that her dismissal because of her refusal to work on some Sundays infringed her rights under Article 9? Probably not, because it was held by the Human Rights Commission that she was dismissed not because of her religious beliefs but because she refused to sign a contract obliging her to work on some Sundays. This is strangely narrow logic, for Louise Stedman's only reason for refusing to work on Sundays was her religious belief that it was wrong to do so. The

Commission decision therefore neatly sidestepped the need to weigh up an employee's right to religious freedom against an employer's right to insist on a contract which denied such rights: *Stedman v UK*.[5]

## What exactly is meant by the right to 'manifest' one's beliefs under Article 9(1)? In particular, does this include the right to proselytize? If so, does this interfere with the freedom of others to believe what they want?

As indicated above, Article 9 is in two parts, the first of which protects the beliefs themselves, or what is sometimes called the *forum internum*, and the other the 'manifestation' of these beliefs 'in worship, teaching, practice and observance'.

Could one person's rights to manifest his or her beliefs interfere with the rights of another? In Greece the law protects the established Orthodox church and makes it a criminal offence for the adherents of other religions to proselytize. A Jehovah's Witness who had been arrested more than 60 times and imprisoned on several occasions for proselytism claimed that this violated his right under Article 9 to manifest his religion: *Kokkinakis v Greece*.[6] Despite the doctrine of margin of appreciation, Minos Kokkinakis won in the Human Rights Court by six votes to three. But it was nevertheless held that the Greek legislation in question was 'prescribed by law' and intended 'for the protection of the rights and freedoms of others' under Article 9(2), although not 'necessary in a democratic society' for this purpose as was required by Article 9(2). The Greek law was also held not to have been justified by a 'pressing social need' nor 'proportionate to the legitimate aim pursued'.

The Greek government drew a distinction between 'bearing witness' and 'unacceptable proselytism', and the Strasbourg court accepted that proselytism would be unacceptable if conducted by means of exerting improper pressure on people whose psychological or economic condition made them especially suggestible, or by means of violence or brainwashing. However, there was no evidence in this case that Mr Kokkinakis had employed any such improper pressure.

## How does the right under Article 9(1) to 'manifest' one's beliefs relate to the right to free expression under Article 10? Is there any potential conflict here?

'Manifestation' of belief is an extremely broad concept which includes acts of observance, worship, ritual, teaching and preaching. It is not always easy to determine where Article 9 protection of 'manifestation' ends and where Article 10 'freedom of expression' begins. These rights inevitably overlap to some extent, especially as Article 10 covers not only the right to make known one's opinions to others but also the right to 'hold' them. It does not really matter under which heading a particular claim falls, as applications are commonly brought on a scatter-gun basis, citing as many articles as possible.

In the case involving publication of the allegedly obscene *Little Red Schoolbook*[7] a distinction was drawn between the holding of beliefs - which under Article 9 is an absolute right - and the dissemination of those beliefs - which fell under Article 10 and which are subject to the limitations set out in Article 10(2).

## How do the rights under Article 9 relate to the prohibition of discrimination contained in Article 14?

Not surprisingly, many Article 9 cases have also prayed Article 14 in aid. However, the Strasbourg court has taken the opportunity from time to time to stress that Article 14 does not stand alone but merely complements the other Convention rights. For a fuller discussion of Article 14 see under Discrimination in Chapter 12.

One case where the complementary role of Article 14 was stressed involved an application by a strict orthodox Jewish organization: *Ch'are Shalom VeTsedek (Jewish Liturgical Association) v France*.[8] This body had more exacting standards of kosher slaughter (known as *glatt* kosher) than the majority body, the Jewish Consistorial Association of Paris, whose abattoirs were the only kosher slaughter-houses recognized by the French government. The applicant body claimed that its non-recognition amounted to violation of its Article 9 rights. The Human Rights Commission found in its favour, holding by 14 votes to 3 that there had been a violation of the applicants' rights under Articles 9 and 14 combined. However, the ECHR took a different line. By 12 votes to 5 it held that there was no breach of Article 9 and by the narrower margin of 10 votes to 7 that there had been no breach of the applicants' combined Article 9 and Article 14 rights.

The chief basis of the majority decision was that there was no infringement of the applicants' rights because if *glatt* kosher slaughter was disallowed in France, *glatt* kosher meat was still available from Belgium! This is hardly a legal argument. And what if Belgium decided to follow the French example and also refuse to sanction *glatt* kosher slaughter? Even the Strasbourg court admitted that ritual slaughter was a form of 'manifestation' of religious belief within Article 9. Yet, as we have seen, the only permissible restrictions on this right must be 'necessary in a democratic society in the interests of public safety, for the protection of public order, health or morals, or for the protection of the rights and freedoms of others'. It is hard to see how a ban on a particular form of kosher slaughter could possibly be justified under any of these heads.

After a majority of the Strasbourg court had satisfied themselves that there was no infringement of Article 9, a smaller majority, stressing the complementary nature of Article 14 – which just happened to suit their unreasonable stance on Article 9 – concluded that there was no violation of Articles 9 and 14 taken together. Yet even they admitted that there was a 'difference of treatment' involved here, but held that its effect was 'limited'.

Another case where discrimination was alleged was *Ahmad v United Kingdom*.[9] A Muslim primary school teacher claimed that his Article 9 rights had been violated by his not being allowed time off for prayer on Friday afternoons. He resigned his position because of this, but his claim for constructive unfair dismissal failed. The Human Rights Commission in Strasbourg likewise rejected his claim under Article 9 on the basis that the article did not exempt him from taking into account 'his particular professional or contractual position'. One problem was that Mr Ahmad had not formally raised the question of time off for Friday prayers until he had been employed for six years. The reason for this was that the first school where he worked was close to a mosque and he was allowed to take off about 45 minutes after the lunch break on Fridays. However, when he moved to another school he needed longer, which is where the problem began.

The case may be taken as an illustration of what is meant by the provision in Article 9(2) that manifestation of one's religious freedom must be subject to 'the protection of the rights and freedoms of others'.

## *Is there freedom to 'manifest' anti-social, revolutionary or violent thoughts?*

The freedom to think whatever one likes can hardly be restricted. The term 'manifestation' has generally been applied chiefly to religion. The 'manifestation' of political and social views would normally be considered under Article 10. See the discussion on freedom of expression in Chapter 6.

## *Can Article 9 be applied horizontally as well as vertically?*

In *Stedman v UK*[10] the applicant was employed by a private company. How then could she have brought her case to Strasbourg? Because she blamed the United Kingdom for not protecting her right to refuse to work on Sundays. This may therefore be seen as a case with indirect horizontal effect. Although Louise Stedman did not succeed before the Human Rights Commission, the partial horizontal dimension of the case was not the reason for this.

### Supplementary note

Beliefs or opinions are much less of a problem than either the 'manifestation' or, even more so, the publication of such views. Until technology is considerably more advanced than at present it will not be possible to detect the privately held opinions of others. Manifestation of those news, however, shades into expression, and it is here that the problems generally arise. This is the distinction drawn by Queen Elizabeth I in saying: 'I will not make windows into men's souls' (see below).

## TRADITIONAL ENGLISH LAW

The right of freedom of thought, conscience and religion long predates the ECHR. The question of religious toleration occupied a central position in English history from the time of John Wycliffe (1328–84) until the mid-19th century. It was to the credit of English society that Wycliffe, unlike the Czech reformer Jan Hus (1369–1415), was not himself burnt at the stake for heresy, although Wycliffe's followers, the so-called Lollards, were outlawed by Act of Parliament in 1401 and their later rebellion was put down in 1414.

The reigns of Henry VIII (1509–47), Edward VI (1547–53) and Mary I (1553–58) were marked by savage religious intolerance, culminating in the burning at the stake of the Archbishop of Canterbury, Thomas Cranmer, and Bishops Latimer and Ridley under Mary. Elizabeth I (1558–1603) declared that she 'would not make windows into men's souls'. In other words, she would not pry into private beliefs, but she did take action against those who sided with her enemies, notably Spain. By the Act of Uniformity (1559) penalties were stipulated for departure from the practices of the Church of England, but its beliefs were so vaguely defined as to allow a wide latitude to divergent views.

Elizabeth's Stuart successors, James I (1603–25, as James VI King of Scots 1567–1625) and Charles I (1625–49) were less politic. Charles's conflict with the Puritan-dominated Parliament led to the English Revolution or Civil War (1642–47), resulting in the ultimate deposition and execution of the king. The establishment of a so-called Commonwealth and later a Protectorate under Oliver Cromwell (1599–1658) was a victory for Puritanism rather than for general toleration. This was particularly noticeable in Ireland, where Cromwell's anti-Catholicism was given full expression. By contrast, Cromwell allowed Jews back into England for the first time since their expulsion by Edward I in 1290.

The Restoration of the Stuarts in the shape of the 'Merry Monarch' Charles II (1660–85) marked a return to a middle-of-the-road established Church of England coupled with wide toleration of other Protestant beliefs. James II (1685–89) was a practising Roman Catholic, but unlike Mary I (1553–58), whose persecutions earned her the sobriquet 'Bloody Mary', James II was remarkably tolerant, especially of extreme Protestants like the Quakers. In fact, the Quaker leader William Penn, founder of the American colony Pennsylvania, was a close friend and confidant of the king's. James II's 'Declaration of indulgence' published in 1687 and reissued in 1688 under the title 'Declaration for liberty of conscience' marked a milestone in religious toleration:

> We cannot but heartily wish, as it will easily be believed, that the people of our dominions were members of the Catholic church; yet we humbly thank Almighty God, it is, and has long time been our constant sense and opinion (which upon divers occasions we have declared) that conscience ought not to be constrained, nor people forced in matters of mere religion.[11]

Cynics have attributed James II's toleration of Protestant dissenters to his concern to protect Roman Catholics, which it would have been impossible to do in isolation. Yet he continued to reiterate the same views while in exile, although that could also perhaps be explained away as a political gambit.

Nevertheless, just how far ahead of his time James II's views were became clear from their hostile reception at the hands of the bishops, seven of whom specifically petitioned the King, expressing their 'averseness' to the Declaration and claiming that it was illegal.[12] This led directly to the Seven Bishops' Case[13] and ultimately to the so-called Glorious Revolution of 1688, culminating in the replacement of the autocratic Roman Catholic James II with his Protestant daughter and son-in-law as joint monarchs in a parliamentary regime: William III (1689–1701) and Mary II (1689–94).

The Toleration Act 1689 passed under the new regime was a far cry from what James II had offered, as it specifically excluded Roman Catholics, who had to wait until 1829 for what was termed Catholic emancipation, and it was only in 1871 with the repeal of the University Test Acts that the disabilities previously applicable to non-Anglicans were abolished.

As far as political views are concerned, Britain has long been regarded as one of the most tolerant of countries. The reason Karl Marx chose the British Museum's reading room to do his research for *Das Kapital* was not only the fact that it was one of the world's best libraries but perhaps even more so that he would not be persecuted for his political views in England. Not surprisingly, Britain became a magnet to political activists from all over the world, including anarchists, communists and revolutionaries of various persuasions.

The rise of 'political correctness' in recent years undoubtedly poses a threat to freedom of thought and even more so to freedom of expression.[14]

## Notes

1 *Kokkinakis v Greece* (1994) 17 EHRR 397 93/18, para 31.
2 *Arrowsmith v United Kingdom* (1978) 3 EHRR 218.
3 *Darby v Sweden* (1990) 13 EHRR 774.
4 *Manoussakis v Greece* (1996) 23 EHRR 387.
5 *Stedman v UK* (1997) 23 EHRR CD 169.
6 *Kokkinakis v Greece* (1994) 17 EHRR 397 93/18.

7 *Handyside v UK* (1979–80), EHRR 737 76/5.
8 *Ch'are Shalom VeTsedek (Jewish Liturgical Association) v France* 00/167.
9 *Ahmad v UK* (1982) 4 EHRR 126.
10 See above.
11 State Trials xii, 234.
12 State Trials xii, 318.
13 State Trials xii, 183.
14 See *Esther Thomas v News Group Newspapers* (Lawtel, 18 July 2001 – CA).

# 8

# Privacy

Is privacy protected under English law? It has always been said that no such protection was afforded by the common law, although, as we shall see, this is not completely true. But what about Article 8 of the European Human Rights Convention?

There are two problems here. First, what Article 8 protects is not privacy but everyone's 'right to respect for his private and family life', which is not quite the same thing. Secondly, in common with the rest of the Convention, Article 8 is meant to have vertical effect only, not horizontal. In other words, it is intended to protect individuals not against other individuals but only against 'public authorities'. So most of the Strasbourg cases brought under this article concern allegations of unlawful activities by state agencies. Such activities include surveillance, search and seizure, interception of correspondence, telephone tapping and the like. However, as with other Convention rights, there has been a trend towards extending the scope of Article 8 so as to give it horizontal effect as well.

**Q. Is there a right of privacy under English common law?**

***A. It is generally believed by lawyers and laypeople alike that there is no protection for privacy under the common law of England. This is not quite true.***

## *PRINCE ALBERT v STRANGE*

The United States has a highly developed law of privacy, but the foundation stone of this elaborate edifice is nothing other than the old English case of *Prince Albert v Strange*.[1]

So proud was the Prince of the family portraits that Queen Victoria and he had sketched that he engaged an engraver to turn the drawings into etchings for easy duplication. But the etchings fell into the wrong hands, those of a man called Strange, a villain on the make, who bought the etchings, probably through the good offices of the palace printer. He then produced a printed catalogue of the etchings, announcing a forthcoming exhibition of them. Prince Albert sought an injunction to stop the exhibition from being held and, more important, to prohibit the publication of the catalogue.

'The principle', said Sir John Romilly, the Solicitor General, who appeared for the Prince, 'is that the court will restrain any person from making use of the property of another, contrary to the will and disposition of the owner.' This view was endorsed both by Knight-Bruce V-C at first instance and by Lord Cottenham LC on appeal. Property, what property? Romilly made it clear that the property rights he was talking about had nothing to do with copyright and that there had been 'the abstraction of one attribute of property, which was often its most valuable quality, namely privacy'. This left the field open for further development, which occurred with the publication of the seminal article, 'The right to privacy', by Samuel Warren and Louis Brandeis,[2] which upon citation in courts throughout the United States gave rise to the fully fledged protection of privacy that is in force there today.

## TRESPASS

Another strand of privacy derives from trespass, the oldest and most important of the ancient 'forms of action', dating back to 1250. Trespass is in fact the origin of all the modern torts, and, for that matter, even of contract.[3]

We normally associate the word 'trespass' with land and real property. Unauthorized entry on to land is the earliest form of tort. By extension, we soon also find trespass to the body or person that is, assault and battery, and in addition trespass to goods. A writ of trespass could therefore be used to protect a person's body, his or her house and his or her goods from interference by others, including interference by the state and its officers.[4]

It is not hard to see how trespass could be extended to cover a right of privacy. A good example of this is to be found in the case of *Hurst v Picture Theatres Ltd*.[5] A perfectly law-abiding and inoffensive citizen who had duly paid his sixpence for a seat in the defendants' cinema was suddenly unceremoniously and forcibly ejected on the false assumption that he had not paid. He sued the cinema proprietors for assault and false imprisonment, and succeeded in the Court of Appeal by a majority of two to one on the ground that, by virtue of buying his sixpenny ticket, he had a licence coupled with an interest in the land (presumably the area occupied by his seat in the cinema). Since the passing of the Judicature Act 1875, it was pointed out, a deed was not necessary in order to grant an interest in land. In other words, the cinema ticket gave Mr Hurst a proprietary interest in land, which, according to one of the most elementary rules of law, is by its very nature irrevocable. But what the case really gave Mr Hurst was the right to be allowed to sit in the cinema without disturbance.

*Hurst* was not cited in the case involving the television actor Gordon Kaye. Mr Kaye was badly injured when a piece of wood smashed his car windscreen and hit him on the head. After spending three days in intensive care he was moved to a private ward. Ignoring notices in the corridor and on the ward door itself, a newspaper reporter and photographer entered the actor's room. Mr Kaye apparently agreed to talk to them and did not object to their photographing his badly scarred head. However, according to medical evidence, the injured actor, who had undergone brain surgery, was in no fit state to give informed consent.

At first instance Potter J granted Gordon Kaye an injunction restraining the newspaper from publishing any statement by him or photograph of him. Was this an invasion of Gordon Kaye's privacy? Lord Justice Bingham in the Court of Appeal was prepared to stigmatize it as 'a monstrous invasion of his privacy'. But he regretted that an invasion of privacy alone, however gross, did not give rise to a cause of action under the existing law. As a result, Potter J's decision was reversed except that the newspaper was prohibited from claiming that Gorden Kaye had 'voluntarily permitted' them to interview or photograph him. The basis of this was that any such claim would amount to a malicious falsehood. But they could still publish the picture.[6]

Gorden Kaye must clearly have had as much of a proprietary interest in his hospital ward as Mr Hurst in his cinema seat. This made the journalists trespassers – trespassers not only as against the hospital but also as against Mr Kaye.

How could this have helped the actor to prevent the newspaper from printing the photographs they had taken of him? Here another fundamental principle of the law comes into play: 'No one may benefit from his own wrong' (Co Litt 148b). This does not only apply to criminal offences, as the word 'wrong' (Latin: *injuria*) clearly indicates. So once the journalists' intrusion was seen for what it was, namely the tort of trespass, they could be restrained from profiting from it by publishing any remarks or photographs which they had obtained as a result of it.

## IS THERE A RIGHT OF PRIVACY UNDER THE HUMAN RIGHTS ACT?

When Michael Douglas and Catherine Zeta-Jones tied the knot at the Plaza Hotel in New York in November 2000 they had already sold the exclusive rights to photograph their wedding to *OK!* magazine. Under the contract bride and groom were each to be paid £500,000 and were given the right to choose their own photographers (paid for by themselves) and copyright in the photographs, together with the right to select the photographs for publication as well as the right to approve the captions and accompanying text.

The wedding guests all received a notice with their invitation reading: 'We would appreciate no photography or video devices at the ceremony or reception.' There was a security checkpoint through which all guests had to pass, and guards kept a lookout for any guests armed with cameras, video recording machines or transmitting devices. Six cameras were actually confiscated during the reception.

Despite these elaborate precautions, a freelance photographer managed to slip into the reception and secretly take his own pictures, which he sold to *Hello!* magazine, *OK!*'s bitter rivals. The nuptial pair and *OK!* sought an urgent injunction to stop *Hello!* from publishing these 'unauthorized' photographs.

It just so happened that on 2 October 2000, shortly before the wedding, the Human Rights Act 1998 had come into force in the United Kingdom. One of the convention rights (Article 8) incorporated in the Act protects the 'right to respect for private and family life' and another (Article 10) the 'right of freedom of expression'. Was this case not a classic example of a conflict between these two rights?

Not quite, because the Convention is supposed to be confined to claims against what are termed 'public authorities', that is, the government and other state agencies; and however prosperous and successful *Hello! Ltd* may be, it can hardly be regarded as a public authority. Technically speaking, the Convention is meant to operate 'vertically', in the sense that the claimant, who is generally a private person or company, is going against some public authority.

On what basis, then, was the application by the Douglases and *OK!* launched? For this would amount to a 'horizontal' application of the Convention, which is not supposed to be allowed. In fact, although an injunction was immediately granted by a High Court judge over the telephone, it was discharged by a unanimous Court of Appeal. However, as was stressed repeatedly in the Court of Appeal, this was not a trial of the action on its merits. An injunction would have killed the relevant issue of *Hello!* magazine completely. While not being prepared to do this, at least one judge in the Court of Appeal (Sedley LJ) nevertheless expressed the view that the Douglases had 'a powerfully arguable case to advance at trial'.[7] The same judge even went so far as to suggest that 'we have reached a point at which it can be said with confidence that the law recognises and will appropriately protect a right of personal privacy'.[8]

This was based at least partly on a 1985 decision of the Strasbourg court, in which it was held that 'although the object of Article 8 is essentially that of protecting the individual against arbitrary interference by the public authorities', an essentially negative obligation, 'there may be positive obligations inherent in an effective respect for private or family life. These obligations may involve the adoption of measures designed to secure respect for life even in the sphere of the relations of individuals between themselves'.[9]

Not only does this passage suggest the possibility of a law of privacy, it also allows for Article 8 to have horizontal as well as vertical effect. But set against Article 8 is section 12 of the HRA, which accords special protection to freedom of expression, the right most likely to come into conflict with privacy, as for example in cases of media intrusion, 'doorstepping', long-lens photography and other forms of what the press rather loosely term 'investigative journalism'. Sedley LJ was of the opinion that, like Article 8, section 12 has horizontal effect and that it does not simply 'prioritise' the freedom to publish over other convention rights. 'Everything', he concludes, 'will ultimately depend on the proper balance between privacy and publicity in the situation facing the court'.[10]

However, Sedley LJ's view that there is already a right of personal privacy under English law has not been widely shared. It was not followed, for example, by any members of the Court of Appeal in *Wainwright v Home Office*[11] decided soon after. Moreover, the judge in the substantive trial of *Douglas v Hello!* expressly declined what he called the invitation to hold 'that there is an existing law of privacy' under which Michael Douglas, Catherine Zeta-Jones and *OK!* magazine were entitled to relief.[12]

It is to this finding that the media confusion over the outcome of the case is probably chiefly attributable, with some reports claiming that the film stars had won, while others were saying that they had lost. The truth is that though the claim based on privacy failed, they succeeded under the law of confidence (discussed below).

At the time of writing therefore there is still no comprehensive protection of privacy under English law. But Strasbourg has just issued a severe blast against the United Kingdom, calling for such protection to be provided. So it is probably just a matter of time before a privacy law is introduced into Parliament – something that the naysayers have long claimed was an impossibility.

## STRASBOURG TO THE RESCUE?

As we have just seen, English law still does not provide protection for personal privacy – even after the coming into force of the HRA, which of course incorporates Article 8 of the Convention. Yet the Strasbourg court now appears to be interpreting Article 8 as providing such protection. In other words, the same article of the Convention is interpreted differently by the UK domestic courts from the way it is understood in Strasbourg.[13]

Does this make any difference in practice? The English courts keep stressing that in most cases the law of confidence will provide an adequate remedy for invasion of privacy. A good example of this is *Douglas v Hello!* discussed above, where although the claim based on privacy failed, the claimants succeeded under breach of confidence. There is no reason to believe that the damages awarded to them would have been any greater had their claim for invasion of privacy been successful. It is never possible to obtain double recovery, so whatever happened, they could only ever have been awarded damages under one head. It would have made no difference to the claimants whether this was labelled 'privacy' or 'confidence', as their legal representatives had made sure to frame their claim under both.

However unlikely a claim for breach of confidence might appear on the facts of *Hello!*, there are some privacy cases that still could not possibly be covered even by the strained interpretation given by the English courts to the concept of 'confidence'. In such cases no remedy is available under the common law, and the English courts have set their faces against interpreting the protection of 'private life' in Article 8 of the Convention as equivalent to the protection of 'privacy' as such.

Until recently the Strasbourg court likewise fought shy of recognizing privacy rights, as is well illustrated by their dismissal of the application brought by the Earl Spencer (brother of the Princess of Wales) and his wife. Their complaint related to a 1995 front-page article in a mass circulation tabloid Sunday newspaper under a banner headline reading 'Di's sister-in-law in booze and bulimia clinic'. The article was accompanied by a photograph taken with a telephoto lens showing Lady Spencer walking in the grounds of the private clinic, with the caption 'So thin: Victoria walks in the clinic grounds this week'. Similar stories appeared in two other mass circulation Sunday tabloids and a tabloid daily.

The Spencers' case was dismissed by the Strasbourg Human Rights Commission as 'inadmissible', but this was only because it was held that the Spencers had not exhausted all domestic remedies, notably breach of confidence.[14]

## *PECK*

But the Strasbourg approach has become more daring. So, for example, in *Peck v UK*, decided in 2003, the Strasbourg court upheld a complaint against the United Kingdom brought by an applicant whose image, picked up on closed circuit television (CCTV), was widely disseminated by the media.[15]

Geoffrey Peck was filmed late one night holding a large knife in his hand in the centre of Brentwood, Essex, just after he had attempted to commit suicide by slashing his wrists. The CCTV operator called the police, who gave Mr Peck medical assistance, detained him briefly under the Mental Health Act 1983 and then drove him home. In short, the presence of the CCTV camera and the efficient monitoring of the film footage saved Geoffrey Peck's life.

The problem began with press releases put out by Brentwood Borough Council to publicize the success of its CCTV system. The first such release included still photographs from the CCTV footage showing Geoffrey Peck holding the knife. The heading was 'Defused – the partnership between CCTV and the police prevents a potentially dangerous situation'. There was no indication of the purpose for which Mr Peck had the knife, although the article did make it clear that he had not been looking for trouble. Several local newspapers ran articles along the same lines with the same pictures. The story was then picked up by Anglia Television, which showed some of the CCTV footage on its local news. Some of the footage was later broadcast on the BBC's *Crime Beat* programme watched by over 9 million viewers. Geoffrey Peck's face was masked, but the Broadcasting Standards Commission later found the masking to be inadequate, and many of Mr Peck's friends and relations who saw the programme claimed to be able to recognize him.

Geoffrey Peck took serious umbrage at all this unwanted publicity, in none of which, however, was his name ever revealed. To counter the negative CCTV images he then launched his own publicity campaign, appearing on radio and national television and disclosing his name for the first time.

The Broadcasting Standards Commission (BSC) upheld Geoffrey Peck's complaint of unwarranted invasion of his privacy and his allegation of unjust and unfair treatment. The BSC expressly added that the fact that Geoffrey Peck had later chosen to speak out publicly about the incident himself did not diminish the infringement of his privacy.

His complaint to the Press Complaints Commission (PCC) was less successful. Indeed, the PCC rejected his complaint out of hand without a hearing. The fact that the CCTV filming was done in a place open to public view was taken as justification for its subsequent publication.

Geoffrey Peck applied for judicial review of Brentwood Council's decision to disclose the CCTV footage on the ground that it was either illegal or irrational. But he was unsuccessful, and his application for leave to appeal was dismissed:

> [T]he judge was plainly correct in his interpretation of the relevant statutory provisions and the Council was neither acting outside its statutory authority nor irrationally in making the film and photographs available to the media. The injury of which complaint is made arises from a failure on the part of the media to sufficiently disguise the applicant when making the film and photographs visible to the public. That is and has been the subject of complaint against the media involved but is not capable of supporting a claim for a declaration against Brentwood Borough Council.[16]

Success was finally achieved in Strasbourg, where a unanimous court upheld Geoffrey Peck's complaint that his Article 8 rights had been infringed and that no effective domestic remedy was available to him, which amounted to a violation of Article 13.

In what sense could the disclosure of the CCTV footage be said to have infringed Geoffrey Peck's private life? The incident took place in a public place and could have been witnessed by any passer-by. Would it have been in any way unlawful if such a passer-by had described the incident in a newspaper article? And what if the passer-by had chosen to photograph the incident and then to publish the photographs?

There are jurisdictions, such as those of France or Belgium, where even photographing a person innocently riding a bicycle along the street is not allowed without their consent. That is not the case under English law. Indeed, a photographer standing on a street corner was once a common sight. He would snap people at random, handing his subjects a card with his studio address where they could purchase prints of their street snapshot or sit for a photographic portrait.

Any curb placed on the right to take photographs in public places would be strongly resisted by the media as an infringement of their freedom of expression under Article 10 and HRA section 12. So to return to Geoffrey Peck, how could the capture of his image on CCTV amount to an infringement of his privacy?

The Strasbourg court in *PG and JH v UK*[17] draws the line at the point where 'a systematic or permanent record' is created:

> A person who walks down the street will, inevitably, be visible to any member of the public who is also present. Monitoring by technological means of the same public scene (e.g. a security guard viewing through closed circuit television) is of a similar character. Private life considerations may arise however once any systematic or permanent record comes into existence of such material from the public domain.

In the *Peck* case the applicant's complaint was not about the fact that he was filmed by CCTV cameras nor that this was done by the creation of a permanent record. 'Indeed, he admitted that that function of the CCTV system together with the consequent involvement of the police may have saved his life. Rather he argued that it was the disclosure of that record of his movements to the public in a manner which he could never have foreseen which gave rise to such an interference.'[18]

Because 'the relevant moment was viewed to an extent which far exceeded any exposure to a passer-by or to security observation . . . and to a degree surpassing that to which the applicant could possibly have foreseen when he walked in Brentwood on 20 August 1995 . . . the Court considers that the disclosure by the Council of the relevant footage constituted a serious interference with the applicant's right to respect for his private life.'[19]

Was this interference justified by any of the restrictions contained in the second part of Article 8 itself? In particular, was the disclosure of the CCTV footage 'necessary in a democratic society'? The test applied here was whether the reasons given to justify the disclosure were 'relevant and sufficient' and whether the measures were 'proportionate to the legitimate aims pursued'.[20] After paying lip-service to 'the strong interest of the State in detecting and preventing crime' and the 'important role' played by CCTV in this regard,[21] the court held that this did not justify Brentwood Council's disclosure of the pictures without Geoffrey Peck's consent or without ensuring that his face was masked. As for Mr Peck's self-publicization of the matter, this, the court held, did not 'diminish the serious nature of the interference or reduce the correlative requirement of care concerning disclosures'.[22]

What about the United Kingdom's margin of appreciation? This too got short shrift:

> In cases concerning the disclosure of personal data, the Court has also recognised that a margin of appreciation should be left to the competent national authorities in striking a fair balance between the relevant conflicting public and private interests. However, this margin goes hand in hand with European supervision . . . and the scope of this margin depends on such factors as the nature and seriousness of the interests at stake and the gravity of the interference.[23]

The court concluded that 'the disclosure constituted a disproportionate and therefore unjustified interference with his private life and a violation of Article 8 of the Convention.'[24]

Geoffrey Peck was also successful in claiming that his Article 13 rights were violated on the ground that there was no 'effective remedy' available to him in the English courts for the infringement of his Article 8 rights. Here again, after some lip-service to the principle of the margin of appreciation, the Court rounded on the inadequacy of the remedy provided under English law by judicial review:

> [T]he Court considers that the threshold at which the High Court could find the impugned disclosure irrational was placed so high that it effectively excluded any consideration by it of the question of whether the interference with the applicant's right answered a pressing social need or was proportionate to the aims pursued . . . . The Court finds therefore that judicial review did not provide the applicant with an effective remedy in relation to the violation of his right to respect for his private life.[25]

The *Peck* case was, to say the least, unusual. So, what use, if any, is it as a guide to the law's attitude to privacy? Would Brentwood Council's release of the CCTV footage have passed muster if it had been specifically publicized as an example of how CCTV could save the life of someone in need of medical assistance? Geoffrey Peck freely admitted the debt he owed to the CCTV camera and its efficient monitoring. But would he still have been able to claim that the release of the footage to the media breached his Article 8 rights? It is quite possible that, in the absence of adequate masking of his identity or his consent to publication of the pictures, Strasbourg might still have ruled in his favour.

In a throwaway *obiter dictum* the Strasbourg court in *Peck* remarked: '[T]he Court would note at the outset that the applicant was not charged with, much less convicted of, an offence. The present case does not therefore concern disclosure of footage of the commission of a crime.'[26] Does this mean that had Geoffrey Peck been engaging in criminal activity when filmed, the Strasbourg court world have dismissed his claim? If so, that is good news for law enforcement.

**Q. What protection is there for privacy under the law of confidence?**

**A.** ***At first sight the law of confidence or confidentiality may appear a poor substitute for a true right of privacy. But the English courts have strained the***

***meaning of 'confidence' to such an extent that it has come to cover some pretty unlikely scenarios while still falling well short of becoming coextensive with a general right to privacy.***

If the courts were prepared to stretch the meaning of 'confidence' to breaking point, why could they not rather have extended the scope of the patchy but very real elements of genuine privacy rights that have long existed in English law? The reluctance of the courts to try to develop a law of privacy in the way that, say, the law of negligence was developed, stands in marked contrast to their radical approach to the law of confidence. Why should this be so? It may not be entirely coincidental that the concept of privacy is anathema to the press and the media generally, whose activities would inevitably be severely curbed by a fully fledged right of privacy. By contrast, confidence or confidentiality appears an innocuous concept.

In *A v B*[27] the Court of Appeal set out an elaborate set of guidelines for use in cases involving considerations of confidence or privacy. The sixth of these guidelines reads as follows:

> (vi) It is most unlikely that any purpose will be served by a judge seeking to decide whether there exists a new cause of action in tort which protects privacy. In the great majority of situations, if not all situations, where the protection of privacy is justified, relating to events after the 1998 [Human Rights] Act came into force, an action for breach of confidence now, will, where this is appropriate, provide the necessary protection. This means that at first instance it can be readily accepted that it is not necessary to tackle the vexed question of whether there is a separate cause of action based upon a new tort involving the infringement of privacy.[28]

This less than reassuring 'guideline' at one and the same time admits the uncertainty of the law in this area while asserting that breach of confidence will serve as a substitute for a privacy suit 'in the great majority of situations, if not all situations, where the protection of privacy is justified'. First, as we have already seen, in regard for example to the *Peck* case, no matter how much it is stretched the scope of breach of confidence is certainly not coextensive with that of invasion of privacy. Moreover, this 'guideline' leaves a question mark hanging over the question of when and in what circumstances 'the protection of privacy is justified'.[29]

The definition of 'confidence' provided in *A v B* is hardly more illuminating:

> A duty of confidence will arise whenever the party subject to the duty is in a situation where he either knows or ought to know that the other person can reasonably expect his privacy to be protected.[30]

The case of *A v B* itself involved the extramarital affairs of a well-known football player with two women, who offered their stories for sale to the tabloid press. To prevent his wife from finding out, the footballer took out an interim injunction to stop publication. This was initially granted by a judge but was set aside by the Court of Appeal.

The question before the court was whether adulterous relationships impose a duty of confidentiality on the parties involved. The Court of Appeal, disagreeing with the judge, said no:

> Relationships of the sort which A [the footballer] had with C and D are not the categories of relationships which the court should be astute to protect when the other parties to the relationships do not want them to remain confidential. Any injunction granted after a trial would have to be permanent. It is most unlikely such an injunction would ever be granted.[31]

And:

> (47) We do not go so far as to say that relationships of the class being considered here can never be entitled to any confidentiality. We prefer to adopt [the] view that the situation is one at the outer limits of relationships which require the protection of the law. The fact that it attracts the protection of the law does not mean, however, that an injunction should be granted to provide that protection. In our view to grant an injunction would be an unjustified interference with the freedom of the press.
> (48) Once it is accepted that the freedom of the press should prevail, then the form of reporting in the press is not a matter for the courts but for the Press Complaints Commission and the customers of the newspaper concerned.[32]

We can only wonder how the law could have reached such a pass as even to be considering whether an extramarital fling could possibly impose a duty of confidentiality on the parties concerned.

Yet this is not the only case of its kind. In *Theakston v MGN*[33] the issue was whether Jamie Theakston's visit to a brothel had the quality of confidence about it. The prostitute in question had offered her story to a Sunday tabloid, together with candid photographs taken at the brothel without Mr Theakston's knowledge or consent. When contacted for his reaction, Jamie Theakston, a television presenter, sought an injunction to restrain publication of the photographs. The application was successful, with the judge holding that at trial an injunction restraining publication of photographs was more likely to succeed than one applicable to the written word.

It is hard to understand why the outcome in *Theakston* was different from that in *A v B*, where the initial interim injunction was discharged. Does the relationship between a prostitute and her 'client' have the inherent quality of confidentiality about it? The suggestion is laughable and was not accepted in *Theakston* (with the rider that it might become confidential in the unlikely event of a contractual stipulation between the two parties that it should be kept secret). Why then was an injunction granted? In particular, it was recognized that, even though a brothel could hardly be regarded as a private place, publication of the pictures would be particularly intrusive into Jamie Theakston's private life. It was also relevant that the photographs had been taken without his knowledge, let alone his consent, and that a brothel was not the sort of place where a man could reasonably expect to be photographed without his express consent. Moreover, it was held, there was no public interest in publishing the photographs. So far as the pictures were concerned, therefore, Mr Theakston's Article 8 rights outweighed the newspaper's right of freedom of expression under Article 10. But the balance was reversed when it came to publication of the article itself.

This decision was dictated more by common sense than by law. For, as the judge pointed out, confidentiality as applied to sexual encounters varies according to the degree of intimacy of the relationship:

> [60] Sexual relations within marriage at home would be at one end of the range or matrix of circumstances to be protected from most forms of disclosure; a one night stand with a recent acquaintance in a hotel bedroom might very well be protected from press publicity. A transitory engagement in a brothel is yet further away.

The judge in *Theakston* expressly labelled the *Flitcroft* situation as 'the outer limit of what is confidential', an opinion endorsed by the Court of Appeal in *A v B* itself.[34]

The judge in *Theakston* specifically distinguished the 'relationship' between prostitute and client from the relationship in an extramarital affair as in *A v B*.[35] And 'I do not consider it likely that the nature or detail of the sexual activities engaged in within the brothel are confidential.'[36] In addition, 'Any confidentiality would be one-sided.'

But if a brothel visit has nothing of the quality of confidentiality about it, what possible basis could there be for granting an injunction (albeit in regard to the photographs but not the text)? The judge made the point that this

> involved no particular extension of the law of confidentiality and that the publication of such photographs would be particularly intrusive into the Claimant's own personality. I considered that even though the fact that the Claimant went to the brothel and the details as to what he did there were not to be restrained from publication, the publication of photographs taken there without his consent could still constitute an intrusion into his private and personal life and would do so in a peculiarly humiliating and damaging way. It did not seem to me remotely inherent in going to a brothel that what was done inside would be photographed, let alone that any photographs would be published.[37]

Although the judge was careful not to say so, in the absence of confidentiality the only basis for any kind of injunction, however narrow, is privacy – a concept that is supposedly non-existent in English law.

In Garry Flitcroft's case there were no pictures involved. Would the Court of Appeal have upheld the judge's decision to give him an injunction had there been any? There is no reference to this point in the judgment. But, as cited above, there is a good deal on freedom of the press.

Tribute is also paid to the newspaper's 'public interest' defence, the last refuge of every scandalmongering 'investigative' journalist.[38] The relevant passage is quoted in full on page 138f.

The concept of 'public interest' proper, namely legitimate right, is here first distinguished from 'interest' in the sense of mere curiosity. But there then seems to be a suggestion that if the public have an 'understandable interest' in something then this somehow gives them a 'legitimate interest' in being informed of it. Yet the word 'interest' actually has a very different meaning in the phrase 'understandable interest' (where 'interest' really just means 'curiosity') from its sense in the phrase 'legitimate interest' (where 'interest' is equivalent to 'legitimate right').

Does this mean that if the public are curious about something, they have a legitimate right to be kept informed of it? And if so, does this mean that the press have a legally protected right to pander to the public's prurient imagination and insatiable appetite for scandal? No explanation is given for this conceptual slide. But if it is accepted as authoritative, it can only bolster yet further the privileged position of the press as enhanced by section 12 of the HRA.

The underlying reason for the knots that the courts have tied themselves into over this is the increasingly strained definition that they have given to the concepts of 'confidence' and 'confidentiality', which in turn appears to be motivated by a dread of developing the law so as to afford genuine protection for privacy.

The classic statement of the criteria for an action for breach of confidence still remains an oft-quoted passage from the judgment of Sir Robert Megarry J in *Coco v AN Clark (Engineers) Ltd*:[39]

> In my judgment three elements are normally required if, apart from contract, a case of breach of confidence is to succeed. First, the information itself, in the words of Lord Greene MR . . . must 'have the necessary quality of confidence about it'. Secondly, that information must have been imparted in circumstances importing an obligation of confidence. Thirdly, there must be an unauthorised use of that information to the detriment of the party communicating it.[40]

What is meant by, information having 'the necessary quality of confidence about it'? This was further explained by Lord Greene MR in the cited passage:

> The information, to be confidential must, I apprehend, apart from contract, have the necessary quality of confidence about it, namely, it must not be something which is public property and public knowledge.[41]

The second requirement was explained a little later in *Coco* itself:

> It seems to me that if the circumstances are such that any reasonable man standing in the shoes of the recipient of the information would have realised that upon reasonable grounds the information was being given to him in confidence, then this should suffice to impose upon him the equitable obligation of confidence.[42]

The original meaning of breach of confidence is well illustrated by the old case of *Pollard v Photographic Co*, in which a woman engaged a photographer to produce a portrait of herself for her own private use. When she discovered that the photographer had used her image in Christmas cards which were on sale in his shop to the general public, she successfully sued him for both breach of contract and breach of confidence, or what the judge termed 'a gross breach of faith'.[43]

It is not hard to see how this case qualifies under Megarry J's threefold set of criteria. First, did the information have the necessary quality of confidence about it? The relevant information here is Mrs Pollard's photographic likeness. Although she was not photographed in the nude or in any compromising situation, her image was not in the public domain and so could easily be held to have been confidential in nature. Secondly, ought the photographer to have realized that he was under a confidential obligation in regard to the photograph? Even if Mrs Pollard had not spelled out the precise purpose for which she wanted her picture taken, it must have been obvious to the photographer that he could not simply use the photograph for his own purposes without her express permission. Thirdly, did the photographer's unauthorized use of the photograph cause the subject to suffer any detriment? Anyone seeing her picture adorning commercially produced Christmas cards was likely to assume not only that she had given her consent but also that she was being paid for doing so – very possibly damaging her reputation as a result.

What if, instead of going to the photographer's studio and sitting for a portrait, Mrs Pollard had been secretly photographed by him in her own home and he had then used the pictures on Christmas cards? Clearly, this would have made the photographer even more culpable than in the actual scenario. But the absence of any kind of relationship between photographer and subject places tremendous strain on the very concept of confidentiality.

This was recognized by Lord Denning in regard to the old case of *Wyatt v Wilson*,[44] concerning an engraving of King George III 'during his illness'. The Lord Chancellor, Lord Eldon, is quoted as remarking in his judgment in that case: 'If one of the late king's physicians had kept a diary of what he heard and saw, this Court would not, in the king's lifetime, have permitted him to print or publish it.' Lord Denning's comment is illuminating:

> That observation is significant. It is the first instance I know of a right of privacy as distinct from a right of confidence. The King had not given any confidential information to the physician. But by publishing the diary the physician would infringe the King's right of privacy. King George III, as you will remember, went off his head. Suppose the physician had written in his diary: 'The King walked into the garden and behold, like the Emperor in the fable, he had no clothes' and he proposed to publish it. Lord Eldon would, I am sure, have granted an injunction to restrain the publisher. To bring it to modern times: Suppose a photographer with a long-distance lens took a picture of a prominent person in a loving embrace in his garden with a woman who was not his wife. Surely an injunction would be granted to stop it being published. The only cause of action, so far as I know, would be for infringement of privacy.[45]

Here, as always, Lord Denning was ready to grasp the nettle. He recognized that, although there is a good deal of overlap between confidentiality and privacy, there comes a point where confidentiality is no longer applicable but privacy rights still need protecting.

The obvious thing for the courts to do in these circumstances would have been to extend the common law to cover privacy rights, as happened in the United States, which now boasts an impressive body of privacy laws – all ultimately resting on the English case of *Prince Albert v Strange*.[46] But this course has been deliberately eschewed by the English judiciary, who have remained as loath to develop a law of privacy as they have been eager to expand the scope of breach of confidence. It may not be entirely irrelevant to note that, though the press is no lover of the law of confidentiality, a fully fledged privacy law would be total anathema to them.

Lord Denning's analysis of the hypothetical case of the long-lens photographer has not been widely followed. Here is a contrasting recent comment by a contemporary judge on the same situation:

> If someone with a telephoto lens were to take from a distance and with no authority a picture of another engaged in some private act, his subsequent disclosure of the photograph would, in my judgment, as surely amount to a breach of confidence as if he had found or stolen a letter or diary in which the act was recounted and proceeded to publish it. In such a case, the law would protect what might reasonably be called a right of privacy, although the name accorded to the cause of action would be breach of confidence.47

The implication here is that it makes little difference whether the cause of action is labelled 'invasion of privacy' or 'breach of confidence'. There is an air of unreality about debates over whether the 'relationship' between a prostitute and her 'trick' could possibly have the quality of confidentiality about it. But the real problem is that, even with the definition of 'confidence' or 'confidentiality' stretched to breaking point, there comes a stage where privacy rights cannot possibly be covered by it. The case of Geoffrey Peck is a good example, and his victory in Strasbourg may perhaps point towards the eventual creation – preferably by statute rather than by judge-made law – of a true law of privacy in the United Kingdom.

## PRIVATE LIFE

Where privacy can be brought under the 'right to respect for private and family life' it will of course be covered by Article 8, but the dividing line between privacy proper and 'private life' is narrow indeed, as was shown in a recent case involving homosexual sex.[48]

The applicant was a practising homosexual. His house was searched by police, and videos showing the applicant engaged in group homosexual sex were seized. He was convicted of gross indecency between men under the Sexual Offences Act 1956, s 13 and the Sexual Offences Act 1967, s 1(2)(a) . He was conditionally discharged for two years. He applied to Strasbourg claiming that his conviction constituted a violation under Article 8 and was also a breach of Article 14 by discriminating against homosexuals by comparison with heterosexual sexual activity.

The Strasbourg court held that his conviction was based not on the videos but on his own involvement in sex acts, thus engaging Article 8. It was also found that there was no risk of injury to anyone in the acts concerned. The doctrine was enunciated that the greater the degree of privacy, the narrower the margin of appreciation. There was no 'pressing social need' justifying legislation or proceedings against the applicant. The court found unanimously in his favour under Article 8, so there was no need to consider Article 14. He was awarded damages of £20,000 plus £12,000 in costs.

In *Sutherland v UK*[49] the complaint was that by fixing the age of consent for homosexual sex at 18 rather than 16 the United Kingdom was discriminating against homosexuals. The Strasbourg Commission held that this constituted a violation of Article l4 in conjunction with Article 8. The argument that reducing the age of consent would expose young boys to 'recruitment' by older homosexuals was rejected. This case is particularly interesting in view of the fact that the applicant had not been prosecuted or even threatened with prosecution, thus giving a very wide interpretation to the requirement in Article 34 that an applicant had to be a 'victim' of the alleged violation complained of.

## PRIVACY PROTECTION FOR KILLERS

As so often in human rights law, it is murderers whose rights have been in the vanguard. Despite all the dithering about the privacy rights of decent law-abiding citizens, some of the most notorious murderers and killers have had no trouble in claiming such rights.[50]

### Notes

1 *Prince Albert v Strange* (1848) 2 De G & Sm 652. See Michael Arnheim (1988) Computer software and the law, *Solicitors Journal*, vol 132, p 674.
2 Samuel Warren and Louis Brandeis (1890) The right to privacy, *Harvard Law Review*, 4 December, pp 193–220.
3 See F W Maitland (1936) *The Forms of Action at Common Law*, Cambridge, pp 53 ff.
4 See *Entick v Carrington* (1765), State Trials xix, 1044–Pratt CJ.
5 *Hurst v Picture Theatres Ltd* [1915] 1 KB 1.
6 *Kaye v Robertson and Another* [1990] *The Times*, March 21 (Court of Appeal).
7 *Douglas v Hello!* [2001] 2 All ER 289 at 316, §125.
8 *Douglas v Hello!* [2001] 2 All ER 289 at 316, §110.
9 *X v Netherlands* (1985) 8 EHRR 235 at 239–240, §23.
10 *Douglas v Hello!* [2001] 2 All ER 289 at 316, §136.
11 *Wainwright v Home Office* [2002] 3 WLR 405.
12 *Michael Douglas and Catherine Zeta-Jones v Hello!* [2003] EWHC 786 (Ch), §229 per Lindsay J.
13 See Peck UK 28/01/2003, No. 44647/98.
14 *Earl Spencer and Countess Spencer* 16/01/1998 28851/95; 28852/95.

15 *Peck v UK* 28/01/2003, no 44647/98.
16 *Ibid*, cited §33.
17 *PG and JH v UK* no 44787/98 S57, (2001) *The Times*, 19 October.
18 *Peck v UK* 28/01/2003, no 44647/98, §60.
19 *Ibid*, §62–63.
20 *Ibid*, §76.
21 *Ibid*, §79.
22 *Ibid*, §86.
23 *Ibid*, §77.
24 *Ibid*, §87.
25 *Ibid*, §106–107.
26 *Ibid*, §79. Cf *Stephen Arthur Perry v UK*, ECtHR, 17 July 2003, Application no 00063737/00. The use in evidence of a secretly filmed videotape was held to constitute a breach of ECHR Article 8(1), but this was not a case involving CCTV.
27 *A v B* [2002] 2 All ER 545.
28 *A v B* [2002] 2 All ER 545 at 552, §11(vi), per Lord Woolf CJ.
29 *Peck v UK* ECtHR 28/01/2003, no 44647/98.
30 *A v B* [2002] 2 All ER 545 at 553, §11(ix), per Lord Woolf CJ.
31 *A v B* at 563 §45.
32 *A v B* at 563 §§47–48.
33 *Theakston v MGN Ltd* [2002] EWHC 137 (QB) [2002] All ER (D) 182 (Feb).
34 *Theakston v MGN Ltd* [2002] EWHC 137 S61 cited in *A v B* §47.
35 *A v B* [2002] 2 All ER 545 at §61.
36 *Ibid*, at §74.
37 *Theakston v MGN Ltd* [2002] EWHC 137, §78.
38 *A v B* [2002] 2 All ER 545, 554–555, §11(xii).
39 *Coco v AN Clark (Engineers) Ltd* [1969] RPC 41.
40 *Ibid*, at 47 cited in *Douglas v Hello!* (Lindsay J – 11 April 2003) [2003] EWHC 786 (Ch) §182.
41 *Saltman Engineering v Campbell Engineering* (1948) 65 RPC 203 at 215.
42 *Coco v AN Clark* [1969] RPC 41 at 48.
43 *Pollard v Photographic Co* (1889) 40 ChD 345.
44 *Wyatt v Wilson* (1820 – unreported).
45 Lord Denning, (1982) *What Next in the Law?*, p 222.
46 *Prince Albert v Strange* (1849) 1 Mac & G 25 (LC).
47 *Hellewell v Chief Constable of Derbyshire* [1995] 4 All ER 473 at 476, per Laws J.
48 *ADT v UK EHRR* (31/7/2000–00/198).
49 *Sutherland v UK* (1998) EHRLR 117.
50 See *Venables and Thompson v News Group Newspapers* [2001] 1 All ER 908 at 913. Cf *Iveson v Harris* (1802) 32 ER 102 at 104, per Lord Eldon LC. On Venables and Thompson see Chapter 6; on Mary Bell see Chapter 3. Another example of special treatment for a killer is the luxury accommodation provided in prison to Abdel al Megrahi, the Lockerbie mass-murderer. The *Guardian*, 20 November 2003.

9

# Property rights

**Q. Are property rights protected by the Convention?**
*A. Yes – to some extent.*

Article 1 of Protocol 1 to the Convention, which is one of the articles incorporated into UK law by the HRA, reads as follows:

## THE FIRST PROTOCOL

**Article 1**
***Protection of property***

Every natural or legal person is entitled to the peaceful enjoyment of his possessions. No one shall be deprived of his possessions except in the public interest and subject to the conditions provided for by law and by the general principles of international law.

The preceding provisions shall not, however, in any way impair the right of a State to enforce such laws as it deems necessary to control the use of property, in accordance with the general interest or to secure the payment of taxes or other contributions or penalties.

The way this right is interpreted by Strasbourg is perhaps best explained by *Sporrong and Lönnroth v Sweden*.[1]

**Q. Can a compulsory purchase order amount to a violation of Art 1, Protocol 1 even if it is never acted upon?**
***A. In certain circumstances, yes.***

The case of *Sporrong and Lönnroth v Sweden* is a classic example of the way the Convention can be used to protect private property rights. The case concerned permits that had been issued by the Swedish government allowing the City of Stockholm to expropriate certain land owned by the applicants and prohibiting the applicants from building on that land in the meantime. Although one of the permits remained in force for no less than 23 years the land in question was never taken over by Stockholm. The applicants did not challenge the lawfulness of the expropriation permits or the ban on construction, but their case was that the very existence of the permits and prohibition amounted to an infringement of their right to the 'peaceful enjoyment' of their property contrary to Article 1, Protocol 1. In addition, they claimed, there was no effective recourse to the Swedish courts on this matter, so there was a violation of Article 6(1) (right to a fair trial) as well.

The applicants won in spectacular fashion on both counts. But the real interest of the case lies in the Strasbourg court's now classic analysis of Article 1, Protocol 1:

> The Article comprises three distinct rules. The first rule, which is of a general nature, enounces [sic] the principle of peaceful enjoyment of property; it is set out in the first sentence of the first paragraph. The second rule covers deprivation of possessions and subjects it to certain conditions; it appears in the second sentence of the same paragraph. The third rule recognises that the States are entitled, amongst other things, to control the use of property in accordance with the general interest, by enforcing such laws as they deem necessary for the purpose; it is contained in the second paragraph.[2]

The court considered each of these rules separately. The expropriation permits, it was held, constituted an interference within rule one. However, as there was no actual expropriation in this case the second rule did not apply. As for the third rule, it was held that this was breached by the prohibition on construction.

This case also contains classic statements on the fundamental Strasbourg principles of proportionality and margin of appreciation, stressing that the key to both is a balancing exercise. Proportionality required that:

> a fair balance was struck between the demands of the general interest of the community and the requirements of the protection of the individual's fundamental rights. The search for this balance is inherent in the whole of the Convention and is also reflected in the structure of Article 1 (Protocol 1).[3]

On the margin of appreciation the position was put in these terms:

> In an area as complex and difficult as that of the development of large cities, the Contracting States should enjoy a wide margin of appreciation in order to implement their town-planning policy. Nevertheless, the Court cannot fail to exercise its power of review and must determine whether the requisite balance was maintained in a manner consonant with the applicants' right to the 'peaceful enjoyment of [their] possessions', within the meaning of the first sentence of Article 1.[4]

Another basic point established in this case was that the applicants' property rights were 'civil rights' within Article 6(1) . This meant that the applicants were entitled to access to 'an independent and impartial tribunal established by law'. It was held that although the Swedish government's decision to issue the expropriation permits could have been challenged by judicial review in the Swedish Administrative Court, this was a very restricted remedy and the Administrative Court was not allowed to determine the merits of the government's decision. So there was a violation of Article 6(1) as well.

**Q. Does Article 1, Protocol 1 apply only to land or real property, or is it also applicable to movable property?**

***A. It is applicable to both.***

**Q. Can confiscation of movable property amount to a violation of Article 1, Protocol 1?**

***A. Yes, but only if it is a permanent deprivation and is not lawful and not in pursuit of a legitimate aim.***

Perhaps the best illustration is provided by *The Little Red Schoolbook*,[5] which is best known as a case about obscenity but is also of interest in regard to property rights, in two respects. First, copies of the book were seized by the police and then, after the conviction of its publisher, Richard Handyside, under the Obscene Publications Acts 1959 and 1964, the print matrix and the remaining copies of the book were also ordered to be confiscated and destroyed.

Richard Handyside's application to Strasbourg claimed a violation of his rights not only under Article 10 (freedom of expression) but also under Article 1, Protocol 1. However, he was no more successful under this head than under Article 10. As far as the initial seizure was concerned, the Strasbourg court found no violation of the article as this was only temporary and the books would have been returned if the publisher had been acquitted. But does the article in question not use the phrase 'deprived of his possessions'? And could this not apply to a temporary seizure just as well as to permanent forfeiture? The court here made an interesting observation. The phrase 'deprived of his possessions', it was pointed out, was really a mistranslation of the original French text, which should more accurately be translated 'deprived of ownership'. So only a permanent deprivation would qualify under that rule.

A temporary seizure would however qualify as 'control of the use of property' in the second paragraph of the article. But it was held that the Contracting States are here allowed a wide margin of appreciation, as it is for them to decide on the 'necessity' for interference with these rights: 'Consequently, the European Court must restrict itself to supervising the lawfulness and the purpose of the restriction in question.' The court accepted that the seizure was lawful, so leaving only the question of whether it pursued a 'legitimate aim'. As the purpose of the forfeiture was the protection of morals and this was within the 'general interest', there was no violation.[6]

What then about the forfeiture and destruction ordered by the English court after the publisher's conviction? For similar reasons no violation of property rights was found here either.[7]

The aim of the British legislation was 'the protection of morals' within Article 10(2). But was this 'necessary in a democratic society'? By a majority of 8 to 5 the Human Rights Commission found that there was no violation of Article 10 ('freedom of expression'), and the Strasbourg court agreed with this result by 13 votes to 1: *Handyside v United Kingdom*.[8]

This case represents the high water mark of the margin of appreciation. Convention protection, it was held, was subsidiary to national systems safeguarding human rights. In the absence of a uniform conception of morals there had to be a considerable domestic margin of appreciation, subject to European supervision.

In addition, the fact that *The Little Red Schoolbook* was intended for a teenage market no doubt told against it. But it is worth noting that the book had been published in Denmark and several other countries without incident – and that even in Scotland, where a bookseller was charged under Scots indecency laws, he was acquitted because the court found that the book was neither obscene nor indecent.

**Q. Can landowners be forced to sell their land to other private persons?**
***A. Yes, if it is deemed to be in 'the general interest'.***

The Leasehold Reform Act 1967 gave long leaseholders the right in certain circumstances to compel the freeholder of the property in question to sell it to them. Among the freeholders worst hit by this legislation was the Duke of Westminster, who owned about 2,000 houses in Belgravia alone. Eighty Belgravia leaseholders exercised their rights under the 1967 Act to purchase the freehold. Besides the fact that he had been forced to sell against his will, the Duke of Westminster claimed that he had lost well over £1 million as a result, this being the difference between the purchase price actually paid and the market value.[9]

The Duke took the matter to Strasbourg, claiming violation of his rights under Article 1 of Protocol 1 and also under Article 6(1) (right to a fair trial) and Article 14 (discrimination) of the Convention. The Strasbourg court found against him, however. The case is interesting from several points of view, not least by way of contrast with the *Sporrong* case discussed above, where the applicants were successful.

The Duke of Westminster asked the court to examine each transaction to determine whether it complied with Article 1 of Protocol 1 or not. But the court rejected this approach in favour of a much more radical one, focusing instead on whether the 1967 Act itself was compatible with the Convention. It was undeniable that the Duke had been 'deprived of his possessions' within Article 1 of Protocol 1, but the question was whether this was 'in the public interest'. This phrase was given a wide meaning. The problem was that the purchase of the freeholds (that is, enfranchisement) did not benefit the public at large but only a number of private individuals. How then could it possibly be in the public interest? But the court held that 'a taking of property effected in pursuance of legitimate social, economic or other policies may be in the public interest, even if the community at large has no direct use or enjoyment of the property taken'.[10]

Enfranchisement was therefore 'in the public interest', and the Strasbourg court further justified its decision by reference to the curiously-named doctrine of the margin of appreciation, referring to the latitude given to the national authorities in each state. In this case the Strasbourg court held that the UK national authorities were in a better position to know what was 'in the public interest' than an international court like itself. In Strasbourg-speak, the court here allowed the United Kingdom a wide margin of appreciation:

> The margin of appreciation is wide enough to cover legislation aimed at securing greater social justice in the sphere of people's homes, even where such legislation interferes with existing contractual relations between private parties and confers no direct benefit on the State or the community at large.[11]

The 1967 Act therefore passed the test of pursuing a 'legitimate aim', another Strasbourg buzz-phrase. It also satisfied the requirement of *proportionality*, yet another Strasbourg favourite. The relevant test here was whether a 'fair balance' had been struck 'between the demands of the general interest of the community and the requirements of the protection of the individual's fundamental rights'.[12]

The Duke also lost on his claim that the enfranchisement law *discriminated* against him and therefore violated his rights under Article 14. Here too the Strasbourg court produced a classic definition:

> For the purposes of Art 14, a difference of treatment is discriminatory if it has no objective and reasonable justification, that is, if it does not pursue a legitimate aim or if there is not a reasonable relationship of proportionality between the means employed and the aim sought to be realised.[13]

The Duke's complaint under Article 6(1) (right to a fair trial) was no more successful. Here his objection was that the individual merits of an enfranchisement could not be challenged in a court or tribunal. But the court held that access to a tribunal to consider any alleged non-compliance satisfied Article 6(1).

**Q. Is taxation subject to human rights law?**
***A. Not usually, but it can be in special circumstances.***

Who was responsible for repairs to the chancel of a parish church? This was the unlikely subject of a recent human rights case. What made it all the more unlikely is that it was essentially a case about taxation, which had always been held by Strasbourg to be a matter for individual national legislatures unless their decision was 'devoid of reasonable foundation'.[14] In other words, this is an area in which there is a wide margin of appreciation.

Mr and Mrs Wallbank were the lay rectors of a parish church in Warwickshire. This meant that they were the freehold owners of a field allotted to a previous lay rector in 1743. The purpose of the grant of land to lay rectors was to enable them to defray the costs of certain church repairs out of the rents and profits which they derived from their allotted piece of land.

When the Parochial Church Council (PCC) served a notice on the Wallbanks under the Chancel Repairs Act 1932 calling upon them to finance chancel repairs to the tune of over £95,000 the Wallbanks took the matter to court. They disputed their liability to pay, contending that the payment demand violated their right to protection of their property under Article 1 of Protocol 1 to the Convention and that it was also contrary to the prohibition of discrimination under Article 14.

At first instance their defence was rejected out of hand. It was the settled law of England, held the judge, that a lay rector was responsible for chancel repairs even though the property owned by that lay rector formed only part of a larger parcel of rectorial land. It was also held that the obligation to repair did not infringe any of the Wallbanks' Convention rights.

This decision was reversed on appeal. Was the PCC a 'public authority' within HRA s 6? The Court of Appeal held that it was, though this was by no means clear-cut. During the debate in Parliament on HRA s 13, the then Home Secretary, Jack Straw, remarked that:

> Much of what the churches do is, in the legal context and in the context of the European Convention on Human Rights, essentially private in nature . . . . For example, the regulation of divine worship, the administration of the sacrament, admission to church membership or to the priesthood and decisions of parochial church councils about the running of the parish church are, in our judgment, all private matters. In such matters the churches will not be public authorities; the requirement to comply with Convention rights will not bite on them.[15]

The Court of Appeal concluded that Article 1, Protocol 1 protected the Wallbanks' property from arbitrary taxation, which the demand for payment of the chancel repairs was seen to be.

As usual, everything was up for grabs. Long-standing domestic precedent was cast aside; a somewhat dubious definition of 'public authority' was relied upon; and a Convention right about the protection of property was reinterpreted to apply to a purely financial demand.[16]

**Q. Do you have the right to live in a caravan on your own land?**
***A. Not necessarily, especially if you fall foul of planning laws.***

June Buckley was a gypsy. She lived with her three children in caravans parked on land owned by herself. She applied to the local council for planning permission for the caravans but was refused and was ordered to remove them within a month. Her appeal to the Secretary of State for the Environment was dismissed. She never removed the caravans and was prosecuted several times. She took her case to Strasbourg, claiming that the council had violated her right to respect for her private and family life under Article 8(1) by prohibiting her from living in caravans on her own land as required by the traditional gypsy lifestyle. The United Kingdom countered this in terms of the restrictions contained in Article 8(2), namely that the enforcement notice requiring the caravans to be removed was 'in accordance with the law' and 'necessary in a democratic society' in the interests of 'public safety', 'the economic well-being of the country', 'the protection of health' and 'the protection of the rights of others'.

The case was decided on the basis of the margin of appreciation. In this case a wide margin was allowed to the United Kingdom, but subject to review by the Strasbourg court to determine whether the national decisions were compatible with the Convention and proportionate to the legitimate aims pursued. Surprisingly perhaps, in this case it was held by a majority of six votes to three that the national authorities had not exceeded their margin of appreciation, so that there was no violation of Article 8.

June Buckley had also put in a linked Article 14 plus Article 8 claim on the ground that her treatment at the hands of the UK authorities had discriminated against her in her attempt to follow a traditional gypsy lifestyle. This claim was also rejected by Strasbourg, which accepted the United Kingdom's submission that, far from discriminating against the gypsy lifestyle, national policy actually encouraged them to cater for their own needs.[17]

## Notes

1 *Sporrong and Lönnroth v Sweden* (1982) 5 EHRR 35.
2 *Ibid*, at para 61.
3 *Ibid*, at para 69.
4 *Ibid*, at para 69.
5 *Handyside v UK* (1976) 1 EHRR 737.
6 *Ibid*, at para 62.
7 *Ibid*, at para 63.
8 *Ibid*.
9 *James v UK* (1986) 8 EHRR 123.
10 *Ibid*, at para 45.
11 *Ibid*, at para 47.
12 *Ibid*, at para 50. See *Sporrong and Lönnroth v Sweden* (1982) 5 EHRR 35.
13 *James v UK* (1986) 8 EHRR 123, at para 75.
14 See *Gasus Dosier- und Fordertechnik GmbH v Netherlands* (1995) 20 EHRR 403 (S60) 95/6.
15 312 House of Commons Official Report (6th series) col 1015 (20 May 1998).
16 *Aston Cantlow PCC v Wallbank* [2001] EWCA Civ 713. This decision has now been reversed by the House of Lords: [2003] UKHL 37.
17 *Buckley v UK* (1997) 23 EHRR 101 96/35.

# 10

# Liberty and equality

It is sometimes assumed that the legal basis of individual liberty is the European Human Rights Convention, incorporated as it is into the Human Rights Act 1998. In fact liberty, or freedom of the individual, has since time immemorial formed the bedrock of the common law, and still does. Ironically, however, the interpretation now favoured by the courts makes the law less protective of the liberties of ordinary citizens than it used to be.

'Liberty and security of person' are guaranteed under Article 5 of the Human Rights Convention, but this right is subject to six exceptions where 'lawful arrest or detention' is sanctioned.

**Article 5**

***Right to liberty and security***

1. Everyone has the right to liberty and security of person. No one shall be deprived of his liberty save in the following cases and in accordance with a procedure prescribed by law:
   a) the lawful detention of a person after conviction by a competent court;
   b) the lawful arrest or detention of a person for non-compliance with the lawful order of a court or in order to secure the fulfilment of any obligation prescribed by law;
   c) the lawful arrest or detention of a person effected for the purpose of bringing him before the competent legal authority on reasonable suspicion of having committed an offence or fleeing after having done so;
   d) the detention of a minor by lawful order for the purpose of educational supervision or his lawful detention for the purpose of bringing him before the competent legal authority;

e) the lawful detention of persons for the prevention of the spreading of infectious diseases, of persons of unsound mind, alcoholics or drug addicts or vagrants;
f) the lawful arrest or detention of a person to prevent his effecting an unauthorised entry into the country or of a person against whom action is being taken with a view to deportation or extradition.

2. Everyone who is arrested shall be informed promptly, in a language which he understands, of the reasons for his arrest and of any charge against him.
3. Everyone arrested or detained in accordance with the provisions of paragraph 1.c of this article shall be brought promptly before a judge or other officer authorised by law to exercise judicial power and shall be entitled to trial within a reasonable time or to release pending trial. Release may be conditioned by guarantees to appear for trial.
4. Everyone who is deprived of his liberty by arrest or detention shall be entitled to take proceedings by which the lawfulness of his detention shall be decided speedily by a court and his release ordered if the detention is not lawful.
5. Everyone who has been the victim of arrest or detention in contravention of the provisions of this article shall have an enforceable right to compensation.

## IS INDIVIDUAL LIBERTY NOT ALREADY SUFFICIENTLY PROTECTED UNDER THE COMMON LAW, WITHOUT THE NEED TO INVOKE THE CONVENTION?

Perhaps the most important provision in the whole of the Human Rights Act is section 11:

**11. Safeguard for existing human rights**

A person's reliance on a Convention right does not restrict –

(a) any other right or freedom conferred on him by or under any law having effect in any part of the United Kingdom; or
(b) his right to make any claim or bring any proceedings which he could make or bring apart from sections 7 to 9.

The effect of this is to preserve the rights and freedoms that were in existence before the coming into force of the Human Rights Act, including the right to enforce any such rights by means of legal action.

Article 53 of the Convention, which has not been incorporated into the Human Rights Act, contains a similar guarantee:

**Article 53**
***Safeguard for existing human rights***

Nothing in this Convention shall be construed as limiting or derogating from any of the human rights and fundamental freedoms which may ensured under the laws of any High Contracting Party or under any other agreement to which it is a Party.

What these two provisions chiefly protect are the rights enshrined in the common law. (See the discussion in Chapter 1.) It is generally assumed that these rights are inferior to those of the Convention. Common law rights, it is said, are essentially negative, while Convention rights are positive. The reason for this is supposedly that English law traditionally operated on the basis that anything that was not expressly forbidden was allowed, while the Convention provides guarantees protecting the rights that it enshrines.

This is somewhat misleading. So, for example, the famous old concept that 'An Englishman's home is his castle', discussed below, is negative in the sense that it allows you to do in your own home anything that is not specifically forbidden, for example having sex with a sheep. But it can also be seen as a guarantee of the right of citizens to go about their lawful business, as against anyone who interferes with that right, such as an intruder.

It should also be possible to read these broader considerations into Article 5 of the Convention. Most of the cases under Article 5 have been complaints about detention or imprisonment, and this is the way the article is generally understood. But does the wording not admit of a broader construction? 'Everyone has the right to liberty and security of person.' 'Liberty' is open to several interpretations, one of which is the right to do whatever you like as long as it does not interfere with anyone else's rights. 'Security' comes from a Latin root meaning 'lack of worry', or 'lack of anxiety'. What it means is the right to stay at home and go about your business without let or hindrance – and without having to look over your shoulder all the time.

Whether this broader interpretation can be read into Article 5 or not, it is part of the English common law – and has been since time immemorial. Eighteenth-century Britain was renowned for its high degree of liberty coupled with a high degree of inequality. This combination is not a paradox at all. It was the French Revolution that lumped 'liberty' and 'equality' together – adding 'fraternity' for good measure. In a very real sense, however, far from being complementary, liberty and equality are at loggerheads with each other.

One only has to think of such revolutionary egalitarian regimes as Maoist China to recognize this. China after the so-called 'Cultural Revolution' was arguably the most egalitarian society that the world had ever seen. Doctors were moved from the hospitals and the cities to work as peasants in the paddy fields – hence the term 'barefoot doctors' – and uneducated peasants took their places in the hospital wards and operating theatres up and down the country. It was a remarkably successful experiment in social engineering, levelling down and creating a uniformly dull and unquestioning Chinese society – with the one exception of Mao Tse-tung himself, who stood with a huge ladle stirring the social cauldron to make it as homogeneous as possible. The resultant equality was artificial and only produced by tight central control. In other words, equality was produced at the expense of liberty.

Also, one person's liberty may actually benefit from someone else's loss of liberty – another example of the way in which liberty and equality are at loggerheads with each other. The liberty of society as a whole benefits from the deprivation of the liberty of criminals. This is so obvious that it should hardly need stating, except for the fact that certain elements of the judiciary appear now to have become unduly solicitous of the rights of burglars and other criminals, including convicted murderers.

## DOES THE OLD MAXIM 'AN ENGLISHMAN'S HOME IS HIS CASTLE' HAVE ANY LEGAL STATUS?

The well-known adage 'An Englishman's home is his castle' is a modification of a maxim cited by Sir Edward Coke in a report of *Semayne's* case heard in 1605, but it was clearly a well-established principle by that time.[1]

> That the house of every one is to him as his castle and fortress, as well for his defence against injury and violence as for his repose; and altho' the life of a man is a thing precious and favoured in law; so that altho' a man kills another in his defence, or kills one *per infortun'*, ('by accident'), without any intent, yet it is felony, and in such case he shall forfeit his goods and chattels, for the great regard which the law has to a man's life; but if thieves come to a man's house to rob him, or murder, and the owner or his servants kill any of the thieves in defence of himself and his house, it is not felony, and he shall lose nothing, and therewith agree [there follow citations of some old cases]. So it is held in 21 Henry VII c. 39 every one may assemble his friends and neighbours to defend his house against violence: but he cannot assemble them to go with him to the market, or elsewhere for his safeguard against violence: and the reason of all this is, because *domus sua cuique est tutissimum refugium* ('Everyone's home is to him the safest refuge').

This remarkable statement reflects the sanctity in English law not only of private property, and in particular of the home, but even more so of the liberty of the law-abiding citizen. Coke is here in expansive mode, explaining that although killing a man in self-defence or even accidentally is normally a felony, this is not the case when a householder or his servants kill 'in defence of himself and his house' a thief who has come to rob or murder him. Backing this up with authority he then goes on to cite a statute dating from the reign of Henry VII (1485–1509), a century earlier, which specifically allows a householder to assemble his friends and neighbours 'to defend his house against violence'. The statute draws a sharp distinction between gathering supporters together at the house – which is allowed – and taking them on a vigilante expedition around the streets.

There are two key concepts here: those of home and of self-defence. First, Coke is at pains to distinguish the legal position if you kill someone threatening your home from that if you kill someone anywhere else. Second, he stresses the importance of self-defence. But what exactly is meant by that term? The Henry

VII statute is instructive here, as it permits a householder to 'assemble his friends and neighbours to defend his house against violence'. This can only mean that you are allowed under the law to prepare a welcoming party for the intending thieves or burglars and that you are exculpated if you kill them in the process.

## WHAT IS THE CURRENT LEGAL POSITION OF A HOUSEHOLDER WHO KILLS AN INTRUDER IN DEFENCE OF HIS OR HER LIFE OR PROPERTY?

Although the Henry VII law does not appear ever to have been repealed, it was not prayed in aid in a recent much-publicized case, and even if it had it would probably have been waved aside by the court. The case involved a householder, Tony Martin, who shot at two intruders to his remote home, aptly named Bleak House, killing one and wounding the other. Tony Martin based his case on self-defence, but by a majority of nine to two he was convicted of murder and wounding with intent, and was sentenced to life imprisonment.

On appeal his conviction was downgraded from murder to manslaughter and his sentence reduced from life to five years' imprisonment.[2] The basis of this decision was a finding of diminished responsibility in reliance upon psychiatric evidence which had not been adduced at trial. The judgment of the Court of Appeal was delivered by Lord Woolf CJ, who remarked that: 'At the time the offences were committed, Mr Martin was being burgled by the two people whom he shot. Because he was being burgled at the time there was considerable public sympathy for Mr Martin and media interest in his case. There were also suggestions that the law was in need of change.'

To say that Tony Martin had attracted 'considerable public sympathy' was an understatement. The reaction to his conviction for murder was little short of a public outcry. But his application for early release was rejected by the parole board, and his challenge of this decision by way of judicial review also failed, even though it turned out that there was evidence of Tony Martin's remorse that the Home Office had never before made available to Mr Martin's lawyers. The chairman of the parole board, a magistrate of 10 years' standing, was quoted as saying in reference to Mr Martin 'The man is dangerous. Our job, irrespective of what the press think, is to protect the public.' And again: 'Everyone should know that the most important consideration is the safety of the public. That is first, second and third, and comes before considering the liberty of the individual.'[3]

Tony Martin a threat to the public? This is tantamount to equating burglars with 'the public'. It may now be 'politically correct' to insist on the rights of burglars, but it obscures the fact that the safety of the public in general is threatened far more by burglars than by Tony Martin.

The main authority cited by the Court of Appeal was *Beckford v R*,[4] a Privy Council advice on an appeal from Jamaica. Solomon Beckford was a police officer who had shot and killed a suspect in the belief that the man was armed and posed a threat to the police officer's life. Like Tony Martin, therefore, Solomon Beckford pleaded self-defence but was found guilty of murder. However, his conviction was quashed by the Privy Council on the ground that the trial judge had misdirected the jury on the test for self-defence.

The correct test for self-defence was enunciated by the Court of Appeal in *Martin* as follows:

> When this defence is raised, the prosecution has the burden of satisfying the jury so that they are sure that the defendant was not acting in self-defence. A defendant is entitled to use reasonable force to protect himself, others for whom he is responsible and his property. In judging whether the defendant had only used reasonable force, the jury has to take into account all the circumstances, including the situation as the defendant honestly believes it to be at the time, when he was defending himself. It does not matter if the defendant was mistaken in his belief as long as his belief was genuine. Accordingly, the jury could only convict Mr Martin if either they did not believe his evidence that he was acting in self-defence or they thought that Mr Martin had used an unreasonable amount of force.[5]

In short, the test for self-defence enunciated here is twofold. First, the defendant has to have a 'genuine belief' that he or she was acting in self-defence. This is subjective. He or she may be mistaken, or his or her belief may be unreasonable. That makes no difference. As long as he or she really believes that he or she was acting in self-defence, this limb of the test is satisfied. But then comes the objective limb: did the defendant use a reasonable amount of force in the circumstances? In Lord Woolf's words, 'It is only if the jury are sure that the amount of force which was used was unreasonable that they are entitled to find a defendant guilty if he was acting in self-defence.'

Overarching these two limbs is the crucial matter of the burden and standard of proof. It is for the prosecution to prove either that the defendant did not have a genuine belief that he was acting in self-defence, or that the amount of force he used was not reasonable in the circumstances. Proving a negative is difficult at the best of times. Proving that a person did not have a certain belief is virtually impossible, especially as the reasonableness or rationality of that belief is immaterial. Deciding whether the amount of force used was excessive is a little easier. But even this has to be proved to the criminal standard of proof beyond reasonable doubt if a plea of self-defence is to be rejected.

Despite the heavy evidential burden involved in disproving a plea of self-defence, the Court of Appeal made no attempt to disturb what they took to be the jury's rejection of this defence on the part of Tony Martin. Moreover, no distinction was drawn between self-defence in a home situation and self-defence in any other situation. The *Beckford* case mentioned above was the only authority on self-defence cited by the Court of Appeal. Yet the circumstances of that case were very different from those of *Martin*. In particular, Solomon Beckford was not in his own home at the time of the shooting. Yet even in that case it was specifically stated by the Privy Council that '[A] man about to be attacked does not have to wait for his assailant to strike the first blow or fire the first shot: circumstances may justify a pre-emptive strike.'

Was it not relevant that the man shot dead by Tony Martin was an intruder in the process of burgling his home? To the law of self-defence in homicide as stated by the Court of Appeal this fact would appear to be of no consequence. It is true that the relevant statute law, section 3 of the Criminal Law Act 1967, makes no specific mention of protection of the home either:

> (1) A person may use such force as is reasonable in the circumstances in the prevention of crime, or in effecting or assisting in the lawful arrest of offenders or suspected offenders or of persons unlawfully at large.
> (2) Subsection (1) above shall replace the rules of the common law on the question when force used for a purpose mentioned in the subsection is justified by that purpose.

The key words here are 'in the circumstances'. What this means is that the amount of force that is to be regarded as reasonable will vary according to circumstances. Is this not where protection of one's home against burglars comes in? Is this not a relevant circumstance justifying greater force than might otherwise be the case? But does the provision in subsection 3(2) that subsection 3(1) replaces the rules of the common law not abrogate the old principle that a man's home is his castle? No, because 3(1) has built into it a variable in the words 'in the circumstances'. This is tailor-made to accommodate the old common law rule. And what about the statute of Henry VII? If, as appears to be the case, it was never repealed, the applicable principle would be *leges posteriores priores contrarias abrogant* – 'later statutes repeal earlier incompatible ones'. This is the doctrine of implied repeal, according to which an earlier statute will be deemed to have been repealed if incompatible with a later one. However, it is not a principle that is lightly invoked, and is only to be used subject to another ancient principle: *generalia specialibus non derogant* – 'general words do not detract from specific ones'. In short, if the old statute was not expressly repealed, then it must still be deemed to be in force, as the provisions of the 1967 act cited above do not contradict it, and even if they did, the 1967 Act, couched as it is in general terms, cannot overrule the very specific provisions of the Henry VII statute.

## IS IT TRUE THAT HOUSEHOLDERS ARE BETTER PROTECTED BY THE LAW IN THE UNITED STATES?

A comparison with the situation in the United States is instructive. The relevant law is stated as follows in *American Jurisprudence 2d*:

> The right of a person to defend his home from attack is a substantive right governed by rules analogous to those applicable to defense of the person, with the major exception that a person faced with danger of attack in his own home is under no duty to retreat. The modern rule as to homicide in defense of the habitation is that if an assault on a dwelling and an attempted forcible entry are made under such circumstances as to create a reasonable apprehension that it is the design of the assailant to commit a felony or to inflict on the inmates a personal injury which may result in the loss of life or great bodily harm, and the danger that the design will be carried into execution is imminent and present, the lawful occupant of the dwelling may lawfully prevent the entry, even by the taking of the life of the intruder. In such case, the occupant may meet the assailant at the threshold and prevent him from breaking in by any means rendered necessary by exigency, and upon the same ground and reason that one may defend himself from peril of life or great bodily harm by means fatal to the assailant, if rendered necessary by the exigency of the assault. This permits the taking of life in case the assailant purposes the commission of any felony, or other crime of violence to the person. In some jurisdictions statutes have been enacted expressly justifying homicides committed in defense of the habitation. Generally, however, a householder is deemed to have no right to take life to prevent a mere unlawful entry into his house, if the entry is not under such circumstances as to afford reasonable grounds for apprehension that the intruder's purpose is to take life, or to inflict serious bodily harm on the inmates, or to commit a felony.[6]

Under US common law, therefore, Tony Martin would have been entitled to kill the intruder as he did. This becomes all the clearer if we take each test individually:

**Q. Was there a forced entry to Mr Martin's property?**
*A. Yes.*

**Q. Were there 'reasonable grounds for apprehension that the intruder's purpose' was 'to commit a felony'?**
*A. Yes.*

Not only was there an 'apprehension' on Tony Martin's part, but it was accepted by the courts that the purpose of the intruders' visit to Bleak House was theft, and they had already committed the full offence of burglary by the time any shots were fired. (The term 'felony' is no longer used in English law, but burglary and robbery would both fall into this category.)

**Q. Was there a danger that this purpose was likely to be carried out imminently?**
*A. Yes. The shooting took place as the two intruders were in the process of breaking in.*

## THE BURGLAR'S REVENGE

Tony Martin was refused legal aid, but his surviving victim, a man of 33 with 37 convictions to his name, was allowed access to public funds to sue Mr Martin for damages for loss of earnings! At the time of writing the case had been abandoned in return for Tony Martin's undertaking not to counterclaim.

**If the English courts now come down hard on householders who kill intruders, why have they been so lenient towards real murderers?**

In further marked contrast to the way Tony Martin was treated by the English legal system was the treatment received by the young murderers of the two-year-old toddler, Jamie Bulger. Both were high-profile cases arousing very strong public feeling. In the case of Tony Martin public sympathy was plainly largely on his side; in the Bulger case the public were equally plainly revulsed by the brutal and senseless murder of an innocent baby. Yet in both cases the legal system was on the opposite side from that of public opinion.

Tony Martin, it is true, was partially successful in his appeal, as his conviction for murder was quashed and his sentence reduced from life to five years. But he was still branded a criminal, guilty of manslaughter, and left with a considerable amount of time to spend behind bars – in a situation where in the United States he would not have been guilty of any crime. A further indignity was visited upon Tony Martin by the grant of public funding (what used to be known as legal aid) for the surviving burglar, a man with a string of convictions, to sue Tony Martin in a civil action for trespass to the person. By contrast, Tony Martin's own appeal against his murder conviction was privately funded, and it was only once his appeal had been (partially) allowed that his counsel was able successfully to request costs out of central (public) funds.

The two killers of Jamie Bulger were only 10 years old at the time, yet it was an unbelievably brutal and horrific murder described by the trial judge as an act of 'unparallelled evil and barbarity' and by Lord Woolf MR (in 1997) as 'exceptionally horrific'. The murderers lured the innocent little child away from his mother at a shopping centre, abducted him, dragged him over two miles and subjected him to indescribable torture, including beating him over the head with a 28 lb iron bar and subjecting him to sexual abuse, before battering him to death and then laying his body on a railway line to make the murder look like an accident. They later even returned to the scene to join the many people laying flowers near where Jamie's body had been found.

After being convicted of murder, these two boys, Robert Thompson and Jon Venables, were sentenced to 'detention during Her Majesty's pleasure' under s 53(1) of the Children and Young Persons Act 1933, a mandatory indeterminate sentence with a tariff to be fixed by the Home Secretary for retribution and deterrence (that is, punishment). The trial judge expressed the view that the murderers would remain in custody for 'many, many years' until the Home Secretary was satisfied that they no longer posed a danger to the public. He suggested eight years as the minimum tariff period, Lord Chief Justice Taylor recommended 10 years and the Home Secretary finally set it at 15 years, but it was expected that the murderers would actually spend longer than this in custody.

The two young killers challenged this by means of judicial review – and won. The case went all the way to the House of Lords, where by three votes to two it was decided that the Home Secretary had acted 'unlawfully' by applying a tariff. By four votes to one it was decided that in fixing the tariff the Home Secretary was exercising a judicial power and, like a sentencing judge, should therefore have remained detached from the pressure of public opinion![7]

The one law lord who was in the minority throughout was Lord Lloyd, who stressed that the question before the court was not whether they agreed with the Home Secretary's decision but only whether that decision was lawful or not. Lord Goff joined him in holding that there was nothing unlawful in the Home Secretary's policy to employ a tariff nor in the setting of the tariff period at 15 years. As for the *way* in which the Home Secretary had chosen to exercise the power entrusted to him by Parliament, Lord Lloyd made the trenchant remark that:

> If the courts are going to tell the Home Secretary how to perform a function which has been entrusted to him, and to him alone, by Parliament, then there would appear to be no limit to the bounds of judicial review. Of course, the court will interfere if the Home Secretary acts unlawfully or abuses his powers, or behaves unfairly, or on any of the other well established grounds of judicial review. But there was nothing remotely unfair in the Secretary of State assessing the tariff on the information which he already had, without calling for further reports.[8]

Lord Lloyd's was a voice of fairness, logic and common sense crying in the wilderness. But the majority in the House of Lords did nevertheless admit that a sentence of 'detention during Her Majesty's pleasure' was meant to have a punitive element and was not purely intended to rehabilitate youthful offenders. The Home Secretary's power to set a tariff was also accepted, provided it was sufficiently flexible to enable him to vary it in the light of the development of the young offender in question. However, the 15-year tariff imposed on the two Bulger killers was quashed, and in the end they spent less than eight years in detention, none of it in an adult prison.[9]

The case went to Strasbourg, where the very right of the Home Secretary to be involved in the sentencing of Venables and Thompson was challenged – again successfully. The Strasbourg court pointed out that the fixing of the tariff amounted to 'a sentencing exercise', to which Article 6(1) of the Convention was therefore applicable. Article 6(1) guarantees a fair trial 'by an independent and impartial tribunal established by law'. 'Independent', said the Strasbourg court, meant 'independent of the parties to the case and also of the Executive. The Home Secretary, who set the applicant's tariff, was clearly not independent of the Executive, and it follows that there has been a violation of Art 6(1).' In addition, as the young murderers had been 'deprived' since their conviction 'of the opportunity to have the lawfulness of [their] detention reviewed by a judicial body in accordance with Article 5(4)', there was a violation of that article as well.[10]

## CAN DETENTION AS A MENTAL PATIENT BE REGARDED AS A VIOLATION OF ARTICLE 5?

After being convicted of dangerous driving and unlawful possession of firearms Mr Leonard Ashingdane was placed in a secure psychiatric hospital, where he languished for eight years before his transfer to an 'open' psychiatric hospital was authorized. However, as there was no room for him there he was kept at the secure hospital. By the time his case was heard by the Strasbourg court he had been locked up there for some 15 years - longer than the time most murderers serve in prison. He took the case to Strasbourg alleging a violation of his right to liberty under Article 5(1) and of his right of access to the courts under Article 6(1). He failed under both heads: *Ashingdane v UK*.[11]

How did Mr Ashingdane come to be treated in this brutal fashion in the first place? It was on the basis of medical reports received on his conviction. Unluckily for him, this was at a time when mental patients were routinely locked up. Only a few years later many psychiatric institutions were closed down and their patients were exposed to 'care in the community'.

## IS IT A BREACH OF A PATIENT'S HUMAN RIGHTS FOR HIM TO BE AT LARGE WHEN HE OUGHT TO BE CONFINED TO AN INSTITUTION?

Amazingly, a psychiatric patient went to court to object to the fact that he was not confined to an institution. This is the flip side of the *Ashingdane* situation.[12] Christopher Clunis, who had received psychiatric treatment for some years on an out-patient basis, was eventually detained at a hospital under the Mental Health Act 1983 for about a month. He failed to keep out-patient appointments arranged for him, and about three months later launched a sudden and unprovoked fatal knife-attack on a stranger, Mr Jonathan Zito, on a platform on the London Underground. Charged with murder, Clunis's defence of diminished responsibility was accepted, and he was convicted only of manslaughter and ordered to be confined indefinitely in a secure psychiatric hospital.

Clunis blamed his killing of Jonathan Zito on his local health authority, which had failed to recognize how dangerous he was! He sued the health authority in negligence. They replied by applying for Clunis's claim to be struck out as disclosing no cause of action on the basis of the old Latin maxim: *ex turpi causa non oritur actio* ('no cause of action arises out of an immoral cause'). This attempt to set the claim aside failed at first instance but succeeded on appeal. The Court of Appeal cited Lord Mansfield's statement of the principle as enunciated over 200 years ago: 'No court will lend its aid to a man who founds his cause of action upon an illegal or immoral act.'[13]

Did it matter whether Clunis was aware that he was committing an illegal and immoral act by killing Jonathan Zito? Yes, but the Court of Appeal drew a distinction here between diminished responsibility and insanity.[14]

**Q. Can a convicted criminal obtain damages for being jailed for knowingly committing a crime?**

***A. Amazingly, yes – in certain circumstances.***

The Clunis case relates to the broader issue of the responsibility of individuals for their own actions. Human rights law has done much to promote what might be termed a 'blame culture', encouraging finger-pointing and enabling people to shrug off responsibility for their own actions.

The Court of Appeal's recourse to ancient principle in *Clunis* was refreshing, all the more so as the court took the opportunity of distancing itself from a decision taken some years ago by the current Lord Chief Justice, Lord Woolf. The case, *Meah v McCreamer*, was a claim for damages for personal injury with a novel twist. Christopher Meah suffered a head injury in a road accident. He was subsequently convicted on two charges of sexual assault and one of rape, for which he was sentenced to life imprisonment. He claimed that he had only become a rapist because of the motor accident, which was the fault of the defendant. Amazingly, he was awarded damages of £60,000 (less 25 per cent for contributory negligence, as he had been a passenger in a car driven by someone he knew was drunk) – a figure specifically intended to compensate him for his imprisonment as well as his injury.[15]

Now that he was in funds, so to speak, two of Meah's victims, including the woman he had raped, sued him for damages, but were only awarded £6,750 and £10,250 respectively.[16]

Meah then decided to have another bite of the cherry and sued McCreamer a second time to recover the amounts that he had had to pay his victims! This time he lost, Woolf J holding that the damages awarded to his victims were 'too remote' to be recoverable by him from McCreamer, and also that it would have been contrary to public policy anyway.[17]

In *Clunis* the Court of Appeal commented on Meah's first case: 'Whilst any decision of that judge (viz. Lord Woolf) must be given the greatest weight, we do not consider, in the absence of argument on the issue of public policy, his decision in *Meah v McCreamer* can be regarded as authoritative on this issue.'[18]

**Q. Is it incompatible with human rights law for a statute to allow foreign nationals suspected of being terrorists to be detained indefinitely without trial or charge?**

***A. Not necessarily.***

The Anti-Terrorism, Crime and Security Act 2001 section 23 allows suspected terrorists to be detained indefinitely without trial or charge. It was challenged by nine foreign nationals held under this law.[19]

The Special Immigration Appeals Commission held that the provision was discriminatory and so breached Article 14 of the Convention, which had been incorporated into English law by the Human Rights Act 1998. In addition, it quashed a proposed derogation order intended to allow the United Kingdom to opt out of Article 5(1) (right to liberty and security of person) in the circumstances following the terrorist outrage in New York on 11 September 2001.[20] As far as s 23 of the Anti-Terrorism Act was concerned, the Commission declared it incompatible with Article 14 of the Convention.

However, this decision was reversed by a unanimous Court of Appeal. In the words of Brooke LJ: 'If the security of the nation may be at risk from terrorist violence, and if the lives of informers may be at risk, or the flow of valuable information they represent may dry up if sources of intelligence have to be revealed, there comes a stage when judicial scrutiny can go no further.'

Both the Commission and the Court of Appeal accepted that it was for the government, not the courts, to decide whether the country was in 'an emergency threatening the life of the nation', which was the basis of the detention orders. But the Court of Appeal did not ask the Home Secretary to disclose the grounds for his suspicion that the people concerned were involved in terrorism, nor was there even a challenge to the provision that suspicion alone was enough to allow them to be detained. The court concluded that the detention powers were not discriminatory, did not infringe the Convention and were also not a disproportionate response to the public emergency threatening the country. Lord Woolf CJ, presiding, did, however, sound a note of warning that the courts should be mindful of the dangers of unjustified discrimination against foreigners. 'This is especially the case if, as here, non-nationals are being detained based on conduct which has not been proved but is only suspected. The mistakes which have been made in the past, in relation to internment of aliens at the outbreak of war, should not be forgotten.'

This is presumably a reference to the famous case of *Liversidge v Anderson,* which surprisingly, however, was not specifically cited. Mr Liversidge (not his original name) had been interned during the Second World War on the basis that the Secretary of State had 'reasonable cause to believe' that he was 'of hostile origin or associations'. Liversidge sought a declaration that his detention was unlawful together with damages for false imprisonment. The case went all the way to the House of Lords, which by four votes to one upheld his detention as lawful. The sole dissenting voice was that of Lord Atkin, noted as a radical judge, who mercilessly attacked his fellow law lords:[21]

> I view with apprehension the attitude of judges who, on a mere question of construction, when face to face with claims involving the liberty of the subject, show themselves more executive-minded than the executive.

Then comes the famous passage which has echoed down the years:

> In England amidst the clash of arms the laws are not silent. They may be changed, but they speak the same language in war as in peace. It has always been one of the pillars of freedom, one of the principles of liberty for which, on recent authority, we are now fighting, that the judges are no respecters of persons, and stand between the subject and any attempted encroachments on his liberty by the executive, alert to see that any coercive action is justified in law. In this case, I have listened to arguments which might have been addressed acceptably to the Court of King's Bench in the time of Charles I.
>
> ... [I]n English law every imprisonment is *prima facie* unlawful, and ... it is for a person directing imprisonment to justify his act. The only exception is in respect of imprisonment ordered by a judge, who, from the nature of his office, cannot be sued, and the validity of whose judicial decisions cannot, in such proceedings as the present, be questioned.

Though Lord Atkins was a lone voice, it is his dissenting opinion that has come to be treated as representing the law. The Court of Appeal's decision in the Anti-Terrorism Act case may possibly have dented the authority of Lord Atkins's powerful plea.

The real problem here, in both *Liversidge v Anderson* and the recent Anti-Terrorism Act case, is the inconsistency of the different views adopted by different judges in interpreting the same statute. Consistency of thought is demanded by logic. Even more important, without consistency the law becomes unpredictable and therefore uncertain, which inevitably leads to injustice. Nevertheless, the judicial self-restraint demonstrated in this decision cannot but be applauded by all those who believe that unelected judges should avoid straying into political decision making, which they should leave to Parliament and the government.

Perhaps it is time to resuscitate the majority speeches in *Liversidge v Anderson*. Most modern commentaries give the impression that the law is to be found in Lord Atkins's opinion, but his was the one dissenting speech out of five. As the majority decision was never overruled, it must still be considered to be good law together with all the earlier authorities upon which it rests. So, for example, during the First World War, Lord Parker held that:

> Those who are responsible for the national security must be the sole judges of what the national security requires. It would obviously be undesirable that such matters should be made the subject of evidence in a court of law or otherwise discussed in public.[22]

And the Lord Chancellor, Lord Finlay, similarly:

> It seems obvious that no tribunal for investigating the question whether circumstances of suspicion exist warranting some restraint can be imagined less appropriate than a court of law.[23]

## Notes

1 5 Rep 92.
2 *R v Anthony Edward Martin* [2001] EWCA Crim 2245, [2002] 2 WLR 1.
3 *The Times* 27 May 2003.

4 *Beckford v R* [1987] 3 All ER 425.
5 See Note 2, above.
6 40 AmJur 2d §174, 1968 as updated to 2000.
7 *R v Secretary of State ex parte Venables and Thompson* [1997] 3 All ER 97.
8 *Ibid*, at 137.
9 For Lord Woolf's reduction of the sentence see [2001] 1 All ER 737. Jamie Bulger's father's attempt to challenge this decision was unsuccessful. See Chapter 3, Note 66. By contrast, the intruder wounded by Tony Martin was consulted on Mr Martin's release condtions. See www.ananova.com, 30 April 2001.
10 *T v United Kingdom; V v United Kingdom* 99/121–22 7 BHRC 659 (15/9/99 & 16/12/99). [2000] 2 All ER 1024. Note: Venables and Thompson were also successful in Strasbourg in claiming that they had not had a fair trial. See Chapter 11. The Home Secretary's power to set a 'tariff' for convicted murderers has also been successfully challenged. See Chapter 1.
11 *Ashingdane v UK* (1985) 7 EHRR 528 85/6.
12 *Clunis v Camden and Islington HA* [1998] 3 All ER 180.
13 *Holman v Johnson* (1775) 1 Cowp 341 at 343, (1775–1802) All ER Rep 98 at 99.
14 *Clunis v Camden and Islington HA* [1998] 3 AER 180 at 188h/j.
15 *Meah v McCreamer* [1985] 1 All ER 367.
16 *W v Meah; D v Meah* [1986] 1 All ER 935.
17 *Meah v McCreamer (No 2)* [1986] 1 All ER 943.
18 *Clunis v Camden and Islington HA* [1998] 3 All ER 180 at 189.
19 *A and others v Secretary of State for the Home Department* [2002] EWCA Civ 1502, [2003] 1 All ER 816.
20 Human Rights Act 1998 (Designated Derogation) Order 2001.
21 *Liversidge v Anderson* [1941] 3 All ER 338.
22 *The Zamora* [1916] 2 AC 77 at 107 cited by Lord Macmillan in *Liversidge v Anderson* [1941] 3 All ER 338 at 367.
23 *R v Halliday, ex parte Zadig* [1917] AC 260 at 269, cited by Lord Macmillan in *Liversidge v Anderson* [1941] 3 All ER 338 at 367.

# 11

# Judicial rights

## Article 6
### *Right to a fair trial*

1. In the determination of his civil rights and obligations or of any criminal charge against him, everyone is entitled to a fair and public hearing within a reasonable time by an independent and impartial tribunal established by law. Judgment shall be pronounced publicly but the press and public may be excluded from all or part of the trial in the interests of morals, public order or national security in a democratic society, where the interests of juveniles or the protection of the private life of the parties so require, or to the extent strictly necessary in the opinion of the court in special circumstances where publicity would prejudice the interests of justice.
2. Everyone charged with a criminal offence shall be presumed innocent until proved guilty according to law.
3. Everyone charged with a criminal offence has the following minimum rights:

   a) to be informed promptly, in a language which he understands and in detail, of the nature and cause of the accusation against him;
   b) to have adequate time and facilities for the preparation of his defence;
   c) to defend himself in person or through legal assistance of his own choosing or, if he has not sufficient means to pay for legal assistance, to be given it free when the interests of justice so require;
   d) to examine or have examined witnesses against him and to obtain the attendance and examination of witnesses on his behalf under the same conditions as witnesses against him;
   e) to have the free assistance of an interpreter if he cannot understand or speak the language used in court.

**Article 7**
***No punishment without law***

1. No one shall be held guilty of any criminal offence on account of any act or omission which did not constitute a criminal offence under national or international law at the time when it was committed. Nor shall a heavier penalty be imposed than the one that was applicable at the time the criminal offence was committed.
2. This article shall not prejudice the trial and punishment of any person for any act or omission which, at the time when it was committed, was criminal according to the general principles of law recognised by civilised nations.

## PRINCIPLES IN PRACTICE

1. Article 6 (1) covers the right to a fair trial in both civil and criminal cases.
2. However, Articles 6(2) and 6(3) cover only criminal trials.
3. Because a defendant in a criminal trial is given more protection than a litigant in a civil case, the determination whether a case is civil or criminal can be crucial. This distinction is not as clear-cut as may be thought.
4. The rights applicable to both civil and criminal trials are:
   - A fair and public hearing
   - within a reasonable time
   - by an independent and impartial tribunal established by law.
   - A publicly announced judgment.
5. These rights are specifically qualified by the right to hold trials in camera in part or whole where justified by circumstances.
6. The additional rights for defendants in criminal trials are:
   - The right to be informed of the nature and cause of the accusation against them,
   - which must be given to them promptly
   - and in detail
   - in a language which they understand;
   - adequate time and facilities for the preparation of their defence
   - the right to defend themseves in person or
   - through legal assistance of his or her own choosing
   - and, if they cannot afford to pay for legal assistance, free of charge 'when the interests of justice so require';
   - the right of the defendants or their lawyers to cross-examine witnesses against them;
   - the right to call witnesses 'under the same conditions as witnesses against him';

- if they cannot speak the language used in court, the right to the free assistance of an interpreter.

7. Article 7 prohibits retrospective criminal convictions. It is intended to prevent a situation where someone is found guilty of an offence that was not an offence at the time when it was committed.
8. Similarly, no one must be subjected to a heavier penalty than was applicable at the time when the offence was committed.
9. However, there is a broad exception to this which allows people to be tried and punished 'for any act or omission which, at the time when it was committed, was criminal according to the general principles of law recognised by civilised nations'. This would cover 'crimes against humanity' even if there was no law against them at the time they were committed.

## Q&A: SUMMARY

**Q. Is there not a guarantee of a fair trial under English common law? If so, what, if anything, does Article 6 add?**

A. *The common law does indeed provide a guarantee of a fair trial, but Article 6 has been interpreted by the Strasbourg court in a way that goes a lot further. Whether this has always served the interests of justice is a matter of opinion.*

**Q. Does Article 6(1) guarantee a right of access to a court?**

A. *Yes, although there is no specific mention of this right in the article.*

**Q. What guarantee is there that a particular court or judge will be 'an independent and impartial tribunal'?**

A. *In practice, none. The Strasbourg guidelines have been applied mostly in cases where a judge has exercised a dual role in the same case.*

**Q. Is it a violation of the right to a hearing by 'an independent and impartial tribunal' for a judge to double as a member of the legislature or executive?**

A. *The Strasbourg court has certainly taken this line, followed by the UK courts.*

**Q. What about the principle that justice must not only be done but must also be seen to be done?**

A. *This is still supposedly the law, but it is interpreted more narrowly by the English courts than elsewhere.*

**Q. Does it make any difference whether a case is classified as civil or criminal?**

A. *Yes, because defendants in criminal eases enjoy many more rights than civil litigants. As a result there have been some challenges to the classification of cases, some of which have been successful.*

**Q. What is meant by 'civil rights' and are these protected by the European Convention on Human Rights?**

A. *'Civil rights' are supposedly protected by the ECHR, but what this means is now more uncertain than ever.*

**Q. Are decisions relating to planning and other policy matters determinations of 'civil rights and obligations' which have to be heard by 'an independent and impartial tribunal', that is, by a judge or court?**

A. *No, although Strasbourg has got itself into an awful tangle over this question.*

# PRACTICAL PROBLEMS

**Q. Is there not a guarantee of a fair trial under English common law? If so, what, if anything, does Article 6 add?**

A. *The common law does indeed provide a guarantee of a fair trial, but Article 6 has been interpreted by the Strasbourg court in a way that goes a lot further. Whether this has always served the interests of justice is a matter of opinion.*

## *Venables and Thompson*

There have clearly been some cases decided under ECHR Article 6 which would not have succeeded without the extra boost of the Convention. The best known of these is probably the Strasbourg victory of Venables and Thompson, the 10-year-old murderers of the little toddler Jamie Bulger. The young killers had no trouble in persuading the Strasbourg Commission and court that they had been denied a fair trial by being tried in an adult court. Their complaint was that they had had to endure a three-week public Crown Court trial with a judge presiding in full panoply. How frightening the judge's wig and red robes must have been to a pair of killers who had just committed one of the most brutal and vicious murders imaginable! A wig and red robes – oh dear! And how different was this from Santa Claus or a pantomime Captain Hook? Moreover, as the UK government pointed out, the courtroom had been specially modified to make it less intimidating to the young defendants, who had had the procedure explained to them and been given a tour of the court in advance, and for whose benefit the hearing times had been shortened. One modification, a raised dock, designed to give the defendants a better view, was actually fastened on as a specific cause of complaint in itself, as it was claimed that this exposed the defendants to the gaze of the public and the press. As a result of all these supposed indignities, it was claimed, although their legal representatives were seated 'within whispering distance', the whole situation was too tense for them to be able to participate effectively in the proceedings and they had therefore been denied a fair trial. Amazingly, these flimsy arguments carried the day in Strasbourg. The

Commission found a violation of Article 6(1) by 14 votes to 5, and the court by the even greater margin of 16:1.[1]

The two killers also raised several other issues. They claimed that the way their trial was conducted also amounted to discrimination within Article 14 in conjunction with the Article 6(1) claim. The Strasbourg Commission held that this did not raise a separate issue, and the killers dropped this particular complaint before the court. Another claim was that the ordeal of the trial itself amounted to 'inhuman or degrading treatment' within Article 3. This was the only claim to be rejected, which it was by both the Commission and the Court. Then came their objection to their sentence, which is discussed in Chapter 10.

One claim that Venables and Thompson never raised in Strasbourg was that the reason they had had an unfair trial was because they were not guilty! Nor was it ever suggested to them that, in view of the overwhelming evidence against them, perhaps they should have pleaded guilty. Then they would not have had to endure the supposed horrors of a three-week trial. One of the bases of their successful claim was psychiatric evidence that they had been suffering post-traumatic stress and would therefore have had great difficulty in discussing the murder with their legal team and concentrating on the proceedings. This is hardly surprising, but was this the fault of the court system or of their perpetration of a horrific crime?

## PRESUMPTION OF INNOCENCE

The presumption of innocence is one of the most fundamental principles of the common law of England, and it is really from there that it found its way into ECHR Article 6(2). Linked to it is the right of silence and the ancient privilege against self-incrimination, which subsequently entered the US Constitution and is constantly invoked by Hollywood gangsters in the well-worn phrase 'taking the Fifth (Amendment)'.

Here again the ECHR has added a new and not entirely welcome dimension. So, for example, Ernest Saunders, convicted of conspiracy, false accounting and theft in the well-known Guinness trial and sentenced to five years' imprisonment, went to Strasbourg to complain that his indictment had been largely based on statements taken from him under compulsion by inspectors from the Department of Trade and Industry.

Article 6 does not expressly include the right of silence or privilege against self-incrimination, but it was read into Article 6(2), and by 14:1 in the Strasbourg Commission and 16:4 in the Court itself Ernest Saunders's rights under that article were found to have been violated.

William and Karen Condron were charged with supplying heroin. They replied 'no comment' to police questions but at trial explained that the heroin found in their flat was purely for their own use. The judge directed the jury that they could if they wished draw inferences from the defendants' silence at interview. Both of them were convicted and sentenced to terms of imprisonment, and this outcome was confirmed by the Court of Appeal. The judge's direction was perfectly in keeping with English law as it then was, as the previous ban on drawing such inferences had been lifted. The Condrons complained to Strasbourg that the judge's instruction had denied them a fair trial.

They won. A unanimous Strasbourg court found a violation of Article 6(1) on the ground that the judge's direction to the jury had been flawed. He should not have left the jury at liberty to draw an adverse inference from the Condrons' refusal to answer police questions as the jury may have believed the Condrons' subsequent explanation. Would the jury really have convicted the Condrons of supply if they had believed the Condrons' explanation?

However, not every application of this kind has succeeded. In the case of John Murray, arrested under anti-terrorism legislation, he was warned by the arresting police officer that a court, judge or jury would be entitled to draw an inference from his failure or refusal to answer questions. He refused to answer any police questions and chose not to testify at trial. The judge drew adverse inferences from this and he was subsequently convicted of conspiracy to murder and other offences and sentenced to eight years' imprisonment. After losing his appeal he applied to Strasbourg. His claim in regard to the right of silence under Article 6(2) was, however, rejected by a large majority both in the Commission and in the court itself, which held that, as the applicant could not be compelled to speak against his will, it was acceptable for adverse inferences to be drawn where necessary, and the system in place contained a number of safeguards protecting the rights of criminal defendants. But John Murray did not go away entirely empty-handed. A claim brought under Article 6(1) succeeded on the ground that he had been denied access to a lawyer for 48 hours.[2]

## ENGLISH DOMESTIC LAW

When the Convention came into existence in the immediate aftermath of the Second World War its intention was to offer the peoples of former fascist and other authoritarian regimes the blessings of democracy. Much of the drafting of the Convention was done by British lawyers, who tried to codify some of the principles already long accepted and practised in the United Kingdom. Among these was the right to a fair trial. It never occurred to anyone in 1951 that the scope of this right as enshrined in Article 6 was any wider than that long embedded in English law and practice, nor for that matter that there was any need for the common law right to be augmented.

Trial by jury was traditionally considered to be the best safeguard of fairness and 'a bulwark of liberty'. But the right to this mode of trial has gradually been whittled away in English law. Civil juries are now very largely a thing of the past, in practice available only in cases of libel, false imprisonment, malicious prosecution and the like, and even there with very reduced powers. With the disappearance of the jury in most civil cases the judge was left sitting alone.[3]

What guarantee of fairness is there if a single person is allowed to decide a case on his or her own? This is not the way the system was ever supposed to work. Except in the old Court of Chancery, now the Chancery Division of the High Court, which was traditionally concerned with trusts, wills and company law and where cases were decided by a single judge (originally the Lord Chancellor himself) sitting alone, the normal pattern was for a judge to sit with a jury.

So hallowed was the principle of trial by jury – which goes back to Magna Carta, signed in 1215, and beyond – that it came to be enshrined in the US Constitution. To this day the US Constitution guarantees the right to trial by jury not only in criminal prosecutions but also in all civil cases worth more than twenty dollars. In most European countries cases are usually decided by benches of three or more judges or by a judge sitting with lay assessors, and in France there also are juries in some criminal cases – sitting with three judges!

Do judges not have their own views, opinions and prejudices just like anyone else? Unlike the continental system, where being a judge is a separate profession from that of a lawyer, British judges are appointed from the ranks of practising lawyers, who have spent their whole previous careers acting for one party against another in an adversarial capacity. It is often possible to predict the outcome of a case purely on the basis of the judge who is deciding it.

What then of the right guaranteed by Article 6 of a hearing 'by an independent and impartial tribunal'? One of the many problems associated with the Human Rights Convention is that it carries a certain element of prejudice within itself. A judge who comes out openly in opposition to the Convention will soon find him- or herself in trouble, as the Scottish judge Lord McCluskey discovered. Four men found guilty of shipping three tonnes of cannabis resin on a ship, the *Isolde*, boarded by customs officials, appealed against their conviction on the basis, inter alia, of alleged breaches of their Convention rights. At a preliminary hearing some of their grounds of appeal were rejected by Lord McCluskey, who was a member of the court. Shortly before the substantive hearing was due to take place an article by Lord McCluskey appeared in a Scottish Sunday newspaper describing the Human Rights Convention as a 'Trojan horse' resulting in a 'crackpot's field day, a pain in the neck for judges and a goldmine for lawyers'. The judge also expressed the view that suspected drug dealers should not have privacy rights under Article 8 of the Convention, one of the grounds of appeal relied upon by the *Isolde* appellants. On the basis of the article the appellants successfully applied for the decision in which Lord McCluskey had participated to be set aside and for a fresh bench of judges to rehear their appeal.[4]

There was no suggestion that Lord McCluskey was actually biased against the appellants: only that he could not be relied upon to be impartial in deciding on Convention rights. But what about judges who approve of the Human Rights

Convention and tend to find in favour of the claimed rights of such special interest groups as convicted criminals, transsexuals and asylum seekers? No one would suggest that such judges are biased, but can they be relied upon any more than Lord McCluskey to be impartial? Yet it can be confidently predicted that judges with views diametrically opposed to those of Lord McCluskey will be in no danger of disqualification.

**Q. Does Article 6(1) guarantee a right of access to a court?**

***A. Yes, although there is no specific mention of this right in the article.***

Sidney Golder, a prisoner serving 15 years for robbery with violence, petitioned the Home Secretary for permission to consult a solicitor with a view to suing a prison officer for libel. Permission was refused. The issue before the Strasbourg court was whether there was a 'civil right' of access to a court within Article 6(1) although not specifically mentioned there. As the article guaranteed the right to a fair trial, it was held that the right of access to a court must be implied. By nine votes to three the court held that there had been a violation of Golder's rights under Article 6(1).[5]

He was even more successful in claiming that the Home Secretary's refusal to allow him to communicate with a solicitor was a breach of Article 8 ('respect for private and family life'). Here a unanimous court held that the refusal was not 'necessary in a democratic society' within Article 8(2).

**Q. What guarantee is there that a particular court or judge will be 'an independent and impartial tribunal'?**

***A. In practice, none. The Strasbourg guidelines have been applied mostly in cases where a judge has exercised a dual role in the same case.***

The Strasbourg court has laid down a twofold test: 'a subjective approach, that is endeavouring to ascertain the personal conviction of a given judge, and an objective approach, that is determining whether he offered guarantees sufficient to exclude any legitimate doubt in this respect'. This second, objective, approach was explained in *De Cubber v Belgium* by citing the old English maxim 'Justice must not only be done: it must also be seen to be done.'[6]

Despite the generality of the right to 'an independent and impartial tribunal', most of the Strasbourg cases of alleged violation of this right have been about judges exercising a dual role in the same case. In both *Piersack* and *De Cubber* one of the judges who convicted the applicant of a criminal offence had previously been involved in that person's case as part of the prosecution. In both cases this was held by the Strasbourg court to be a violation of the right to a hearing by 'an independent and impartial tribunal'.

There have been a number of similar UK cases. In *Findlay v United Kingdom* a member of the Scots Guards successfully objected to the fact that he had been convicted by a court martial composed of members who were under the command of the 'convening officer' who had also selected both prosecuting and defending officers.[7]

However, *Findlay* was distinguished by the House of Lords in a recent case in which it was held that the appointment of permanent presidents and part-time judge advocates to courts martial did not amount to a violation of the right to 'an independent and impartial tribunal', that the three men concerned had had a fair trial in terms of the common law and Article 6 alike, and that their convictions were safe.[8]

**Q. Is it a violation of the right to a hearing by 'an independent and impartial tribunal' for a judge to double as a member of the legislature or executive?**

***A. The Strasbourg Court has certainly, taken this line, followed by the UK courts.***

In *McGonnell v United Kingdom*[9] it was held to be a violation of Article 6 that the same person who had presided over the legislature when enacting certain planning regulations subsequently presided over a court hearing a planning appeal under those same regulations. Strictly speaking, this was not a UK case at all, as it concerned Guernsey, whose government, laws and judiciary are quite separate from and independent of the United Kingdom. The problem involved the Deputy Bailiff, who was president of the island's legislature, the States of Deliberation, and also presided over the Royal Court. There was no suggestion that the Deputy Bailiff was 'subjectively' biased, but under the 'objective' test the Strasbourg court reached a unanimous finding of a violation of Article 6. The appearance of a possible lack of impartiality was enough.

This decision is the launching pad for the imposition of a far-reaching 'separation of powers' doctrine, under which members of the executive or legislature are banned from exercising judicial functions. The main casualties of this doctrine are the Lord Chancellor and the Home Secretary. It is not for nothing that the Lord Chancellor is the highest paid member of the British government, as he or she has traditionally occupied three positions rolled into one. Not only is he or she a very senior Cabinet Minister with the power to appoint the judges, but he or she also presides over the House of Lords in its legislative capacity, and is the head of the judiciary, with the right to preside over the House of Lords in its judicial capacity. With the recent onslaught on this supposedly unholy trinity of functions, Lord Irvine, who held the post from 1997 to 2003, eschewed his right to sit in judgment as a law lord. So great was the pressure that the UK government actually decided to abolish the Lord Chancellorship altogether, though this was so badly botched up that at the time of writing there is still a Lord Chancellor. However, it can safely be said that, for however long or short a time the office survives, no Lord Chancellor will ever act as a judge again. At the same time there are plans to uncouple the judicial functions of the House of Lords from its role as a branch of the legislature by giving the law lords control over a new 'Supreme Court'. However justifiable this may appear in terms of the doctrine of the separation of powers, what it will amount to in practice is yet more power for an unelected and increasingly activist judiciary.

## ANDERSON

The Home Secretary has already come under more direct attack. In a recent case brought by Anthony Anderson a unanimous seven-judge panel of the House of Lords decided that it was incompatible with Article 6 of the European Convention on Human Rights for the Home Secretary to have the right to determine how long a convicted murderer serving a mandatory 'life' sentence should spend in prison for purposes of punishment.[10] The Home Secretary's sentencing power was granted to him by Act of Parliament, namely section 29 of the Crime (Sentences) Act 1997. The significance of this case is therefore that it represents a successful challenge by convicted murderers to an Act of Parliament. This decision is a good illustration of the way in which human rights law has given the already staggering power of the judiciary a yet further boost.

The basis for the House of Lords decision in Anderson's case was that the Home Secretary's right to set sentencing tariffs was contrary to Article 6 of the Convention. But where does Article 6 say that there is a right 'to have a sentence imposed by an independent and impartial tribunal'? The answer is that it does not. In fact, there is no mention of sentencing at all. What it says is that 'everyone is entitled to a fair and public hearing within a reasonable time by an independent and impartial tribunal established by law'. The House of Lords decision depends on characterizing the sentencing process as part of the trial. But what about the provision, then, for a 'public hearing'? If the Home Secretary is to lose the power of fixing the tariff for convicted murderers, then this decision will presumably go to the Parole Board – who do not hold public hearings either.

Why should this decision not be applauded as a victory for human rights? Because what it really is a victory for the judiciary over the executive and legislature alike. The immediate beneficiary is Anthony Anderson, convicted of two brutal murders. In the words of Lord Bingham:[11]

> In September 1986 the appellant [ie Anthony Anderson] murdered a 60 year old man in obviously poor health who had allowed the appellant into his house. Once in the house the appellant punched and kicked the victim who suffered cardiac arrest and died. The appellant stole some of the victim's property. In May 1987 the appellant murdered at 35 year old homosexual who had invited the appellant back to his house after a chance meeting. The appellant attacked and kicked his victim, who died from his injuries, and stole his property. The appellant denied both murders but was convicted before Kenneth Jones J and a jury at the Central Criminal Court.

The key word in Article 6(1) of the convention is 'fair'. Fairness must surely apply to both sides, not only to convicted murderers but also to their victims. Current English criminal procedure does not allow the prosecution to ask for a particular sentence or indeed to become involved in the sentencing process in any real sense at all. On the basis that Anderson 'had deliberately picked on vulnerable victims' the trial judge had recommended a minimum term of 15 years for both murders. The Lord Chief Justice made the same recommendation, but the Home Secretary set the term at 20 years.[12]

Was this really too severe? Norman Brennan, Director of the Victims of Crime Trust, was quoted in the press as saying: 'Members of the public see sentences handed out by the judiciary as very inadequate.'[13] The argument on the other side is twofold. First, as a politician the Home Secretary is likely to be susceptible to the pressures of public opinion. Secondly, it is a breach of the principle of the separation of powers for a member of the executive to perform a judicial function.

Is it so wrong for public opinion to be taken into account in sentencing? The US Supreme Court has recently ruled as unconstitutional an Arizona requirement for 'aggravating circumstances' to be found by a judge before a convicted murderer could be sentenced to death. This was a function that only a jury could perform, it was held, in conformity with the guarantee of jury trial contained in the Sixth Amendment to the US Constitution. Breyer J, concurring with the majority, went even further, holding that the Eighth Amendment (prohibiting 'cruel and unusual punishments') 'requires that a jury, not a judge, make the decision to sentence a defendant to death'.

Moreover:

> Nor is the fact that some judges are democratically elected likely to change the jury's comparative advantage in this respect. Even in jurisdictions where judges are selected directly by the people, the jury remains uniquely capable of determining whether, given the community's views, capital punishment is appropriate in the particular case at hand.[14]

From the perspective of the UK judiciary this argument may appear topsy-turvy. Juries are Justice Breyer's first preference in determining the death penalty, with democratically elected judges second and appointed judges bringing up the rear. The point Breyer J is making is precisely the desirability and indeed the necessity for public opinion to be taken into account in these life-and-death decisions. Does this argument not apply also where not the life but the liberty of a convicted murderer is at stake?

What about the doctrine of the separation of powers? Lord Diplock famously remarked that 'the British Constitution, though largely unwritten, is firmly based on the separation of powers'.[15] This is plainly wrong. The legislature and executive are so closely intertwined that the Prime Minister and Cabinet owe their position precisely to the fact that they command a majority in the House of Commons, and legislation in practice originates with the executive, which can generally ensure that any bill it wishes Parliament to pass will become law and any bill it opposes will be defeated. Even the fact that the law lords not only concern themselves with judicial business but can also participate in the legislative business of the House of Lords as a Parliament – more so now than was traditionally the case – flies in the face of the doctrine of the separation of powers.

What then was Lord Diplock thinking of? He went on to explain: 'Parliament makes the laws, the judiciary interpret them.' In this respect Lord Diplock was quite right. This division of power is indeed an important part of the British constitution. But it rests not so much on the doctrine of the separation of powers as on that of the legislative supremacy of Parliament, dating back to the 'Glorious Revolution' of 1688–89 and beyond. However, it is now honoured more in the breach than in the observance, as judge-made law has made increasing inroads on the fabric of the law. The Home Secretary's power to fix a tariff for convicted murderers was granted to him by Act of Parliament. It could therefore be argued that any interference with it by the courts should be rejected as amounting to a challenge to Parliamentary legislative supremacy.

Separation of powers entails a system of checks and balances, as indeed there is in the US Constitution, for example, which enshrines that principle in a very real sense. In the United Kingdom, however, although the judiciary can strike down decisions of the executive and in certain circumstances even set aside Acts of Parliament, the judges of the High Court and above are not subject to any real controls by either the executive or the legislature.[16] Election of judges is unknown and impeachment effectively long abolished, although it originated in England and has been successfully used against many judges in the United States (including only one Supreme Court Justice, Samuel Chase, who was acquitted).

**Q. What about the principle that justice must not only be done but must also be seen to be done?**

***A. This is still supposedly the law, but it is interpreted more narrowly by the English courts than elsewhere.***

The literal meaning of this doctrine is only a starting point. If anyone who is a party to a lawsuit also has the right to decide its outcome, that would be a clear breach of the principle. By extension we come to the category of cases where the person sitting in judgment is not a party but is nevertheless associated in one way or another with one of the parties. What we are dealing with here is partiality or bias, which leads us to our next category, namely cases where, although there may be no actual bias, there may well be an appearance, or at least a suspicion, of partiality.

## THREE PRINCIPLES

In *Webb and Hay v The Queen*,[17] decided by the High Court of Australia in 1994, Deane J suggested a fourfold classification of these cases, based on three related but separate principles. First, there is the principle that no one should be in a position to decide a matter in which he or she has an interest, whether pecuniary or otherwise. Secondly, there is the principle of avoidance of partiality or bias. What this means is that a judge must not be a respecter of persons, which is related to the principle of equality before the law, which in turn can be seen as forming part of the fundamental principle of the rule of law. Thirdly, we have the principle that justice must not only be done but must also be seen to be done.

## *Pecuniary interest*

One of the most straightforward cases illustrative of the first of these three principles is *Dimes v Grand Junction Canal Co.*[18] The case involved a dispute between a canal company and a landowner. At first instance the Vice-Chancellor found for the company. This decision was affirmed by the Lord Chancellor, Lord Cottenham. The matter then went to the House of Lords, where the issue was the legality of the Lord Chancellor's decrees in favour of the company.

The problem was that Lord Cottenham, who held the office of Lord Chancellor between 1846 and 1850, was a major shareholder in the canal company at the time when he made the decrees, a fact that was unknown to the defendant in the case. When Lord Cottenham's decision was challenged, all the judges were summoned to Westminster Hall to advise the House of Lords on this sensitive issue. This was an ancient procedure which was adopted only in very important cases. Following the judges' unanimous opinion, the House of Lords declared Lord Cottenham's decrees voidable and duly annulled them.

The *nemo judex* principle was simply explained in *Dimes* by Lord Campbell (who was himself to become Lord Chancellor a few years later):

> No one can suppose that Lord Cottenham could be, in the remotest degree, influenced by the interest he had in this concern; but, my Lords, it is of the last importance that the maxim that 'no man is to be a judge in his own cause' should be held sacred. And that is not to be confined to a cause in which he is a party, but applies to a cause in which he has an interest. . . . We have again and again set aside proceedings in inferior tribunals, because an individual, who had an interest in a cause, took a part in the decision. And it will have a most salutary effect on these tribunals when it is known that this High Court of last resort, in a case in which the Lord Chancellor of England had an interest, considered that his decree was on that account a decree not according to law, and should be set aside. This will be a lesson to all inferior tribunals to take care, not only that in their decrees they are not influenced by their personal interest, but to avoid the appearance of labouring under such an influence.

Lord Cottenham was spared the indignity of this decision: he had died just a few months before his decrees were struck down.

## *Non-pecuniary interest*

Lord Cottenham's interest in the *Dimes* case was financial, but as has now been recognized by the English courts, there is no need for the principle to be confined to such instances. For:

> there could be cases where the interest of the judge in the subject matter of the proceedings arising from his strong commitment to some cause or belief or his association with a person or body involved in the proceedings could shake public confidence in the public administration of justice as much as a shareholding (which might be small) in a public company involved in the litigation.[19]

This was said by Lord Hutton in the second *Pinochet* case. A law lord was found to have sat on the first *Pinochet* case in the outcome of which he had a non-pecuniary interest. The case in question was an application for the arrest and extradition to Spain of the former Chilean dictator, General (or Senator) Augusto Pinochet, to stand trial for certain crimes against humanity allegedly committed while he was head of state of Chile. The question before the House of Lords was whether a former head of state enjoyed immunity from arrest and extradition.[20] Besides the parties themselves, three human rights groups were given leave to participate in the hearing as 'interveners'. One of these bodies was Amnesty International, which had not only put in written submissions but was also represented by a team of four counsel, who addressed the court in favour of extradition.

By a majority of three to two the House of Lords decided against General Pinochet, one of the three law lords forming the majority being Lord Hoffmann, whose wife had worked for Amnesty International since 1977 and who himself was an unpaid director and chairman of a connected body known as Amnesty International Charity Limited.[21] The information about Lord Hoffmann's personal association with Amnesty International came to light only about a fortnight after the House of Lords decision to extradite General Pinochet. The General's solicitors received an anonymous telephone call and on the following day it was headline news. However, ignoring the rising tide of criticism of Lord Hoffmann's participation in the decision, the Home Secretary duly signed the authority for the General's extradition to proceed. General Pinochet's lawyers then lodged a petition asking for Lord Hoffmann's opinion to be declared invalid or, alternatively, for the decision of the House of Lords to be sit aside.

A fresh panel of law lords was summoned to hear this petition.[22] Delivering the leading speech, Lord Browne-Wilkinson adopted a low-key approach:

> It is important to stress that Senator Pinochet makes no allegation of actual bias against Lord Hoffmann; his claim is based on the requirement that justice should be seen to be done as well as actually being done.[23]

Lord Hope of Craighead struck a more critical note:

> I think that the connections which existed between Lord Hoffmann and Amnesty International were of such a character, in view of their duration and proximity, as to disqualify him on this ground. In view of his links with Amnesty International Charity Ltd he could not be seen to be impartial. There has been no suggestion that he was actually biased. He had no financial or pecuniary interest in the outcome. But his relationship with Amnesty International was such that he was, in effect, acting as a

judge in his own cause. I consider that his failure to disclose these connections leads to the conclusion that the decision to which he was a party must be set aside.[24]

The House of Lords stressed that in this class of case the disqualification of the judge in question was automatic. It is not necessary to show a 'real danger' or even a 'reasonable suspicion' of bias, let alone any actual bias on his part.

But what exactly is the appropriate test? It was stated by the Court of Appeal in these terms in *Locabail v Bayfield Properties*:

[I]f a judge has a personal interest in the outcome of an issue which he is to resolve, he is improperly acting as a judge in his own cause; and . . . such a proceeding would, without more, undermine public confidence in the integrity of the administration of justice. In the context of automatic disqualification the question is not whether the judge has some link with a party involved in a cause before the judge but whether the outcome of that cause could, realistically, affect the judge's interest.[25]

How much of a personal interest does a judge have to have in the outcome of a case before he or she is automatically disqualified? It used to be held that any interest, however small, would disqualify him or her, but there has been a recent drift away from this. In Locabail, for example, it was maintained that there is a 'de minimis exception':

This seems to us a proper exception provided the potential effect of any decision on the judge's personal interest is so small as to be incapable of affecting his decision one way or the other.[26]

This remark looks very much like an exercise in back-tracking. For how can the potential effect on a judge's personal interest be measured? Lord Hoffmann presumably thought that his association with Amnesty International was irrelevant to his sitting on the Pinochet case. However, the Locabail judgment does go on to add: 'But it is important, bearing in mind the rationale of the rule, that any doubt should be resolved in favour of disqualification.' But where the judge is not personally involved disqualification becomes very difficult to obtain:

In any case where the judge's interest is said to derive from the interest of a spouse, partner or other family member the link must be so close and direct as to render the interest of that other person, for all practical purposes, indistinguishable from an interest of the judge himself.

There are other dicta which muddy the waters further. In the *Pinochet* case Lord Browne-Wilkinson was at pains to stress that that decision did not mean automatic disqualification from any case involving a charity with which the judge happened to be connected:

Only in cases in which a judge is taking an active role as trustee or director of a charity which is closely allied to and acting with a party to the litigation should a judge normally be concerned either to recuse himself or disclose the position to the parties.[27]

This is arguably too protective of judges. It is hard to understand why a judge should not routinely be required to disclose any such interest to the parties.

But what if disclosure is made and no party objects to the judge's continuing to hear the case? Can such parties adopt a 'wait and see' approach, challenging the judge's decision only after he or she has found against them? That was the way the Court of Appeal described the application made by Mrs Emmanuel, the claimant in *Locabail*, against the decision of a solicitor sitting as a deputy High Court judge who, on the eighth day of the hearing, disclosed that he had just discovered that 'the firm of which I am a partner seems to have had something to do with attempting to get a bankruptcy order against' Mrs Emmanuel's husband.[28]

Mrs Emmanuel's lawyers lodged their objection only after an adverse judgment was handed down by the deputy judge over four months later. Her initial application for the deputy judge's decision to be set aside on the ground of his firm's involvement with the case against Mr Emmanuel was heard by the very deputy judge whose decision was being queried, who dismissed the application. The matter then went to the Court of Appeal, which upheld this decision. The Court of Appeal understandably objected that 'Mrs Emmanuel wanted to have the best of both worlds'.[29] But should the deputy judge not have had to recuse himself of his own accord?

It was held by the Court of Appeal that this was not a case of automatic disqualification at all. The reason given for this was that, although the deputy judge was head of the litigation department of the firm of solicitors concerned, he did not have any personal knowledge of his firm's involvement in the case against Mrs Emmanuel's husband. But why should the state of the deputy judge's knowledge be the determining factor? Perhaps a more pertinent question is: why did he not know? The Court of Appeal admitted that although he had conducted a 'conflict search' in regard to Mrs Emmanuel, he had not done so in regard to her husband. So perhaps he ought to have known of the potential conflict. Moreover, surely the very existence of this potential conflict should have been enough to disqualify him, regardless of his state of knowledge? Or, failing that, how could his judgment possibly be squared with the requirement that justice must not only be done but must also be seen to be done (see below)? Above all, is it really a good idea to allow a judge to hear an application for his own disqualification in a particular case? For is this not an almost literal example of someone being a judge in his own cause?

## *'A real danger of bias'*

Three other cases were heard by the Court of Appeal together with *Locabail*. Coming as it did so soon after the House of Lords decision to set aside the judgment of a law lord in *Pinochet* and in view of the sensitive nature of the issues involved, the Court of Appeal was made up of its three most senior judges: the Lord Chief Justice (Lord Bingham), the Master of the Rolls (Lord Woolf) and the Vice-Chancellor (Sir Richard Scott). In the interests of certainty and clarity only one judgment was delivered, which was the judgment of the Court as a whole.

Only one of the four appeals heard on that occasion was successful. This was *Timmins v Gormley*, a personal injury case, where the application was for setting aside the judgment of a recorder on the ground of bias. Besides having largely a claimant personal injury practice as a barrister – a fact he had disclosed to the parties – the recorder was a prolific writer on the subject of personal injury litigation, in which he expressed 'pronounced pro-claimant anti-insurer views'. Though there was 'no suggestion of actual bias on the part of the recorder', it was found by the Court of Appeal that there was 'a real danger' that someone holding the views expressed by the recorder might 'unconsciously have leant in favour of the claimant and against the defendant in resolving the factual issues between them'.[30] On this basis, the appeal against the recorder's decision was allowed and a retrial ordered.

At the time of writing the 'real danger' test applied in *Timmins* was supposedly the correct standard under English law. This was established by the House of Lords in *R v Gough*,[31] in which several competing tests were analysed and evaluated. The fact that this test itself was stated in several different ways in that case alone is not particularly helpful. Lord Goff, concluding his speech, with which his brother law lords all agreed, described the appropriate test as whether 'there was a real danger of bias on the part of the relevant member of the tribunal in question'.[32] In his brief concurring opinion, Lord Woolf endorsed 'the proper test which Lord Goff has identified',[33] yet the wording he used in describing it was not quite the same as Lord Goff's, Lord Woolf's test being 'whether there is a real danger of injustice having occurred as a result of the alleged bias'.

This wording places the emphasis not on the alleged bias itself but on its effect on justice. Though intended to be the same test as Lord Goff's, it could easily lead to a different conclusion when applied to the facts of a specific case. In addition, Lord Goff himself used a different formulation of his test elsewhere in his speech in *Gough*, asking whether 'there was a real likelihood, in the sense of a real possibility, of bias'.[34] But is 'a real likelihood of bias' the same thing as 'a real possibility of bias'? 'Likelihood' surely means 'probability', whereas 'possibility' represents a considerably lower level of expectation, even with the word 'real' in front of it. In the concluding paragraph of his speech Lord Goff appears to equate 'real danger' with 'real possibility' rather than with 'real likelihood', which he identifies with 'real probability'. It is not easy to tell from this what the requisite level of possibility is. As a result the test is not as clear as it might be. Indeed, it is surprising that the House of Lords should have been content with it after the problems resulting from its lack of clarity in a case involving a juryman just a few years earlier.[35]

## 'Justice must not only be done but must be seen to be done'

Lord Goff was at pains to reject the test suggested by Lord Hewart CJ in *R v Sussex Justices, ex parte McCarthy*[36] that even a suspicion of bias was sufficient to vitiate the proceedings.[37] The *Sussex Justices* case arose out of a road traffic accident in which McCarthy's car had collided with another vehicle. McCarthy was charged with the criminal offence of drunken driving, and the driver of the other car also instituted civil proceedings against him for damages. At his criminal trial the magistrates' clerk was none other than the solicitor acting for the plaintiff motorist in the civil case. When the magistrates retired to consider their verdict this clerk withdrew with them in case they needed to consult him on a point of law. This was customary at the time, although the practice now is for the clerk to join the magistrates only if expressly invited to do so. In fact, the Sussex magistrates did without their clerk's assistance. But Lord Hewart was in no doubt that McCarthy's conviction had to be quashed nevertheless:

> It is said, and, no doubt, truly, that when that gentleman retired in the usual way with the justices, taking with him the notes of the evidence in case the justices might desire to consult him, the justices came to a conclusion without consulting him, and that he scrupulously abstained from referring to the case in any way. But while that is so, a long line of cases shows that it is not merely of some importance but is of fundamental importance that justice should not only be done but should manifestly and undoubtedly be seen to be done. The question therefore is not whether in this case the deputy clerk made any observation or offered any criticism which he might not properly have made or offered; the question is whether he was so related to the case in its civil aspect as to be unfit to act as clerk to the justices in the criminal matter. The answer to that question depends not upon what actually was done but upon what might appear to be done. Nothing is to be done which creates even a suspicion that there has been an improper interference with the course of justice.[38]

This passage has been invoked on many occasions, not least by Lord Denning MR, who restated it in his own characteristically robust manner:

> [I]n considering whether there was a real likelihood of bias, the court does not look at the mind of the justice himself or at the mind of the chairman of the tribunal, or whoever it may be, who sits in a judicial capacity. It does not look to see if there was a real likelihood that he would, or did, in fact favour one side at the expense of the other. The court looks at the impression which would be given to other people. Even if he was as impartial as could be, nevertheless, if right-minded persons would think that, in the circumstances, there was a real likelihood of bias on his part, then he should not sit. And if he does sit, his decision cannot stand.[39]

Lord Hewart's dictum was criticized in *R v Camborne Justices, ex parte Pearce*:

> While indorsing and fully maintaining the integrity of the principle reasserted by Lord Hewart CJ, this court feels that the continued citation of it in cases to which it is not

applicable may lead to the erroneous impression that it is more important that justice should appear to be done than that it should in fact be done.[40]

This rather mealy-mouthed comment combines criticism of Lord Hewart's statement with purported support for the principle it embodies. What exactly is that principle? Lord Hewart leaves us in little doubt: it is the principle 'that justice should not only be done but should manifestly and undoubtedly be seen to be done', which he describes as 'of fundamental importance' and which, he stresses, is supported by 'a long line of cases'.

While claiming to uphold this principle, the court in the *Camborne Justices* case effectively subverted it. Henry Pearce had been found guilty of selling watered-down milk in a prosecution brought by the Cornwall County Council. The magistrates' clerk at his trial, a certain Donald Thomas, also happened to be an elected member of the county council. This fact came to Pearce's knowledge only after the trial, and he then applied for *certiorari* to quash the conviction. Unlike the *Sussex Justices* case, the clerk here did not retire with the magistrates, but he was sent for to advise the justices on a point of law. The facts of the case were not discussed in his presence, and, after advising the magistrates he returned to court. On the basis of these facts the court held that 'there was no real likelihood of bias', and the application for *certiorari* was dismissed. But perhaps the most illuminating comment came from Lord Goddard CJ in the course of argument, when he conceded that: 'If the court were asked to express an opinion they would say that it were better if Mr Thomas were not to sit when prosecutions were conducted on behalf of the council of which he was a member.'

The 'long line of cases' referred to by Lord Hewart in support of the principle applied in the Sussex Justices includes *Eckersley v Mersey Docks*, in which Lord Esher MR, one of the great Victorian judges, stated as the rule applicable to judges 'that not only must they not be biased, yet if the circumstances are such that people – not reasonable people, but many people – would suspect them of being biased, they ought not to sit as judges.'[41]

Some confusion has arisen from the fact that the actual decision in *Eckersley*, which did not involve either a judge or a juror, was an exception to this general rule. Lord Esher MR explained extremely clearly why the very strict rule that is applicable to judges of all degrees did not apply to the situation in the case before him. The point is that the test for judges does not depend on actual bias but merely on a suspicion of bias – and not necessarily even reasonable suspicion. Moreover, it cannot be stressed enough that Lord Esher did not invent this doctrine: it was already well established by his day.

Has this time-honoured principle now been swept away in England? The House of Lords in *Gough* certainly disapproved of it, without, however, expressly overruling Lord Hewart's judgment in the *Sussex Justices* case, and without so much as mentioning *Eckersley v Mersey Docks* or any of the other cases on which Lord Hewart's judgment was based.

## *Uniform standard?*

It is not even clear to whom the 'real danger' test applies. In *Gough* Lord Goff thought it 'possible, and desirable, that the same test should be applicable in all cases of apparent bias, whether concerned with justices [viz justices of the peace, or magistrates] or members of other inferior tribunals, or with jurors, or with arbitrators'.[42] Does this mean that the same standard is to apply across the board from the highest to the lowest level? If so, why is there no mention of High Court judges or the higher echelons of the judiciary? Is this because Lord Goff thought that a different standard was applicable to them? Or because it was unthinkable to him that their judgments would ever have to be set aside for bias? The *Pinochet* episode was of course as yet in the future at the time of *Gough.*

By contrast, in the *Mersey Docks* case both Lord Esher and Lopes LJ expressly stated that the same test – what we might call the 'suspicion of bias' test – was applicable to judges of all degrees (though not necessarily to arbitrators appointed in a contract). Indeed, Lord Esher specifically mentions 'judges of the Superior Court'.

## *Jurors*

Although Lord Esher did not refer directly to juries, the same test used to be applied to them, most recently by the Court of Appeal (Criminal Division) in *R v Morris* (1991).[43] This decision was expressly disapproved in Gough by Lord Goff, who remarked that in Morris 'it appears that *R v Spencer* was not cited to the court'.[44] In *R v Spencer*[45] three nurses at a secure mental hospital were charged with ill-treating patients. A member of the jury whose wife happened to work as a cleaner at another psychiatric hospital made no secret during the trial of his belief in the guilt of the defendant nurses. As a result, this juror was discharged by the judge, but he then gave a lift to three other jurors, who disobeyed the judge's instructions not to discuss the case with the discharged juror. The trial judge decided not to accede to the defence request to discharge the rest of the jury. The test he applied was 'that the jury should not be discharged unless it could be shown that there was a very high risk that the apparently biased juror had influenced any of his fellows'. This test was characterized by both the Court of Appeal and the House of Lords as too strict. The Court of Appeal offered instead the following test:

> . . . [I]n this type of circumstance this court must ask itself whether it thinks there is anything in the events which ex hypothesi should not have occurred which leads it to the conclusion that an injustice may have been done, or that there is a real danger that the appellant may have been prejudiced by what has gone on. In the instant case, we do not think that we should come to that conclusion.[46]

This is a somewhat vague and long-winded version of the 'real danger' test, which was restated rather more pithily by Lord Ackner in the House of Lords:

'The correct test is . . . whether there was a real danger that the appellant position had been prejudiced in the circumstances.'[47] However, although the test applied by the House of Lords was essentially the same as that used by the Court of Appeal, the result was exactly the opposite – which hardly inspires confidence in the 'real danger' test.

## *Australia*

The 'real danger' test was expressly rejected by the High Court of Australia in *Webb and Hay v The Queen*.[48] The case involved the trial of two men for the brutal murder of a certain Lance Edward Patrick. During the trial the mother of the murder victim's fiancée was approached by a member of the jury, who handed her a bunch of daffodils with a request that she give them to Mr Patrick's mother. The two defendants immediately objected and asked for a 'mistrial', that is, for the jury as a whole to be discharged. The trial judge refused this request and also decided not to excuse the juror in question. After conviction and an unsuccessful appeal the defendants were given special leave to appeal to the High Court of Australia on two grounds, one being that, on the basis of the 'flower incident', the trial judge should have discharged the jury.

The trial judge applied a version of the 'real danger of bias' test. But the correct test under Australian law was held to be very different:

> When it is alleged that a judge has been or might be actuated by bias, this Court has held that the proper test is whether fair-minded people might reasonably apprehend or suspect that the judge has prejudged or might prejudge the case.

This is in fact our old friend the doctrine espoused by Lords Denning, Hewart and Esher. It asks not whether it is likely that the judge or juror concerned actually is biased, but whether his or her conduct is likely to create an impression of bias on an outside observer. Mason CJ and McHugh J in Webb go on to explain, quoting Lord Hewart:

> The principle behind the reasonable apprehension or suspicion test is that it is of 'fundamental importance that justice should not only be done, but should manifestly and undoubtedly be seen to be done'.

## *The United States*

In the United States there is a large body of law devoted to the question of the disqualification of judges. American law has remained true to the ancient common law principle requiring not only what has been termed 'the cold neutrality of an impartial judge' but also the appearance of neutrality.[49] It is accepted that whether a judge is disqualified is a question not of fact but of law.[50]

In a number of states of the United States this whole matter is governed by statute. It is generally held that such statutes should be broadly construed so as to afford maximum protection of the public against biased judges. So, for example, it has been held that the grounds for disqualification enumerated in a statute should not be regarded as exhaustive; also, that a judge's disqualifying interest need not be directly involved in the case in question; and moreover, that the term 'party' in a disqualification statute should not be narrowly interpreted but should include all parties 'in interest'.[51] This last point is particularly instructive in the light of the disqualification of a law lord in England in the *Pinochet* case.

The Federal statute on the subject provides that: 'Any justice, judge, or magistrate of the United States shall disqualify himself in any proceeding in which his impartiality might reasonably be questioned.'[52] This places the onus on the judge him- or herself to stand down wherever his or her impartiality might 'reasonably' be impugned. Once again, the emphasis is on the impression of bias rather than on the existence of bias. The section then goes on to enumerate a number of specific circumstances in which a judge should recuse him- or herself. These, it should be emphasized, are not by way of explanation of the general provision quoted above but in addition to it:

> (b) He shall also disqualify himself in the following circumstances:
> (1) Where he has a personal bias or prejudice concerning a party, or personal knowledge of disputed evidentiary facts concerning the proceeding;
> . . .
> (5) He or his spouse, or a person within the third degree of relationship to either of them, or the spouse of such a person:
> (i) Is a party to the proceeding, or an officer, director, or trustee of a party;
> (ii) Is acting as a lawyer in the proceeding;
> (iii) Is known by the judge to have an interest that could be substantially affected by the outcome of the proceeding;
> (iv) Is to the judge's knowledge likely to be a material witness in the proceeding.

What if the judge discloses his or her interest? If the parties do not object, should he or she be permitted to hear the case anyway? This appears to be taken for granted in England.[53] However, the US Federal statute does not allow this in respect of the specific grounds for disqualification listed in subsection (b) but only in relation to the general grounds identified in subsection (a):

> (e) No justice, judge, or magistrate shall accept from the parties to the proceeding a waiver of any ground for disqualification enumerated in subsection (b). Where the ground for disqualification arises only under subsection (a), waiver may be accepted provided it is preceded by a full disclosure on the record of the basis for disqualification.

In keeping with the original spirit of the English common law, another Federal Statute provides that the mere filing of an affidavit by a party alleging bias on the part of the judge is enough in itself to disqualify him or her.[54] No proof of bias is needed, and there is no determination of the truth or falsehood of the allegation. All that is required is a certificate of counsel of record to say that it is made in good faith.

There is a similar provision in some state statutes. However, it has to be said that in certain other states this kind of provision has been held unconstitutional on the ground that it transfers judicial power from the court to the parties.[55]

## *United States – juries*

By contrast with Britain, in the United States prospective jurors are routinely subjected to examination on the voir dire, which is a crucial part of jury selection.

In England it is not possible to question jurors at all. At the time of writing it is still possible to challenge at juror for cause, but this is extremely rare, as it has to be based on information about him or her obtained from some source other than the juror him- or herself. In practice such challenges are limited to a situation where a juror recognizes the defendant.

That is why British cases concerned with alleged prejudice on the part of a juror tend to arise only after the trial. By contrast, the general practice in the United States of jury selection on the basis of voir dire examination leaves little room for any dispute about the fairness of a verdict after it has been returned. Indeed, it is a general rule of US procedural law, whether in a state or federal court and whether in a civil or criminal trial, that once a verdict has been rendered it is too late to apply to disqualify a juror. The rule is not invariable, but the key test is whether the losing party has been prejudiced by the presence of a juror who ought not to have been impanelled in the first place. There is also an understandable reluctance to allow such matters to be decided by an appeal court, which, unlike the trial judge, will not have had the opportunity of seeing and hearing the testimony of the juror concerned and determining his or her demeanour.[56]

One of the grounds on which a juror may be challenged in the United States is *propter affectum*, that is, on the basis that the juror was likely to be biased. Where a juror is connected with one of the parties by blood, marriage or commercial ties there is a presumption that he or she will be biased, so a juror who is related to one of the parties is automatically disqualified. This ancient rule extends to the ninth degree of relationship! A challenge on this ground is characterized as a challenge 'for principal cause'. Other principal causes include situations where a juror is the employer or employee of either party or their attorney. In such situations the relationship or association between the juror and the party is conclusive, and no court has any discretion to disregard it.[57]

The other form of challenge *propter affectum* is what is termed a 'challenge to the favor'. Does this mean that a juror who shows sympathy for one of the parties can be challenged under this head? It has been held that this in itself will not necessarily disqualify the juror concerned, provided the juror claims that this will not affect his or her ability to reach a verdict dispassionately.[58]

The key question here is whether the relevant juror has prejudged the case. But how is it possible to tell? Is it enough if the juror has placed a bet on the outcome of the case? However, where a juror made a $1 bet on the penalty in a murder case before the juror knew that he would be called in that case, it was held that there was no prejudice. The fact that the position taken by the juror was contrary to his small financial interest in the outcome no doubt contributed to this result.[59]

In only very rare cases have counsel been allowed to question jurors upon voir dire on their political views or affiliation. A challenge on political grounds was even disallowed in a quo warranto case challenging the election of a particular official, where the jurors in question were members of a political club which had opposed the defendant in the disputed election.[60]

The reason for the reluctance of US law to allow political prejudice to disqualify a juror is no doubt because of the openness of political party affiliation in American life, in a way that is unimaginable in Britain or Europe.

Voir dire examination of jurors on their religious beliefs has, however, been allowed in certain cases. But the most frequent type of bias on which questioning is permitted is racial prejudice. However, even where a juror has admitted holding a prejudice against a particular race or nationality, this has not disqualified him or her if he or she can credibly assert that he or she harbours no prejudice against the party in question, or that his or her prejudice against the race or nationality concerned is not so extreme as to affect the fairness of his or her verdict.[61]

## Conclusion

English law, it turns out, has fallen out of step with the rest of the common law world. In England alone the test is whether there was a real danger of bias. In the United States and Australia, as we have seen, as well as in Canada and New Zealand, some form of the 'reasonable suspicion' test holds sway. This is hardly surprising, as that was the original English test as well. Why then have the English courts seen fit to depart from it?

The justification given for this is essentially that it would be unjust for the mere impression of bias to be enough to set aside a decision. However, this argument can easily be countered:

- Bias is insidious. It is impossible to tell whether someone actually is biased or not, so conduct which might give that impression cannot be ignored.
- Even if a decision is set aside on this basis, the case can always go to a retrial. But the more alert judges are to the need to avoid doing anything that could give the impression of partiality, the fewer decisions there will be that have to be set aside. Had the time-honoured principle enunciated by Lords Esher,

Hewart and Denning not been discredited by the English courts the *Pinochet* debacle would probably never have occurred. For although it was not realized that Lord Hoffmann was automatically disqualified from sitting on that case, it should nevertheless have been obvious that his doing so would be likely to give an impression of partiality. But as this did not matter under the already prevailing 'real danger of bias' test, those who knew of Lord Hoffmann's association with Amnesty International presumably considered that there was no obstacle to his sitting.

- The abandonment of the traditional doctrine in favour of the 'real danger' test may, ironically, itself be seen as a breach of the principle that no one should be a judge in his or her own cause. For in changing the rules in this way, the English courts have taken it upon themselves not only to act as legislators – which has become increasingly common – but to do so in a matter that affected their own position. The 'real danger' criterion makes a judge's decision much harder to challenge on grounds of bias than it would have been under the old test.

**Q. Does it make any difference whether a case is classified as civil or criminal?**

***A. Yes, because defendants in criminal cases enjoy many more rights than civil litigants. As a result there have been some challenges to the classification of cases, some of which have been successful.***

The prime example is an English case involving failure to pay the community charge: *Benham v UK*.[62] Although the amount involved was only £325, because it was held by the magistrates' court that non-payment had been the result of 'culpable neglect' Stephen Benham was committed to prison for 30 days. This decision was reversed on appeal, but by that time he had already spent 11 days in prison. Under English law these proceedings were classed as civil, not criminal, so Mr Benham was not entitled to free legal representation, and, as he could not afford a lawyer, he had to defend himself.

He took the case to Strasbourg, where the court held that as the original case had been brought by a public authority and the magistrates had the power to imprison for non-payment, it was really a criminal case, which meant that free legal representation ought to have been available. As a result, it was held by a unanimous Strasbourg court, there had been a violation of Articles 6(1) and 6(3)(c) taken together.

By contrast, in a domestic decision it was held that an application by a local authority for an anti-social behaviour order under the Crime and Disorder Act 1998 was a civil rather than a criminal matter.[63]

**Q. What is meant by 'civil rights' and are these protected by the European Convention on Human Rights?**

***A. 'Civil rights' are supposedly protected by the ECHR, but what this means is now more uncertain than ever.***

The term 'civil rights', which occurs in Article 6(1), has become a buzz-phrase with the English courts. What exactly does it mean? Its context in Article 6 makes that pretty clear: 'In the determination of his civil rights and obligations or of any criminal charge against him, everyone is entitled to a fair and public hearing . . . '. The article is concerned with the right to a fair trial; and the juxtaposition of 'civil right' with 'criminal charge' surely indicates that all this means is simply that everyone has the right to a fair trial whether civil or criminal. It is important to note that the relevant phrase is not 'civil rights' but 'civil rights and obligations'.

So far so good. It is perhaps worth noting that 'civil rights' has a much wider meaning in the United States, where it is used as a synonym for what is generally referred to in the United Kingdom as 'human rights'. It is possibly under the influence of this broader concept that the courts have made such a meal of 'civil rights' in recent years.

As recently explained by Lord Hoffmann:

> The term 'civil rights and obligations', was originally intended to mean those rights and obligations which, in continental European systems of law, were adjudicated upon by the civil courts. These were, essentially, rights and obligations in private law. The term was not intended to cover administrative decisions which were conventionally subject to review (if at all) by administrative courts.[64]

The extension of the concept of 'civil rights' started as long ago as 1971. The applicant in a case against Austria complained to the Strasbourg court that the determination of an administrative matter by a so-called Regional Commission constituted a violation of his civil rights. The Strasbourg court accepted that the applicant's rights in what could be regarded as an administrative matter were 'civil rights', although the application failed as it was held that the Commission qualified as 'an independent and impartial tribunal' within Article 6(1).[65]

This marked a breach with the principle that 'civil rights and obligations' in Article 6(1) meant just that: rights and obligations in a civil legal suit, as distinct from a criminal prosecution and also from public law. In continental Europe there had long been a clear-cut distinction between public law and private law. However *Ringeisen's* case blurred the distinction as far as human rights law was concerned, leading to inconsistency and ultimately to confusion.

*Ringeisen* was followed in a later Austrian case involving government expropriation of land for the purpose of building a highway. The firm whose property had been compulsorily purchased took the case to Strasbourg on the ground that it had been denied access to 'an independent and impartial tribunal' as guaranteed under Article 6(1) . However, the Strasbourg court held unanimously that access to the Austrian Administrative Court, which had jurisdiction over such matters, did indeed fulfil the requirements of Article 6. So no violation of Article 6 was found.[66]

The issue in such cases is twofold. First, does an administrative matter like this entail a determination of 'civil rights'? Second, does the domestic court or tribunal qualify as an 'independent and impartial tribunal'?

In essence the question is whether it is an infringement of Article 6 for administrative decisions in regard to such matters as planning applications, housing and welfare to be taken by administrators or administrative tribunals rather than by the ordinary law courts.

In general judges tend jealously to cling to and extend the scope of their own jurisdiction. It is hardly surprising therefore to find them insisting that Article 6(1) demands that it must be possible for an administrative decision to be challenged by a court exercising 'full powers' or 'full jurisdiction'.

With one or two hiccups along the way, the initial modest extensions of the concept of 'civil rights' by the Strasbourg court became more and more daring, culminating in a case brought against the United Kingdom by Max Kingsley, a casino manager whose 'certificate of approval' had been revoked by the Gaming Board. Mr Kingsley challenged this decision by applying to the High Court for judicial review of the Gaming Board's decision. After a hearing lasting 16 days his application for judicial review was refused. No fewer than three judgments were delivered, all of them unfavourable to Mr Kingsley, the last of these (165 pages in length) being on Mr Kingsley's allegations that the Gaming Board had been biased against him and that its decision had been *Wednesbury* unreasonable.[67]

After being refused leave by the Court of Appeal to appeal against this decision, Mr Kingsley took his case to Strasbourg. Surprisingly perhaps, the UK government did not contest the claim that Mr Kingsley's 'civil rights' were engaged here, as under English law Mr Kingsley had no right to sue the Gaming Board directly but only to seek to have its decision set aside by judicial review.

The Strasbourg court held unanimously that there had been a violation of Mr Kingsley's 'civil rights' under Article 6(1). The chief basis for this decision was that in judicially reviewing the decision of the Gaming Board the High Court did not have 'full jurisdiction' to substitute its own decision on the facts for that of the Gaming Board.

This really amounts to a fundamental attack on the whole English system of judicial review. Unlike an appeal, where the court in question has the power to consider the merits of the case afresh and reach its own conclusion, judicial review is limited to determining whether the decision under review is lawful. For the reviewing court to substitute its own decision for that of the original decision maker is strictly forbidden. So in this case, if the court had substituted its own decision for that of the Gaming Board on whether Mr Kingsley was 'a fit and proper person' to hold a gaming licence, the court would have been usurping the position of the Gaming Board, which was entrusted by statute with the power and duty to decide such matters.[68]

Does this mean that judicial review will no longer satisfy the requirement in Article 6(1) that civil rights and obligations be determined by 'an independent and impartial tribunal'? Not quite. It is worth comparing *Kingsley's* case with that of *Bryan,* which had an opposite outcome in Strasbourg. This was a planning case in which there was no dispute of fact. Mr Bryan had received an enforcement notice from the local authority requiring him to demolish two buildings that had been constructed in a conservation area without planning permission. Mr Bryan exercised his statutory right under planning law to appeal to the Secretary of State for the Environment, who appointed a planning inspector to conduct an inquiry and determine the appeal. Mr Bryan's appeal was rejected by the inspector. Mr Bryan then appealed to the High Court, as he was entitled to do, and this appeal was also dismissed. But though described as an appeal, this process is restricted to an appeal 'on a point of law' and is therefore more akin to a judicial review. Nevertheless, because there was no dispute over the primary facts a unanimous Strasbourg court found that 'the scope of the High Court was therefore sufficient to comply with Article 6(1)' and that there was accordingly no violation of that article.[69]

The Strasbourg court in *Kingsley* recognised the similarity between that case and *Bryan*:

> The subject matter of the decision appealed against was thus a classic exercise of administrative discretion, and to this extent the current case is analogous to the case of Bryan. . . . The Court does not accept the applicant's contentions that, because of what was at stake for him, he should have had the benefit of a full court hearing on both the facts and the law.

If a 'full court hearing on both the facts and the law' is not called for in 'civil rights' matters involving 'administrative discretion', what then is meant by the requirement of 'full jurisdiction'?

At the time of writing the leading authority on this is a House of Lords decision in a housing case. The applicant, Runa Begum, sought accommodation for herself and her child from a local authority on the basis that she was threatened with homelessness. She was offered a secure tenancy of a two-bedroom flat, which she turned down, on the grounds that the area was 'drug addicted', 'racist' and violent and that her estranged husband frequently visited the block in question. Runa Begum requested a review of the council's decision, which was conducted by the council's rehousing manager, Sue Hayes, who rejected her reasons for refusing as 'unreasonable': 'I consider that the area in which [the block] is located is no different to any other area within the [borough].'[70] Runa Begum then exercised her statutory right to appeal on a point of law to the county court. After an initial victory she lost in the Court of Appeal and took the matter to the House of Lords.

The House of Lords was confronted by three issues:

1. When Sue Hayes decided that Runa Begum's refusal was unreasonable, was this a determination of Runa Begum's 'civil rights' within Article 6(1)?
2. If so, did Sue Hayes constitute an 'independent and impartial tribunal' as required by Article 6(1)?
3. If not, did the county court possess 'full jurisdiction' to determine the matter?

The result was inconclusive. The House of Lords chose not to answer the first question at all but dealt with the remaining questions on the assumption that the case did concern 'civil rights'. Question two had to be answered in the negative, as there was no way that Sue Hayes, an employee of the housing authority, could possibly be regarded as independent, although the court expressed confidence that she had been impartial. As for the third question, the answer given by Lord Bingham was cryptic: '"full jurisdiction" means "full jurisdiction to deal with the case as the nature of the decision requires"'.[71]

Lord Bingham summed the whole position up in a delphic formula:

> The narrower the interpretation given to 'civil rights', the greater the need to insist on review by a judicial tribunal exercising full powers. Conversely, the more elastic the interpretation given to 'civil rights', the more flexible must be the approach to the requirement of independent and impartial review if the emasculation (by over-judicialisation) of administrative welfare schemes is to be avoided.[72]

This appears to mean that the level of powers exercised by the domestic courts in judicial review applications should vary in accordance with the scope of the definition of 'civil rights': hardly a satisfactory solution, especially as the definition of 'civil rights' was left uncertain. Lord Bingham did, however, at least recognize the danger of 'over-judicialisation', or undue control by the courts.

Likewise Lord Hoffmann in *Alconbury*: 'The 1998 [Human Rights] Act was no doubt intended to strengthen the rule of law but not to inaugurate the rule of lawyers.' This is a fundamental distinction and one regrettably all too often glossed over.[73]

Lord Clyde made a similar point. Considering the suggestion that 'the scope of judicial review might somehow be enlarged so as to provide a complete remedy' to cover Article 6(1), he remarked: 'The point in the event does not arise, but I consider that it might well be difficult to achieve a sufficient enlargement to meet the stated purpose without jeopardising the constitutional balance between the role of the courts and the role of the executive.'[74]

Lord Clyde here puts his finger on a serious problem, namely judicial activism or what is sometimes termed judicial supremacism. For every increase in the power of unelected judges reduces that of the democratically elected government.[75] However, Lord Clyde then continues in a different vein:

> The supervisory jurisdiction of the court as it has now developed seems to me adequate to deal with a wide range of complaints which can properly be seen as directed to the legality of a decision. It is sufficient to note the recognition of the idea of proportionality, or perhaps more accurately, disproportionality, and the extent to which the factual areas of a decision may be penetrated by a review of the account taken by a decision-maker of facts which are irrelevant or even mistaken.[76]

Having flagged up the danger of over-judicialization, Lord Clyde here praises the extension of the principles governing the scope of judicial review in two directions: to proportionality and to consideration of 'mistaken' facts. On whose authority were these two major new principles added? The judges decided on it themselves. Is this not therefore in itself an example of judicial supremacism?[77]

## *Conclusion*

The upshot of all this is that the law is more uncertain than ever. The courts have made a meal of the term 'civil rights' but have spat it out without digesting it. The cases of *Alconbury* and *Runa Begum* have both allowed a certain latitude to administrative decisions, but this comes after a major expansion of the scope of judicial review decided on by the judges themselves.

**Q. Are decisions relating to planning and other policy matters determinations of 'civil rights and obligations' which have to be heard by 'an independent and impartial tribunal', that is, by a judge or court?**

***A. No, although Strasbourg has got itself into an awful tangle over this question.***

Article 6(1) says that everyone is entitled to a hearing 'by an independent and impartial tribunal established by law' 'in the determination of his civil rights and obligations or of any criminal charge against him'. This provision started life as a standard guarantee of a fair trial, but it has now become bogged down in a quagmire over the question of what is meant by 'civil rights and obligations'. Do planning decisions and other policy matters fall under this heading? That was the question before the House of Lords in the leading *Alconbury* case.[78] *Alconbury* itself, which was concerned with a planning application, was heard together with several other cases involving compulsory purchase, railways and highways. Are such matters really determinations of 'civil rights and obligations'? Lord Hoffmann held that this type of case required a decision 'as to what the public interest requires' and not a determination of civil rights and obligations. 'It may affect civil rights and obligations but it is not, and ought not to be, a judicial act such as art 6 has in contemplation.' He went on to hold that:

> a decision as to the public interest (what I shall call for short a 'policy decision') is quite different from a determination of right. The administrator may have a duty, in accordance with the rule of law, to behave fairly ('quasi-judicially') in the decision-making procedure. But the decision itself is not a judicial or quasi-judicial act. It does not involve deciding between the rights and interests of particular persons. It is the exercise of a power delegated by the people as a whole to decide what the public interest requires.[79]

Amazingly, the authority relied upon for this crucial distinction between 'policy decisions and determinations of right' was a judgment by Lord Greene MR dating from 1947 – the same judge and the same year as the famous but now frequently disparaged *Wednesbury* case![80] The case relied upon in *Alconbury* is a largely forgotten case about a compulsory purchase order made by a local authority and confirmed by the Minister of Health.[81] The owners of the land challenged the order on the ground that the Minister had failed to act in a 'quasi-judicial' manner as he was required to do. This argument succeeded at first instance but was reversed by a unanimous Court of Appeal, which held, as Lord Greene put it, that:

> the functions of the Minister in carrying these provisions into operation are fundamentally administrative functions. In carrying them out he has the duty which every Minister owes to the Crown, viz. to perform his functions fairly and honestly and to the best of his ability. But his functions are administrative functions, subject only to the qualification that at a particular stage and for a particular and limited purpose there is superimposed on his administrative character a character which is loosely described as quasi-judicial. . . . His action in so deciding is a purely administrative action, based on his conceptions as to what public policy demands. His views on that matter he must, if necessary, defend in Parliament, but he cannot be called on to defend them in the courts.

In his usual careful manner Lord Greene went on to explain that:

> As a Minister, if he acts unfairly his action may be challenged and criticised in Parliament. It cannot be challenged and criticised in the courts unless he has acted unfairly in another sense, viz. in the sense of having, while performing quasi-judicial functions, acted in a way which no person performing such functions, in the opinion of the court, ought to act.[82]

This is a fine distinction but an important one. As in *Wednesbury*, Lord Greene is concerned that judges do not usurp powers belonging to others by substituting their own decisions for the decisions of those properly entrusted with the right to make those decisions. In *Johnson* the Minister was entrusted with the power to decide whether a particular piece of land should be compulsorily purchased or not. That, said Lord Greene, is an administrative decision and the courts cannot interfere with it – unless, viewed objectively, the way that the Minister reached his decision was unlawful or improper.

Does the endorsement of this kind of language and thinking by the House of Lords in *Alconbury* mean that we are now back in what activist judges and their supporters would see as the 'bad old days'?

On the face of it *Alconbury* represents a rejection of judicial activism in regard to administrative decisions. Lord Hoffmann even remarks that the Human Rights Act 'was no doubt intended to strengthen the rule of law but not to inaugurate the rule of lawyers'.[83] This rejects the all-too-frequent assumption made by lawyers that the more power that is concentrated in the hands of the judiciary the better. Lord Nolan goes even further than Lord Hoffmann, remarking: 'To substitute for the Secretary of State an independent and impartial body with no central electoral accountability would not only be a recipe for chaos: it would be profoundly undemocratic.'[84]

The cases to which these remarks are applicable are administrative law cases involving public rather than private rights. The vehicle for bringing such cases to court is judicial review, where the role of the court has always been strictly limited. A judge engaged in a judicial review is not supposed to substitute his or her own decision for that of the minister or official entrusted with the power to make that decision, but only to determine whether the decision of the minister or official concerned is lawful.

By stressing this fundamental point, the House of Lords in *Alconbury* was not saying anything new as far as English law was concerned. But it was still important to say it, for two reasons:

- This limitation on the power of the judges in judicial reviews has often been honoured more in the breach than in the observance.
- The Strasbourg court has not followed a consistent line on this, allowing the UK authorities a much wider margin of appreciation in some cases than in others.

But there is a sting in the tail to this apparent judicial self-restraint. For, as emerges particularly from Lord Slynn's speech in *Alconbury*:

- '[I]t is not right to say that a policy maker cannot be a decision maker or that the final decision maker cannot be a democratically elected person or body.'[85]

But:

- Where this is the case, there has to be 'a sufficient judicial control to ensure a determination by an independent and impartial tribunal subsequently'.[86]

However:

- 'Judicial control' does not mean that the court has to have '"full jurisdiction" to review policy or the overall merits of a planning decision'.[87] 'This principle does not go as far as to provide for a complete rehearing on the merits of the decision. Judicial control does not need to go so far. It should not do so unless Parliament specifically authorizes it in particular areas.'[88]

Nevertheless:

- The scope of judicial review should be expanded to include the principle of proportionality and the doctrine that a court should be permitted to quash a decision reached on 'a material error of fact'.[89]

The decision in *Alconbury* itself and its conjoined appeals upheld the right of government ministers to decide policy matters of this kind, but subject to certain stringent conditions.

Instead of resulting in more judicial self-restraint Alconbury could easily lead to more judicial activism. 'Judicial control' is a tell-tale phrase. What Alconbury is really saying, therefore, is that it is all right for administrative decisions to be taken by officials or elected politicians – as long as ultimate 'control' is in the hands of judges who, though not permitted to substitute their own decision for that of the original decision maker, are vested with expanded powers of judicial review.

## Notes

1 *V v UK* 99/122; *T v UK* 99/121–16 December 1999.
2 *Saunders v UK* (1997) 23 EHRR 313 96/59; *Condron v UK* 00/143–2 May 2000; *John Murray v UK* (1996) 22 EHRR 29 96/2.
3 The quotation is from *Ford v Blurton* (1922) 38 TLR 801 at 805, per Atkin LJ (later Lord Atkin). At the time of writing there is a threat to jury trials even in criminal cases. The British government of Tony Blair has expressed the intention of depriving the defendant of the right to a jury trial in prosecutions for 'offences triable either way', including burglary, theft and assaults short of grievous bodily harm.
4 *Lieuwe Hoekstra, Jan van Rijs et al v HM Advocate (No. 1)* (2000) UKHRR 578.
5 *Golder v UK* (1979–80) 1 EHRR 524 75/1.
6 *Piersack v Belgium* (1983) 5 EHRR 169, (1985) 7 EHRR 251 82/6; *De Cubber v Belgium* (1985) 7 EHRR 236, (1991) 13 EHRR 422 84/13.
7 *Findlay v UK* (1997) 24 EHRR 221 97/8.
8 *Boyd and others v Army Prosecuting Authority and others* [2002] UKHL 31; *R v Spear, Hastie and Boyd* [2001] 2 WLR 1692 (Courts Martial Appeal Court).
9 *McGonnell v United Kingdom* 00/66.
10 *R in Secretary of State for the Home Department, ex parte Anthony Anderson* [2002] UKHL 46.
11 [2002] UKHL 46 at §9.
12 *Ibid*. The Strasbourg court has now specifically held that it is a breach of Article 5(4) of the ECHR for a convicted murderer's 'tariff' to be set by the Home Secretary, as the minister is not a judge or a judicial body with the power to order the murderer's release: *Egon von Bulow v UK*, ECtHR, 7 October 2003, Application no 00075362/01.
13 *BBC News* Web site, 21 October 2002.
14 *Ring v Arizona* Case no 010–488, 24 June 2002 <http://laws.findlaw.com/us/000/01–488.html>.
15 *Duport Steels v Sirs* (1980) 1 All ER 529 at 541.
16 Circuit judges may be removed by the Lord Chancellor for incapacity or misbehaviour: Courts Act 1971, s 17(4). High Court judges and above may be removed by the Crown on an address by both Houses of Parliament. But even a criminal conviction, for driving with more than the permitted level of alcohol in his blood, did not trigger any such consequences for a High Court judge in 1975. And a recent finding by the House of Lords that a law lord ought not to have been sitting on a particular case owing to his association with a pressure group involved in the case as an intervener did not result in the law lord's resignation nor in any action being taken against him.

17 *Webb and Hay v The Queen* (1994) 181 CLR 41, (1994) 122 ALR 41.
18 *Dimes v Grand Junction Canal Co* (1852) 3 HL Cas 759, 10 ER 301.
19 *R v Bow Street Metropolitan Stipendiary Magistrate, ex parte Pinochet Ugarte (No 2)* [1999] 1 All ER 577 at 589.
20 *R v Bow Street Metropolitan Stipendiary Magistrate, ex parte Pinochet Ugarte* [1998] 4 All ER 897.
21 After the first House of Lords judgment in *Pinochet*, so closely involved was Amnesty International in the case that it actually sought judicial review to forestall any attempt by the Home Secretary to block Senator Pinochet's extradition to Spain: *R v Secretary of State for the Home Department, ex parte Amnesty International* (Queen's Bench Divisional Court, 9 December 1998) Lawtel 10/12/98.
22 *R v Bow Street Metropolitan Stipendiary Magistrate, ex parte Pinochet Ugarte (No 2)* [1999] 1 All ER 577.
23 *Ibid* at 583.
24 *Ibid* at 595 f.
25 *Locabail v Bayfield Properties* [2000] 1 All ER 65 at 70 f.
26 *Ibid* at 71.
27 *R v Bow Street Metropolitan Stipendiary Magistrate, ex parte Pinochet Ugarte (No 2)* [1999] 1 All ER 571 at 589.
28 *Locabail v Bayfield Properties* [2000] 1 All ER 65 at 81.
29 *Ibid* at 87.
30 *Ibid* at 92.
31 *R v Gough* [1993] 2 All ER 724.
32 *Ibid* at 737–738.
33 *Ibid* at 740.
34 *Ibid* at 735.
35 *R v Spencer* [1985] 1 All ER 673 (CA), (1986) 2 All ER 928 (HL).
36 *R v Sussex Justices, ex parte McCarthy* [1923] All ER Rep 233.
37 *R v Gough* [1993] 2 All ER 724 at 731.
38 *R v Sussex Justices, ex parte McCarthy* [1923] All ER Rep 233 at 234.
39 *Metropolitan Properties v Lannon* [1968] 3 All ER 304 at 309–310.
40 *R v Camborne Justices, ex parte Pearce* [1954] 2 All ER 850 at 855.
41 Lord Esher MR in *Eckersley v Mersey Docks* [1891–4] All ER Rep 1130 at 1132, [1894] 2 QB 667.
42 *R v Gough* [1993] 2 All ER 724 at 737.
43 *R v Morris* (1991) 93 Cr App R 102.
44 *R v Gough* [1993] 2 All ER 724 at 736.
45 *R v Spencer* [1985] 1 All ER 673 (CA), [1986] 2 All ER 928 (HL).
46 [1985] 1 All ER 673 at 685.
47 [1986] 2 All ER 928 at 939.
48 *Webb and Hay v The Queen* (1994) 181 CLR 41, (1994) ALR 41.

49 See for example *Commonwealth v Murphy*, 295 **Ky** 466, 174 SW2d 681, *Hughes v Black*, 156 **Me** 69, 160 A2d 113.
50 See for example *Suttles v Northwestern Mut L Ins Co*, 193 **Ga** 495, 19 SE2d 396, 21 SE2d 695, 143 ALR 343.
51 See *Lynip v Alturas School District*, 29 **Cal** App 158 158, 155 P 109, and 30 **Cal** App 794, 160 P 175.
52 28 United States Code §455(a)
53 See *R v Bow Street Metropolitan Stipendiary Magistrate, ex parte Pinochet Ugarte (No 2)* [1999] 1 All E 577 at 593, per Lord Hope.
54 28 USC §144.
55 See *Diehl v Crump*, 72 **Okla** 108, 179 P 4, 5 ALR 1272. 28 USC §144–46 Am Jur 2d S215, p. 237.
56 47 Am Jur 2d #219 ff, p 808 ff.
57 See *Alabama Fuel & Iron Co v Powaski*, 232 **Ala** 66, 166 So 782.
58 *Commonwealth v Webster*, 59 **Mass** (5 Cush) 295.
59 *Fugate v State*, 169 **Neb** 420, 99 NW2d 868.
60 *Gray v State*, 19 **Tex** Civ App 521, 49 SW 699.
61 *State v Giudice*, 170 **Iowa** 731, 153 NW 336; *Johnson v State*, 88 **Neb** 565, 130 NW 282.
62 *Benham v UK* (1996) 22 EHRR 293 96/21.
63 *R v Manchester Crown Court, ex parte McCann* (22 November 2000).
64 *Runa Begum v Tower Hamlets LBC* [2003] UKHL 5 [2003] 1 All ER 731, §28, citing the dissenting opinion in *Feldbrugge v Netherlands* (1986) 8 EHRR 425 at 444 (§19–21).
65 *Ringeisen v Austria (No 1)* (1971) 1 EHRR 455 2614/65.
66 *Zumtobel v Austria* (1993) 17 EHRR 116 93/37.
67 *R v Gaming Board for Great Britain, ex parte Kingsley QBD* (Jowitt J) 11/1/96 (Lawtel).
68 *Kingsley v United Kingdom* (2000) 33 EHRR 13 35605/97.
69 *Bryan v UK* (1996) 21 EHRR 342 19178/91. Cf *R (on the application of Alconbury Developments Ltd) v Secretary of State for the Environment* [2001] UKHL 23, [2001] 2 All ER 929.
70 *Runa Begum v Tower Hamlets LBC* [2003] UKHL 5 [2003] 1 All ER 731, §9.
71 *Ibid*, §5, quoted from Lord Hoffmann's speech in *R (on the application of Alconbury Developments Ltd) v Secretary of State for the Environment* [2001] UKHL 23, [2001] 2 All ER 929, §87.
72 *Runa Begum v Tower Hamlets LBC* [2003] UKHL 5 [2003] 1 All ER 731, §5.
73 *R (on the application of Alconbury Developments Ltd) v Secretary of State for the Environment* [2001] UKHL 23, [2001] 2 All ER 929 at 995, §129.
74 *Ibid* at 1008, §169.
75 *Ibid*. Sedley LJ has argued that 'Ministers are no more elected than judges': The common law and the constitution, in Nolan and Sedley (1997) *The Making*

*and Remaking of the British Constitution*, p 27. This is at least a recognition of the need for the judiciary to claim that it has democratic accountability. The whole argument is based on the appointment by Harold Wilson of two ministers, Patrick Gordon Walker and Frank Cousins, who were not members of either House of Parliament. But this only lasted a short time, and the gyrations Wilson went into to secure a seat in Parliament for his two ministers shows just how exceptional a situation this was. Moreover, when Gordon Walker lost the by-election that was intended to bring him back into the House of Commons, he promptly resigned his ministerial position – a further recognition that it was simply not possible to continue without a seat in Parliament. This is more fully discussed in Arnheim, *Principles of the Common Law* (forthcoming).

76 *Ibid*, referring to *R v Criminal Injuries Compensation Board ex p A* [1999] 2 AC 330 at 344–345.

77 Irrelevancy had long been recognized as a basis for deciding on the legality of a decision. See *Associated Provincial Picture Houses v Wednesbury Corp* [1947] 2 All ER 680.

78 *R (on the application of Alconbury Developments Ltd) v Secretary of State for the Environment* [2001] UKHL 23, [2001] 2 All ER 929.

79 *Ibid*, para 74.

80 *Associated Provincial Picture Houses v Wednesbury Corporation* [1948] 2 All ER 680.

81 *Johnson & Co v Minister of Health* [1947] 2 All ER 395.

82 *Ibid*, at 400.

83 [2001] 2 All ER 929 at 995. Whether consciously or not, this echoes the wag in the early days of US independence who, in response to the claim that the US constitution would introduce 'a government not of men but of laws', retorted 'a government not of laws but of lawyers'.

84 [2001] 2 All ER 929 at 978, §60.

85 *Ibid* at 975, §48.

86 *Ibid*, §49.

87 *Ibid*, §50.

88 *Ibid*, §52.

89 *Ibid*, §53.

# 12

# Social rights

### Article 11

#### *Freedom of assembly and association*

1. Everyone has the right to freedom of peaceful assembly and to freedom of association with others, including the right to form and to join trade unions for the protection of his interests.
2. No restrictions shall be placed on the exercise of these rights other than such as are prescribed by law and are necessary in a democratic society in the interests of national security or public safety, for the prevention of disorder or crime, for the protection of health or morals or for the protection of the rights and freedoms of others. This article shall not prevent the imposition of lawful restrictions on the exercise of these rights by members of the armed forces, of the police or of the administration of the State.

### Article 12

#### *Right to marry*

Men and women of marriageable age have the right to marry and to found a family, according to the national laws governing the exercise of this right.

### Article 14

#### *Prohibition of discrimination*

The enjoyment of the rights and freedoms set forth in this Convention shall be secured without discrimination on any ground such as sex, race, colour, language, religion, political or other opinion, national or social origin, association with a national minority, property, birth or other status.

## THE FIRST PROTOCOL

**Article 2**

***Right to education***

No person shall be denied the right to education. In the exercise of any functions which it assumes in relation to education and to teaching, the State shall respect the right of parents to ensure such education and teaching in conformity with their own religious and philosophical convictions.

**Q. Does the right to join a trade union include the right to refuse to join one?**

***A. Yes.***

The milestone case here was *Young, James and Webster v UK*,[1] one of the boldest and arguably one of the most sensible human rights cases ever decided. It involved three British railwaymen who had been sacked for refusing to join one of the rail unions. Strasbourg held that the 'closed shop' was incompatible with ECHR Article 11.

The case is interesting for other reasons as well. First, the reasoning process by which a negative right was read into an article guaranteeing a positive right. But, as always, this approach cannot be relied upon in every case. In *Gustafsson v Sweden*[2] a Swedish youth hostel proprietor refused to sign a collective agreement with a trade union and was then driven out of business as a result of a boycott organized by the trade union. The Strasbourg Court, disagreeing with the Strasbourg Human Rights Commission, rejected the applicant's claim that the pressure to get him to join a collective agreement was a violation of his rights under Article 11 (freedom of assembly and association) and also under Article 13 (right to an effective remedy). Article 13, which is not actually incorporated into the HRA, as the HRA itself effectively takes its place as far as the United Kingdom is concerned, reads as follows:

> Everyone whose rights and freedoms as set forth in this Convention are violated shall have an effective remedy before a national authority notwithstanding that the violation has been committed by persons acting in an official capacity.

*Young* is also of interest from the point of view of the fundamental Strasbourg doctrine of the margin of appreciation.[3] Although closed-shop agreements were perfectly legal under UK law at the time when the three railwaymen lost their jobs, and although the Strasbourg court accepted that there was a 'legitimate aim' behind such agreements, it was not prepared to allow the matter to be determined in accordance with UK law, thus effectively depriving the United Kingdom of its 'margin of appreciation'. It was irrelevant to the Strasbourg decision that between the sacking of the railwaymen and the Strasbourg hearings there had been a change of government in the United Kingdom, the new Thatcher administration being totally opposed to the whole idea of the closed shop and all that it stood for.

Finally, *Young* is an example of the Convention's indirect horizontal effect.[4] The three railwaymen's quarrel was with their employer, British Rail, which had dismissed them. Under UK law as it was at the time no redress was available. But precisely for this reason the United Kingdom was held responsible for failing to have legal guarantees in place that would have prevented such dismissals from taking place in the first place. And it was the state that was ordered to pay compensation: £18,626 to Ian Young, £46,215 to Noel James and £10,076 to Ronald Webster.

**Q. Do convicted prisoners have the right to marry?**
*A. Yes.*

Prisoners have the same right to marry as anyone else, and this applies even to life prisoners: *Draper v UK*.[5] In *Hamer v UK*[6] there were no facilities for conducting a marriage ceremony available inside the prison and a prisoner was refused permission to get married outside. The Human Rights Commission held that this amounted to a breach of Article 12. However, in certain cases placing a delay on a prisoner's marriage may be justified in the public interest: *Draper v UK*.

**Q. Does the right to marry include a right to divorce?**
*A. No.*

In *Johnston v Ireland*[7] the Strasbourg court held that the right to marry guaranteed by Article 12 did not imply a right to divorce. This marks an interesting contrast with the ruling that the right under Article 11 to join a trade union does include the right to refuse to join one: *Young, James and Webster v UK*.[8] *Johnston v Ireland* was decided at a time when divorce was not permitted under the Irish constitution. Since that time this provision has been changed on the basis of a popular referendum. Prior to this change the only legal remedy available in Ireland for a failed marriage was a judicial separation. *Airey v Ireland*[9] concerned a married woman who wanted a judicial separation but could not afford to hire a lawyer to obtain the decree. Legal aid was not available for this in Ireland at the time, and the Strasbourg court held that this constituted a breach of Article 6(1) guaranteeing a fair trial. Legal aid is specifically mentioned in Article 6, but only Article 6(3)(c) in regard to criminal trials. On the basis of the ancient rule of statutory construction, *expressio unius est exclusio alterius* ('the express mention of one thing implies the exclusion of another'), this should mean that the provision of legal aid does not apply to civil trials.

**Q. Do same-sex couples have the right to marry?**
***A. Not yet, but . . .***

Article 12 confers the right to marry and the right to found a family on 'men and women of marriageable age'. Could this possibly be interpreted so as allow a marriage between two men or two women 'of marriageable age'? This thought would not have crossed the minds of the drafters of the Convention. At the time of writing the conventional interpretation of 'marriage' still holds sway in Strasbourg.[10]

Unlike Articles 8 to 11, Article 12 has no second paragraph containing a list of exceptions, but the rights in Article 12 are subject to 'the national laws governing the exercise of this right'. This must presumably mean that there was intended to be a wide margin of appreciation accorded to the individual states.

Same-sex relationships are now interpreted as protected under Article 8 as 'private life' but not as 'family life', and Article 12 is not interpreted as including same-sex marriages.

## TRANSSEXUAL RIGHTS

The rights of transsexuals are one of the most obvious areas of law where the margin of appreciation has visibly shrunk in recent years.

In *Rees v UK*[11] a female-to-male transsexual applied to have his birth certificate amended. His request was refused on the ground that the register of births was meant to be a historical record, and that as Mark Rees was a physical and biological female at birth and given the name Margaret Rees, it would be falsifying the past to change the register. However, the same restrictions did not apply in regard to names. Under the general law, anybody in the United Kingdom has always been able to change their first name or surname at will. As far as transsexuals are concerned, this also entitled them to be issued with official documents – including passports, but not birth certificates – indicating their new gender.

The Strasbourg Human Rights Commission found unanimously that this refusal to change a transsexual's birth certificate was a violation of Article 8 ('respect for private and family life') but not of Article 12 ('right to marry'). The Strasbourg court agreed on Article 12 but took a far less liberal line on Article 8, holding by 12 votes to 3 that there had been no violation. This view was reached on the basis of a wide margin of appreciation.

This contrasts with the outcome in *B v France*[12], where a French male-to-female transsexual who had been refused an amendment on the official register of births was successful – in both the Commission and the Strasbourg court – in claiming a violation of Article 8.

Transsexual marriage was a more intractable question, and a wide margin of appreciation was in evidence in *Cossey v UK*.[13] Caroline Cossey was a male-to-female transsexual who had gone through a ceremony of marriage at a London synagogue which was declared void by the English High Court. This time the Strasbourg Commission was again more liberal-minded than the Strasbourg court. The Commission found a violation of Article 12 by 10 votes to 6, but by 14 votes to 4 the court disagreed.

The position was still in flux in *Sheffield and Horsham v UK*,[14] involving two male to female transsexuals who had undergone 'gender reassignment' operations. Kristina Sheffield had been married as a man and had a daughter. Her former wife got a court order to stop contact. Rachel Horsham was issued with a passport in her new name but was refused a new birth certificate. Both applicants claimed that their treatment at the hands of the UK authorities was discriminatory. The Human Rights Commission agreed with them, but by a narrow majority the Strasbourg court held that there had been no violation of Article 8 or Article 14 ('Prohibition of discrimination'). No breach was found under Article 12 either, and it was held that the right to marry was subject to the laws of the contracting states.

## Transsexual triumph

Christine Goodwin's case is now the leading Strasbourg authority on transsexual rights. Born male, she felt, as transsexuals often put it, that she was a woman in a man's body. After living as a woman for some time she underwent 'gender reassignment' surgery. She claimed that she then suffered harassment and discrimination at work together with numerous other social and financial handicaps arising from the fact that her birth certificate and other official documents continued to describe her as male.[15]

Did this amount to a violation by the United Kingdom of Christine Goodwin's 'right to respect for [her] private and family life' under Article 8? The Strasbourg court said yes. In view of the changing views on transsexualism, it was held that the United Kingdom could 'no longer claim that the matter falls within their margin of appreciation, save as regards the appropriate means of achieving recognition of the right protected under the Convention'.

## Marriage

Christine Goodwin's signal success under Article 8 was reinforced by an equally complete victory under Article 12. A unanimous Strasbourg court found that her rights under both articles had been violated by UK law, and the UK government subsequently announced its intention of passing legislation to recognize transsexual marriages.[16]

Her complaint under Article 12 was that UK law effectively prevented her from exercising her right to marry. Article 12, drafted at a time before 'gender reassignment' surgery, accords 'men and women of marriageable age the right to marry and to found a family, according to the national laws governing the exercise of this right'. This wording was given a wide – not to say elastic – interpretation by the Strasbourg court. The first obstacle to be got over was the specific reference to 'men and women'. But having already found in Christine Goodwin's favour on Article 8, the court cleared this hurdle quite effortlessly:

> It is true that the first sentence [of Article 8] refers in express terms to the right of a man and woman to marry. The Court is not persuaded that at the date of this case it can still be assumed that these terms must refer to a determination of gender by purely biological criteria.

European Union law is then prayed in aid:

> The Court would also note that Article 9 of the recently adopted Charter of Fundamental Rights of the European Union departs, no doubt deliberately, from the wording of Article 12 of the Convention in removing the reference to men and women.

There is a careful (deliberate?) omission here of a crucial part of the quoted Charter article, which reads as follows:

> The right to marry and the right to found a family shall be guaranteed in *accordance with the national laws governing the exercise of these rights*. [Emphasis added]

The italicized words allow a wide margin of appreciation to the individual EU member states, some of which recognize transsexual marriages and others of which do not. The full wording does not therefore help to take matters forward in the way that the Strasbourg court would have liked, as it leaves it to each state to decide in what circumstances, if any, non-standard marriages are to be recognized. For the United Kingdom, therefore, this would justify the status quo, under which there is no recognition for any but the conventional kind of marriage between a biological male and a biological female.

The next obstacle standing in the way of the desired goal is the association in Article 12 between marriage and the founding of a family. Indeed, the word 'right' occurs only once, suggesting that 'the right to marry and to found a family' is a single right embracing both. Article 9 of the EU Charter gets away from this concept by repeating the word 'right', to make it clear that the right to marry is distinct from the right to establish a family. Here the Strasbourg court is careful not to invoke the EU Charter, because the contrast would be glaring.

Nothing daunted, the judgment simply asserts that there are two separate and distinct rights in Article 12 itself, which is of course absolutely essential if transsexual marriages are to be recognized, as there can of course never be any natural issue of such a marriage:

> Reviewing the situation in 2002, the Court observes that Article 12 secures the fundamental right of a man and a woman to found a family. The second aspect is not however a condition of the first and the inability of any couple to conceive or parent a child cannot be regarded as per se removing their right to enjoy the first limb of this provision.[17]

The strongest argument in the court's armoury in favour of transsexual marriage is the apparently incontrovertible point that if a male-to-female transsexual is not allowed to marry a man, her right to marry is effectively non-existent:

> The applicant in this case lives as a woman, is in a relationship with a man and would only wish to marry a man. She has no possibility of doing so. In the Court's view, she may therefore claim that the very essence of her right to marry has been infringed.[18]

But this argument too is less persuasive upon closer examination. If the term 'marriage' extends to transsexual unions, why not then also to homosexual ones? This would clearly be impossible on the current wording of Article 12 or Article 9 of the EU Charter. However, if – as is already the case in certain countries – homosexual unions were legally recognized as equivalent to marriages without actually being called marriages, then transsexual unions could be recognized without straining the law. This would not of course satisfy transsexuals, who do not wish to be regarded as anything less than full members of their 'new' gender. But such recognition could facilitate fraud, where a particularly convincing transsexual is able to persuade a prospective mate that he or she is biologically of the desired gender. This possibility also contradicts the assertion made by Strasbourg (in regard to Article 8) that 'there are no significant factors of public interest to weigh against' the interests of transsexuals in obtaining legal recognition of their gender reassignment.

That such fraud is a real possibility is shown by the case of *S-T v J*,[19] in which a female-to-male transsexual went through a ceremony of marriage with a woman, declaring that there was no impediment to the marriage. The couple even had two children as a result of persuading a fertility clinic to provide artificial insemination by donor. The marriage eventually broke down and the wife petitioned for divorce. Indeed, it was only when the husband's birth certificate was produced at the hearing of the divorce petition that the wife learned the true situation. The husband was convicted of perjury and his claim for ancillary relief was rejected.

Besides harming others, full recognition of their 'new' gender could actually do harm to transsexuals themselves – and, even more so, to prospective transsexuals, because such recognition would only reinforce the popular misconception that there is such a thing as a 'sex-change' operation which can literally change a man into a woman or a woman into a man: a cruel deception indeed!

Finally, what about the margin of appreciation? The Strasbourg court was prepared to admit that 'fewer countries permit the marriage of transsexuals in their assigned gender than recognise the change of gender itself.'[20] But:

> The Court is not persuaded however that this supports an argument for leaving the matter entirely to the Contracting States as being within their margin of appreciation. This would be tantamount to finding that the range of options open to a contracting State included an effective bar on any exercise of the right to marry.[21]

The fact that the 'gender reassignment' surgery had been performed under the National Health Service was specifically used as a stick to beat the United Kingdom:

> The Court is struck by the fact that . . . the gender reassignment which is lawfully provided is not met with full recognition in law, which might have been regarded as the final and culminating step in the long and difficult process of transformation which the transsexual has undergone . . . . Where a State has authorised the treatment and surgery alleviating the condition of a transsexual, financed or assisted in financing the operations and indeed permits the artificial insemination of a woman living with a female-to-male transsexual (as demonstrated in the case of *X, Y & Z v UK* – 22/4/97) it appears illogical to refuse to recognise the legal implications of the result to which the treatment leads.[22]

What if it had not been possible to have 'gender reassignment' surgery on the National Health Service? Would Strasbourg then have considered it 'logical' to refuse to recognize transsexuals as belonging to their 'new' gender? Almost certainly not.

Another interesting type of logic occurs a few paragraphs down. The Strasbourg court admits that, despite 'increasingly sophisticated surgery and types of hormonal treatments' it is still not possible for a transsexual to 'acquire all the biological characteristics of the assigned sex' and 'the principal unchanging biological aspect of gender identity is the chromosomal element'.[23] The judgment then goes on to stress that 'chromosomal anomalies may arise naturally', as in 'intersex' cases, where 'some persons have to be assigned to one sex or the other as seems most appropriate in the circumstances of the individual case'. On this basis, the judgment goes on: 'It is not apparent to the Court that the chromosomal element, amongst all the others, must inevitably take on decisive significance for the purpose of legal attribution of gender identity for transsexuals.' Then comes the rather surprising conclusion: 'The Court is not persuaded therefore that the state of medical science or scientific knowledge provides any determining argument as regards the legal recognition of transsexuals.'[24]

Setting this argument out in syllogistic form, what we get is something like this:

1. There is a limit to the degree of sex-change that can be achieved by surgery and hormone treatment: in particular, chromosomes cannot be changed.
2. Chromosomal anomalies sometimes occur naturally, as with intersex births.
3. Therefore chromosomes should not be decisive in determining the legal identity of transsexuals.

It was also held that there were no significant factors of public interest to weigh against the interests of this individual applicant in order for a 'fair balance' to be struck.[25]

**Q. 'Can a person change the sex with which he or she is born?'**
***A. Yes, but not for the purposes of marriage.***

'Can a person change the sex with which he or she is born?' In the words of Lord Nicholls, this was essentially the issue before the House of Lords in *Bellinger v Bellinger*.[26] More specifically, the question was whether the marriage of a man to a male-to-female transsexual was valid.[27]

The relevant law is contained in section 11(c) of the Matrimonial Causes Act 1973, which provides that 'a marriage . . . shall be void' if 'the parties are not respectively male and female'.

After considering the recent Strasbourg decision in *Christine Goodwin v UK*,[28] Lord Nicholls nevertheless concluded that:

> Recognition of Mrs Bellinger as female for the purposes of section 11(c) of the Matrimonial Causes Act 1973 would necessitate giving the expressions 'male' and 'female' in that Act a novel, extended meaning: that a person may be born with one sex but later become, or become regarded as, a person of the opposite sex. This would represent a major change in the law, having far reaching ramifications. (§36–37)[29]

The other law lords agreed. What then about the duty of the courts in section 3(1) of the HRA to read and give effect to legislation in a way that is compatible with the Convention rights insofar as it is possible to do so?

There are, however, two problems with this. First, the HRA is not retrospective. So, according to Lord Hope, it could not apply to the Bellingers' purported marriage ceremony, which took place in 1981.[30] Lord Hobhouse ignored the question of retrospectivity and simply asked whether it was possible, as a matter of interpretation to:

> 'read down' s 11(c) of the 1973 Act so as to include additional words such as 'or two people of the same sex one of whom has changed his/her sex to that of the opposite sex'. This would in my view not be an exercise in interpretation however robust. It would be a legislative exercise of amendment: making a legislative choice as to what precise amendment was appropriate.[31]

The result of *Bellinger* appears strange. For, while refusing to validate a transsexual marriage on the ground that it was not permitted by s 11(c) of the Matrimonial Causes Act 1973, the House of Lords went on to declare that subsection incompatible with Articles 8 and 12 of the Convention.

**Q. Do illegitimate children have the same rights as legitimate ones?**
***A. Yes.***

*Johnston v Ireland*[32] (discussed above in regard to divorce) is again relevant here. Mr Johnston had separated from his wife but had been unable to have the marriage dissolved and to remarry. At the time of the application he was living with a new partner and the daughter of this union. In addition to Article 12 the application in *Johnston* was brought under Article 8, guaranteeing the 'right to respect for private and family life', the contention being that the unmarried couple and their daughter constituted a family. Because their daughter was classified under

Irish law as illegitimate, with certain resultant disabilities, it was held that this constituted a violation of Article 8.

This followed from *Marckx v Belgium*,[33] in which an unmarried mother successfully contended that Belgian illegitimacy laws amounted to a breach of the right to respect for family life within Article 8 and were also a violation of Article 14 because they were discriminatory.

In *Inze v Austria*,[34] the Strasbourg court held unanimously that an illegitimate son had been deprived of his property, contrary to Article 1 of the First Protocol of the Convention, and that he had also been discriminated against contrary to Article 14. Under Austrian law legitimate children were accorded priority in certain circumstances. Strasbourg maintained that any such discrimination would normally be incompatible with the Convention. In this particular case the Strasbourg ruling actually resulted in an illegitimate son being given preferential treatment over his legitimate sibling. The case involved the inheritance of farmland. Austrian law provided that farms of a stipulated size could not be subdivided. The question was whether the farm in question should go to Mr Inze, who was illegitimate, or to his legitimate half-brother. Austrian law gave it to the legitimate son, but Strasbourg said this was contrary to the Convention: as the illegitimate son was the elder the farm should have gone to him. Is it fairer and more humane to favour legitimacy over illegitimacy than to uphold primogeniture? Surely both are discriminatory.

This case is one of many showing that the way the Convention is interpreted tends to favour certain easily identifiable special interest groups, and tends to promote a particular social and sometimes even a political programme.

**Q. Do children have any rights?**
***A. Yes, implicitly the same as adults.***

Surprisingly, perhaps, there is no specific reference to the rights of children in the Convention at all. The assumption is that all Convention rights apply equally to all, irrespective of age. However, Strasbourg has paid increasing attention to the UN Convention on the Rights of the Child.

**Q. Are natural fathers discriminated against by comparison with mothers?**
***A. Yes, but with some notable exceptions.***

The sad Danish case of Jon Nielsen divided Strasbourg opinion in a fairly typical way.[35] Jon's parents were not married and his father's repeated applications for custody were rejected. Jon lived with his mother who, on medical advice, had him admitted at the age of 12 to the child psychiatric ward of the State Hospital. He was unsuccessful in challenging this decision, through his father, on the ground that it was unnecessary and unlawful and his mother's reason for having him admitted was that he did not want to stay with her. After spending five-and-a-half months in the hospital he was placed in a foster home. His complaint to Strasbourg was that his confinement in the hospital was a violation of Article

5(1) and Article 5(4). Article 5(1) guarantees 'the right to liberty and security of person' except in certain specified circumstances, including, in Article 5(1)(e), 'the lawful detention . . . of persons of unsound mind', which was not relevant here. Article 5(4) entitles 'everyone who is deprived of his liberty' to 'take proceedings by which the lawfulness of his detention shall be decided speedily by a court and his release ordered if the detention is not lawful'.

The Strasbourg Commission found in favour of Jon Nielsen by big majorities: 11 to 1 on Article 5(1) and 10 to 2 on Article 5(4). But the Strasbourg court was less sympathetic, finding Article 5 'not applicable' by 9 votes to 7.

## UK DOMESTIC LAW

By contrast, in a remarkable recent decision the House of Lords allowed an unmarried father to become his infant daughter's sole adoptive parent.[36] The mother had never had any interest in raising the child herself and had never met the child or even seen her, except at a distance. Soon after the birth the child had been placed with foster parents with a view to adoption. On learning of the existence of the child (from social services) the father at once expressed a desire to look after her, and the mother cooperated with him in making the necessary arrangements. From the age of two months the child lived with her father, who gave up his job to look after her. But when he applied to adopt her as sole parent he came up against the Official Solicitor, who in his capacity as the child's guardian opposed the father's application, in spite of the mother's consent. At first instance the father won, but he lost in the Court of Appeal, on the ground that there was no good reason justifying the exclusion of the mother. A unanimous House of Lords, however, reversed this decision and made the father the sole adoptive parent of his daughter.

Is English law so hostile to the rights of fathers that the case had to go all the way up to the House of Lords to get justice? All the more remarkably so, as the father had demonstrated his devotion to his daughter from the outset and the mother consented to his application.

This eminently sensible decision was based in part at least on Article 8 of the Convention. But it provides a good illustration of the different ways in which the same Convention right can be interpreted. Indeed, the interpretation adopted by the House of Lords was diametrically opposed to that put forward by the Court of Appeal. An adoption order, said the Court of Appeal, was an interference by a public authority (that is, a court) with the right to respect for family life under Article 8(1). Interference with this right is permissible under Article 8(2) only if it is 'in accordance with the law and is necessary in a democratic society in the interests of national security, public safety or the economic well being of the country, for the prevention of disorder or crime, for the protection of health or morals, or for the protection of the rights and freedoms of others'.

The Court of Appeal was quite happy to accept that adoption was 'in accordance with the law' and 'necessary in a democratic society'. It must also be in pursuit of a 'legitimate aim', must meet a 'pressing social need' and be 'proportionate' to that need – these all being favourite Strasbourg buzz-words though they do not actually appear in the text of the Convention itself. The Court of Appeal held that it was 'difficult indeed to argue that there is a pressing social need to deprive [the child] of all legal relationship with one half of her family of birth', and to do so would be 'a disproportionate response to her current needs'. The House of Lords disagreed. In the words of Lord Nicholls: 'I do not see how an adoption order made in this way can infringe the child's rights under Article 8'.

## DISCRIMINATION

Article 14 ('prohibition of discrimination') is commonly referred to as a parasitic right, for, as its wording indicates, it is concerned only with discrimination in regard to 'the enjoyment of the rights and freedoms set forth in this Convention'. It cannot therefore be invoked as a separate or freestanding right on its own but only as a rider to one of the other rights. In respect, however, to the grounds of discrimination that it prohibits its scope is vast, as it covers discrimination on a whole range of grounds, introduced by the words 'such as' and ending with the phrase 'or other status', a clear indication that the list of grounds is not to be regarded as closed.

So, for example, when June Buckley complained to Strasbourg about the refusal of planning permission for her and her family to live in three caravans parked on her own land, this was brought both as a claim under Article 8 ('respect for private and family life') and in addition as a claim under Article 14 in conjunction with Article 8. In her case both claims were rejected, but they were examined separately, and this is standard Strasbourg procedure.[37]

A classic Strasbourg case on discrimination is the *Belgian Linguistic Case*,[38] brought by Walloon or French-speaking Belgian parents complaining that the law in the Flemish (or Dutch) speaking parts of the country did not make adequate provision for French-language education. The claim was therefore based on Article 14 ('prohibition of discrimination') in conjunction with Article 2 of the First Protocol ('right to education').

Protocol 1 Article 2 refers specifically to the right of parents to ensure the provision of education 'in conformity with their own religious and philosophical convictions', but there is no mention of language. On the basis of the traditional rules of statutory construction this would give rise to a presumption of the operation of the old principle *expressio unius est exclusio alterius* ('the express mention of one thing implies the exclusion of another'). So, for example, where a statute specifically taxed 'every occupier of lands, houses, coal mines or saleable underwood', it was held that as coal mines were expressly mentioned, iron mines were exempt from the tax. However, the more broad-brush approach used in human rights law led the Strasbourg court to hold that the absence of any mention of the language of instruction did not mean that there was no right in this respect. On the contrary, it held that a 1963 Belgian law that restricted access to French-medium schools was incompatible with Article 14 read in conjunction with the first sentence of Protocol 1 Article 2.

## REVERSE DISCRIMINATION

Interestingly enough, Strasbourg has recently maintained that it is discriminatory not only to 'treat differently persons in analogous situations without providing an objective and reasonable justification' but also the converse, 'to treat differently persons whose situations are significantly different' again of course 'without an objective and reasonable justification'.[39]

This emerged in a Greek case involving a Jehovah's Witness who refused to wear military uniform at a time of general mobilization. He was convicted of insubordination by a court martial and sentenced to four years' imprisonment. Released after serving two years, he sat a public examination to become a chartered accountant. Despite getting the second highest marks of the 60 candidates sitting, he was debarred from practising as a chartered accountant by the Greek Institute of Chartered Accountants on the ground that he was a convicted felon. He failed to persuade the Greek Administrative Court, first, that his conviction had not been for a felony but only for a misdemeanour, and second, that his ban by the accountancy profession was a violation of his right to freedom of religion and equality before the law. In Strasbourg both the Commission and the Court found that he had been discriminated against in relation to his freedom of religion, or in Strasbourg parlance, there had been a breach of Article 14 ('prohibition of discrimination') taken in conjunction with Article 9 ('freedom of thought, conscience and religion'), which meant that it was not necessary to consider whether there had been a breach of Article 9 taken on its own. Both Strasbourg bodies also found a violation of Article 6(1) ('right to a fair trial').

In what way had the Greek Jehovah's Witness been discriminated against? Essentially by being treated by the accountancy institute as a criminal when the only reason for his conviction was a matter of conscience. In other words, he was treated in the same way as ordinary criminals when he ought not to have been – a form of reverse discrimination.

## DISCRIMINATION IN UK DOMESTIC LAW

These cases provides a good illustration of the way that discrimination is treated in Strasbourg jurisprudence. In UK domestic law, of course, several types of discrimination, notably racial and sex discrimination, are the subject of a whole body of law of their own. So as far as UK domestic law is concerned, a case can indeed be based on discrimination alone, or if applicable, it can combine a domestic discrimination cause of action with an Article 14 claim riding on one or more of the substantive Convention rights.

## EMPLOYMENT AND RELIGION

In *Stedman v UK*,[40] a practising Christian employed by a private company complained that she had been discriminated against on grounds of religion, contrary to Article 14, by being dismissed for refusing to work on occasional Sundays on a rota basis. Her Article 14 claim was in conjunction with a claim under Article 9 ('freedom of thought, conscience and religion') and Article 8 ('respect for private and family life'). The Human Rights Commission found that she had not been dismissed because of her religious beliefs but because she had refused to work certain hours. So her complaint under Article 9 was dismissed, as was her claim under Article 14, as she was not treated any differently from employees of any other religious persuasion. Her claim under Article 8 was also rejected, as the Commission held that the requirement to work on occasional Sundays did not constitute an interference with family life.

Louise Stedman was employed by a private company, but, in keeping with the vertical effect doctrine, the Commission first considered whether, had she been employed by the state, her dismissal in similar circumstances would have amounted to an infringement of her rights under Article 9. They held that it would not have done so. *A fortiori*, it was held, the United Kingdom could not be to blame for not having legislation in place that would have protected Ms Stedman against her dismissal by a private employer.

This decision is surprising, as section 101 of the Employment Rights Act 1996 makes dismissal of a shop worker automatically unfair if the reason for the dismissal was that the employee refused to work on Sunday or on a particular Sunday. Louise Stedman did not qualify to bring a claim of unfair dismissal before an employment tribunal. But in any event, the approach of Strasbourg does not always follow that of the domestic courts, despite the margin of appreciation doctrine.

### Notes

1 *Young, James and Webster v UK* (1981) 4 EHRR 38 81/3.
2 *Gustafsson v Sweden* (1996) 22 EHRR 409.
3 See Chapter 1.
4 See Chapter 1.
5 *Draper v UK* (1981) 24 DR 72.

6 *Hamer v UK* (1979) 24 DR 5.
7 *Johnston v Ireland* (1987) 9 EHRR 203 86/15.
8 *Young, James and Webster v UK* (1982) 4 EHRR 38 81/3.
9 *Airey v Ireland* (1979) 2 EHRR 305 79/3.
10 See *Rees v UK* (1987) 9 EHRR 56 86/9 §63.
11 *Rees v UK* (1987) 9 EHRR 56 86/9.
12 *B v France* (1992) 16 EHRR 1.
13 *Cossey v UK* (1990) 13 EHRR 622.
14 *Sheffield and Horsham v UK* (1998) 27 EHRR 163.
15 *Christine Goodwin v UK* 11 July 2002, 28957/95.
16 At the time of writing no such legislation had yet been introduced.
17 *Christine Goodwin v UK* 11 July 2002, 289S7/95, §98.
18 *Ibid*, §101.
19 *S-T v J* [1998] 1 All ER 431.
20 *Christine Goodwin v UK* 11 July 2002, 28957/95, §103.
21 *Ibid*, §103.
22 *Ibid*, §78.
23 *Ibid*, §82.
24 *Ibid*, §83.
25 *Ibid*, §93.
26 *Bellinger v Bellinger* [2003] UKHL 21.
27 *Ibid*, §1.
28 *Christine Goodwin v UK* 11 July 2002, 28957/95.
29 *Bellinger v Bellinger* [2003] UKHL 21, §§36–37.
30 *Ibid*, §65.
31 *Ibid*, §78.
32 *Johnston v Ireland* (1987) 9 EHRR 203 86/15.
33 *Marckx v Belgium* (1979) 2 EHRR 330 79/2.
34 *Inze v Austria* (1988) 10 EHRR 394 87/23.
35 *Nielsen v Denmark* (1989) 11 EHRR 175 88/16.
36 *In Re B (A Minor)* [2001] UKHL 70, [2002] 1 All ER 641 at 650 (§31).
37 *Buckley v UK* (1997) 23 EHRR 101 96/35.
38 *Belgian Linguistic Case* (1968) 1 EHRR 252.
39 *Thlimmenos v Greece* 00/123–6 April 2000 S44.
40 *Stedman v UK* (1997) 23 EHRR CD 168.

# References

The following are references to the secondary sources (books and articles) quoted in the text.


Arnheim, Michael (1988) Computer software and the law, *Solicitors Journal*, **132**

Arnheim, Michael (forthcoming) *Principles of the Common Law*

Baker, Christopher (1998) *Human Rights Act 1998: A practitioner's guide*

Barendt, Eric, Lustgarten, Laurence, Norrie, Kenneth and Stephenson, Hugh (1997) *Libel and the Media: The chilling effect*

Bork, Robert (1996) *Slouching towards Gomorrah*

de Smith, Stanley, Woolf, Lord and Jowell, J (1995) *Judicial Review of Administrative Action*

Denning, Lord (1982) *What Next in the Law*?

Dershowitz, Alan (2002) *Shouting Fire*

Dicey (1959) *Introduction to the Study of the Law of the Constitution (1885–1914)*, 10th edn

Drzemczewski, Andrew Z (1983) *European Human Rights Convention in Domestic Law: A comparative study*

Irvine, Lord (1996) Judges and decision-makers: the theory and practice of *Wednesbury* review, *Public Law* 59

Laws, Sir John (1993) Is the High Court the guardian of fundamental constitutional rights?, *Public Law* 59

Lester, Lord and Pannick, David (1999) *Human Rights Law and Practice*

Loveland, Ian (2000) *Constitutional Law: A critical introduction*, 2nd edn

Maitland, F W (1936) *The Forms of Action at Common Law*

Nolan, Lord and Sedley, Sir Stephen (1997) *The Making and Remaking of the British Constitution*

Reid, Lord (1972) The judge as lawmaker, 12 *Journal of the Society of the Public Teachers of Law* 22

*Rights Brought Home: The Human Rights Bill* (HM Government) White Paper (Cm 3782)

Starmer, Keir (1999) *European Human Rights Law*

Steyn, Lord (1998) Incorporation and devolution: a few reflections on the changing scene, *European Human Rights Law Review* 153

Warren, Samuel and Brandeis, Louis (1890) The right to privacy, *Harvard Law Review*, 4 December, pp 193–220

Weir, Tony (1996) *A Casebook on Tort*, 8th edn

Williams, Glanville (1963) *The Proof of Guilt*, 3rd edn

# Index